THE
GIANT
BOOK OF
WHAT DO YOU
KNOW?

THE FACT–PACKED
INFORMATION BOOK IN COLOUR

THE

GIANT

BOOK OF

WHAT DO YOU

KNOW?

THE FACT-PACKED

INFORMATION BOOK IN COLOUR

Galley Press

First Published in Great Britain in 1980 by
The Hamlyn Publishing Group Limited
under the title
*The Hamlyn Children's Giant
Book of What Do You Know?*

This revised edition published in 1988 by Galley Press
in association with Octopus Books Limited
59 Grosvenor Street, London W1

ISBN 0 86136 022 2

Printed in Czechoslovakia

The material in this book originally appeared in the following
Hamlyn titles: *What do you know about The Earth?* by Neil Curtis;
What do you know about Animals? by Ian Jackson and *What do you
know?* by Kenneth Allen, Neil Ardley, Alan Blackwood, Jean Stroud
and Arthur Thomas.
51160/8

Contents

The Earth

What is the Earth?

You and I already know a great deal about the Earth, because it is the place on which we live. The Earth is a *planet*; that is, an almost spherical ball of rock, soil, and water, surrounded by an envelope of gases which we call *air* or the *atmosphere*.

The shape of the Earth is more correctly called an *oblate spheroid* which is a complicated way of saying that the planet is slightly flattened at the *north* and *south poles* and bulges slightly at the *equator*. This modification of the spherical shape occurs as a result of the Earth's rotation about an axis through the poles. As the Earth spins, its materials tend to be forced outwards. This force is greater at the equator than at the poles.

The Earth, together with its twin planet, or *satellite*, the Moon, are suspended in space and move in an *orbit* around the fiery ball of the Sun at the rate of one complete circuit every year—to be exact every $365\frac{1}{4}$ days. It is because this period of rotation is not exactly 365 days that every four years we need to have a *leap year* of 366 days. This makes up for the quarter days lost in the normal 365 day year.

We have said that the materials of the planet tend to be flung outwards as the Earth goes round. When you look at

Above:
The Earth supports life in a multitude of forms, organized into communities.

Right:
The planet Earth is a partly solid *sphere* about two-thirds covered by water — the seas and the oceans. It provides us with everything we need to live.

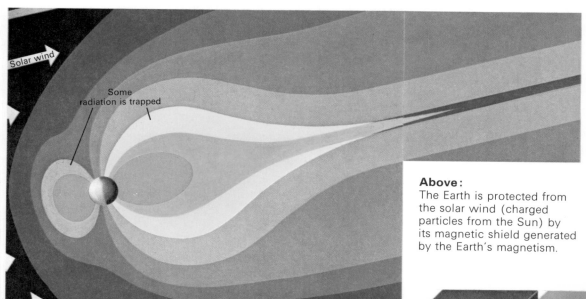

Some radiation is trapped

Solar wind

Magnetic shield

Above:
The Earth is protected from the solar wind (charged particles from the Sun) by its magnetic shield generated by the Earth's magnetism.

Above:
The Earth's present atmosphere was formed from original gases at the Earth's beginning, gases from the surface and volcanoes, and oxygen released by plants.

the ground beneath your feet or take hold of a piece of rock in a quarry it is hard to imagine that the shape of the whole Earth can change, as you might mould a piece of plasticine. But it is simply a question of the scale of things. The Earth seems to us to be very hard and solid because we are so tiny by comparison. But the forces locked up within the planet are more than a match for the strength of the rocks. It has been said that if we could reduce the Earth to the size of a football and its hardness by an equivalent amount it would have a consistency something like that of toothpaste.

It is upon this base that the whole range of familiar and not so familiar life forms have developed, from the tiny, single-celled amoeba up to and including the most advanced life form the planet has yet known – man. Although man certainly is the most intelligent of Earth's animals, he must remember that he has developed as just one part of the complex network of life and that he is not removed from it.

Perhaps you have heard the expression 'spaceship Earth'. You can understand that if you were isolated in a tiny spaceship for the rest of your life it would be very important to make the best use of all your resources and not to foul the compartment with your waste. This is also true of the Earth, but because it is so big we sometimes tend to forget it.

Where is the Earth?

If you have ever been lost in a city or even a large town without the help of a street plan you will have some idea of the problems which confronted scientists of old when they tried to imagine exactly where Earth was in the Universe. You might be able to work out where you were in the city if you could climb on to a very tall building and have a bird's eye view of the city as a whole. In the same way, if you could detach yourself from Earth and look at it from space you would be able to see where it is.

We have explained that the Earth moves around the Sun in the previous question but this was not at all obvious to our ancestors and it has taken many generations of scientific thought to devise an accurate 'street plan' of space which pinpoints the Earth's position correctly.

Like us, our forefathers could look up at the night sky and observe a constantly changing pattern of bright objects including the much larger Moon. We know now that the Earth is just one of nine planets which together with their satellites (moons), a belt of smaller rocky bodies called *asteroids*, some *meteors* which appear to us as shooting stars, and one or two *comets* are all orbiting around the Sun some 140 million kilometres away.

Right and centre:
The Earth seems very large indeed to us, but this picture shows the position of our solar system in the known Universe and how tiny even the solar system is.

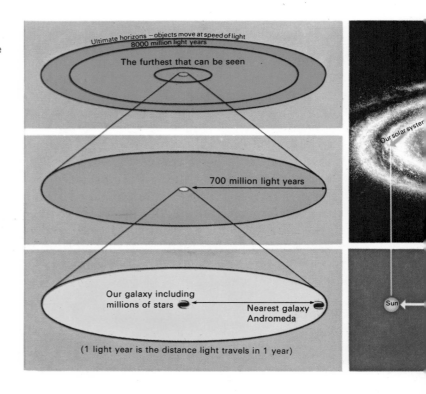

Ultimate horizons – objects move at speed of light
8000 million light years
The furthest that can be seen

700 million light years

Our galaxy including millions of stars

Nearest galaxy Andromeda

(1 light year is the distance light travels in 1 year)

Our solar system

Sun

This arrangement of various heavenly bodies is called the *solar system*. But what of all the other myriad points of light which we usually refer to simply as stars? From the vantage point of Earth, these stars appear to be arranged in patterns which have been given names like the *Plough* because of their resemblance in outline to more familiar objects. These patterns are called *constellations* but they may be made up of stars which are many millions of kilometres from each other.

In fact, each one of these pin-pricks of light is a sun very similar to our own except that some of them are younger and cooler and appear to be red in colour and others are hotter, older, and blue. Our solar system is just one of many similar systems which all fit into a larger arrangement called a *galaxy*, and there are millions of other galaxies in the Universe.

It has only been with the coming of the telescope in the 1600s and more recently radio telescopes and satellites that we have been able to establish our 'street plan'. Our ancestors believed that the Earth was at the centre of things. Some ancient civilizations believed that our planet was supported by huge animals such as elephants and whales. They could be forgiven for thinking that the sky was like a gigantic domed roof with the Sun, the other planets and the stars suspended from it.

Below right:
In about AD 150, the Greek astronomer Ptolemy believed that the Earth was at the centre of the solar system and that the planets and the Sun revolved around it.

Our galaxy
80 000 light years across

4.2
light years

Centauri,
nearest star neighbour

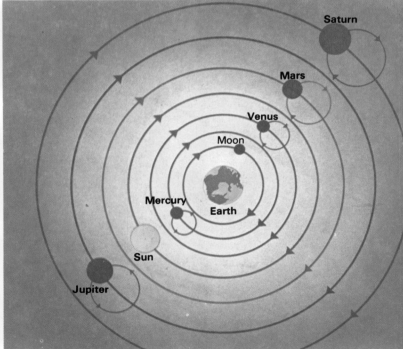

Saturn

Mars

Venus

Moon

Mercury

Earth

Sun

Jupiter

How was the Earth born?

Perhaps you are wondering why we have chosen to ask this question rather than 'How was the Universe born?' Unfortunately, this has been puzzling scientists for many years and has still not been satisfactorily answered.

Many different ideas have been suggested, ranging from the hand of God to the 'Big Bang Theory'. 'Big Bang' suggests that the Universe was formed about 20,000 million years ago by the sudden explosion of a small mass of material which was incredibly heavy. But where did this 'primaeval atom', as it has been called, come from in the first place? It seems unlikely that anyone will ever have the final answer.

On the other hand, once we can assume that the Universe does exist, it becomes a little easier to think about the formation of our own planet because we already have the building materials available.

For many years, the most accepted idea concerning the formation of the Earth was the result of the work of a scientist called Kelvin in 1862. He suggested that the Earth has cooled from a melted, that is, a molten, mass. He put forward this idea partly because it had been proved definitely by that time that the Earth is losing heat, and also because this seemed to provide an explanation for the origin of volcanoes spewing their red hot lava from the interior.

More recently, however, a great deal of evidence has been gathered, indicating that the planet was probably never completely melted. In fact, the most popular theory nowadays is that the Earth, and also the rest of the solar system, were formed from the coming together of a cloud of dust and gas. This was probably a result of the gravitational

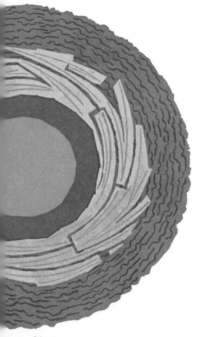

Above:
It was once thought that the Earth was formed hot and that it cooled from the outside towards the centre. This made the surface crack to build mountains and valleys.

Right:
About 450 million years ago (a mere tenth of the age of our planet) the surface of the Earth may have looked like this.

attraction which all objects have for each other. We think this occurred about 6000 million years ago. This means that the Earth probably formed cold rather than as a molten ball.

We know from the evidence of deep mines, however, that the Earth becomes very much hotter towards the centre. Where does the heat come from? Certainly, it must have become hot enough to melt many of the original materials. We think this heat has a twofold origin. When the Sun contracted at the very beginning, its centre became hot. This set off the decay of certain radioactive substances which released a great deal more heat. It seems likely that the first of the Earth's rocks were formed from their molten parent materials about 4500 million years ago.

Left:
This picture illustrates the traditional idea of the creation of the Earth as related in the Old Testament of the Bible.

13

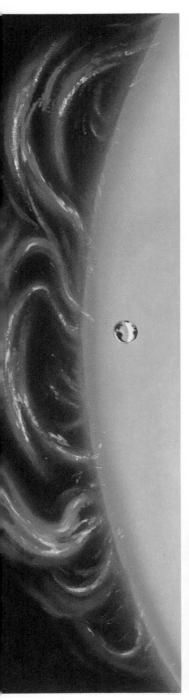

How does the Earth keep warm?

This is a question that you have answered for yourself every time that you have been sunbathing. Almost all of the Earth's heat, and this means its energy, must come from the Sun. In addition to this the interior of the Earth has retained much of the heat which was generated at the formation of the Earth. This internal heat came from energy released as the Earth contracted as well as from heat given off by the decay of certain types of radioactive materials. But more of this later. For the moment we are concerned with the Sun. No plants would grow without the Sun, and therefore, no animals and no man. Without the Sun, our planet would be a frozen, barren waste.

What is the Sun?

In an earlier question, we explained that the Sun is a star like many millions of others in the Universe, but why does the Sun or any other star shine and give out its warmth?

The Sun is more than one hundred times larger in diameter than the Earth, and over a million times larger in volume, but its mass is only about 330,000 times more.

You know that the Earth is solid and that gases are usually lighter than solids, so that if you were to guess that the Sun was made up mostly of gas you would be correct. By using an instrument called a *spectrograph*, which carefully examines the kind of light which the Sun is emitting, scientists have

Above:
Look at this illustration and see how tiny the Earth is, compared to the Sun.

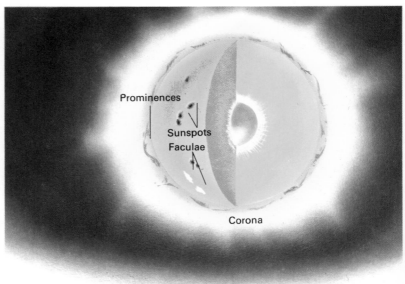

Prominences

Sunspots

Faculae

Corona

been able to prove that 70 or 80 per cent of the Sun is made up of hydrogen, which is the lightest material that we know of. The rest is mainly another very light gas called helium, from the Greek word *helios* meaning sun because it was first noticed there. You may have come across these two gases because they have been used to fill airships and balloons.

Why is the Sun able to burn for so long without ever seeming to use up its fuel? The process is simple to explain, but cannot successfully be repeated on Earth even in a controlled way.

All elements are made of tiny particles called *atoms*. The atoms of different elements are made up of different numbers of other particles, such as *protons, neutrons,* and *electrons,* giving each element its own special properties. In the Sun, atoms of hydrogen are constantly combining by a process called *fusion* into atoms of helium. This happens at a temperature of about fourteen million degrees Centigrade (remember that water boils at only 100°C) and a tremendous amount of heat and light is liberated. There is so much hydrogen fuel that it will last a very long time, particularly because so little hydrogen releases so much heat.

Right:
A view of the Sun showing faculae and sunspots.

Left:
A section through the Sun showing what the various parts are called. Faculae are bright areas and sunspots are dark spots that both appear on the surface. Prominences are clouds of intensely hot gas which appear to shoot up like flames from the surface of the Sun.

Faculae

Sunspots

Umbra

Penumbra

Above:
A close up of a sunspot shows that it has a darker inner part called the umbra and a lighter outer part called the penumbra.

How do we travel the Earth?

Being able to live in Britain and holiday in the United States of America is something that has been taken for granted for some years by those who are able to afford an air-ticket. Even the least well-off think nothing of seeing and hearing a jet aircraft rushing at speeds of more than 800 kilometres an hour to the other side of the world. Many families in the industrial countries of western Europe and America own some kind of motor vehicle. Even those of us who do not own a car are able to take advantage of the various forms of public transport. Travelling large distances with ease and comfort is something that has become commonplace.

The ability to travel quickly and safely has meant that people are able to work in the big cities and live in more pleasant surroundings out of town. But it is not only for our own travel that we have come to rely so heavily on transport systems. How would our milk arrive on the doorstep each morning without them? Or how would oranges or more exotic fruit and vegetables be so readily available? Or how would people living in Europe be able to buy Japanese motor cycles or cameras? How would children living in remote districts be able to get to school? How would farmers be able to get their produce to market? The list is almost endless.

But travel and transport of goods has not always been so easy. It is worth remembering that it is little more than twenty years since jet aircraft were a novelty and less than a hundred years since the first motor car, a German Daimler Benz, chugged and coughed its way out of the inventor's

Above:
An open boat powered by oars and a single sail is a far cry from the fast, luxurious, ocean-going liners we are used to.

Right:
An old London bus.

16

Above:
Modern aircraft are powerful enough to carry cars and passengers.

Above right:
Many people rely on fast electric trains to carry them to and from work.

workshop. Although steam driven railway engines were already quite common in industrialized countries in the late 1800s, it was the realization of the properties of petrol and the invention of the internal combustion engine that made the most impact.

For more than half a century, motor cars and the availability of cheap petrol have changed our way of life in

Right:
A nuclear submarine may remain submerged for months. It produces all the air its crew needs.

industrialized countries. Fast, cheap transport has brought commodities from all over the world to our shops. Recently, however, it has been brought to our attention very dramatically that fossil fuels are fast running out. Scientists are hurriedly trying to invent new forms of power, and in the meantime people are beginning to return to a much older form of transport, the horse.

What makes the ground tremble?

Perhaps you have seen science fiction films in which great cracks suddenly appear in the ground, and the land seems to roll like the sea. Of course, if you live in Britain or Europe this does not seem very realistic, does it? But, even though

these scenes may be exaggerated to make the film more exciting, there are many places around the world, such as Los Angeles in America or Tokyo in Japan, where the ground could tremble at any time, with terrible effects.

This shaking of the Earth is called an *earthquake*. You know that if you throw a stone into a pond, waves spread through the water in all directions from the point where the stone fell. In a similar way, if some rocks in the Earth are somehow disturbed, movements like waves are set up in the ground itself. The land can be felt to shake close to where the rocks were disturbed, and depending on the force of the earthquake, buildings may come tumbling down, water pipes may be broken, roads torn up, and huge fires started by the breaking of gas mains or electricity cables. Last, but certainly not least, thousands of people may lose their lives.

Try placing a brick on a plank of wood and slowly tilt the plank from one end until the brick slips. You will find that you can tilt the plank quite a lot before the brick eventually slips, and when it does it slips suddenly. This is because both the brick and the piece of wood have rough surfaces and tend to grip together. Before the brick can move, this tendency has to be overcome by tilting the plank more and more until the brick suddenly slides. Similarly, inside the Earth, if rocks are pushed more and more they will break, or move very suddenly along existing cracks. Your brick and plank were quite small and you would feel very little when the brick slips, but in the Earth the rock masses are so big that even if they move a little an earthquake is caused.

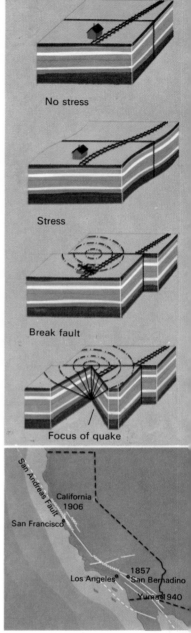

No stress

Stress

Break fault

Focus of quake

If you were to make the surfaces of your brick and plank more slippery (perhaps by rubbing them with soap) you would find that the plank need not be tilted so much before the brick moved, and that it would slide more slowly. In America, scientists are testing the effects of pumping thousands of gallons of water into the ground in the hope that rocks can be made to move more slowly, and in this way prevent earthquakes.

Apart from the harmful results of earthquakes the ways in which earthquake waves pass through the Earth can tell scientists quite a lot about what the inside of our planet is like. But they have to be able to detect and measure these waves. An instrument which measures earthquakes is called a *seismometer*. Simply, it consists of a masonry column bedded into the solid rock to which is attached an arm loaded with a heavy weight called a *boom*. On the end of the boom is a pen which marks a line on to a piece of paper wrapped round a drum which rotates when the seismometer is in operation. Because of its weight, the boom tends to remain still during an earthquake but the rest of the instrument is shaken and these movements are recorded as a squiggly line on the paper as it rotates.

Top:
This illustration shows how the stress builds up along a fault line, the rocks eventually fracturing, causing an earthquake.

Above:
This map shows the fault systems in California and the epicentres of historic earthquakes in the area.

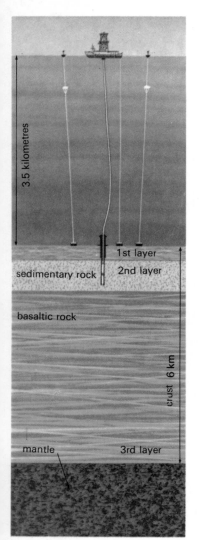

3.5 kilometres

1st layer

sedimentary rock | 2nd layer

basaltic rock

crust 6 km

mantle | 3rd layer

Above:
Drilling ships like this one can yield a great deal of information about the composition of the Earth.

Right:
This illustration shows how nitrogen is continuously cycled through animals, plants, and the atmosphere.

What is the Earth made of?

There are really two questions here. Not only 'What is the Earth made of?' but also 'How do we know what the Earth is made of?'. We can find out about the materials that make up the surface of our planet by simply taking samples of all the rocks and soils which are exposed and carefully examining them. But the Earth measures almost 6600 kilometres from the surface to its centre. The deepest holes which man has been able to drill in his search for oil are a little over seven kilometres and the deepest mines still less. An attempt was made by scientists from the United States of America to drill a hole right through the Earth's crust. They knew that the crust was at its thinnest under the oceans, but they soon discovered the enormous cost and the project was abandoned. This attempt was called the 'Mohole project' in honour of a famous geologist called Mohorovičić. So how do we know what is in the innermost parts of our planet?

Scientists have been able to piece together evidence from a variety of sources to give a picture of the composition of the Earth as a whole but first we should look at some of the more common materials of which the Earth is made.

Let us begin with the air we breathe. It can be shown quite easily that air is mainly a mixture of three gases. There is

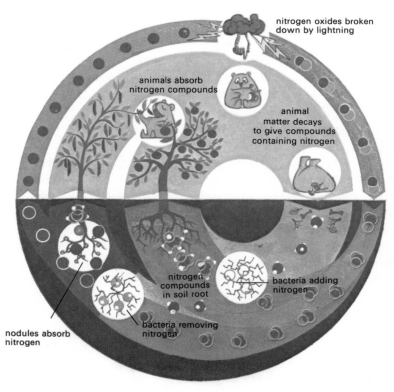

nitrogen oxides broken down by lightning

animals absorb nitrogen compounds

animal matter decays to give compounds containing nitrogen

nitrogen compounds in soil root

bacteria adding nitrogen

bacteria removing nitrogen

nodules absorb nitrogen

about 78 per cent of the total volume occupied by the gas nitrogen. Nitrogen is fairly inert which means that it does not easily combine with other materials in chemical reaction but it is very important when it does combine because of the variety of substances formed that are so essential to life. These substances are the *proteins*. There is about 21 per cent of oxygen in the air. This is the gas which we need to breathe. There are also small amounts of argon, a number of rare gases and some carbon dioxide is the gas which plants need.

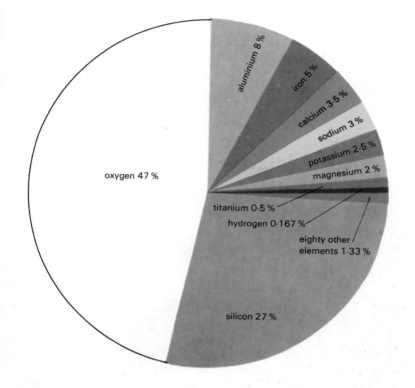

oxygen 47 %

aluminium 8 %

iron 5 %

calcium 3·5 %

sodium 3 %

potassium 2·5 %

magnesium 2 %

titanium 0·5 %

hydrogen 0·167 %

eighty other elements 1·33 %

silicon 27 %

Left:
This diagram shows the main elements found in the Earth's crust.

Almost 99 per cent of the Earth's surface rocks are made up of eight basic substances or *elements*. These are oxygen, silicon which is the important component of glass, aluminium found in clays, iron which you are very familiar with, calcium which you need to form your bones, sodium found in common salt, and potassium and magnesium. Apart from oxygen and silicon all of these are metals. We shall look at the depths of the Earth in the next question.

What would you see on a journey to the centre of the Earth?

In the previous question we looked at what the surface materials of the Earth were made of. While we know a good deal about the composition and structure of the interior of the planet it is more difficult to understand how we can gain such knowledge.

We have seen when we talked about earthquakes and what happens to the waves from them, that these waves may be bent or even blocked altogether by the different materials making up the depths. Another very important piece of evidence in our efforts to build up a thorough understanding of our planet is the density of the Earth.

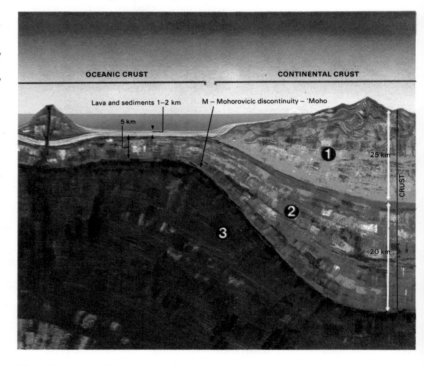

OCEANIC CRUST   CONTINENTAL CRUST

Lava and sediments 1–2 km   M – Mohorovicic discontinuity – 'Moho

5 km

①   25 km

②   CRUST

3   20 km

Density simply means the weight of an object divided by its volume. The density of the surface rocks can easily be measured at an average of about 2.7 grams per cubic centimetre, but the density of the Earth as a whole seems to be about 5.5 g/cm^3. This clearly means that the materials which make up the interior of the Earth are very much more dense than the rocks on the surface.

There are two other clues. Firstly, the lavas which are spewed out from volcanoes and other types of rocks which arise from greater depths are an indication of what is going on at quite shallow depths. Finally, meteorites are thought

Right:
A look into the centre of the Earth.

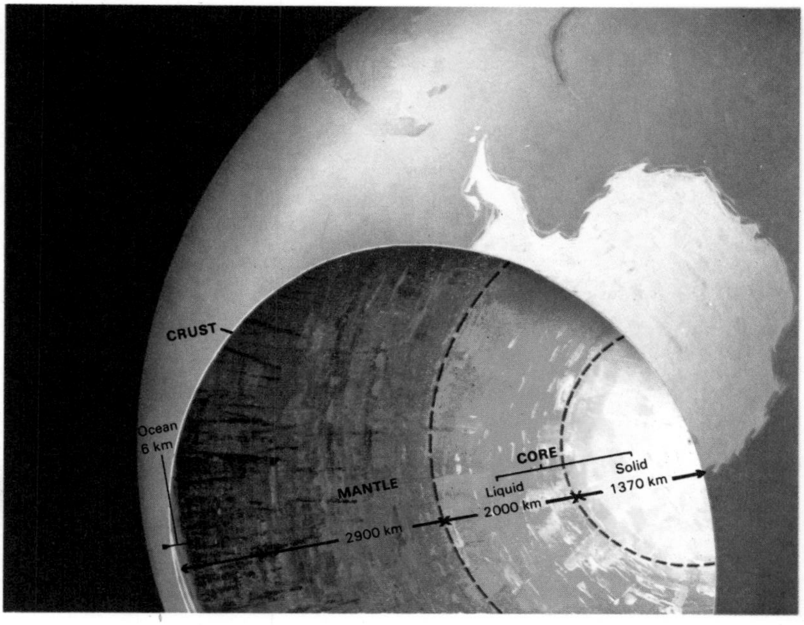
CRUST
Ocean
6 km
MANTLE
CORE
Liquid
2000 km
Solid
1370 km
2900 km

to be composed of materials which are representative of planetary composition. But it has been the coming of earthquake studies (seismology) that has given us such a clear picture of the Earth.

The Earth is generally divided into three main zones. The surface zone is the *crust* which has been found to average 6 kilometres thick under the ocean floor and about 35 kilometres thick under the continents. Below this there is a zone which we usually call the *mantle* and may also be called the zone of heavy rock.

The heavy rock is called peridotite and is composed of minerals containing mostly elements such as silicon, magnesium, and iron. This zone continues to a depth of about 2900 kilometres and has a density of 3.4 g/cm^3. In fact the crust and topmost layer of the mantle have often been given the names sial and sima. The sial is composed of light rocks such as granite and its name comes from the chemical symbols for silica and alumina (silicon and aluminium oxides) which make up these rocks. The sima is composed of dark heavy rocks such as basalt containing silica, iron oxides, and magnesia. The centre zone of the Earth is called the *core* which has metallic properties probably composed of metals such as iron and nickel under very great pressures.

Why does the Earth look so young?

As we have seen, the Earth has kept many secrets about herself. Geologists have been able to learn some of these secrets by looking carefully at the way in which the processes within and at the surface of the planet are constantly in motion. One of these secrets has been called the Earth's secret of eternal youth. This really means that while, for example, a person is born; grows up, grows old, and eventually dies, the Earth seems to look as young as it always has, at least, during man's short stay. This does not mean that the Earth always stays exactly the same. On the contrary, it is changing all the time.

Have you ever looked into a kaleidoscope? If you have you will know that the ever-changing patterns as you turn it are made up of different combinations of the same pieces of coloured glass. In the same way, the basic building blocks of the Earth are the same now as they ever were and the only thing that is being added is energy in the form of the Sun's rays. This is the fuel of the Earth's 'boiler'.

But if the materials stay the same, why does the Earth not grow old and die? In fact, the Earth is ageing, but this is happening so slowly as far as we are concerned that it is not easily noticeable. Of course, geologists can look back into the past and see that over a very long time changes have taken place to the planet as a whole and especially in any one area of the globe. But these changes take place in the way which scientists call *geological cycles*.

There are lots of different geological cycles. For example, the Sun's warmth heats up the sea, driving some of it up into

Right:
This diagram shows the water cycle.

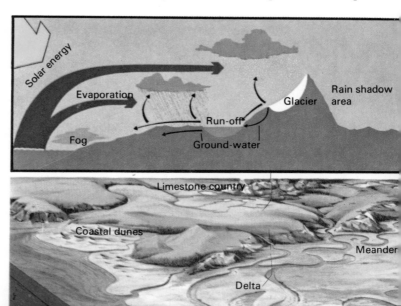

Solar energy

Evaporation

Fog

Run-off

Ground-water

Glacier

Rain shadow area

Limestone country

Coastal dunes

Meander

Delta

the sky as water vapour. (This is called *evaporation*.) This water comes together into the clouds we see, and then falls as rain, some on the land and some straight back into the sea. The rain that falls on land forms the streams and rivers and again returns to the sea, so completing the 'cycle'.

Other cycles wear away mountains and build new ones elsewhere, or take animal wastes into the soil to fertilize plants which feed the animals, and so on. We need these cycles which keep the Earth looking so young because through them many of the materials we use in our industries are brought to the surface, reborn, or even made by them. Of course, some of these cycles take millions of years to complete and we may consume their products in our factories in hundreds or sometimes even tens of years.

Below:
A landscape sculptured by some of the surface processes such as the effects of water, wind and ice.

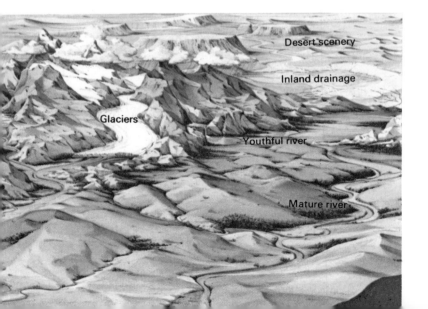

Desert scenery

Inland drainage

Glaciers

Youthful river

Mature river

25

Right:
As you know, the movement of water between the land, the atmosphere, and bodies of water is the very important water cycle.

What makes the rain fall?

You will remember from the last question that rain plays an important part in helping the Earth to keep her youthful face. It is only one stage in one of the cycles mentioned, and is called the *hydrologic* cycle. But how does water rise into the sky to form the many different clouds you know so well and why does it fall again as rain?

The water, or water vapour as it is more scientifically called, gets into the air by *evaporation*. Plants also lose water through their leaves and stems, and this follows the same path into the sky.

Before rain can fall the air must cool so that the water vapour can *condense*. This means that it turns into water droplets. When you have a bath some of the steam that rises from the hot water forms a thin film of water on any of the cold surfaces in the bathroom, such as the mirror or the window. It is a little more complicated than just cooling, however. Water vapour needs to have something to form on so that it can condense into droplets. In the air this is usually the tiny particles of dust which are ever present. This means, of course, that our industries can affect the rainfall in an area because of the smoke and other substances which usually accompany them.

The clouds which develop from these water droplets are of many different kinds, and not all of them will give rise to rain. You may have noticed some of the kinds of clouds. They have interesting names like stratus or cumulonimbus.

If you have spent a holiday in an area where there are high hills or mountains, it is likely that it will have been cloudy or have rained a lot. This is because the air which flows across the hills is forced rapidly upwards by them, causing it to cool as it expands. And if this air is very moist as it is, for example, when it reaches the Lake District of England, the water quickly condenses so that this area will usually have a very high rainfall.

You have seen how the clouds occur, but this does not explain why this water should suddenly fall as rain, or even snow or hail. The main difference between a cloud droplet and a raindrop seems to be size – a cloud droplet is very tiny and floats in the air and a raindrop is larger and heavy enough to fall as it is pulled by gravity. It is not easy to see why the droplets should grow to raindrop size but one reason may be that there are always a few larger droplets present which may fall and bump into other droplets to grow still larger, and so on.

Below:
Raindrops may grow by bumping into one another and may eventually fall to the ground.

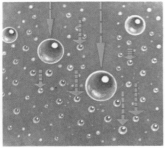

Right:
When water falls as snow ten centimetres of snow would be equal to one centimetre of rain.

Why is it hard to make tea on a mountain?

You know that there is more to making a really good cup of tea than just pouring hot water on to a few tea leaves and then pouring it out. The next time your mother makes tea, watch. You will find that she puts the kettle on to heat, and before the water boils she pours a little into the teapot to warm it. She will then dry the pot, carefully put in the correct amount of tea, and when the water is boiling hard she will take the pot to the kettle before pouring in the water. Why does she go to all this trouble for a cup of tea? The answer is that you simply cannot make tea if the water is not at a temperature of 100°C, that is, under normal conditions when the water is boiling. But what is the connection with making tea on mountains?

To understand this, you must know what is meant by boiling. All liquids release a certain amount of vapour. This vapour exerts a pressure; that is, it pushes on its surroundings. As a liquid is heated, the pressure increases until eventually it is the same as the pressure of the air – this is the boiling point.

Below:
The atmosphere pressing on the surface of the mercury is enough to force the mercury to rise about 760 millimetres or to support a column of mercury 760 millimetres long.

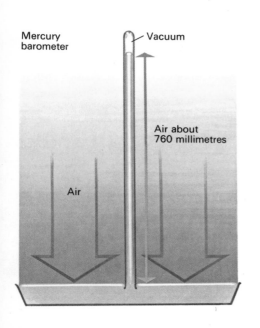

Mercury barometer

Vacuum

Air about 760 millimetres

Air

Above right:
This diagram shows how atmospheric pressure varies with altitude.

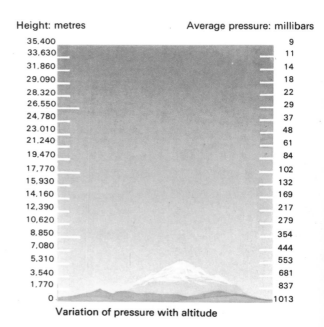

Height: metres	Average pressure: millibars
35,400	9
33,630	11
31,860	14
29,090	18
28,320	22
26,550	29
24,780	37
23,010	48
21,240	61
19,470	84
17,770	102
15,930	132
14,160	169
12,390	217
10,620	279
8,850	354
7,080	444
5,310	553
3,540	681
1,770	837
0	1013

Variation of pressure with altitude

What is air pressure? We do not feel the air pressing down on us. But in fact, every square centimetre of the Earth's surface at sea-level feels an air pressure of about one kilogram. This is really the weight of a column of air measuring one centimetre by one centimetre by the height of the column.

And that is quite a lot of air!

What happens when you climb a mountain? Obviously, the column of air becomes shorter and the pressure of the air is reduced. For example, if you were to climb to a height of 6000 metres, the air pressure is about half the air pressure that you would feel at sea-level. If you try to make tea at this height you will find that because the air pressure is lower, the pressure of the water will be lower when the water boils and it will not be so hot. You cannot make the water any hotter because it simply turns into steam. This all leads to a rather poor cup of tea!

If you have watched the weather forecast on television you will have seen that the forecaster's charts have lots of lines on them. The air pressure along any one line or *isobar* as it is called is exactly the same, but different lines indicate different pressures.

Right:
Some barometers record the
variations in pressure from
day to day on a chart like
the one shown here.

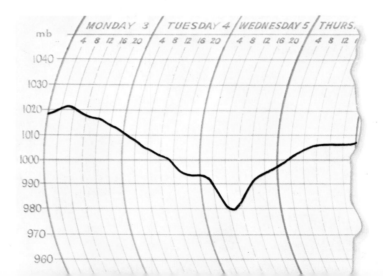

Can a rock rot?

Above:
A visit to a cemetery will prove to you that rocks can rot.

The answer is yes! If you have ever looked at a china clay pit and seen the soft, white, sticky china clay it is hard to imagine that it was once hard rock. For example, the china clay found in South Devon, England is the result of the rotting of the granite underlying the moors of Dartmoor and Bodmin.

But what happens to make the granite rot into clay? Rocks rot by the process known as *weathering*, and all rocks suffer from its effects, whether they are found in the tropics or the frozen wastes of the Antarctic. Weathering is the sum total of all the effects on the surface materials caused by the processes of heating and cooling, freezing and thawing, and so on.

There are two main types of weathering given special names by geologists:

1. Physical Weathering These are the processes by which rocks are broken down by actions such as change of temperature on the materials themselves, and also the effects of water freezing and thawing in contact with the rocks.

2. Chemical Weathering This is the term used to describe what happens when the chemicals that make up the rocks change as a result of the action of water and air.

It is also worth noting that plant growth can have a

Below:
Trees and other plants can help to prise rocks apart.

Below right:
The freezing and thawing of water in joints can cause rocks to shatter. Heating and cooling can lead to 'onion skin' weathering.

considerable effect on rock materials, as can *bacteria* – tiny
organisms which are not like any other plant or animal.
In fact, without these bacteria which release essential
nourishment from the rocks there could be no more advanced
life forms, including man himself.

Physical Weathering
In areas of the world where it is damp enough to have rain
and becomes cold enough for the water to freeze, rocks can
be prised apart by the action of ice as it freezes and expands.
In hot, dry deserts rocks may become very hot during the
day only to cool very quickly as soon as the sun goes down,
so that they expand and shrink suddenly. This can cause the
rocks to split with explosive force.

Chemical Weathering
When rain falls it may carry gases from the air such as
oxygen and *carbon dioxide*. The carbon dioxide makes the rain
slightly acid; acid enough to be able to dissolve rocks like
limestone. The Karst district of Yugoslavia, for example,
where the rocks are worn into blocks and channels and
swallow holes and caves, shows the effects of this very well.

You have seen, then, that, like a piece of wood or an
apple, a rock can become rotten when its materials may
fall victim to rain and wind.

When is a rock a soil?

Most of us think of soil as the black or brown substance in which we grow our vegetables in the back garden; the substance which gets wet and sticky when it rains and makes our shoes dirty. But what is it that gives soil the special property which allows us to grow many of the plants that we and other animals need?

We have already seen from the previous question that rocks can break down in various ways. When the products of this breakdown are mixed with a material called *humus* the result is known as soil. If you were to look at a quarry you would probably find that on top of the solid rock there is a band of broken and partly rotted rock, and then as you move upwards there are different layers of soil. What you would actually see depends upon the type of rock, the climate and the way in which the water in the soil moves, and the type of vegetation growing there. Of course, plants also reflect the climate and the type of soil, so that you can see each depends upon the other in a very complicated relationship.

Right:
Bacteria can extract nutrients from rocks. Mosses and lichens would then be able to grow. Grasses could then grow in cracks where tiny amounts of soil have formed.

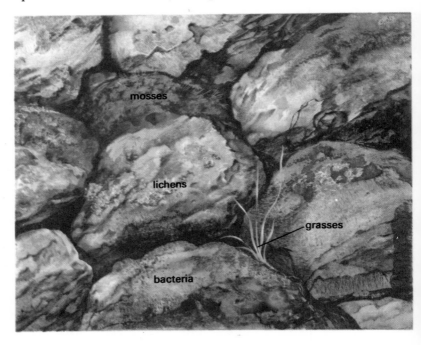

What is humus? Humus is a jelly-like acid material which results from the decay of the remains of plants and animals. You may ask where the first humus came from if humus comes from plants and animals. Animals need plants which grow in the soil. Soil needs humus. As you read in the last question bacteria can break down rock, and the substances thus

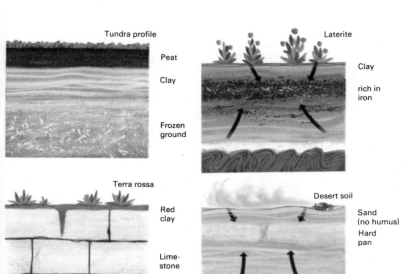

Tundra profile
Peat
Clay
Frozen ground

Laterite
Clay
rich in iron

Terra rossa
Red clay
Lime-stone

Desert soil
Sand (no humus)
Hard pan

Above and right:
Some of the major soil types of the world.

top soil

rich in humus

rich in mineral salts

sub-soil – weathered rock

solid rock

Above:
A soil section.

released provide nourishment for the first specialized plants such as lichens and mosses. When these plants decayed their remains mixed with the rock particles to form the first soils.

Scientists who study the soil are called pedologists. This word is derived from the Greek, *pedion*, meaning the ground, and *logos* meaning discourse or speech. In an effort to understand the complicated world of the soil, pedologists use *soil profiles* which are simply vertical sections through old, well-established soils showing the various layers. These layers are formed as the soil ages by the action of rainwater moving material downwards (*leaching*), the concentration of humus by plant growth, and so on.

As climate influences soils, pedologists recognize that there are a number of main types of soil that can be seen in the various climatic regions around the world. *Podzols* and *brown earths*, for example, are found in Britain and Europe where the climate is temperate.

How are mountains worn away?

When we talked about geological cycles we said that mountains can be worn away. You have already learned that hard rocks can become soft and rotten by weathering and may even dissolve completely. Eventually, all the materials which result from this weathering process may be transported from their place of formation by the Sun-driven carriers such as rain, wind, or sea.

The Earth's gravity can also play an important part in removing these weathered materials, particularly on hills and mountains. On hills, helped by the action of the rain, or even by plants and animals, the soil can slowly *creep* downwards. And of course, as the soil is removed, more rock is exposed to the elements so that weathering can once more take its toll of the bare surface.

In dry deserts where there is not enough moisture to hold the weathered material together, the wind may pick up particles of sand and hurl them against any rocks which may be still standing and slowly wear them away thus providing even more ammunition for the sand-blasting wind.

Water, in its various forms, is probably the most important of the Earth's many transport systems. We have seen that rain can accelerate the process of soil creep, even though occasionally a particularly hard rock can protect what lies beneath it from further decay so that earth pillars result. But much of the rock debris, as it is sometimes called, finds its way into the rivers and streams where it may travel great distances. It is carried by rolling along the river bed,

Below left:
At first water runs down the slope in sheets; it then forms a channel and deep gulleys may develop.

Below right:
Severe rain erosion can cause the land to look like this. A landscape like this is known as *badlands*.

Bottom left:
Ripples may be formed on the river bed and particles may be carried in suspension or may be rolled and dragged along the river bottom.

Bottom right:
A dried river bed may expose pot holes.

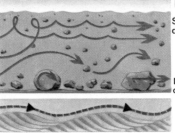

Suspended debris

Debris rolling on bed

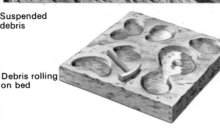

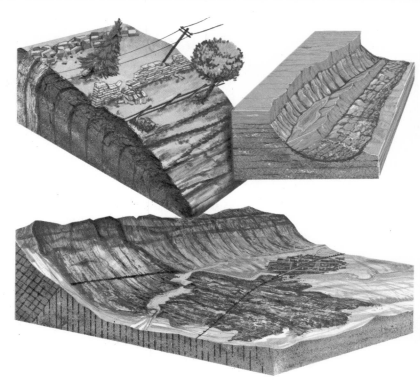

Right:
The effect of soil creep.

Far right and below:
Landslips can cause severe erosion particularly in coastal areas where cliffs are undercut by the sea.

Below left:
A hard rock may protect the underlying rocks from erosion resulting in earth pillars.

Below:
These dramatic screes are to be found at Wastwater in the English Lake District.

Inset:
A raindrop can have a considerable impact on wet soil.

Below right:
Erosion of these folded rocks have caused older rocks to be exposed in the core of this anticline.

by bouncing, or by complete suspension in the water itself. The dissolved materials may move also in the form of solutions.

Particles of rock wear away by bumping into one another and hitting the sides and bed of the river. They are rounded and polished as they are carried along and may further widen and deepen the river valley itself. As the river deepens its valley, gravity plays an increasingly important part in carrying material down the valley sides into the river. Ice, too, can trap rock fragments within it and carry them down valley as we shall see later. Most of the material eventually finds its way into the sea where the tides and currents may sweep it many kilometres from the original mountain or hill.

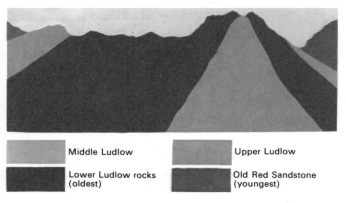

Middle Ludlow	Upper Ludlow
Lower Ludlow rocks (oldest)	Old Red Sandstone (youngest)

Where does all the rain go?

You have read from some of the previous questions why rain falls from the skies, and the importance of rain in wearing away rocks and transporting the debris far from its place of origin.

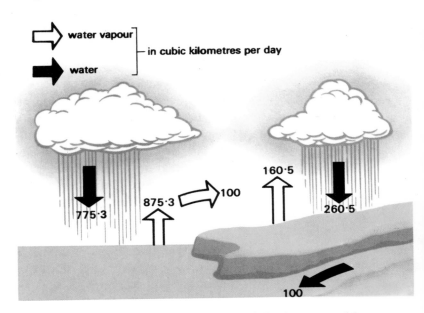

Right:
This picture shows the quantities involved in the water cycle.

Two-thirds of the surface of the globe is covered by water. This water is found in the world's oceans and much of the fresh water which is essential for all life has evaporated from them. But what happens to all the rainwater that falls on land? Some is evaporated straight back again, some soaks into the ground, some is taken up by the plants of the Earth. All the water in the Earth's rivers and streams, however, comes from *meteoric* water, that is water that falls from the atmosphere as rain. Of course, we use a great deal of the rain which falls on to the land surface, not only for washing and drinking but also in our industries and as a means of transport and disposal of our waste products. Here is another case where man's demands on the resources of the planet are beginning to show signs of wear, as you would soon notice

Right:
Some of London's water is drawn from wells drilled into the chalk aquifer. The rain originally fell on the North Downs and Chilterns some kilometres away.

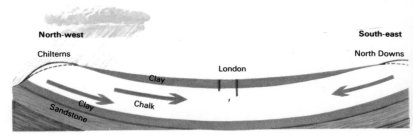

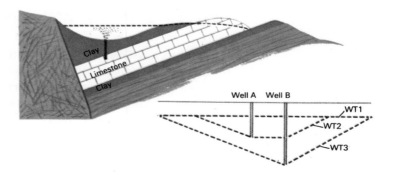

Well A Well B

WT1
WT2
WT3

if you were to look at the dead, stinking waters of many of the rivers in industrial regions of the United States and elsewhere, where fish can no longer live.

The rain which eventually forms rivers falls on to hills where it first runs downwards as a sheet of water. Soon the water cuts out channels which then come together to form larger streams and rivers. The way in which a river and its valley develop, depends upon the amount, frequency, and violence of the rain, the type of rocks and the slope upon which it falls. It depends also on the plant cover.

When the river flows down hill on a land surface which has been newly uplifted by earth movement, it is called a *consequent* stream, and the smaller streams which run down its valley sides to join it are called *tributaries* or *subsequent* streams. In this way a river system is formed.

We mentioned that some of the rain soaks into the ground – it becomes *groundwater*. Most rocks, such as sandstone, have many tiny holes between the grains which allow water to pass through them, and they may also be cracked which aids the flow. Other rocks, like clay, (clay is certainly a rock) do not allow the passage of water, and act as a barrier, so that water may build up against it forming an *aquifer*. The top surface of this water-bearing layer of rocks (resembling a wet sponge) is called the *water-table*. We drill our wells providing us with much of our water into this layer, but of course, if we take out more water than is flowing into the aquifer, the well will eventually run dry.

How can a river grow old?

We have explained how some of the rain which falls on to the land surface finds its way into the rivers and how a river system is born, but now we have a chance to look at another one of these familiar geological cycles. This time it is the cycle of *erosion*. This really means the way in which a river

Right:
This illustration shows how a river and its surrounding scenery evolves:
(1) Davis's youthful stage;
(2) maturity;
(3) old age. The dotted lines on the waterfall show the original position of the resistant rock indicating how the fall has been cut back. It is not certain why meanders develop, but they may become so extreme that the two parts of the meander neck may join, leaving the cut-off channel as an ox-bow lake.

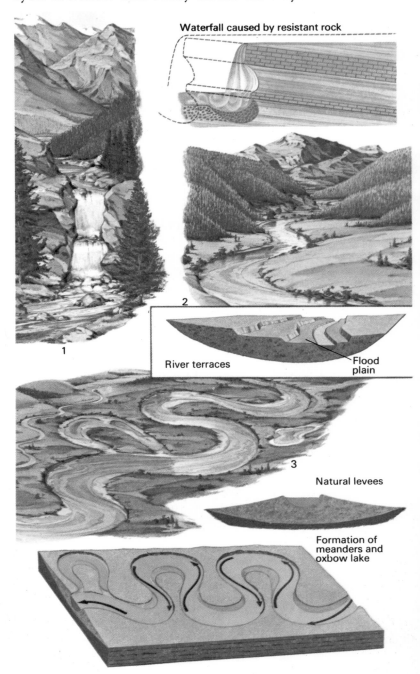

Waterfall caused by resistant rock

River terraces

Flood plain

Natural levees

Formation of meanders and oxbow lake

1

2

3

system works upon and moulds the land forms. It has been suggested by an eminent scientist called W. M. Davis that there is a sequence of stages. He suggested that a river valley system can pass through three major stages provided that there is no interruption by further uplift of the land. He called these stages *youth, maturity,* and *old age.*

In practice, it is now thought not to be quite as simple as this, but you would still be able to recognize these stages if you saw them in the countryside. Davis suggested that in the youthful stage when the land has only just been uplifted the water rushes down the steep slopes carving deep, narrow valleys with many waterfalls.

Eventually the rate at which these valleys are carved slows down and the river becomes wider, particularly where the rocks are less resistant to this wearing away. At this stage the action of the main rivers and their tributaries have begun to wear down and flatten the original surface. This is the mature stage.

At old age the landscape has been worn to that of a flat or very gently sloped region called a *peneplain.* The main rivers wind their way slowly towards the sea in a series of loops called *meanders.* Those hills which do survive are called *monadnocks.* This time of old age, or the *senile* stage as it is sometimes called, may take a very long time to develop fully and in addition to the meanders you may be able to see that the river channel may eventually become raised above the level of the surrounding plain. The embankments holding back the waters are made up of fine silty or sandy material called *alluvium* deposited there during times of flooding. They are called *levees.*

Sometimes, the meanders may curve around so far that the river finds it easier not to flow around the bend and the neck of the bend is cut off, leaving the remaining bend as an *ox-bow lake.*

Finally, it may happen that the sea-level may fall or the whole or part of the peneplain may be uplifted again and the river may be *rejuvenated.* That is, new rapids may be born, and the meander channels may be cut much more deeply by the fast flowing waters which then flow down to the sea.

Right:
This illustration shows some of the land features associated with river development.

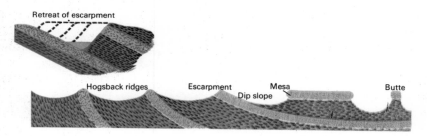

Retreat of escarpment

Hogsback ridges   Escarpment   Mesa   Butte

Dip slope

Top:
The extent of the ice in the north polar region today.

Above:
Icebergs in the north polar seas today.

Right:
A glacier flowing down from the snowfield.

Far right:
During the last Ice Age the ice, shown in white, extended much farther than it does today.

Inset:
This diagram shows how the centre of a glacier flows faster than it does at its margins.

What are glaciers and icebergs?

You have probably been told about the huge masses of ice that exist at the north and south poles today. You may also have heard that thousands of years ago great tongues of ice stretched southward from the north as far as Britain and northern Europe, and that millions of years before many of the countries of the southern hemisphere were similarly affected by an *Ice Age* as these periods of extremely harsh conditions are called. But how do these tongues of ice occur and what effects can they have on the face of the Earth?

It has already been mentioned that some of the water falling from the sky may do so as snow rather than rain. This is particularly likely to happen at the tops of mountains and in the regions closer to the north and south poles, where the temperatures are generally lower. Of course, we quite often wake up on a cold winter's morning to find everything outside shrouded by a glistening, soft, white mantle, but our snow soon melts again. In some parts of the world, however, such as in Greenland or the Himalayas, not all of the snow which falls in the winter is melted during the short, cool summer months and the snow tends to build up into *snowfields*. This is the first condition necessary for the formation of the frozen sculptors of our planet, the *glaciers*. As the snow builds up in the snowfield, it becomes compacted into bluish ice rather than the familiar, white snowflakes.

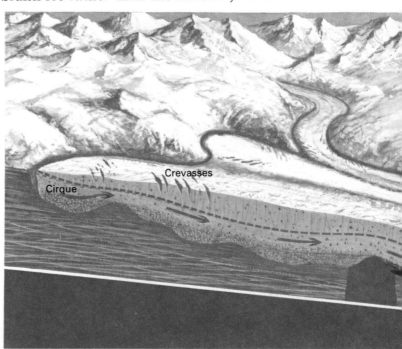

Cirque

Crevasses

The glaciers often flow down-hill from the snowfields where they are formed and only come to rest when the rate of melting of the ice-fronts, or snouts, as they are often called, is greater than the amount of ice which can be provided by the snowfield.

When the snout of a glacier meets the sea as often happens in Alaska, for example, great chunks of ice may break from the parent glacier by a process called *calving* to send an *iceberg* out into the icy seas. If you have seen photographs of these great blocks of ice you will know what an impressive sight they are, but it is as well to remember that the mountain of ice which you see rising grandly out of the water is only the tip of the iceberg, and that nine-tenths of it is under water. It is not surprising then that it was an iceberg that was responsible for the tragic sinking of the great steam ship which was thought to be unsinkable, the *Titanic*. She foundered and sank very quickly on her maiden voyage with the loss of over 1000 lives after a collision with an iceberg.

Top and above:
This illustration shows the extent of the ice in the south polar region today. Note that penguins only live in the south polar region.

Left:
Parts of Europe may have looked like this during the last Ice Age.

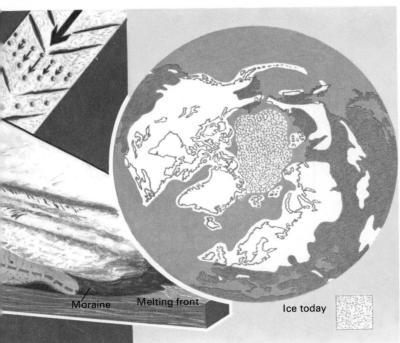

Moraine   Melting front   Ice today

Can glaciers move mountains?

Try taking an ice-cube from the refrigerator and rubbing it against a stone from the garden. You will find that not only does the ice melt where it has been in contact with the warmth of your hand, but that it also quickly melts where you have been rubbing it, and it has no effect on the stone. You might think, then, that this is rather a silly question. Of course, you know that glaciers and icebergs are much bigger than ice-cubes, and that it is much colder in their surroundings than in your garden. But even the largest glaciers can only push about a fiftieth as hard as would be necessary to break a piece of granite.

In reality the movement and accompanying processes of a glacier in a valley are much more complicated than that of water. In the warmer regions where large amounts of ice still occur there may be a lot of water melting from the ice which might trickle into the underlying rock and on freezing again would exert enough pressure to shatter it. There are many scientists who study glaciers, however, who

Right:
Louis Agassiz was the first geologist to study the extent of glaciation in former Ice Ages. This illustration is based on a sketch he made in about 1841 which he used in connection with his early studies.

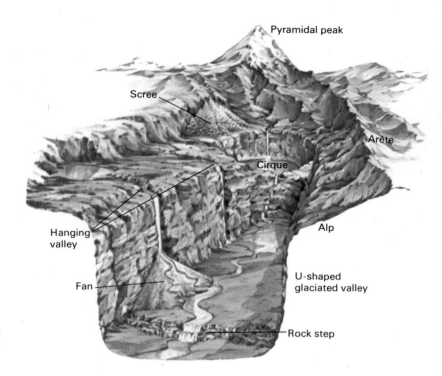

Pyramidal peak

Scree

Arête

Cirque

Hanging valley

Alp

Fan

U-shaped glaciated valley

Rock step

Right:
These are just some of the
features which a glacier can
leave behind as marks of its
power of erosion.

believe that this cannot happen. In any event, these effects
are only important in the top few centimetres of the rock
and would not account for the removal of a significant
amount of rock.

You know that if you compress a spring and then release
it, it springs back into its original shape quite violently. In a
similar way, all rocks have forces stored within them like
a compressed spring, and by removing the top few inches
of surface rock these forces may be released with such vigour,
so far as the rock is concerned, that the rock may shatter
still further. This allows the ice to pick up and carry away
more material.

We have said that rock debris is removed by ice. This
occurs because as the ice presses upon the fragments of rock,
the ice tends to melt forming a cavity. The fragment lodges
into the cavity and the ice eventually carries it away.
These suspended stones can also aid the erosive power of the
glacier in the manner of a piece of glass- or emery-paper. If
you have built balsawood model aircraft, you know the
way in which you smooth and round off the leading edges
of the wings by rubbing them with glass-paper. In a similar
way, a glacier may carry a large block of rock which might
easily break off other rocks jutting from the valley wall, so
that smaller fragments can begin their task of smoothing and
polishing the remainder.

How do you know when ice has been at work?

As we have already explained, in certain parts of the world, snowfields are formed and glaciers extend from them. These glaciers wear away the valleys in which they are confined, transport rocks, and deposit clay and rocks when they melt. In many ways the glaciers affect the landscape. In the past, sheets of ice were sculpturing the surface of the Earth in areas which are quite mild in climate today. Areas such as the English Lake District, Snowdonia of North Wales, and the Alps are all good examples of glaciated landscapes. But what features do all these areas have in common to allow us to tell that they have been affected by ice?

An area that has been glaciated is marked out by two distinctive sets of land features:

1. Features resulting from erosion of the area by the glaciers.

2. Features which result from deposition of material which had been carried by the ice.

We shall deal with features resulting from erosion first. The ice may carry rock fragments within it and those in contact with any rock surface will scratch it as the glacier passes over the rocks. These grooved rocks are called *striated surfaces*. If some of the rocks are harder than others, they may remain raised above the valley floor as ice-moulded hummocks which are smooth on the side facing the direction

Right:
A glacier may also leave behind material which it has been carrying in character-istic forms such as those shown in the illustration.

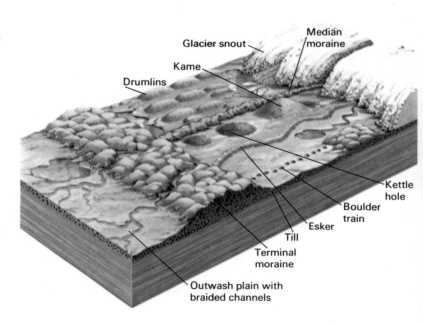

Glacier snout

Median moraine

Kame

Drumlins

Kettle hole

Boulder train

Esker

Till

Terminal moraine

Outwash plain with braided channels

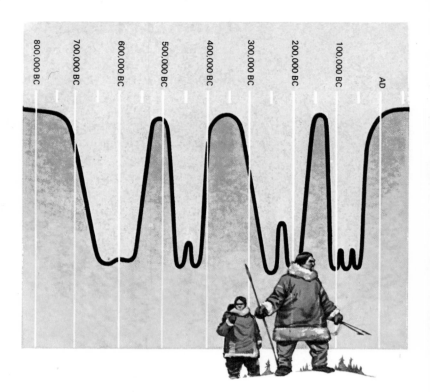

Right:
There have been four glacial phases or Ice Ages during the last 800,000 years as indicated by the troughs in this picture.

of the flow of ice and jagged on the other side. These are called *roches moutonnées*.

Snowfields formed in mountain hollows are cut back and deepened by the processes which are associated with the ice and then small glaciers move downslope. This commonly happens in existing valleys. The armchair-like hollows which are formed at the head of the valley are called *cirques, cwms*, or *corries*. When two or more of these cirques occur on different sides of a mountain, the erosion may cause them to meet, and an *arête* or a *pyramidal peak* will remain. The Matterhorn in the Alps is a very famous peak of this kind.

The glacier moving down the valley will cause the valley to become deeper and U shaped leaving the original tributaries hanging, and any spurs left by the meanderings of the river will be worn away or *truncated*.

Deposits of rock fragments and clay left behind after a glaciation may be dropped from the ice itself or from any of the melt waters accompanying it. The haphazard mixture of rock and fine clay is known as *drift* or *till*. It may be dropped at the nose of the glacier as it melts giving rise to *moraine*. Sometimes a block of one kind of rock may be carried many kilometres only to fall on a completely different type of rock. This is an *erratic*.

These and many other features give us very strong clues that ice has been at work.

What are tides?

If you live by the sea or you have had a holiday at the seaside, or even if you have spent some time by the mouth of a river, you will know that at certain times of the day the waters rise and fall. These ups and downs of the seas are called *tides*. In fact, on average, the rise and fall occurs every twelve hours and twenty-six minutes.

Why should tides occur? You know that everything on the Earth's surface is attracted towards the Earth by a force called *gravity*. Actually all objects are attracted towards each other by this force by an amount which can be worked out by a simple rule called the *inverse square law*. Roughly, this means the greater is the distance between two objects the smaller is the attraction, but the larger the objects the greater the attraction.

As the Moon passes around the Earth it attracts the waters of the oceans on the side facing it and causes them to bulge. On the opposite side from this bulge there is another one. Because the Earth is closer to the Moon than the oceans, the Earth is attracted towards the Moon more than the waters. This means that a bulge of water is left behind. These bulges pass around the Earth with the motion of the Moon and give rise to the tides.

There are two other things which help in the formation of the tides. You know that if you cause the water in your bath to rock, it may rise and fall against the side of the bath for some time. In the same way, once the tides have begun, the waters tend to continue to rock up and down and they are given an extra push by the attraction of the Moon. The Sun also tends to attract the Earth's oceans towards itself, but

Right:
The gravitational attraction of the Sun and Moon produces the daily tides.

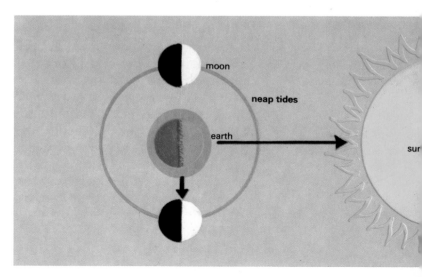

because it is so very much further away the attraction is much less important. At certain times of the year, however, the Sun, the Moon and the Earth are all in a straight line. When this happens, the attraction of the Sun is added to the attraction by the Moon, and the tides are particularly high. These are called *spring tides* and only happen when the Moon is new or full.

At other times, the Sun, the Earth, and the Moon are in positions which look like the corner of a square, with the Earth at the point. When this happens the attraction of the Sun tends to cancel out some of the pull of the Moon and the tides are much lower. These are called *neap tides*.

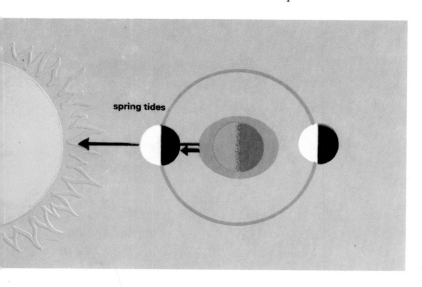

spring tides

Why are there waves on the sea?

Only very rarely are the seas completely still. These were the times that sailors on the old sailing ships feared the most – even more than they feared the worst storms. They became becalmed, which meant that no wind was blowing to fill the great sails to carry them to their next port of call. The sea would be motionless and mirror-like and no rain would fall. If the sailors were held fast for too long their food would begin to run out, and perhaps more important fresh water would become scarce.

You may have guessed by now the connection between waves on the sea and the wind. In fact, waves are almost wholly the result of the wind blowing across the surface of the water. Perhaps you have played 'blow' water polo at home. You need a table tennis ball, two pieces of tube and a bowl full of water. Float the table tennis ball in the bowl and blow through the tubes. As you blow on to the water you will notice that the surface is stirred up into ripples – the harder you blow the bigger the ripples.

It is very similar on the sea. The wind drags the water to form waves which slowly move forward and get larger. Although the wave shape moves forward, each particle of water moves round in circles and does not change its average position. The height of a wave depends upon three factors. How hard the wind is blowing (you will realize why gale warnings are so important to sailors), how long the wind has been blowing, and the *fetch*. The word fetch means the length of the stretch of open water over which the wind is blowing.

Right:
Breaking waves can exert tremendous force and cause cliffs to be eroded away.

What happens when a wave reaches the shore?

When a wave approaches shallow water – shallow means that the depth is less than half the distance between two wave tops – it is slowed down by dragging on the sea bed. The first waves to approach the shore are slowed first and the ones behind pile up. The amount of water in each wave increases, the wave grows taller until eventually it topples over or *breaks*. It is these waves and *breakers* that are responsible for the many processes of erosion and deposition that are typical of every shoreline and beach.

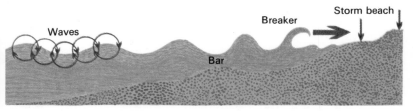

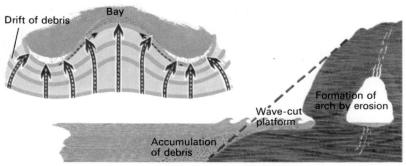

Left:
These diagrams show the movement of waves at sea and the way in which they break as they approach the shore. Waves may curve to erode a headland, and they can cause considerable erosion.

What are groynes?

When you have visited the seaside, you may have seen what look like garden fences running straight down the beach into the sea, and then coming to a halt. But they do not seem to be fencing anything off, do they? These barriers are called groynes. If you look more closely at them you will probably find that they are covered with various types of seaweeds and barnacles (small limpet-like shells but with a hole in the top). More important than this, however, you should be able to see that the sand or shingle has built up higher on one side of the groyne than the other. In fact, on the south coast of Britain, it is very likely that the sand will be higher on the western side, and on the east coast it will probably be higher on the north of the groyne. Why should this be happening? And why are the groynes there in the first place?

Right:
Groynes prevent sand and shingle from being transported very far by the action of longshore drift. Longshore drift may cause a spit to form at an estuary and salt marshes then develop behind it.

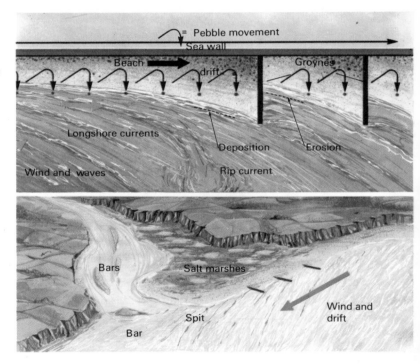

We have already explained how waves are formed by the wind and how these waves break when they reach the shore. Although it is only the wave shape that moves in the open sea, on the shore the breaking waves of water tend to have a motion shorewards. This motion is called the *swash*. But as you will have seen, after the swash up the beach, the water runs back again – this is called the *backwash*. If the force of the swash is greater than the force of the backwash, the

Right:
When the amount of sediment that is being carried by a river is greater than the amount that can be removed by longshore drift and other currents, a delta may form. The inset shows how the sediments in a delta build up.

waves are called *constructive*, and the sand, mud, and shingle that may be carried with the wave tends to be moved in the direction of the wave. When the reverse occurs the waves are called *destructive*. Generally, constructive waves are formed in quiet weather conditions and destructive waves during storms.

Generally, the waves do not come straight up the beach in Britain. This is because the wind most commonly blows from the west, that is, the *prevailing* winds are the westerlies. Therefore, on the south coast, for example, the waves travel up the beach and along from west to east. The sand and shingle is carried diagonally up the beach by the swash and directly down the beach by the backwash. This means that sand and shingle tend to move from west to east. What would happen if this were allowed to carry on unchecked? Of course, the beaches in the west would be washed away and those in the east built up. To prevent this the groynes are erected and the sand builds up on one side. Sometimes, the movement of shingle and sand may build up material into bars and spits. This is called *longshore drift*, and a good example of this is Chesil Beach near Weymouth in Dorset, England.

What are the main types of coasts?

In 1952, a scientist called H. Valentin grouped all the coasts of the world into two main divisions. He called these two types *advancing coasts* and *retreating coasts*. Advancing coasts may be the result of the uplift of the coastal land or they may be built outwards by deposition. Retreating coasts occur when the land is sinking or when it is being eroded by the force of the waves. Both these processes may be taking place at the same time on many beaches, and it is only by carefully observing an area over a period of many years that scientists are able to tell which process is the more important in that area.

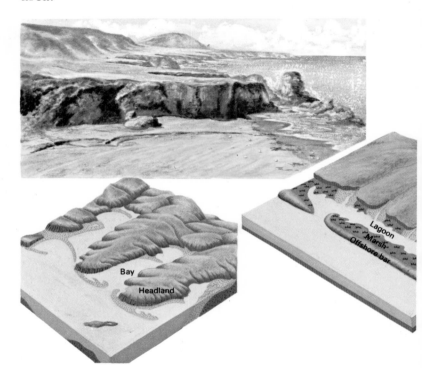

Right:
A raised beach like this one is typical of the Isle of Arran.

Right:
A coast line showing the features of bays and head-lands characteristic of submergence.

Far right:
An emerging coastline.

Bay

Headland

Lagoon

Marsh

Offshore bar

There are many features associated with these two main types of coastline which enable you to recognize them quite easily. For example, if the sea-level rises or the land sinks, it is clear that many of the features that were present on the land and formed by terrestrial processes will become flooded by the sea and drowned. If it was a hilly area before the sea advanced, you might expect to see bays, estuaries, rias (drowned river valleys), and gulfs separated by projecting areas of dry land called headlands and peninsulas. The *fjords* of Scandinavia are typical of submergence.

If you were to go to many parts of the north-west coast of Scotland, you might notice a different situation, however. On the Isle of Arran for example, behind the present beaches you might be able to recognize what appear to be other typical sea beaches. These beaches are higher than the level of the highest seas there today. They are called *raised beaches* and are old sea beaches which have been raised above the present sea level. Sometimes, as many as four levels of raised beaches can be seen.

Right:
The Temple of Serapis, near Naples, once stood on dry land. It has since been sub-merged and raised several times. Borings made by marine worms can be seen in the columns. The changes in sea level are caused by movements of magma underground.

What causes the changes of sea-level?

We have seen in previous questions how great sheets of ice have extended over many areas of the Earth's surface at certain times during geologic history called Ice Ages. The water which made up these icy masses came from the seas so that the sea-level fell, but at the same time the weight of the ice pressed down upon the Earth and when the ice retreated the land bounced back up again. The areas of the Baltic still seem to be rising from the melting of the ice from the last Ice Age. Local sea-level changes may occur for many other reasons such as earth movements.

Can rocks bend?

When you pick up a pebble on the beach, it is hard to imagine that this solid material rock, can be bent just as though it were toothpaste. Throughout the world, however, you can find large areas of exposed rock that clearly show the evidence of bending. It is also important to realize that it is the bending and upheaval of the surface rocks which give rise to the basic structure from which the landscape is moulded. Some of the *folds* which have been formed in beds of rock are so large that you cannot see their complete shape. Their existence can be proved by other methods, as we shall see later. You will also see later how rocks called sedimentary rocks are deposited in beds that are almost horizontal, but they can be twisted into remarkable shapes and even turned upside down by later Earth movements.

Geologists try to simplify the business of examining folded rocks by giving characteristic forms names. Take a piece of paper to help you learn some of the folds that can be seen in nature. First of all, bend the sheet into a gentle curve and hold it so that the bend is at the top as you look at it. When rocks are bent into this shape it is called an *antiform*.

Now, instead of using just one sheet, do the same thing with a number of sheets held together. Try to imagine that

Right:
This illustration shows a part of a fold. The *dip* of the rocks is important to the geologist who is trying to work out the structure in an area. If you were to walk along the *strike* of a bed of rocks you would be walking along the same bed continuously.

Centre right:
A clinometer is an instrument for measuring the dip of a bed of rocks.

Far right:
This illustrates how a fold may be fractured.

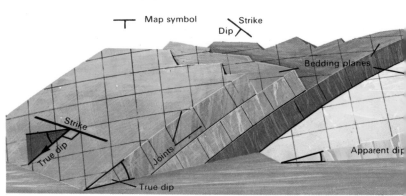

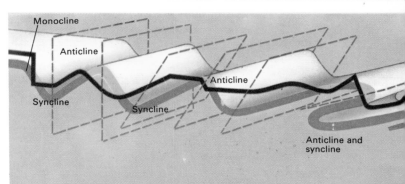

each sheet of paper is a bed of rock and that the bottom sheet was the first bed to be laid down, in other words the oldest. Now hold the fold in one hand and cut off the top of the curve with scissors. You will see that the sheet that was at the bottom is now in two halves at the centre of the sheets of paper. When this happens to folded rocks, and the oldest beds occur in the centre of an antiform, it is called an *anticline*. Sometimes if there is more than one period of movement, what was at first an anticline can be turned upside down, and the situation becomes quite confusing.

Of course, beds of rock in the Earth's crust are rather longer than your piece of paper and you would not expect to find just one fold. Take the sheet of paper and put two gentle folds in it. You will see that one has its bend at the top, the antiform, but the other has its bend at the bottom; this called a *synform*. When there are younger rocks in the centre of the synform it is called a *syncline*.

With many periods of upheaval, then, you can see that there could be synformal anticlines and antiformal synclines. Sometimes, rocks are bent into *dome* and *basin* shapes.

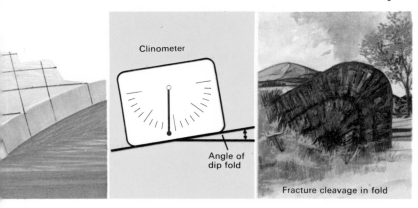

Clinometer

Angle of dip fold

Fracture cleavage in fold

Left:
This diagram shows some of the different types of folds.

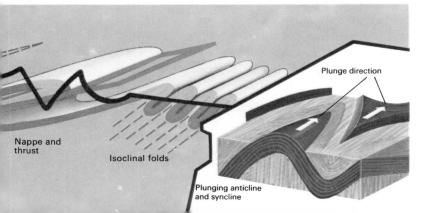

Nappe and thrust

Isoclinal folds

Plunge direction

Plunging anticline and syncline

Can rocks break?

You have seen that the enormous forces locked within the Earth are enough to bend huge masses of rock. Sometimes the rocks may break and great blocks may move quite large distances. This is known as *faulting*. A famous fault in Britain is the Great Glen Fault running across Scotland from the Island of Mull in the south west to the Moray Firth in the north east. This is almost as though Scotland had broken

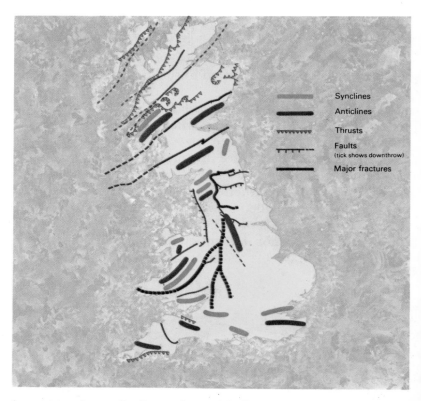

Synclines
Anticlines
Thrusts
Faults
(tick shows downthrow)
Major fractures

into two pieces. In fact, along this line the northern part has moved south westwards relative to the southern half by a distance of as much as 105 kilometres. This type of fault is called a *tear fault*, and they are very important on a global scale as we shall see later. A well-known example is the San Andreas fault in California.

There are many different types of faults, and faults, like folds have their own special names. If you could stretch a bed of rock until it broke, you would probably find that the way it broke would be usually called a *normal fault*. In other words, the surface where the break took place would be quite steep, and one block would move downwards along this plane with respect to the other so that if the plane was inclined to the left the right-hand block would be the lower.

Normal faults, then are usually associated with crustal stretching.

On the other hand *reverse faults* are associated with crustal shortening. In the above situation, a reverse fault would have the lower block on the left. In some cases, reverse faults occur where the fault plane is almost horizontal. This type of fault is called a *thrust*.

As you can see, on any given fault plane there can be vertical movement, that is, up and down, and this is called the *throw* of the fault. There can also be horizontal movement, that is, from side to side, and this is called the *heave* of the fault. Many of these strange terms that have become associated with faulting had their origins in the coal mines of the north of England where faults were particularly important. One way of discovering the presence of a fault is by noticing that there is a sudden change in the beds of rock from one side of the fault to the other. For example, on one side of a fault there might be Carboniferous limestones and on the other older Devonian sandstones. This would mean that the younger limestones had dropped down in relation to the sandstones. Other miners' terms associated with faulting include the word *hade*. The fault plane of a normal fault, for example, slopes towards the fallen block of rock, that is, it 'hades to the downthrow'.

Right:
Some typical types of fault movements.

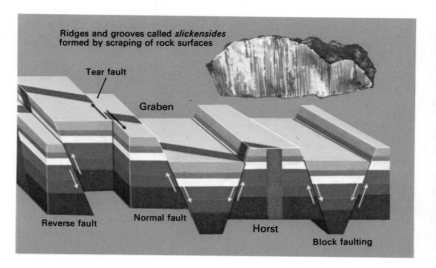

Ridges and grooves called *slickensides* formed by scraping of rock surfaces

Tear fault

Graben

Reverse fault

Normal fault

Horst

Block faulting

Where there are combinations of reverse and normal faults, whole blocks of rocks may be moved up or down. A block which has moved up is called a *horst*, and a block that has moved down is called a *graben*.

What kinds of rocks are there?

If you have been to any of the places where rocks are exposed at the surface of the Earth, such as in cliffs and quarries, or in mountainous areas, you may have already noticed that rocks come in a variety of forms. Even if you have only had the chance to examine the pebbles in your garden, you will probably have seen that the colour, shape, and hardness of the pebbles can vary quite considerably. Remember that soft, white, crumbly chalk and hard, black basalt are both rocks. Even soft, sticky clays are considered to be rocks.

It is important for geologists to be able to pass on information about any particular rock in as brief and accurate a way as possible, so that geological information can be accumulated. In scientific language a rock could be described as *an acid, igneous rock containing more than 10 per cent quartz, and in which the alkali feldspars predominate over the calcic feldspars.* But this is very long-winded and not easy to understand – it would be enough to say that the rock is a *granite*.

It is possible to group all the hundreds of different rock types in the world into families to give an idea of the origin and/or the make-up of those rocks. Every rock can be given a name to convey more particular information. In fact rocks are usually divided into three major groups on the basis of the way in which they were formed. Rocks may be *igneous*, *sedimentary*, or *metamorphic* in origin. The word igneous comes from the Latin *ignis* meaning fire and immediately gives an idea of how these rocks were formed; that is, that the great heat inside the Earth has been involved in their formation. Igneous rocks are formed by the cooling of *magma*, or melted rock which has been made more fluid by gases. A granite is a typical igneous rock.

As the name implies, *sedimentary* rocks are formed from compacted, hardened, and cemented sediments such as sands to form sandstones, clays to form shales and limey oozes to form chalk. As you have seen the sediments arise from the wearing away of other rocks. *Metamorphic* rocks are rocks that have been changed by heat and pressure. A slate is the metamorphic version of a shale.

What are rocks made of?

You could answer this question by just saying that rocks are made of minerals. But then there is the question: what are minerals made of? And the answer might be that the basic component of a mineral is a crystal, and so on. In the end we see that rocks are made up of the elements. You have read of the elements in a previous question, and they include oxygen, silicon and aluminium.

Rocks are made up of materials formed by the elements joining together in chemical combination. Some elements, such as gold, do not need to combine with other elements and can exist alone in the Earth's crust. But silicon, for example, can combine with oxygen in the proportion of two atoms of oxygen to one of silicon to form the compound called silicon oxide or silica. In nature silica may be found as the mineral called quartz. Quartz may occur in a variety of colours depending upon the impurities it contains, ranging from black or pink to glassy clear. You might find quartz as irregularly shaped broken lumps, but if you look at the pieces closely, they are more likely to have straight edges or may end in a pyramid shape. In fact, if the conditions in which the quartz formed were perfect, a crystal might have formed. What you see is the result of many crystals growing and interfering with each other.

Right:
The metal aluminium, which occurs in combination with other elements in rocks, is a good conductor of heat and electricity. It is used for electricity cables and cooking pots. Aluminium is becoming more difficult to find in workable amounts in the Earth's crust.

A crystal is a symmetrical solid. It has flat surfaces that have a direct relationship to the arrangement of the atoms in the crystal. A mineral may then be described as a solid, inorganic substance occurring naturally in the Earth's crust, and having a definite composition and a structure which is consistent throughout. In this definition the word inorganic may be puzzling. It is a chemical term implying that the rocks do not contain the element carbon in the types of combinations which are normally associated with living creatures, or their basic materials.

This brings us back to the first definition in this question: that a rock is a mass of minerals. Unfortunately, nature is rather fickle and as you will find in many of the other natural subjects, the scientific definitions do not always tell the whole story. Some rocks have been formed by the action of living creatures and still others, such as volcanic glass, are not made up of crystals at all.

Right:
An igneous rock, such as granite, is made up of the minerals quartz, mica, and feldspar.

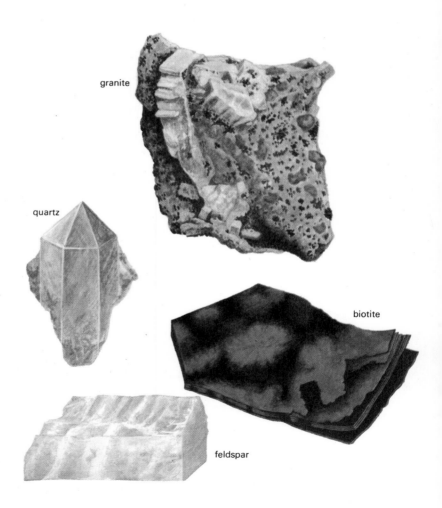

granite

quartz

biotite

feldspar

What shapes of crystals are there?

We have already explained the way in which rocks are made up of minerals, and that minerals take the form of regular solids called crystals that may come in a great many different shapes, hardnesses, and colours. Naturally, you would expect that if you wanted to know more about rocks, you would need to understand more about the way in which crystals develop. The scientific study of crystals is known as crystallography.

The shapes of crystals are very important to anyone wishing to identify a mineral, because these regular forms exactly express the way in which the atoms of that mineral are arranged. This means that if you are able to recognize the shape of the crystal of a mineral, then, with the help of a number of other properties, you could work out what the mineral was by a process of elimination. Other important properties are weight, hardness (which in this case means the resistance to scratching), and so on.

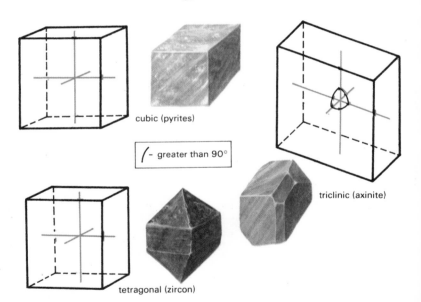

cubic (pyrites)

/ - greater than 90°

triclinic (axinite)

tetragonal (zircon)

The most important property, then, in recognizing crystalline materials is *symmetry*, that is, the regularity of the shape. You can try an experiment in symmetry for yourself. Take a fairly large potato and peel it: Be very careful not to cut yourself with the knife. Then cut the potato into the shape of a cube; that is, a dice shape with six square faces and sharp corners. Some minerals such as iron pyrite (fool's gold) often develop as cubic crystals. Now cut off the corners of the potato cube and you will have a shape with eight more faces. If you continue to make these eight faces larger and larger, you will eventually cut away the six original faces leaving a shape with eight faces only called an octahedron.

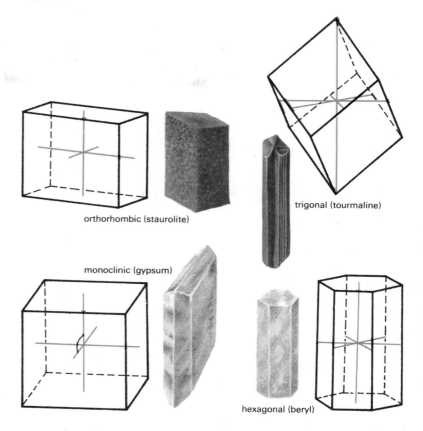

orthorhombic (staurolite)

trigonal (tourmaline)

monoclinic (gypsum)

hexagonal (beryl)

You have now shown for yourself that three seemingly different shapes are related to each other. These relationships occur throughout the world of crystals, so that of all the many crystal shapes there are only seven crystal systems into which they can all be classified. You have already seen one of these systems, the cubic system. The other six are given the names tetragonal, orthorhombic, hexagonal, trigonal, monoclinic, and triclinic. If you can place any crystal that you find into one of these systems then you have gone a long way towards identifying the mineral. With some crystals it is quite easy, but with others it does require considerable practice. We shall explain how to recognize some of the simpler crystals in the next question.

How do you recognize crystals?

In the previous question, we mentioned that there are seven crystal systems. Knowing their names is of little value unless you know how to place a given crystal in its system, and then some of the minerals in each system. The way in which you place a crystal in its class is really quite simple and depends upon what are known as *elements of symmetry*. In fact, each crystal system is actually defined by certain elements of symmetry.

Look at your potato again – the one that you have cut into an octahedron. Hold it between your finger and thumb so that your finger is at one of its points and your thumb at the one exactly opposite. Now turn the potato slowly about these two points, and you will find that each edge or face is repeated by an exactly similar edge or face four times as you turn it through one complete turn. This means that this shape has a fourfold axis of symmetry. You will find that you can hold the potato-octahedron by two other pairs of points and repeat the process so that there are three of these axes. Now hold the potato by two opposite faces instead. When you turn it this time you will find that there are three repeats in one full turn and that there are three other pairs of faces that you can hold. You can see, then that the octahedron has four of these threefold axes of symmetry.

You already know that this shape was cut from a cube. You have now seen how to recognize any cubic crystal. To belong to the cubic system, a crystal must have four threefold axes of symmetry, and you can look for them in exactly the same way as you did with the potato-octahedron.

From left to right:
A plane of symmetry, a centre of symmetry, and a threefold axis of symmetry.

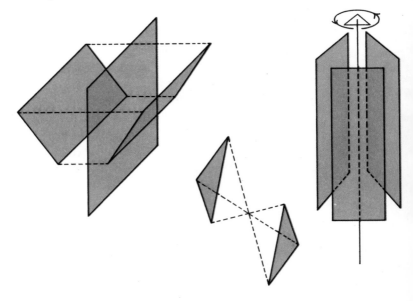

Right:
Any crystal reflects the
arrangement of its atoms;
this simple arrangement of
two different atoms is
typical of a substance such
as common salt.

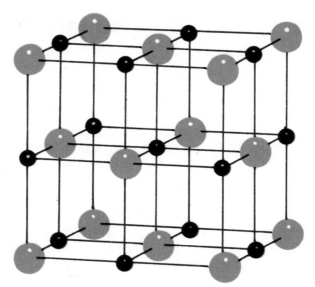

You can soon recognize the other six systems of crystals by working out their axes of symmetry. Each system is defined by a different set of rules. Crystals belonging to the tetragonal system must have one fourfold axis of symmetry and one only. It might also have four twofold axes if it were a very regular example of the system, but there are some that do not. An example of this system is the mineral zircon which is sometimes used as a stone in jewellery. Orthorhombic crystals must have three twofold axes, hexagonal crystals one sixfold axis, trigonal one threefold axis, monoclinic one twofold axis, and finally triclinic with no axes at all.

Right:
Silicon atoms and oxygen
atoms may join together in
chains of tetrahedra like the
one shown. You can see
how the chains are packed
together into the crystal
shape.

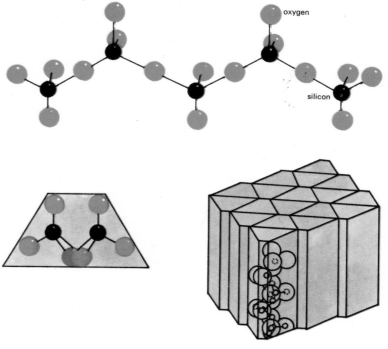

What are the main mineral groups?

We have already explained the way in which the form of a crystal is directly related to its internal atomic structure. You have also seen how the many possible crystal shapes can be grouped into just seven crystal systems. To simplify their study, the Earth's minerals can also be grouped together. The way in which they are grouped depends upon the purpose of the grouping. For example, you might want to group minerals on the basis of the elements which compose them; this would be a chemical classification. On the other hand, you could group together all the minerals of the same colour, or all the minerals which have crystals of the same system, but these groupings would not tell you anything about the ways in which the different minerals were formed.

A simple grouping which is often used by mineralogists (those who study minerals) is into *rock-forming minerals* and *non rock-forming minerals*. Naturally every mineral occurs in a rock, but the rock-forming minerals actually make up the bulk of the igneous rocks. You will remember that igneous rocks are formed by the cooling of magma and they provide the materials for sedimentary and metamorphic rocks.

Right:
Some of the many different silicate minerals that you might come across in rocks.

olivine crystal

granular mass of olivine

augite crystal

hornblende crystal

fibrous mass of actinolite

veins of asbestos in serpentine

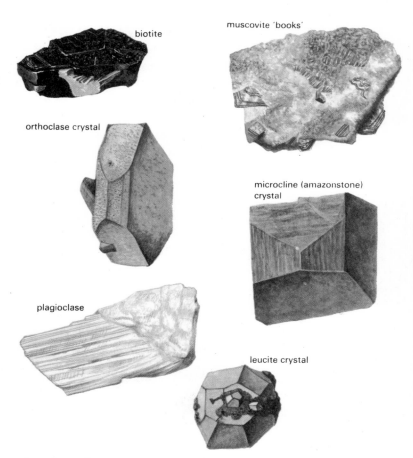

biotite

muscovite 'books'

orthoclase crystal

microcline (amazonstone) crystal

plagioclase

leucite crystal

Right:
Here are some more silicate minerals.

Another important grouping is into *silicates* and *non-silicates*, but this is rather more complicated and the details are beyond the scope of this book. A very great simplification of this grouping would be to say that silicates contain silica in combination with other elements and non-silicates do not contain silica.

The silicates are by far the most important of the rock-forming minerals, and are worth more detailed consideration. These silicate minerals may be further divided into groups which have similar internal, or atomic, make-up. To be more scientific, it has been shown by a researcher called Bowen, how members of a group are formed from molten rock at different temperatures. As you know, heat is just one form of energy. Minerals that are formed at very high temperatures, such as olivine, are formed by a great deal of energy which is reflected by the way in which its atoms are arranged. The other main silicate minerals are given the names pyroxenes, amphiboles, micas, feldspars and quartz. The order in which they have been mentioned exactly corresponds to the temperature at which you would expect them to form from the melted rock material.

How do you identify minerals?

When you recognize a person, the recognition is based on your knowledge of certain characteristics of that person. Without your being consciously aware of it, your brain is very quickly looking at the person's height, build, colour of hair, facial characteristics such as colour of eyes, size and shape of mouth, and so on. Similarly, when you wish to identify any mineral, there are a number of properties that you need to look for. Some of these properties can only be examined with the use of a special microscope, and with many minerals they can only be positively identified in this way. But there are a lot of minerals that can be identified quite accurately by carefully looking at them with the naked eye or with the aid of a simple magnifying lens (one with a magnification of × 10 is ideal).

Right:
The mineral fluorite can occur in a variety of colours. The iron minerals limonite and haematite have different streaks.

fluorite

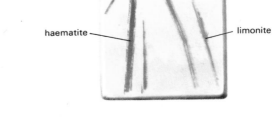

haematite — limonite

When identifying a mineral, you do need to know the features to look for. Each mineral has a different internal make-up which is reflected in its properties. You need to work out the crystal class to which the mineral belongs, its hardness (resistance to scratching), specific gravity, colour, lustre, degree of transparency, streak (colour of powder when crushed), and sometimes the taste or the smell. In the case of taste, you should never try to taste the mineral yourself because many are poisonous. You need to be very experienced before using this test.

We have already explained how to establish the crystal form, and this is very important. There is a scale invented by Mohs to test hardness, which indicates by the numbers one to ten the hardnesses of certain reference minerals. A mineral of hardness 3 will scratch a mineral of hardness 2 but not one of hardness 4 and so on. The softest mineral is talc and the hardest diamond.

Right:
These minerals are exhibiting different lustres.

chalcopyrite

blende

topaz

Specific gravity can be estimated if you are experienced, by holding the specimen in your hand and feeling if it is light or heavy for its size. Colour may be affected by impurities and by weathering. Lustre refers to whether the mineral shines like a metal or looks glassy or pearly and so on. The transparency refers to how well you can see through the

Right:
Minerals can break or *cleave* in a variety of ways – these are just a few.

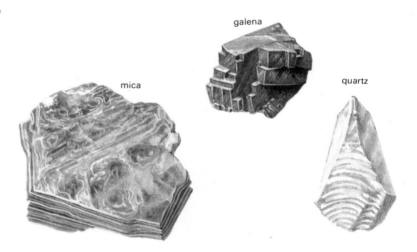

galena

mica

quartz

mineral – is it completely clear or not? To test the streak, simply scratch the sample on a piece of unglazed porcelain and look at the colour of the trace. Another important feature is the way in which the sample breaks – along certain planes or irregularly. These are the properties you look for when you are trying to work out a mineral 'fingerprint'.

Which rock burns?

All rocks will eventually burn or melt at high enough temperatures. The rock we are referring to burns at quite low temperatures and provides us with many chemicals. It can be very soft and crumbly or quite hard; it can be shiny or quite dull. It can be burnt in its natural state or it can be treated so that it burns without smoke; it is usually black. Of course, the rock is coal! Like oil, coal is often regarded as a mineral, although as you will see, it also has living origins.

Certain parts of the world, such as the bogs of Scotland and Ireland, the American swamps and places like Burma are water-logged. Plants that live there do not decay in the normal way when they die. The bacteria and fungi which break down the plant remains under more normal conditions, cannot live because there is not enough oxygen and certain acids are formed which kill them. Under these circumstances, a jelly-like humus is formed and this soaks into the fragments of wood and bark and so on, to form a material called *peat*.

Peat is rich in carbon, and the chemical reactions which occur also produce marsh gas or methane which burns very readily. Methane is the natural gas which is piped into most of your homes. In more remote places, such as the north-west of Scotland, where peat is still being formed, it is dug up during the summer months and stacked to dry so that it can be used for fires during the long, cold winter.

As the peat builds up year after year, the water is squeezed out, and then with further burying under clays and sands it undergoes a change. It becomes more and more compacted and the gases are pressed out. It becomes harder and richer in carbon until eventually it forms a *brown coal*. It has often

Right:
Coal is deposited as one of a sequence of sedimentary events and the rocks that occur above and below a coal seam, together with the contained fossils, indicate the conditions of deposition in the cyclic sequence.

SEDIMENTS	FOSSILS	ENVIRONMENTS
coal	leaves, stems, and spores of trees	swampy forests
seat earth	roots	
mudstone		surface built up to water level
sandstone locally cross-bedded with irregularities		deltaic
		influx of river sands
siltstone	plant debris	deltaic lagoons
mudstone and shale		delta front or estuarine
with ironstone nodules	mussels, fish	brackish water
mudstone	marine molluscs	inundation by the sea
coal		swampy forests

Right:
Coal can be mined by
tunnelling underground or
by digging huge, open pits.
These pits are called open
cast mines.

been shown in coal fields that the greater the thickness of
rock on top of the coal, the higher the carbon content of the
coal. Eventually anthracite results which contains about
95 per cent carbon and is a very high quality and expensive
coal.

Most of the coal fields throughout the world are to be
found in rocks of Carboniferous age. About 300 million
years ago, dense swampy forests occurred because of the very
rich plant life which had by then developed on Earth, and it
is the remains of these forests that gives us most of our coal.

Right:
This was how an eighteenth
century naturalist represented
the coal seams of Somerset,
England.

Which mineral comes from animals and plants?

We have already given a definition of a mineral in a previous question, and two of the properties were that a mineral must be solid and inorganic. There is one material which is always included as a mineral, however, which does not follow the rule. We have mentioned it before. Can you guess what it is?

The mineral to which we are referring is correctly called petroleum from the Greek *petra* meaning a rock and the Latin *oleum* meaning oil. Petroleum is the name given to all the materials which occur in nature and are known chemically as hydrocarbons. This means that they are composed of combinations of carbon and hydrogen. These materials may be gases, such as the natural gas which now supplies some of the domestic gas in Britain. There are also liquid oils from which we obtain our vital petrol (or gasolene as it is known in the United States). Many other important products are derived from petroleum, from perfumes to plastics. You can appreciate, then, the importance of this mineral to our way of life in the industrialized nations.

From the way in which the question is worded, and from what you have read so far, you will have guessed that the mineral that comes from animals and plants is, in fact, petroleum. Actually, many different origins have been suggested for this mineral. They have included the ideas that petroleum has been produced by chemical reaction, from volcanoes, and from the decay of land plants. But the evidence that has been gathered at an enormous rate

Right:
This map shows the distribution of the world's coal and oil fields.

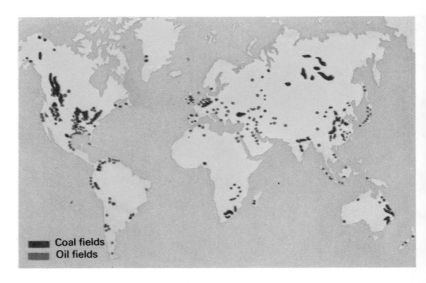

Coal fields
Oil fields

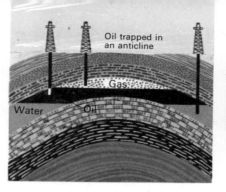

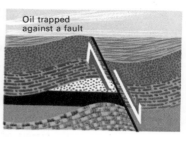

Oil trapped in an anticline

Oil trapped against a fault

Gas

Water Oil

Oil trapped by impervious rocks

Oil trapped against salt dome

Right:
Oil, filling the cavities in a porous rock, may become trapped in economic amounts in a variety of ways. Oil is associated with natural gas and water and is trapped by impervious layers of rock.

because of the economic importance of oil has shown that none of these ideas is likely to be correct. It is much more probable that oil was formed (and is still being formed today) from the decay of tiny marine plants and animals such as algae and the one-celled diatoms.

The two most important conditions for the formation of petroleum are the activities of certain bacteria and time. It is very important to remember that petroleum products take millions of years to form and concentrate into quantities which can be worked. But in 100 years we have consumed a large proportion of the world's oil reserves. Oil, then, formed as tiny droplets among the particles of muddy sediments at the bottom of the sea where the water was stagnant and there was little air.

Right:
An oil pipeline to carry oil from its source to a refinery.

When is a mineral a gem?

A mineral can claim the title of gem if, in its natural state or when cut in certain ways, its properties are thought to be beautiful. Gems are those minerals which are prized throughout the world for their eye-pleasing appearance.

Some gems are very precious indeed. Diamond, for example, has exactly the same chemical composition as graphite, the soft lead-grey material which is used in pencils. Why, then do we value diamond so highly? There are two main reasons. Firstly, diamond has a very high *refractive index*. This means that although diamond is glass clear, it tends to bend the light passing through it much more than glass does. If the diamond is cut in certain ways, it gives a delightful play of colours which no other gem can rival. Indeed, this is the sole reason for cutting a diamond. It is scarcely recognizable in its raw state, and it would certainly be hard to believe that an uncut stone and such gems as the famous Kohinor diamond were the same material. Diamonds are also the hardest known mineral. This has led to its wide use on the cutting edges of oil drill bits, and on saws for cutting the hardest stones or metals. Now, however, diamonds suitable for industrial use can be manufactured artificially, but nature is still needed to furnish us with gem quality stones.

Another property which gives a stone its value is rarity. For example, even if the correct materials are present, it takes conditions of extreme heat, and pressures equivalent to being buried as much as 120 kilometres beneath the surface of the Earth to form a gem.

Other true gems are the deep, green emeralds, the transparent red ruby, and the delicate to deep blue sapphires. Emeralds are a variety of a mineral called beryl which occurs associated with granites. The ruby is a type of corundum

insect in amber

Above:
Amber is actually fossil tree resin so that it is not strictly a gem. It is often used in jewellery, however.

Right:
Some of the most beautiful and valuable gems.

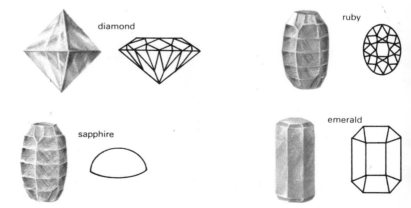

diamond

ruby

sapphire

emerald

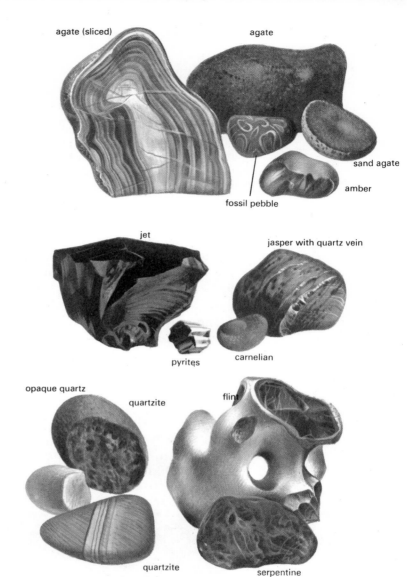

agate (sliced)

agate

sand agate

amber

fossil pebble

jet

jasper with quartz vein

pyrites

carnelian

opaque quartz

quartzite

flint

quartzite

serpentine

which you may know as the hard stone that is used to sharpen
knives and other cutting edges. Sapphire is also a variety of
corundum. All these gems are rare, resistant to scratching,
beautiful in colour, have an attractive lustre and can be cut
to further enhance their beauty.

As well as these very valuable stones there are other less
valuable, but in some ways just as attractive, stones that
are known as semi-precious. These tend to be less hard or
brilliant in colour and lustre, and rather more common.
Many varieties of quartz are semi-precious, such as citrine,
amethyst and the non-crystalline opal; the banded ones such
as onyx and agate are also very pleasing. Even volcanic
glass called obsidian, or the type of soft coal usually called
jet, can be polished and are often used in jewellery.

Why does a volcano erupt?

By now you should be aware that in the bowels of the Earth all is not still. On the contrary, it is very active. One obvious example of the Earth's internal workings is the activity of volcanoes. There are many famous instances of a volcano erupting and spewing white hot, molten rock from its mouth; if you have been to Pompeii or just seen pictures of it you will realize how a whole city and most of its inhabitants can be engulfed in the fiery ash suddenly erupting from what was thought to have been a dead volcano. A more recent example was the eruption of Mount Saint Helens in the United States in 1980. This eruption had the force of 500 of the nuclear bombs dropped on Hiroshima in 1945. Perhaps the most famous of all volcanoes is Krakatoa. This volcano had remained dormant for 200 years, when on 27 August 1883, the volcano exploded with such force that the whole island was ripped apart. The noise was heard almost 5000 kilometres away in Australia, and a tidal wave of 36 metres high was sent across the sea to Java, killing 36,000 people. You can understand, then, that it is a very great force that makes volcanoes erupt.

Volcanoes were once thought to be burning mountains and it is not difficult to understand why. But nowadays, a volcano is usually defined as a direct feed from a magma chamber in the interior of the Earth to the surface. Remember that a magma is any hot material within the Earth which can flow and penetrate into or through the surface

Right:
When Mount Vesuvius erupted in AD 79 to bury the city of Pompeii, many of the 20,000 inhabitants were killed and their remains can be seen preserved in the positions in which they died, trapped by the hot ash and pumice.

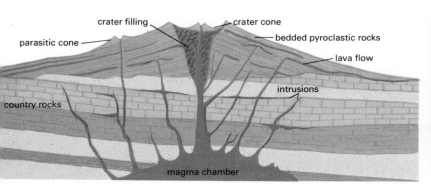

rocks. A magma, then, is usually thought to consist of a kind of 'porridge' of solid rock material, liquids and semi-plastic substances which are made to flow by the lubrication of hot gases under great pressures.

Two main causes are responsible for the birth of a volcano. Explosive eruptions may be caused by pressure resulting from the build up of gases within the Earth or a crack in the crust can be opened up forming a passage or *vent*. Volcanic lava can then flow through it.

It is important to remember that the classic cone shaped body which you might immediately think of as a volcano, only forms as a result of volcanic activity. It is the pile of ash and cooled lava that has flowed or been thrown out of the original fissure or crack. A volcano may erupt only once, and it may not emit enough material to build up the well-known cone. This cone usually occurs when there are successive eruptions from the same vent.

What kinds of volcanoes are there?

You have seen the ways in which volcanoes erupt, and we have already said that volcanoes are not always the simple cones that one usually associates with outpourings of red hot, molten rock. In fact, eruptions vary a great deal in the type of products that are spewed out, in their intensity, and in the form which the volcanic vent takes.

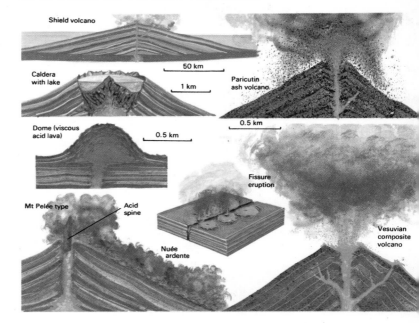

Right:
Typical examples of the main types of volcanoes.

First of all there is the type which is known as the *fissure eruption*. This is simple to describe. Here a flood of lava pours out of a crack in the Earth's crust and flows very freely. When it cools, it hardens into an almost flat sheet. This type of eruption is also known as the Icelandic type, because of the type of lava flows commonly found there.

In the Hawaiian type of volcano, so called for obvious reasons, lava pours out of a pit-like crater, and gas is quietly released most of the time. Occasionally, however, there is a sudden spurt of the volcanic gases blowing out a spray of glowing, burning droplets of lava. The well-known *Pele's hair* is caused by these droplets being caught in the wind and stretched into threads.

If the lava cannot flow easily (and this occurs when the composition of the magma is richer in silica), the gases have more difficulty in bubbling off. They are only released when the pressure builds up enough to force the gases out. In this kind of eruption, which is known as the *Strombolian type* after

Right:
A vent of a volcano may
become plugged with
solidified lava. When the
cone is eroded away the
plug or neck remains, like
this one at Le Rocher-St-
Michel in France.

Stromboli, Sicily, the volcano erupts from time to time
carrying lumps of lava or *volcanic bombs*. Sometimes there are
also lava flows.

If the lava is very thick and almost solid, great gas
pressure is needed before it is released. When it does erupt
it does so with explosive and terrible force, so that hot ash and
fragments of lava are thrown high into the air. This is known
as the *Vulcanian type*, and the characteristic cone is developed.
There are other types of central volcanic types, that is,
where the eruption is from one main centre.

Vulcanology is a very complex study, and, for the more
adventurous, can be an extremely dangerous one, involving
climbing to the very top of an active volcano. Under these
conditions, even if the volcano is not actually erupting the
ground may be so hot that it burns the shoes of the scientists
and the gases may be almost suffocating. Workers have
actually looked into open craters into the bubbling, burning
lava below.

Where do you find volcanoes?

We expect you know where there are some active volcanoes either today or in the very recent past, because when one erupts it always makes the headlines in the newspapers. For example, we have already mentioned the eruption of Mount St Helens, and, of course, Mount Etna in Sicily is still active as are some of the volcanoes on the Hawaiian islands. Perhaps the most spectacular of the recent eruptions took place off the coast of Iceland when suddenly a new island, Surtsey, was born of the eruption. In fact, there are almost 800 volcanoes which are either active today or have been noted as having erupted during recorded history. Are all these volcanoes dotted about the surface of the Earth at random or can we see any sort of pattern in their distribution? And if there is a pattern, is it significant?

The answer to both of these questions seems to be yes. If we look at a map of the world which shows all the active volcanoes, we would see that about two-thirds of them are situated around the edges of the Pacific Ocean including many on the groups of islands. This grouping of the volcanoes is often referred to as the 'Pacific ring of fire'. Of the remaining volcanoes, a number can be seen ranging along the centre of the Atlantic ocean. It has been shown that this line of active volcanoes follows what is known as the mid-Atlantic ridge. This ridge is extremely important as we shall see later, but for the moment let it remain as a line of volcanic activity. There are two other areas where there are concentrations of volcanoes. In and around the Mediterranean area includes Etna and Vesuvius. The other area is east Africa where Mount Kilimanjaro is a good example.

It is also very important to note that although there may

Right:
Volcanic activity usually occurs at the margins of crustal plates, in particular, at those margins where crust is being created or destroyed.

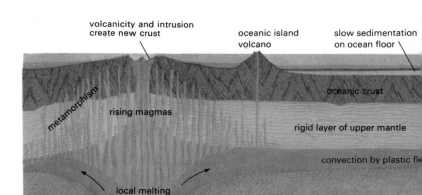

constructive boundary
(mid-ocean ridge)

volcanicity and intrusion
create new crust

oceanic island
volcano

slow sedimentation
on ocean floor

oceanic crust

metamorphism

rising magmas

rigid layer of upper mantle

convection by plastic fl•

local melting

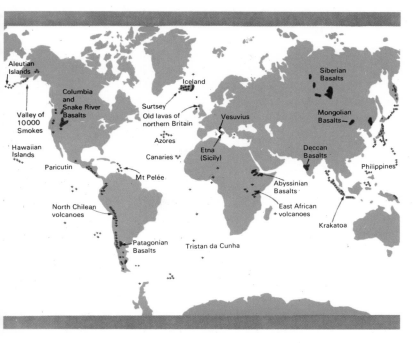

Labels on map:
Aleutian Islands
Columbia and Snake River Basalts
Valley of 10000 Smokes
Hawaiian Islands
Paricutin
North Chilean volcanoes
Iceland
Surtsey
Old lavas of northern Britain
Azores
Canaries
Mt Pelée
Patagonian Basalts
Tristan da Cunha
Vesuvius
Etna (Sicily)
Abyssinian Basalts
East African volcanoes
Krakatoa
Siberian Basalts
Mongolian Basalts
Deccan Basalts
Philippines

Left:
This map shows the world distribution of active volcanoes.

be slight variations from volcano to volcano in any one of these groups, each group tends to erupt similar products with similar compositions. For example, the mid-oceanic ridge volcanoes erupt basalt lavas while volcanoes in the 'ring of fire' often erupt lavas of andesite which contains more silica.

The significance of these patterns of volcanoes is concerned with the drifting of the continents but we shall deal with this more fully in another question. Suffice to say that the Earth's crust is made up of a number of rigid plates 'floating' on the mantle below. Concentrations of volcanoes are usually associated with the margins of these plates.

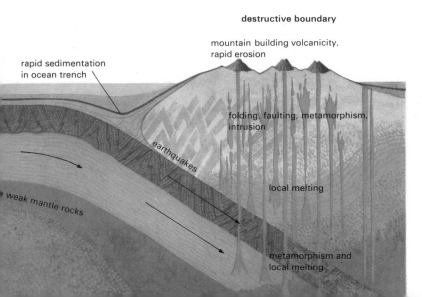

destructive boundary

mountain building volcanicity, rapid erosion

rapid sedimentation in ocean trench

folding, faulting, metamorphism, intrusion

earthquakes

local melting

weak mantle rocks

metamorphism and local melting

What are mountains made of?

From what you have learned already, it is obvious that mountains must be made of rock. But what kinds of rocks and what kinds of mountains are there? How do the mountains get there in the first place? Over the years in which geological thinking has been at its most active, many theories have been put forward to answer these questions. In fact, these types of questions hold the key to some of the most important facts concerning the Earth's whole history. These are the ideas of mountain building.

If you were asked to name a mountain that you know, which one would it be? Perhaps it would be Mount Everest or Mount Etna or perhaps you might suggest the Harz mountains of Germany or the Juras of France and Switzerland. All these mountains are different; made of different types of rock and formed by different processes. Perhaps the simplest and easiest example to understand is the volcano, Mount Etna. Its cone is built up by successive outpourings of lava from the bowels of the Earth. The Harz mountains were formed by block faulting, in other words they are the *horsts* that we have already mentioned.

Right:
The work of the Earth's up-heavals provides challenges to intrepid mountaineers.

Right:
A section across the ridge
that is present in the middle
of oceanic basins. At this
point, new crust is being
formed and it pushes the
land masses further apart.

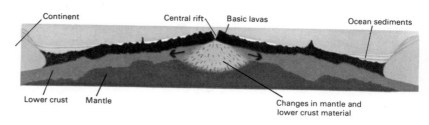

Continent   Central rift   Basic lavas   Ocean sediments

Lower crust   Mantle   Changes in mantle and
lower crust material

In these two examples, the volcanic mountain such as Etna can be made of a variety of volcanic materials such as basalt lava or cinders and ash, or more acid, blocky lavas, and the fault mountains can be uplifted blocks of granite such as those that form the Kharas mountains in south-west Africa.

You probably know that Mount Everest is the highest mountain in the world, standing 8848 metres above sea level. (It is interesting to note that the deepest part of the ocean known to man is the Marianas Trench south-east of Japan, which is 11,033 metres deep).

You might also know that Mount Everest does not stand alone but is part of a great chain of the highest mountains anywhere, called the Himalayas, astride the borders of Tibet and Nepal. Among these lofty pinnacles the Abominable Snowman, the *Yeti*, is said to have his icy home.

Below and below right:
A representation of a folded mountain chain and some typical rocks that might be found in it showing how they become more intensely metamorphosed near the granite core.

1   Shale

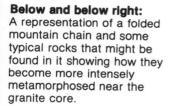

2   Schist

3   Gneiss

4   Granite

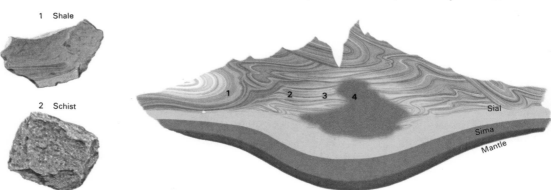

1   2   3   4   Sial

Sima

Mantle

There are many other such chains of mountains; for example, the Alps or the more modest mountains of the Highlands of Scotland. These are the great *fold mountains*, made of sediments laid down in primordial oceans and then uplifted by crumpling of the Earth's crust during periods of crustal shortening. The fact that these mountains occur in long chains in certain areas of the globe is no accident as you will see later, but is associated with one of the most important concepts of the modern Earth sciences, that of continental drift, the almost unbelievable idea of whole continents moving.

How are mountain chains built?

Most of the major mountain chains of the world have been constructed by periods of accumulation of unusually thick deposits of sediments in elongated basins followed by uplift, folding, thrusting of huge masses of rock called *nappes*, and faulting. These processes, known collectively as *tectogenesis* are usually accompanied by intense volcanic activity as well as the forcing into position of huge masses of granite which may continue to rise for a long time after the main movements have ceased and the processes of weathering are active. These regions in which Earth movements are concentrated are usually given the name of *orogenic belts* and the whole process is known as an *orogeny*.

You can see that the process of orogeny involves the sinking of a part of the Earth's crust, followed by sedimentation in the basin that has been formed, and finally uplift of the whole area. It is interesting to note that mountain chains such as the Juras that we have already mentioned are formed by a different process. In this case, certain parts of the nearby Alps had been uplifted by orogeny so that the area now occupied by the Juras was tilted. It so happened that the rocks which now compose the Juras were laying upon a huge bed of salt. In effect this salt acted like a layer of lubricating oil so that the rocks on the top slid very slowly down hill folding and faulting as they went. This is known as *gravity tectonics*.

In 1859, the geologist, James Hall, working in the northern Appalachian mountains of America discovered that the sediments that made up this range were of a type that could only have been deposited in quite shallow water in the sea. At the same time he recorded that the sediments were in some places as much as 12,000 metres thick. How, then, did such a thick deposit accumulate? It is clear that the older

Below:
The theory of isostasy suggests that as mountains are worn away by erosion, the Earth compensates by further uplift.

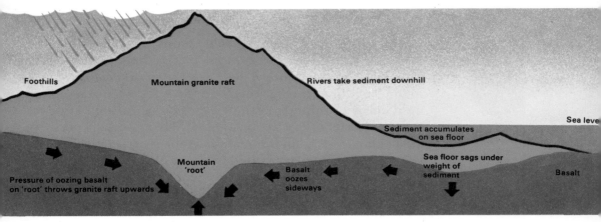

Foothills   Mountain granite raft   Rivers take sediment downhill

Sea level

Sediment accumulates on sea floor

Mountain 'root'

Basalt oozes sideways

Sea floor sags under weight of sediment

Basalt

Pressure of oozing basalt on 'root' throws granite raft upwards

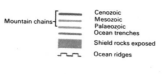
Right:
The positions and ages of
the world's mountain chains.

rocks underneath must have been sinking as fast as the new
sediments were being laid down. This type of elongated,
sinking basin has been called a *geosyncline*. At first, it was
thought that the sinking was caused by the weight of the
sediments being deposited on top but it was soon realized
that this was not so. In fact, it was the famous mineralogist,
Dana, who first suggested in 1873 that the sinking of the
basin was the cause of and not the result of the sedimentation.
Nowadays a new, all-embracing theory seems to provide us
with all the answers to the problems of how and why
mountain building takes place in the way it does. This is the
theory of *plate tectonics*.

Right:
The all-embracing theory of
plate tectonics neatly
accounts for the method of
formation of mountain
chains. The inset shows the
more traditional theory for
mountain building with the
crust being dragged down-
wards, filled with sediment
at a rapid rate, and then
squeezed.

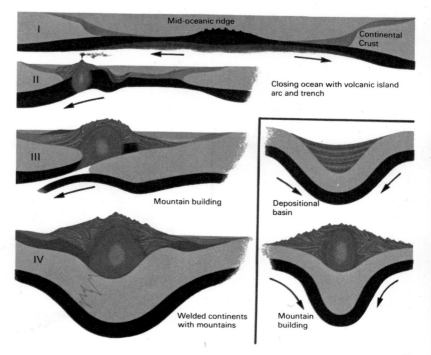

Can whole continents move?

It is almost impossible to believe, but without doubt, the answer to this question seems to be yes. But how do we know, because we cannot see or feel them drifting beneath our feet? In the early days of geology, the drifting of whole continents was certainly not considered to be a possibility, and in fact, in 1846 Dana positively asserted that continents and oceans have always been in the same place throughout geologic time. What happened, then, to change the geological mind?

It was a man called F. B. Taylor who first put forward a convincing argument for the movement of whole continents. He made this statement in the year 1910. During the following two years H. B. Baker and perhaps most famous of all A. Wegener supported Taylor's ideas. Since these pioneer workers first developed their startling suggestion, more and more evidence has been piling up to lend support to them.

It had been noticed 300 years ago that there was a remarkable fit between the outlines of the continents on the

Below and left:
The continental shelf shown here marks the edge of the continental land mass and it is along this edge that Bullard found such a good fit between the continents.

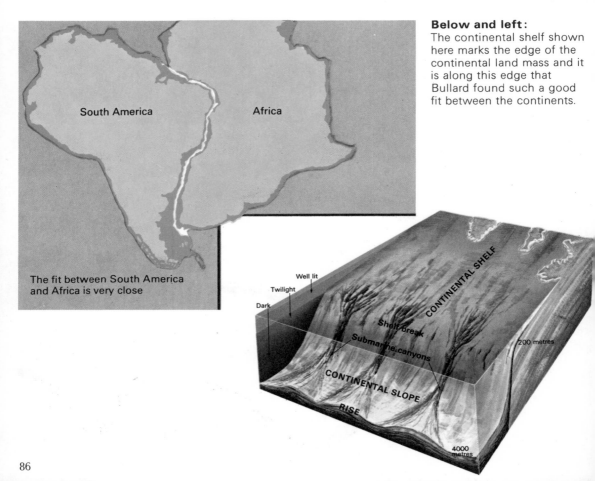

South America

Africa

The fit between South America and Africa is very close

Well lit

Twilight

Dark

CONTINENTAL SHELF

Shelf break

Submarine canyons

200 metres

CONTINENTAL SLOPE

RISE

4000 metres

opposite shores of the Atlantic. It is particularly noticeable how well the coasts of South America and the Nigeria region seem to match up rather like two pieces of a jigsaw puzzle. An even more accurate fit was discovered by Bullard in 1965 when he used a computer to try to match up these continents along the 500 fathom (900 metre) line of their shores.

Perhaps even more surprising is the correspondence of many great formations of rock which are separated by thousands of kilometres of ocean. A particularly good example is provided by sediments deposited by ice sheets during the great Carboniferous Ice Age. Deposits of this age can be found in South Africa, India, Australia, and Assam. Now if the ice sheet had been large enough to cover these areas as they are positioned today, there would have been a world-wide fall in temperature and other evidence proves that this simply was not so. This means, then, that during the Carboniferous these areas must have formed one huge continent and that they have subsequently broken up and drifted apart.

There is yet more evidence provided by palaeontology, which although it is not conclusive in itself, taken with all else is very convincing. Between the continents of Australia and South America, it is noticeable how there are some groups of animals and plants that are obviously very similar and closely related, while others are only found in one continent or the other. It is now thought that the groups showing similarities had evolved before the break up of the continents while the very different life forms had evolved separately afterwards. It is clear, then, that the map of the world has not always been the same as it is today.

What are crustal plates?

Geology, the study of our planet Earth, is essentially a science of keen observation of all of the natural processes of the planet that go on around us all the time. Consequently, a great deal is known about the Earth, although, of course, there is still a great deal to be learned. You have already seen, for example, what makes the rain fall, how rivers form, how volcanoes work, even that whole continents are able to move, and so on. What has been needed, however, is an idea, a theory, which would knit together all that is known about the separate processes into one unified whole. This would be a theory to explain how continents drift, why earthquakes occur only in certain parts of the Earth, why there are deep ocean trenches in some areas or oceanic ridges in others.

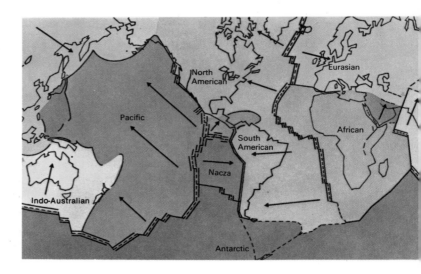

Today we seem to have such a theory explaining all, or most of what has been puzzling the experts for many years. This is the all-embracing theory of *plate tectonics*. The word 'tectonics' comes from the Greek *tecton*, a builder. In other words, tectonics refers to building and structure, in this case of the Earth itself. Thus, the idea of plate tectonics suggests that the surface of the Earth is made up of a number of rigid plates comprising the thickness of the crust and the upper part of the mantle. The plates are free to move, and indeed are doing so today, floating on the plastic substance of the deeper layer of the Earth's mantle, called the asthenosphere. They may well be kept in motion by the convection currents that have been mentioned before.

The important point to remember is that the plates are solid and rigid so that almost all the activities that we have

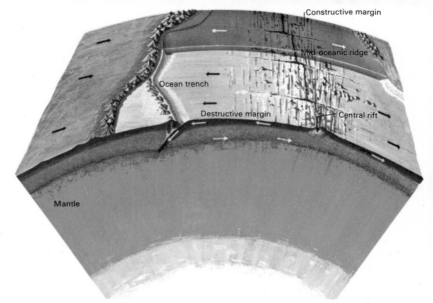

Constructive margin

Mid-oceanic ridge

Ocean trench

Destructive margin

Central rift

Mantle

Right:
This block of the Earth's crust and mantle shows how the movements of plates, the formation of ocean ridges, mountain buildings, etc., are related.

mentioned such as volcanoes and earthquakes, are to be found associated with the edges of these plates, or the plate margins, as they are more usually called.

There are three main types of margin. The plates may just slide past each other, such as the San Andreas fault in California, and this is called a *conservative* margin. The mid-oceanic ridges, where mantle material is welling up from the depths and pushing the sea floor apart, forming new crust, are known as *constructive* margins. In other places, such as the west coast of South America, where the island arcs occur that you have already learned about, one crustal plate is slipping beneath the other at a *destructive* margin. The deep ocean trenches, such as the Marianas trench, are to be found here, where the sea floor is pulled down. Earthquake activity is often concentrated in a zone known as the Benioff zone in these areas.

You can see, then, that in one unifying idea, the Earth's activities can be viewed as a whole, rather than as a number of isolated processes.

Below:
The Earth's magnetism may be 'frozen' into cooling igneous rocks. Its direction changes periodically and these stripes record the changes progressively — older rocks moving away from the mid-ocean ridge. This is more evidence for sea-floor spreading.

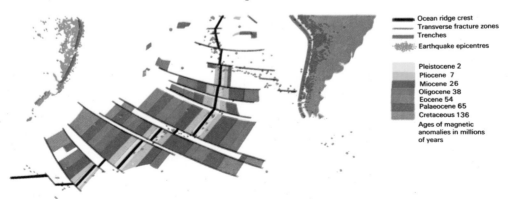

Ocean ridge crest
Transverse fracture zones
Trenches
Earthquake epicentres

Pleistocene 2
Pliocene 7
Miocene 26
Oligocene 38
Eocene 54
Palaeocene 65
Cretaceous 136
Ages of magnetic anomalies in millions of years

Astronomy

Has there ever been a Man in the Moon?

The legend of the Man in the Moon has grown up for a very obvious reason. If you look up at the silvery disc of a full Moon on a clear night the surface features of our satellite could easily give you the impression of a face. Before the coming of space travel many science fiction writers told of strange creatures which inhabited our neighbour. H. G. Wells wrote a very famous story called *The First Men On The Moon* in which he tells of ant-like beings which he called 'Selenites'. These 'men' lived in the craters and caves of the Moon and would break at the lightest blow of a human fist.

Right:
The American Apollo space programme was started to find out more about the Moon. Here we see a manned spacecraft in orbit around the Moon. The Earth can be seen in the distance.

Today, space probes and manned landings on the Moon have given us new clues to its origin and history. Scientists are now almost sure that there has never been life on the Moon. It was once thought that originally the Earth had no Moon, but as a result of a terrific explosion the Moon was shot out into space from what is now the Pacific ocean. Geologists have long since discarded this idea. It now seems to be more likely that the Moon and the Earth were formed at more or less the same time, contracting from a cloud of dust and gas, as we have explained in a previous question.

If this is true, why do they appear to be so different? The answer is one of chance. When the Moon was born it was too small (it has about one-sixth of the Earth's gravity) to retain an atmosphere or any lighter, life-giving materials like water. This means that the Moon is, and always has been a dry, barren waste without life of any kind. You can see, then, that there never has been a Man in the Moon but there has already been more than one man on the Moon!

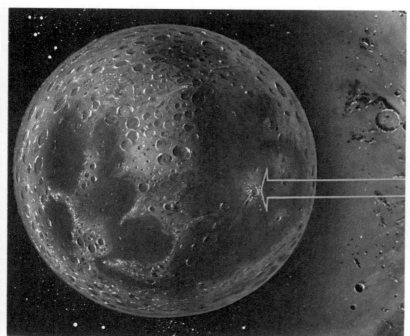

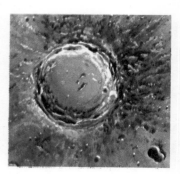

When will the Earth die?

As you have already seen, the very existence of the Earth, and all the other planets in the solar system, depends upon the Sun. You have seen how the Sun provides enormous amounts of energy by the change of the gas hydrogen into the gas helium. But as with any other 'engine' the fuel, that is the hydrogen, must slowly be used up. When this happens, as has already occurred with millions of other stars, the Sun will collapse and explode. The explosion will totally destroy the Earth and its neighbours. There is no need to worry unnecessarily – it will be at least another 5000 million years before the Sun explodes.

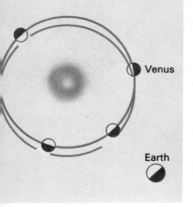

What are our nearest neighbours like?

In our solar system the three bodies that are nearest to us are our own Moon and the planets Venus and Mars. The formation, structure, and surface of the Moon are more closely linked with Earth and we have looked at these similarities in a previous question.

For the moment then, let us concern ourselves with our neighbouring inner planets. Because these two planets are so close to us (in terms of the size of the solar system) they have been the subject of many science fiction stories. But what are these planets really like? And do they really have strange life forms inhabiting them?

Venus is closer to the Sun than the Earth, and orbits at a distance of about 110 million kilometres from the Sun. Sometimes Venus comes as near as 40 million kilometres to Earth. It does seem unlikely, but a year on the planet Venus would be shorter than a day. This occurs because the planet is spinning on its own axis more slowly than it is orbiting around the Sun. In the case of the Earth, of course, it is the other way round so that there are $365\frac{1}{4}$ of our days in a year.

Venus is about the same size and weight as the Earth but because it is much closer to the Sun and does not have our

Venus

Earth

Above and right:
The phases of Venus, that is the ways in which Venus appears to us at different times of the year, are unlike those of the Moon. Venus is the most brilliant of all the planets.

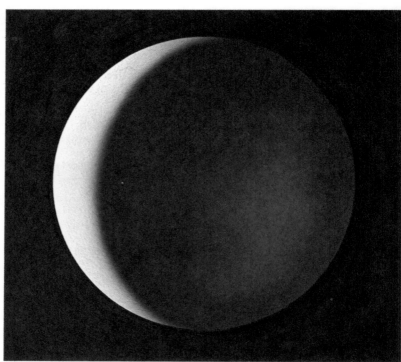

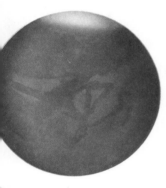

protecting layer of the gas ozone, it is very much hotter. In fact, the surface temperature has been estimated at about 850°C, or more than eight times the boiling temperature of water. Because of the extreme heat, because there does not seem to be a breathable atmosphere apart from a dense covering of carbon dioxide gas, and because there is little evidence of water it would be very surprising if there were any life forms like our own.

Mars has been a particularly favourite haunt of the story-teller's spacemen. H. G. Wells popularized the idea of Martians in his book *The War of the Worlds*. Mars orbits around the Sun at a distance of about 230 million kilometres and is farther away from it than we are. If you look at Mars in the night sky it appears to be red in colour. This reddish tinge seems to be the actual colour of the planet's surface because it is only protected by a thin atmosphere of carbon dioxide.

The surface of Mars is certainly cratered rather like our Moon and also appears to have canal-like scars running across it. It would be very unlikely that any life as we know it could survive there because of the lack of water and free oxygen, and because the temperature may fall low enough during the night to freeze any normal living creature. You can see, then, that Earth is very lucky to have conditions which will support a network of plant and animal life.

Does a comet foretell disaster?

Before we can answer this question, we must look at exactly
what a comet is. As you probably know, a comet looks
rather like a star with a long, milky 'tail' stretching across the
sky. In fact these 'tails' are not tails at all because they
always point away from the Sun and do not trail behind.

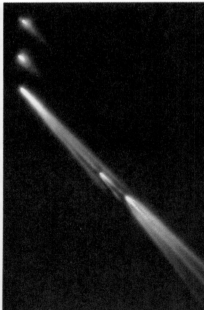

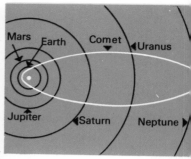

A comet seems to be made up of three main parts. The *nucleus* in the centre of the star-like part is composed mainly of ice and dust particles, surrounded by a *coma* of much smaller particles and gas. The coma results from the melting of the ice and other substances as the comet approaches the Sun on its extremely stretched out elliptical orbit. The Sun's radiation also tends to force some of these tiny pieces of ice away from the comet and out into space, which explains why the tail is always directed away from the Sun.

A scientist called Halley, after whom a particulary bright comet is named, discovered how comets moved. He also predicted when some comets which had already been seen would return. For example, Halley's comet made its closest approach to Earth for 76 years as predicted in 1986.

Why are comets associated with disaster? It is true that a comet appeared before the Norman conquest of Britain in 1066, and that two more comets were seen before the Great Fire of London in 1666 and the Great Plague in the previous year, but in world terms these cannot be regarded as major events. Perhaps it is the result of people's belief that what happens in their own country is of world importance that has led to this idea that comets predict disaster. On the other hand, it has been suggested that the Star of Bethlehem that told of the birth of Christ was in fact a comet. It does seem unlikely, however, that a body of ice and gas moving around the sky in a quite regular orbit can have anything to do with the events here on Earth. This is particularly true of comets because they have such a low density. Although they may have a diameter of as much as 128,000 kilometres they do not have enough gravitational pull to affect the bodies they pass. In fact, their own orbits may be completely changed.

How can you look at the stars and planets?

We have already mentioned what an important part the invention of the telescope has played in man's exploration of the Universe. More recently, of course, you have seen the value of radio telescopes, satellites, and even manned spacecraft. But in astronomy (the science of the planets and stars) and in geology (the science of the Earth) there are still plenty of discoveries to be made by the home scientist with the aid of a few readily available instruments.

If you want to look more closely at the stars and planets yourself you will either need a pair of powerful binoculars, or an astronomical telescope. They will give a much greater magnification; that is, they will make the object you are looking at appear much larger.

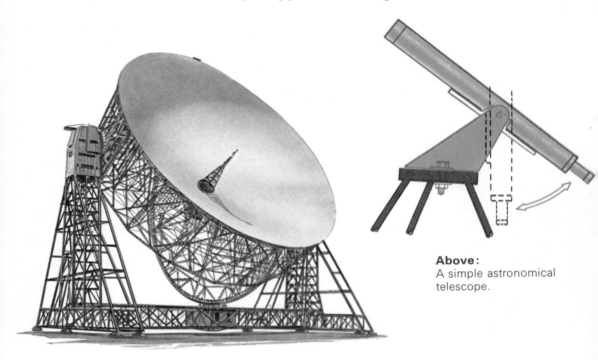

Above:
A simple astronomical telescope.

Above:
Radio telescopes such as this one at Jodrell Bank with its 75 metre dish are used to track satellites.

Let us look at binoculars first. If your family owns a pair or if you are thinking of buying binoculars, you will find that they are usually described by two numbers and that they come in a variety of prices. The price is dependent upon the quality of the lenses and prisms (these are the pieces that gather the light), on how light in weight they are, and on how much rough handling they will take. Usually it is better to buy the very best pair that you can afford, and you should ask for advice on this. The numbers will appear as 8 × 40

Above:
Binoculars can be used for many hobbies as well as astronomy.

These two telescopes were the types used before better quality lenses could be made. As you can see, they were long and ungainly and were raised and lowered by means of a system of pulleys.

Above:
A reflecting telescope works by gathering light and reflecting it to the eyepiece.

or 7 × 50. The first number is the magnification and the second is the diameter of the largest or object lens measured in millimetres. It is not necessarily better to buy those with the greatest magnification because they cannot usually be used at night and they are very difficult to hold steady without a support. The 7 × 50 binocular is very useful and can also be conveniently used for other hobbies such as birdwatching.

An astronomical telescope is more useful for a closer look at the heavenly bodies. (The difference between an astronomical and other types of telescope is that the image which you see in the astronomical type is upside down and back to front.) Of course, this does not matter when you are looking at something like a star, and it means that an astronomical telescope is generally simpler and less expensive than an equivalent terrestrial telescope (one in which the image is the right way round). Basically, a telescope is an instrument which gathers as much of the light as possible coming from a body. This may be achieved either by a system of lenses, as in a *refracting* telescope or by a large, special type of mirror, as in a *reflecting* telescope. There are many detailed books on this subject that you can find in your local library, and the manufacturers will be only too pleased to help you.

Is there life on other planets?

Ever since man has been aware of worlds beyond our own, he has begun to wonder whether he is alone in the Universe. Do other races of creatures very different or perhaps quite similar to ourselves exist on distant planets? This desire to explore beyond the confines of our world and to imagine what possible life forms could exist on other planets has led science fiction writers to describe all kinds of strange creatures. In *The First Men on the Moon*, H. G. Wells tells of a species living in the craters and caves of the Moon that he calls the Selenites. These creatures resemble giant, intelligent ants. Of course, we are aware today that no such creatures exist and there never has been any form of life on the Moon, least of all the 'Man in the Moon'. There have been other creatures from the pages of science fiction such as the Mekons with tiny green bodies and huge heads whom Dan Dare met in his space travels in the *Eagle* comic. More recently, television has brought the terrifying, war-like Daleks who confronted Doctor Who in the programme of the same name.

These are just a few of the imaginary men from outer space, but what are the possibilities of actual life forms? The first point to make is that there is little to be gained from trying to picture weird and wonderful creatures sprouting radio antennae from their heads and breathing liquid ammonia.

Top:
The world's first liquid-fuelled rocket.

Above:
The space craft invented in fiction by Jules Verne.

Right:
Space walks are not just left to the minds of science fiction writers nowadays.

Right:
An artist's impression of the
surface of Mars, the
imagined home of fictional
spacemen.

We should try to confine ourselves to examining whether or
not there is any chance of living systems much like our own
somewhere else in the Universe. It must also be remembered,
however, that a living world elsewhere could be more or
less developed than our own. In other words it could still be
at the stage of a 'primordial soup' of primitive life forms or
thousands of years more advanced than our own world.

Scientists have attempted to calculate how many galaxies
there are in the Universe and how many solar systems are
contained within these galaxies in an effort to work out how
many planets there might be similar to our own. Even the
most cautious would probably agree that the number of
planets in the Universe similar to our own probably runs
into the thousands. This means that the chances are heavily
in favour of there being many other worlds just like our own
in which there are plants and animals and humans breathing
air made up of oxygen, nitrogen, carbon dioxide, and a few
other gases.

Are these intelligent creatures trying to make contact with
us using radio waves? Some people think so, but of course,
they may be thousands of light years away so that by the time
we received any message, they could be extinct. The
possibility exists that we have already been visited by
spacemen and that such wonders of the world as the pyramids
of Egypt were constructed with their help. Perhaps soon
we shall know more of the creatures from outer space.

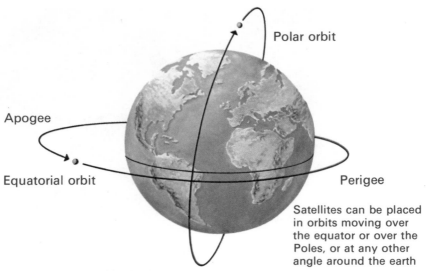

Polar orbit

Apogee

Equatorial orbit

Perigee

Satellites can be placed
in orbits moving over
the equator or over the
Poles, or at any other
angle around the earth

How do satellites stay up in space?

A satellite orbiting the earth is rather like a chestnut being whirled
on the end of a piece of string. The centrifugal force of its motion
forces it outwards, but the earth's gravity (or string) keeps it from
moving away. A satellite continues to circle the earth because there
is no air in space to stop it moving. It will carry on orbiting for
ever unless it moves near the earth and the upper atmosphere drags
on the satellite and slows it down. Satellites move in ellipses rather
than circles. The nearest point to earth is called the perigee, and
the farthest, the apogee.

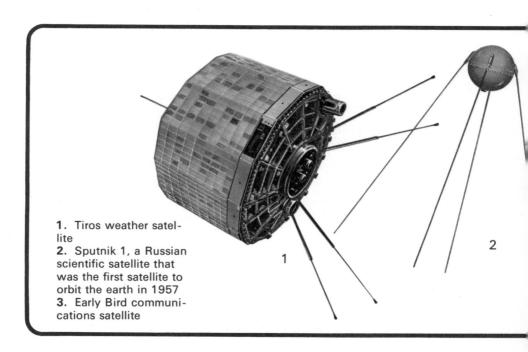

1. Tiros weather satellite
2. Sputnik 1, a Russian
scientific satellite that
was the first satellite to
orbit the earth in 1957
3. Early Bird communications satellite

1

2

How are satellites recovered from space ?

Although satellites can remain in space orbiting the earth for ever, it is useful to have ways of getting them back to earth unharmed so as to recover scientific information or animals making experimental spaceflights. Reconnaissance satellites that take photographs of the earth's surface can eject capsules that are able to re-enter the earth's atmosphere with the photographs aboard. An aircraft with a special scoop chases the capsule as it descends beneath its parachute after re-entry, and captures the capsule before it falls to the ground.

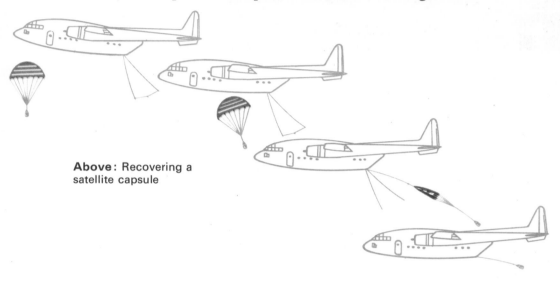

Above: Recovering a satellite capsule

3

What are satellites used for ?

Satellites have many uses. Communications satellites bounce radio signals from one continent to another, making world-wide TV and telephone services possible. Scientific satellites measure conditions in space, and observe the sun, planets and stars from space. Weather satellites send back pictures of the earth's weather, making weather forecasting much more accurate. Other satellites aid navigation and air traffic control, and the latest earth resources satellites are able to detect the presence of oil deposits, shoals of fish, and even diseased crops at an early stage in a disease.

Magnitude	Number of stars
1	20
6	3,000
11	800,000
16	50,000,000
21	1,000,000,000

The numbers of stars of different magnitudes. Bright stars are of first magnitude. Second magnitude stars are $2\frac{1}{2}$ times less bright, and so on. Stars of 25th magnitude are the faintest we can detect. They are 10,000 million times less bright than first magnitude stars

How many stars are there?

If you look up into a clear night sky in the heart of the country well away from town lights, you will be able to see about 2,000 stars. In the entire sky, there are between 5,000 and 6,000 stars visible to the naked eye. But there are millions upon millions of stars to be seen through a powerful telescope. The table shows the numbers of stars of different magnitudes or brightnesses.

How hot is a star?

Stars vary in temperature greatly. The hottest stars have surface temperatures of as much as 35,000°C or more and shine a brilliant blue-white. The less hot stars are, the redder they appear to be. The table shows the surface temperatures and colours of five kinds of stars together with an example of each kind. Stars are classed into various groups according to their surface temperature. The sun is in a group of medium temperature.

Temperature: 25,000°C	11,000°C	6,000°C	4,000°C	3,000°C
Typical star: Spica	Sirius	Sun	Arcturus	Betelgeuse

Do stars have planets?

The sun is surrounded by no less than nine planets, so it is very likely that other stars also have planets. However, other stars are so far away from us that any planets they possess are far too small for us to be able to see, even with the most powerful telescopes. Nevertheless, it is possible to detect the presence of very large planets near other stars. If a star has a massive planet, the planet's

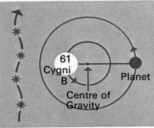

Above: If a star has a very large planet, the centre of gravity of the two bodies lies between them. Both bodies move around the centre of gravity (**right**) and this movement produces a wobble in the star's general motion (**left**)

Left: An impression of the surface of a planet near a red giant star

gravity produces a wobble in the star's motion. In 1944, a wobble was observed in the motion of a star in the constellation Cygnus (the Swan) called 61 Cygni B. By measuring this wobble, astronomers calculated that the planet has a mass about 15 times that of Jupiter. In 1963, a planet was detected around a nearby star called Barnard's Star. The planet has a mass half as big again as Jupiter and revolves once around Barnard's Star in 24 years. This planet is probably very similar to the large planets which are part of our own solar system.

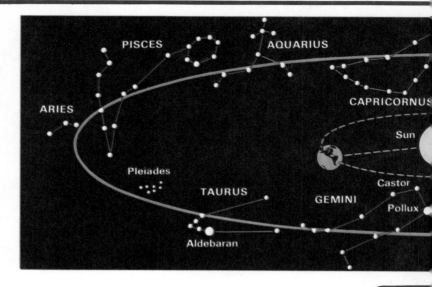

Why are stars grouped in constellations?

People who gazed at the skies in ancient times believed that they could see the shapes of animals and people traced out in the stars. These star groups, or constellations, have the Latin names of the shapes, and astronomers use the names in identifying stars. But the stars in a constellation do not belong to any actual group in space and may be far apart. The twelve constellations lying on the ecliptic, the sun's path through the sky, are called the zodiac.

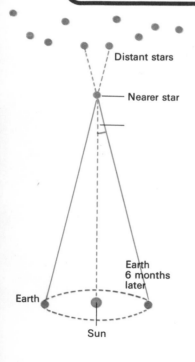

How far away are the stars?

Stars are too far away to use kilometres or miles to measure their distances, so astronomers use light-years instead. One light-year is nearly 10 million million km, and the nearest star, Proxima Centauri, is 4¼ light-years distant. The farthest heavenly bodies are at the unimaginable distance of 8,000 million light-years! As the earth moves round the sun, the nearer stars appear to move very slightly in relation to the distant stars. The farther apart they are, the greater the parallax (apparent movement) appears to be. By observing the various movements, astronomers are able to calculate the approximate distances of the stars from earth.

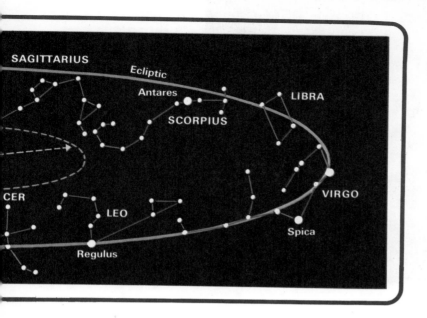

SAGITTARIUS
Ecliptic
Antares
SCORPIUS
LIBRA
VIRGO
Spica
CER
LEO
Regulus

What is a nebula?

One of the most striking objects in the sky is the Great Nebula in the constellation of Orion. It can be seen as a faint greenish patch with the naked eye just below Orion's Belt, but through binoculars or a telescope it is seen as a mass of glowing gas. Nebulae are large clouds of dust and gas in space. Many produce their own light, and others are illuminated by stars. Some are dark, and we see them as black clouds or bands against the stars. Many luminescent nebulae are formed when stars explode into supernovae. The remains of the star move out through space as an expanding shell of glowing gas. Nebulae are among the most striking sights in the heavens. Photographs show them to have beautiful colours, but these colours may not show in a telescope.

The Great Nebula in Orion

Left: The galaxy from above. The red arrow indicates the position of the sun
Below: The galaxy seen edge on

What is the Milky Way?

We see the Milky Way as a band of stars stretching right across the heavens. On a clear night in the country far from towns, it is a spectacular sight. The sun, all the stars we can see in the sky, and 100,000 million more beside, make up a vast group of stars called the galaxy. The stars lie in spiral arms radiating out from a large cluster. Edge on, the galaxy looks like a flat disc with a central bulge. When we look at the Milky Way, we are looking along the arms of the galaxy and so see a belt of stars across the sky. The galaxy formed from interstellar gas 7,500 million to 15,000 million years ago. It is 100,000 light-years across.

The Andromeda galaxy
is a magnificent spiral
galaxy very like our
own galaxy

Where and what are the galaxies?

Our galaxy, vast island of stars though it is, is only one of millions of similar galaxies scattered throughout space as far away as we can see through our telescopes. The nearest galaxies to our galaxy are two small satellite galaxies called the Magellanic Clouds. They can be seen only in the southern hemisphere, and look like pieces torn out of the Milky Way. A large nearby galaxy is the Andromeda galaxy, which can be seen with the naked eye as a faint patch. It is over 2 million light-years away.

Galaxies come in many shapes. Many are spiral. Elliptical galaxies look like globular clusters of stars, and irregular galaxies such as the Magellanic Clouds have no particular structure. About a hundred million galaxies can be seen with the largest telescopes. Galaxies, like stars, tend to form clusters and our galaxy is one of a cluster of over twenty that include the Andromeda galaxy.

Elliptical and irregular
galaxies

How big is the universe?

We cannot say exactly how big the universe is, only how far we can see out into space. But the observable universe is immensely vast – about 200,000 million million million km across, in fact. The farthest objects that we can detect from the earth are 8,000 million light-years distant. They are so far away that, when the light waves or radio waves we detect them by left these bodies 8,000 million years ago, the earth and sun were not even formed. The waves have travelled for this great length of time at a speed of 300,000 km every *second* before reaching us— a practically impossible concept to grasp!

The diagram showing the scale of the universe (right) may give some idea of the immense distances involved. Each division on the scale is 10,000 times bigger than the division above it. From this we can work out that the universe is 10 million million million million times bigger than a man. And a man is 10,000 million times bigger than each atom of which he and everything in the universe is made.

How did the universe form?

Scientists disagree on the origin of the universe. They observe that all the galaxies are moving away from each other, rather like spots painted on a balloon do when it is blown up. The universe is therefore expanding. The 'steady state' theory suggests that the universe is infinitely large, and that it has always existed. As it expands, new galaxies are formed in the spaces left as the existing galaxies move apart. If this theory is correct, the universe would always have looked to us as it does now. The 'big bang' theory disagrees. It suggests that the universe formed about 20,000 million years ago with a gigantic explosion. The galaxies produced started to

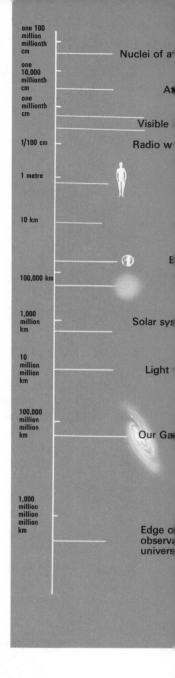

one 100 million millionth cm

one 10,000 millionth cm

one millionth cm

1/100 cm

1 metre

10 km

100,000 km

1,000 million km

10 million million km

100,000 million million km

1,000 million million million km

Nuclei of a

At

Visible

Radio w

E

Solar sys

Light

Our Ga

Edge o
observa
univers

Above: The scale of size in the universe. Each division is 10,000 times greater than the preceding division

The 'steady state' theory of the universe. As existing galaxies move apart from each other **(left)**, new galaxies are formed in the spaces between them **(right)**

move out into space in all directions. Towards the edge of the observable universe, there seem to be more galaxies moving away than astronomers would expect. This evidence suggests that the 'big bang' theory may be correct. But another theory holds that the universe alternately increases and decreases in size.

What are quasars?

The word quasar is short for quasi-stellar object, which means an object that resembles a star. But quasars are not like ordinary stars. Many are thought to be near the edge of the observable universe and moving away from us at nearly the speed of light. But quasars produce intense amounts of light and radio waves, and may be as much as 200 times as bright as an ordinary galaxy. And they appear to be much smaller than a galaxy—about one light-year across. No one can account for how quasars produce such immense amounts of energy. Perhaps they are much nearer, much larger, and not moving so fast.

The quasar 3C 273 was one of the first quasars to be discovered in 1963

Evolution

What is evolution?

To answer the question very simply, evolution is the process by which living things on our planet Earth have changed and developed from the algae-like forms of which there is evidence in ancient rocks, into the many varied plants and animals which we can see around us today. But if we were to leave it at this simple explanation, there would be much that would remain unsaid.

As we have already explained, life first seems to have shown itself on Earth over 3500 million years ago, and if we are to believe what the modern theories of evolution tell us, it has taken all that time for the modern creatures to evolve. It is written in the Christian Bible that God created the Earth and all its inhabitants in six days and nights and on the seventh day He rested. Many books have been written, by men of religion, by men of science, and by men of both religion and science discussing the merits of the ideas of evolution and of religion. In this question, we shall be concerned with the evidence that can be drawn from such sources as the fossil record and Charles Darwins's historic voyage in HMS *Beagle*.

In the 1600s Archbishop Ussher calculated that the Earth was formed in the year 4004 BC and this view held fast until the late 1700s when the science of geology was taken more and more seriously. At this time a scientist called Hutton stated his *Principle of Uniformitarianism*. He said that all the processes of the Earth took place very slowly; this developed into the idea that the present is the key to the past. In other words, if you look at a process's results on Earth today, such as the kind of muds and silts that are deposited in a modern estuary, and you then find similar sediments in an ancient rock, these sediments must have been formed by an estuary. From these ideas it was realized that the Earth must be very old indeed. Then William Smith at the turn of the 1700s to

Above:
Charles Darwin.

Right and far right:
Pigeon fanciers have been able to exploit the processes of evolution by selecting individuals with particular characteristics and breeding from them so that eventually different types emerge like the ones seen here.

Rock Dove

Fantail

Right:
The very early stages in the
lives of very different animals
are quite similar. It is thought
that this is because the
animals had a common
ancestor.

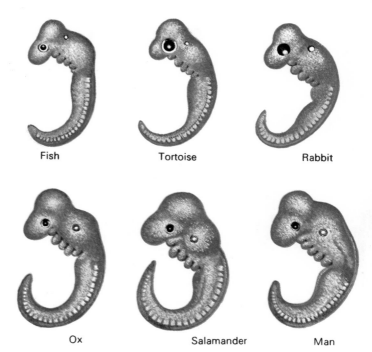

Fish   Tortoise   Rabbit

Ox   Salamander   Man

the 1800s showed how it could be proved that layers of rock
were laid down one on top of the other over long periods.
From this point the value of fossils was recognized because it
could be seen how the older fossils were very simple, becoming more and more complex in the younger rocks.

Charles Darwin and evolution go hand in hand. Darwin
travelled to the Galapagos Islands and noticed that birds
which were all clearly finches had adapted by evolution
to live in a variety of ways. Elsewhere, other species of
birds had filled all the available ecological niches. He said
that this had occurred because the islands were isolated and
the finch had evolved to fill these gaps.

Pouter

Short-faced Tumbler

What is a fossil?

Fossils are any remains of a once living plant or animal that have been preserved by a variety of ways. The trace may be in the form of a complete animal such as the mammoths which were found by Russian scientists frozen into the ice of Siberia. It was said that the meat on the animals was still fresh enough to eat, and indeed Russian geologists were supposed to have dined on mammoth steaks. This form of preservation is very unusual. A more likely way is for the hard parts of the animal to be preserved as a fossil. The fossil is formed when the animal dies because the hard parts are buried by sediments which in turn become compacted into rock, leaving the fossil contained within. Insects have commonly been found preserved in amber which is fossil tree sap. The sap probably ran down the trunk of the tree trapping the insect so that when the sap hardened into the beautiful yellowish brown amber it was preserved complete.

Plants may be found preserved as black traces, particularly in rocks called shales. You may find traces of leaves and stems in this way. More recently it has been discovered that the pollen which all flowering plants release for fertilizing their seeds has been preserved in quite large amounts. In fact, the science of palynology (the study of fossil pollen) as it is called, has become very important in the search for oil.

Animal trails may also become fossils. Trails of worms moving along the sea bed have been found which have become 'frozen' into what has become a rock. Footprints of the long dead dinosaurs are not unusual. In the same way that modern chickens eat grit and retain it in their crops to

chalk

sandstone

limestone

shale

Above:
Some typical sedimentary rocks in which fossils may be found.

Right:
An animal may be fossilized like this if the conditions are suitable.

living animal

hard parts of dead animal

rapid burial

impregnation by minerals from sediments

aid digestion, dinosaurs swallowed quite large stones and they can be recognized by scientists called *palaeontologists,* who study all forms of life in former geological periods through fossils.

Which fossils are you most likely to find?

The animal kingdom is divided into those animals which have backbones, *vertebrates,* and those animals which do not have backbones, *invertebrates.* In terms of the numbers of animals which have ever lived throughout the history of the Earth, the invertebrates are much more common. Many invertebrates had external shells made of chalk-like materials to protect them. Others had internal skeletons made of similar substances.

We mentioned in the previous question that it was usually the hard parts of animals that were preserved. Therefore, you are most likely to find fossils of animals which were numerically common, widely distributed, possessed hard parts, and which lived in conditions suitable for their preservation. In other words you are most likely to find fossil invertebrates.

Right:
A mammoth trapped in soft mud may be fossilized and its bones rediscovered millions of years later.

What are the geologic column and the fossil record?

As you know the Earth is about 4500 million years old. Clearly, this is an immensely long period of time, difficult for us with our life span of about 70 years to imagine. To make consideration of the history of the Earth a little easier, this huge time scale has been divided up into smaller units, and then further divided into still smaller units. The largest unit of time that we use is called an *era*. There are six of these eras, but they do not by any means represent equal lengths of time. They are the Eozoic, Archaeozoic, Proterozoic, Palaeozoic, Mesozoic, and Cenozoic. Palaeozoic, for example, means ancient life, and the rest have equivalent meanings. During any given period of time, however, beds of rocks will have been laid down somewhere around the globe and these must be given names too. The strata or beds of rock deposited during an era are referred to as a Group.

Eras are divided into Periods and the Groups into Systems and it is the Periods and Systems which make up the geologic column shown in the picture. Sometimes confusion arises between time and rock units. If you wish to divide say, the Devonian period you might refer to the divisions as Early, Middle, or Late Devonian time, whereas the equivalent rock units would be the Lower, Middle and Upper Devonian. It is important that these terms should not be mixed up, although they often are, even by experienced geologists.

As you can see from the picture, the last 600 million years only comprise three Eras. This is only a tiny period compared with the 4000 million years that went before, which are usually referred to loosely as the Precambrian, that is, the period of time before the Cambrian, the lowest Period in the Phanerozoic time scale.

At first, it was thought that the first life appeared on Earth at the beginning of Cambrian time because it was in rocks

Right:
Fossils may be used to date rocks of different types in areas some distance apart.

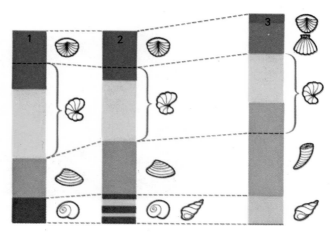

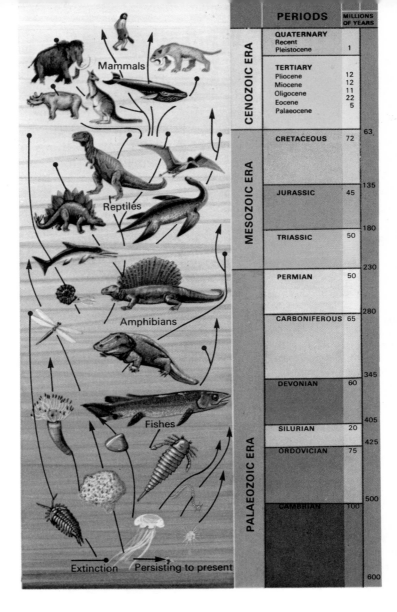

PERIODS		MILLIONS OF YEARS
QUATERNARY		
Recent		
Pleistocene		1
TERTIARY		
Pliocene		12
Miocene		12
Oligocene		11
Eocene		22
Palaeocene		5
		63
CRETACEOUS	72	
		135
JURASSIC	45	
		180
TRIASSIC	50	
		230
PERMIAN	50	
		280
CARBONIFEROUS	65	
		345
DEVONIAN	60	
		405
SILURIAN	20	
		425
ORDOVICIAN	75	
		500
CAMBRIAN	100	
		600

CENOZOIC ERA

MESOZOIC ERA

PALAEOZOIC ERA

Mammals

Reptiles

Amphibians

Fishes

Extinction Persisting to present

Right:
The geologic column and fossil record.

described as Cambrian in Wales that fossils were first found. Later, however, it was discovered that the first life forms may have occurred at least 3500 million years ago, but still the most detailed fossil record exists for the last 600 million years.

The boundaries between the time Periods or rock systems are often established on the appearance of some new form of life. It may be a completely new type of life form or just a distinctive species of an animal or plant form that had existed earlier. In fact, the availability of the fossil plays an important part too. For example, although graptolites had existed in Cambrian times, the Ordovician period is usually subdivided on the basis of the species of these animals.

What was the first life on Earth?

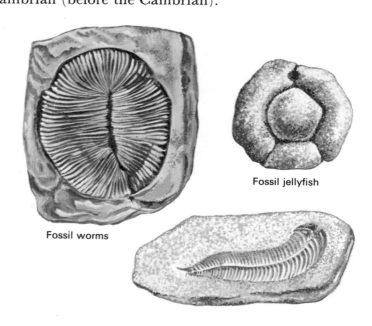

Charnia

Above:
The Precambrian fossil called
Charnia discovered in
Charnwood Forest,
Leicestershire, England.
It may have been an early
seaweed.

Right:
These Precambrian fossils
can be found in the ancient
rocks of South Africa and
Australia.

Until quite recently it was thought that there were no abundant life forms on this planet until about 600 million years ago. When we remember that the Earth itself is at least 4500 million years old, it does seem to have taken a very long time before any animals or plants appeared. Then, geologically speaking, they must have developed very quickly indeed. Probably the reason why 600 million years was thought to be the date of the earliest common life was because a great deal of the pioneer work in geology in the 1800s was done in Britain. Apart from some recently discovered traces in older rocks of Scotland and Charnwood Forest, England, the oldest fossils occur in rocks dating from a period called the Cambrian (*Cambria* Roman name for Wales) found first in Wales and then in Scotland. In these rocks fossils of shellfish called brachiopods, insect-like, sea-dwelling trilobites, cockle-like shellfish, and one or two other groups of animals are all to be found in abundance.

It was obvious, however, from the work of many geologists that these Cambrian rocks were not the oldest in Britain. Unfortunately almost all the earlier beds had been severely altered by heat and pressure as a result of earth movements so that even if there were any traces of life they would have been lucky to survive for the workers of the last century to find. All these older rocks were lumped together, and the period in which they were deposited was called the Precambrian (before the Cambrian).

Fossil jellyfish

Fossil worms

Of course, if many different types of animals had developed by the Cambrian period, it seems reasonable to suppose that they could not all have suddenly arrived on the

Spriggina

Above:
This fossil, called *Spriggina*, may have been an early worm.

Right:
This picture indicates some of the animals that may have existed rather later in the Earth's history, in the Middle Cambrian—a mere 550 million years ago. By this time several animal species had evolved.

scene. This suggested that although few traces had been definitely identified as belonging to more primitive life, there must have been some early life forms developing slowly during the millions of years of the Precambrian.

Later more and more people in countries outside Britain became interested in the geology of their own countries and it was not long before traces of very primitive worms, sponges and other very early invertebrates were found in Precambrian rocks of North America, Australia, and southern Africa. In 1964, a scientist called J. G. Ramsay claimed to have found structures which resemble the algae you might find in a pond, in a series of rocks which have been dated at 3500 million years old. In fact, associations of algae and other life forms, called stromatolites, are the most widespread Precambrian fossils. You can see then that the fossils which you may be able to find quite easily on beaches or in chalk quarries are very old by our standards but newcomers by the standards of Earth's time.

Holocystites Silurian

Above:
A fossil echinoderm called
a cystoid.

Which are the most advanced animals without backbones?

What do we mean by advanced? In this case we mean those invertebrates which are most like animals with backbones including man himself. This does not necessarily mean that all the other groups of animals without backbones are not very efficient living creatures, capable of great variety and different ways of life.

The group of sea-dwelling invertebrates called the Echinodermata are the most advanced in our sense of the word. Echinodermata means spiny skinned. The word refers to the spines which protect these animals and on which they move.

There are two main divisions of the Echinodermata. Both these divisions have modern, living representatives. There are the free-living forms (meaning that they are not doomed to stay in one place) which include the starfish, sea cucumbers, and the sea urchins. There are also the forms which are attached in some way to the sea floor, with names like crinoids and blastoids. All the members of the Echinodermata have skeletons of calcite buried within the soft tissue, although sometimes these skeletons are rather reduced in size.

Many invertebrate shells are used for protection. Because the skeletons of this group are internal, they act as a support for the body like our own framework of bones. This internal skeleton can become fossilized and is of interest to geologists.

The two groups which are of most importance in the fossil record are the sea urchins or echinoids, and the crinoids or sea lilies. It is worth noting here that sea lilies are the common name given to these crinoids. It is an attempt to describe

Right:
Some fossil starfish.

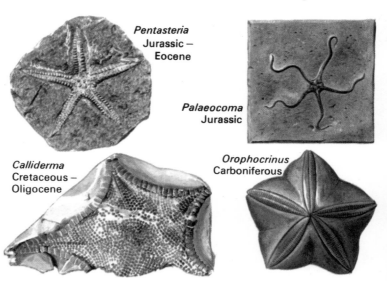

Pentasteria
Jurassic –
Eocene

Palaeocoma
Jurassic

Calliderma
Cretaceous –
Oligocene

Orophocrinus
Carboniferous

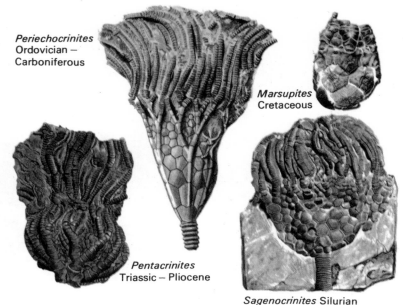

Periechocrinites
Ordovician –
Carboniferous

Marsupites
Cretaceous

Pentacrinites
Triassic – Pliocene

Sagenocrinites Silurian

Left:
Fossil sea lilies or crinoids.

their appearance, and you must remember that they are animals, not plants.

The skeletons of sea lilies are made up of a large number of separate units called ossicles. When the animals die these ossicles often become separated so you would be quite fortunate to find a whole fossil crinoid. You are more likely to find the individual parts, but even these tiny fragments can be positively identified.

The skeleton or test of the echinoid is made of plates of calcite and the animals grow by adding more calcite to each plate. Spines also develop by accumulation of calcite. This skeleton is very strong because of the way in which the plates are arranged, and whole fossils may be found, for example, in flints in the chalk. Echinoids first appeared about 500 million years ago during a period which we refer to as the Ordovician, and there are still sea urchins in modern oceans.

Below:
The fossil on the far right is a fossil echinoid or sea urchin and it is known as an irregular type. These are much more common in the fossil record than the two regular types also illustrated.

Micraster
Cretaceous – Miocene

Hemicidaris
Jurassic – Cretaceous

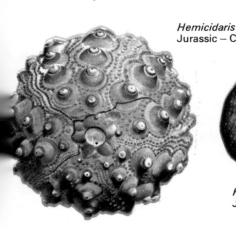

Holectypus
Jurassic – Cretaceous

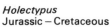

Coccosteus

Pterichthys

Cephalaspis

How have animals with backbones evolved?

You have seen that the animal kingdom is divided up into a number of major groups. Each group is usually referred to as a *phylum*. Man belongs to the phylum Chordata. All animals belonging to this group must possess a *notochord*, that is, a structure like a spine at some stage during their life cycle. In some animals, such as the graptolites that have already been discussed, this notochord remains in its elementary state. In the case of a group of chordates known as the Craniata, this notochord develops into a support for the body, and the skull or cranium which protects the central nervous system. As you might have guessed by now, the Craniata includes all the birds, mammals, and so on, and of course, man himself.

The Chordata are thought to be very closely related to the Echinodermata; the group of animals without backbones which includes sea urchins and starfish. This can be proved by the great similarity of certain chemicals contained in the bodies of both groups. It is certain that all of the ancestors of the chordates lived in the sea.

The earliest vertebrates—animals with backbones—were probably as long ago as 510 million years. Their remains

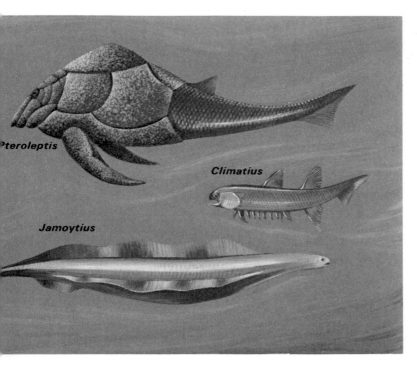

Pteroleptis

Climatius

Jamoytius

Left:
An artist's impression of some of the earliest known vertebrates.

have been found in Cambrian rocks in Arizona in North America. They are fragments of the scales of creatures, called agnathans, which were fishes that had no jaws or teeth. These small animals had skeletons of cartilage and they were covered by armour in the form of bony plates, or scales, and it was these that were found in Arizona. The oldest known vertebrate fossils known in Britain come from central Scotland. They are about 420 million years old.

The first vertebrate remains are, therefore, parts of primitive fish, and it is thought that they lived in the place where they are found. It is interesting to compare these remains with the bones of modern jawless fish. Modern jawless fish do not have effective kidneys because the salts in their bodies are in balance with their surroundings. It is reasonable to suppose that the same was true for their early vertebrate ancestors. This sounds even more likely when we take into account that there is more energy in the form of food available in the sea so that evolution is more likely to come about.

The first backbone simply acted as a support for the fish's muscles, but later it evolved to protect the brain. The first fish were armoured fish. The backbones should not really be called bones at all, because they are made of cartilage, and bone merely provided the fish with protective armour. From that time onwards vertebrates evolved very speedily indeed.

What animals developed from the armoured fish?

You have seen the way in which the early fish had a spine made of cartilage, and that bony plates served to protect them. They probably needed to be armoured because they could not swim particularly well. As they became more mobile, however, the need for the protective armour was reduced. The bone cells slowly began to move inwards, changing the cartilage into bone. Thus, the first fish with a true backbone evolved. It is interesting to note that modern sharks still have a spinal column which is made of cartilage because the ossification, as the change to bone is known, has not occurred in this group.

The first bony fish appeared during early Devonian times, that is, about 380 million years ago. At the end of Devonian times, about 350 million years ago, the bony fish began to evolve very rapidly indeed, and divided into two groups. The groups are the modern bony fish, which account for about 95 per cent of all modern fish, and the remaining five per cent are a group known as lung fish.

The modern bony fish form a group in which there is just one single line of evolution. This evolution takes place as a gradual loss of the heavily armoured scales together with a change in the structure of the jaw. The change in the jaw structure is mainly concerned with the way in which the mouth opens, but it is rather complicated and it is enough to say that modern fish are able to open their mouths far wider than their early ancestors. This ability has obvious advantages when it comes to feeding.

There are still lung fish living today. They differ from more familiar fish in two main respects. Firstly, they have internal nostrils rather than gills, and equally important, the structure of the fins is different.

Right:
An early amphibian.

Below right:
A lobe-finned fish.

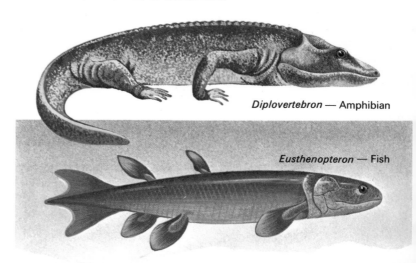

Diplovertebron — Amphibian

Eusthenopteron — Fish

In the true fish, the fins are formed on rays which extend from the body – they are usually referred to as ray finned. In the case of the lung fish, however, the fin rays enter an extension of the body tissue itself – they are known as lobe finned. This means that the fins of the lung fish eventually led to their ability to move on to land because of their development into legs.

Modern lung fish are able to survive for long periods when ponds dry out. They burrow into the mud at the bottom of ponds, only to emerge when the pond fills with water once again.

During Devonian times, the widespread desert climate tended to encourage the development of animals which were able to survive on land as well as in water. These animals were the amphibians. They first appeared in Greenland, which was furthest away from the return of the sea during Carboniferous times some 300 to 350 million years ago.

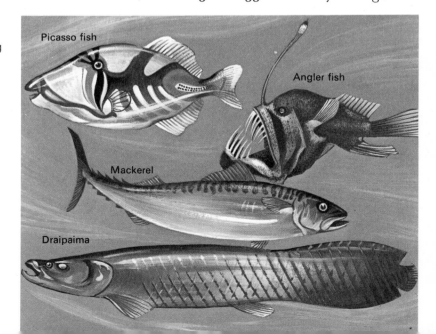

Picasso fish

Angler fish

Mackerel

Draipaima

		Turtles	Snakes	Lizards
Tertiary				
Cretaceous				
Jurassic	To Mammals			
Triassic	Procolophonids	Therapsida		
Permian	Pareiasaurs		Pelycosauria	
Upper Carboniferous				

After the amphibians – what next?

The amphibians were able to survive on land as well as in water, which as we have seen, was of considerable advantage during the arid climates of Devonian times. Nevertheless, all amphibians, even those that survive today, must return to water to breed. In fact, after the amphibians had developed, and seemed to have come to terms with their new way of life, there was a mass return to the sea, and few amphibians still exist. The early amphibians were large, being as much as two metres long, but gradually they became smaller and more variable in appearance.

The amphibians that returned to the sea had limbs and not fins like the fishes. The body became much longer and most species of the newly returned marine forms became predatory, that is, they hunted other animals for food. A new group of animals evolved in the late Carboniferous times, some members of which were to dominate the Earth for a considerable period of time. This new group is the reptiles. Land forms perfected their means of moving in their dry surroundings by increasing the strength of the limbs.

By the end of Carboniferous times drier conditions once more came to the Earth. Thus, those species which were better able to cope with these conditions survived while many became extinct. The reptiles developed an extra outside layer to prevent the body from drying out, and eventually a means of protecting the delicate egg was found. Reptiles' bodies became covered with hard plates, and these

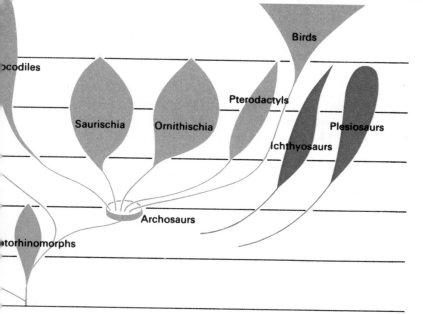

Birds

ocodiles

Pterodactyls

Saurischia   Ornithischia

Plesiosaurs

Ichthyosaurs

Archosaurs

torhinomorphs

are well shown in today's relics of the past, the crocodiles and alligators, for example. It is possible that the protected egg, capable of withstanding dry conditions, came first as a protective adaptation for one group of amphibians, but this is not certain and there is much speculation about these early amphibians and reptiles.

During Permian times where dry conditions were very widespread and deserts were far greater in number and extent than they are today there was a very rapid evolution, in which all the various habitats were occupied. It is worth a mention here that at the same time a group of warm-blooded animals were also beginning to evolve – the mammals. It would be some time, however, before they would be as powerful as they are today. There were also mammal-like reptiles, and in some areas, such as South Africa, these were the dominant species. Instead of the flat scales of the reptiles, the mammal-like reptiles had fine scales standing at an angle from the body and which would eventually become hair. Hair acts as a better insulation against heat loss, so that they could live in cooler climates and eventually develop a warm blood stream so that there would be no need to hibernate during winter. But for 100 million years the reptiles were dominant, and one group, the dinosaurs, were the unchallenged masters of the Earth.

Hylonomus

Left:
Hylonomus, one of the earliest known reptiles.

129

Which animals are among the largest that have ever lived?

It is probably safe to say that some of the largest animals that have ever lived on the surface of this planet are members of a group of animals which have been collectively called dinosaurs. These 'terrible reptiles', as their name means,

Coelophysis

Diplodocus

have excited the imagination of men ever since bones of the first dinosaurs were discovered in rocks of Upper Triassic age – that is, deposits about 200 million years old. Many tales have been told of these monsters sharing the Earth with man, but, of course, as we shall explain later all the dinosaurs had died out long before man appeared.

Dinosaurs evolved into a great variety of different shapes and sizes but they all had a common ancestor. They ranged in size from dinosaurs the size of a chicken, to others which were as much as 30 metres long and weighing more than 30 tonnes. Some dinosaurs, such as *Diplodocus*, lived on plants. Others were hunters. They attacked and killed dinosaurs as much as 15 metres long for food. *Tyrannosaurus* were the largest meat-eating animals that have ever dwelled on land. Bones of these animals have been discovered in rocks about 70 million years old in North America. There were also dinosaurs that lived in the sea. Others such as *pteranodon* developed a kind of wing and they could glide in the upward currents of air that occur above the cliffs on which they must have lived.

Some of the less terrible dinosaurs could escape the predatory ones using their speed, but others were much too clumsy and slow-moving to get away. They developed armoured coverings to their bodies to protect them and had spines and horny plates as well. In fact, *Stegosaurus* was probably able to

Ornithomimus

Brachiosaurus

Plateosaurus

defend itself quite well with the help of spikes at the end of its long tail.

Dinosaurs have presented researchers with many puzzles, not least of which is how giants like *Brontosaurus* managed to live at all. Examination of its bones has shown that its legs were probably not strong enough to support its weight on land, and if it lived partly submerged in water, its rib cage may have collapsed. On the other hand, it did not possess the correct kind of feet to survive in swamps.

There have been many arguments about why the dinosaurs suddenly died out. Perhaps the climate changed. In the 1980s, scientists found evidence of a disaster about 65 million years ago. It may have been caused by the impact a huge meteorite, which threw up dense clouds of dust around the Earth.

Tyrannosaurus

Which were the first animals with warm blood?

The ability to control the body temperature is a considerable advantage to an animal. Even today, reptiles are cold blooded. In practice, this means that their body temperature corresponds with the temperature of the surrounding environment. Now, the efficiency of an animal's body functions is very dependent on its temperature. This means that as the air temperature falls, the animal's body temperature falls and its functions become more and more sluggish. Thus

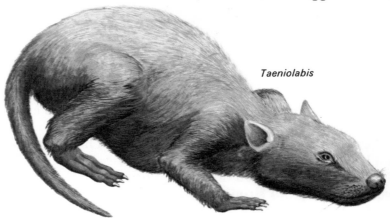

Taeniolabis

reptiles survive perfectly well in warm climates, and even in cooler climates they manage by hibernating during the winter months. But cold blooded land animals cannot survive in the very cold regions of the Earth. You can see, then, that if an animal has the ability to control its body temperature it has a considerable advantage over the reptiles in its adaptability to cold climates. It does mean, however, that in cooler places, animals must have their bodies insulated to prevent loss of heat. This can be achieved by extra layers of fat, hair or fur in the case of mammals, and feathers in the case of birds.

The ability to control body temperature may have evolved separately on two occasions. It is possible that a group of primitive reptiles may have been partly warm blooded and probably the dinosaurs could control their body temperature to some extent.

An animal with warm blood has a very high metabolic rate, as the speed of its body processes is known. But this in turn means that their cells, which make up the bodies of all living things, require more oxygen or they may be damaged. Together with warm bloodedness, then, the blood supply carrying oxygen around the body must be made more efficient. There must be more blood vessels in the bones. It is interesting to note that the bones of dinosaurs have almost as many pores as those of modern mammals.

In late Jurassic times (about 150 million years ago), an animal existed which has great importance in the development of life on Earth. This creature is known as *Archaeopteryx*; we expect that you have heard of it. It seems to be exactly intermediate between a bird and a reptile. It had some feathers and could probably fly, although not very well. In order to be efficient enough to fly it must have been warm blooded. But its skeleton is more like that of certain dinosaurs, and rather than a bill, its jaws were armed with small teeth. This first bird probably developed from some of the reptiles that leapt from tree to tree.

Morganucodon

Ctenacodon

Pantothere

How have mammals evolved?

As you know the group of animals known as mammals are successful, widespread, and very diverse. Modern mammal range in size from animals such as the lesser shrew of Britain at a total length of a little over six centimetres and weighing little more than 4.5 grams to the giants of the oceans such a the blue whale weighing in at up to 150 tonnes.

Modern mammals occupy a range of different habitats they can live in deserts, as does the desert fox, in frozen wastes as does the polar bear, in jungles where many specie abound, in temperate woodlands like the European badger and so on. These are the mammals that live on land. As we have seen, there are those that roam the oceans such as the whales.

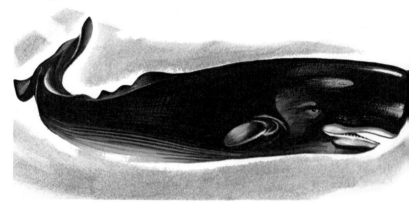

Ocean dwelling mammals have more problems than their counterparts on land because they still have to maintain their body temperature. Obviously hair would be useless to help them retain heat. Consequently, they have evolved thick layers of fat usually known as blubber. On the other hand, because the salt water helps them to support their body weight, they have been able to grow to these enormous sizes. In fact, the largest whales are the largest animals that have ever lived, larger even than the mighty, vegetarian dinosaur, *Brontosaurus*.

Mammals have also conquered the air, perhaps not as efficiently as birds, but nevertheless bats could still be considered to be successful animals in the struggle for survival.

How, then, has this great diversity been achieved? In Triassic times, some 200 million years or so ago, mammal-like reptiles had developed at least partial control of their body temperature and may have been covered in fur or hair rather than scales. It is difficult to say with certainty from fossil evidence, exactly when the first true mammals

The duck-billed platypus (*above*) and the spiny ant-eater (*right*) are the only surviving mammals that lay eggs and they are very primitive indeed.

appeared, but it was certainly not for another thirty or forty million years, when at the end of Triassic times animals, not unlike modern shrews, were alive.

The most primitive mammals probably still laid eggs rather than giving birth to living young, and today there are still mammals surviving which are also egg-laying. The duck-billed platypus of Australia, for example, lays its eggs at the bottom of a burrow. It has been able to survive (it could be described as a living fossil) because the Australian continent has been cut off by the drifting apart of the continents for at least 100 million years. Marsupials, also found mainly in Australia, represent a kind of intermediate stage of evolution with the young being born alive at a very early stage and remaining in the mother's pouch.

From Tertiary times until today, in geologic terms, the evolution of mammals has been very rapid with the development of animals such as the horse and the elephant being the easiest to trace.

Right:
The Tasmanian wolf and the kangaroo are examples of marsupials that have survived in Australasia because this area became separated from the rest of the world by continental drifting. As a result, these animals had little competition from more advanced mammals that were developing elsewhere.

Tasmanian wolf Kangaroo

When did plants first colonize the land?

We know already that the first life on Earth was probably plant and that it lived in water. Indeed, these are the very primitive algae that we have already mentioned. You must bear in mind that these first plants did not have stems, leaves, and roots as do the plants that you might immediately think of as living today. These plants were just collections of living cells.

In rocks of Cambrian age, however, there is evidence of plants which might have lived on land. This was between 500 and 600 million years ago. But it was not until about 150 to 200 million years later that plant life became abundant on land and evidence of this can be found in rocks of the so-called Silurian and Devonian periods.

The first plants that began to encroach the land had to live in shallow water, but they did have roots and could take in the gas carbon dioxide from the primitive atmosphere. But

Above:
An artist's impression of a plant that has been found fossilized in Devonian rocks of Scotland. It lacked the true roots, leaves and seeds of modern plants.

Right:
The modern club moss and the fossilized fragment of a lepidodendron shown here belong to the same group of primitive plants.

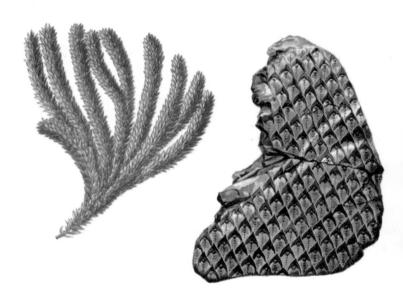

the first true land plants were a group which are called *psilophytes*. They still had to live in damp places, however, and they do not seem to be directly related to any plants living today.

The first trees appeared in the Devonian, although they were not much like the trees that you will be familiar with in a modern country landscape. For one thing these trees, with the group name of *lepidodendrons*, did not produce flowers, and in fact it was not until a mere 135 million years ago that the first flowering plants became abundant. Modern examples of very primitive land plants are the ferns and mosses. About 350 million years ago, however, land plants became so abundant that their remains have left us with the deposits of coal which are so important to our industries and help to warm many of our homes.

Right:
These horsetails, ferns, seed ferns, and tree ferns can be found fossilized in rocks of Carboniferous age.

reconstruction of *Lepidodendron*

Neuropteris leaves

Annularia leaves

Calamites stem

Ptychocarpus leaves

reconstruction of *Calamites*

What is the importance of plants in life's framework?

It is only when we stop to think that we realize the importance of land plants to us. We eat them in our cereals and vegetables, we make use of them for fibres like cotton, we depend on them for many drugs such as penicillin, and as we have already mentioned we need the fossil fuels. But even when we eat meat, we must remember that the animals which produce the meat probably lived on plants.

Plants are nature's producers. From sunlight, oxygen, and other foods from the soil, plants manufacture the foods upon which all animals ultimately depend. It is worth noting that it was with the rise of the land plants in the Devonian, that land animals also began to evolve.

What is known about ancient plants?

We have looked at the ways in which plants first colonized the land surface of the Earth, but perhaps it is time to look at the evolution of plants as a whole in more detail. It is generally easier to follow the trends in the evolution of plants because modern advanced plants may be quite similar in their make up to a more primitive form. Animals, and the development of the animal kingdom are very much more complicated.

As has already been mentioned, plants are made up of *cells*. These cells are the living substance from which all life is composed. It is unnecessary here to discuss the detailed organization of living cells. It is enough to say that they are made up of a dense nucleus surrounded by a watery fluid. The very first plants, of course, were probably just single cells of living matter.

Right:
Two true bacteria. It has been stated that bacteria reproduce so quickly that if an unlimited food supply was available the weight of bacteria produced after twenty-four hours from a single bacterium would be greater than the mass of the Earth.

Bacteria are sometimes thought of as plants. These are tiny (microscopic) single-celled organisms which usually live by feeding on other plants or animals as parasites, or on dead or decaying matter. It has been discovered however, that there are bacteria that will even feed on such unpalatable things as concrete and glass. In fact, without bacteria, no other life would be possible, because it is bacteria that aid in the breaking down of rock debris to form soil, and bacteria that enable waste products to decay. As you might expect, fossil remains of bacteria are rare, although they can be found in the rock called the Rhynie chert of the Scottish Devonian.

Right:
It is thought that these blue-green algae are important in the formation of soils.

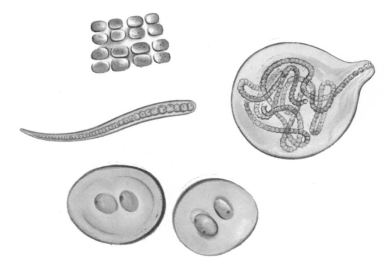

The algae are also a very primitive group of plants, still in existence today, but representing some of the earliest life forms to be found on Earth. The algae are the most diverse plant group both in size and in their ways of life. Remember that seaweeds are algae as is the green film that forms on the glass of a goldfish tank.

The evolution of plants can usually be traced on the basis of their way of multiplying, and the algae are no exception. Their method is very primitive. At a particular time of the year the cell contents become more dense, two cells come together, and new nuclei develop. The rest of the year the cells just divide.

Algae are usually subdivided into groups on the basis of their colour. Green algae are those that can only live in clear, comparatively shallow, marine conditions and they build reefs. Red algae include the seaweeds and live in the deep seas making use of only part of the light that is found at depth. The blue-green algae are thought to be important in the formation of soils. The brown algae live in shallow water marine conditions.

What happened to plants next?

So far we have considered the very first primitive plants that existed on Earth many hundreds of millions of years ago, and we have seen when they first appeared on land and the effects that this had. Now perhaps, we should look at the more advanced forms including most of those plants that we are so familiar with.

The group of ancient plants that forms a link between advanced and primitive plants is known as the *Cordaitales* which first appear in the Lower Carboniferous rocks some 300 to 350 million years ago. This group reached the height of its development in terms of both numbers of individuals and species at the time when the last of the important coal deposits were being laid down, that is, in the Late Carboniferous times about 270 million years ago. They could be thought of as being intermediate in type between epidodendrons mentioned earlier and modern conifers. (Remember that conifers are trees that bear cones, such as larch or Scots pine.) All the members of the Cordaitales were tree-like, and were able to withstand very dry conditions. They had leaves that were not flattened so that less water was lost through them. The outer 'skin' of the leaf became much thickened, and the shape of the tree was such that air became trapped within the branches.

In Middle Permian times, about 250 million years ago, true conifers were becoming quite abundant, and almost 100 million years later in the Jurassic period they had reached their peak. It can be shown that conifers evolved directly from the Cordaitales. Evolution of the conifers occurred in two different directions. Members of the genus *Pinus* became

Below:
A section through a typical flower.

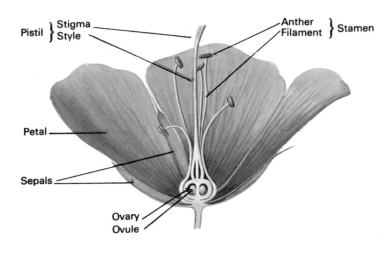

Pistil { Stigma, Style

Anther, Filament } Stamen

Petal

Sepals

Ovary

Ovule

Agathis australis

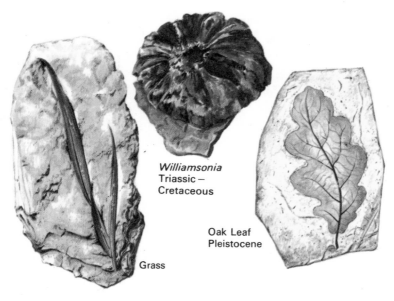

Williamsonia
Triassic –
Cretaceous

Oak Leaf
Pleistocene

Grass

Left:
Here are some fossil remains of flowering plants. Remember that trees such as oaks and horsechestnuts are flowering plants as well.

Below:
Some common coniferous plants that can be found today.

Yew

more and more able to withstand drying, indeed, would not survive in damp conditions.

Another group, known as the *Taxus-Macrocarpa* group, continued to retain the more primitive type of flattened leaf. Members of this group could not withstand drying but could survive in very poor soils where there were strong winds and high rainfall or snow – that is, mountain conditions. All conifers must live in association with a root fungus because they do not have root hairs.

There are two other groups of plants that seem to have developed from the early types, but this is not certain. They are both palm-like types, but one group, the *Bennetitales* became extinct during the Cretaceous period, about 100 million years ago.

The plants that you are probably most familiar with are the flowering plants. These probably evolved indirectly from the conifers at some point during the Jurassic, but they did not become important until the Tertiary, between 50 and 70 million years ago. They have not yet reached their maximum development.

Scots Pine

Juniper

Monkey
Puzzle

Which animals are among the tiniest that have ever lived?

Among the tiniest animals that live independently today are members of the *plankton* which inhabit the seas everywhere. These *zooplankton* as they are more properly called are very important to the whole life of the sea because, together with the tiny plants upon which they feed, the *phytoplankton*, they provide the nourishment for all the other animals which live in the sea. Even giant whales feed upon plankton.

Right:
Some modern foraminiferids viewed with the aid of a microscope.

Right:
Radiolarians like the ones shown here are planktonic marine animals which may feed on tiny plants.

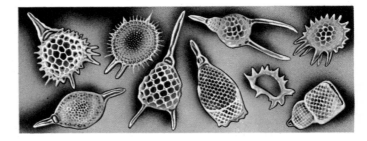

For the geologist, however, there are other groups of microscopic animals (this means that they can only be clearly seen with the aid of a microscope) that are more important. Firstly, there is a group of animals called *ostracods* which range in size from one millimetre to two centimetres so that they could be seen with the naked eye. Ostracods belong to the arthropods which include insects and spiders. Do you remember where you have seen this word before? Remember that insects and spiders are arthropods, but which fossil group do they belong to?

Right:
These are the parts of the radiolarians that may collect on the sea floor to form a radiolarian ooze. This only forms at great depths — perhaps greater than 4500 metres.

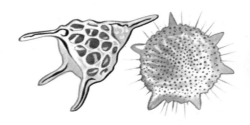 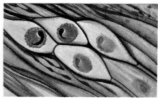

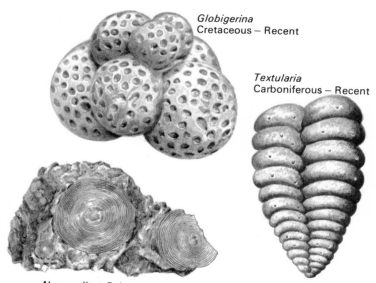

Globigerina
Cretaceous – Recent

Textularia
Carboniferous – Recent

Nummulites Palaeocene – Oligocene

Right:
Some fossil 'forams'.

Ostracods are different from all the other arthropods in that they have an external hard shell in the form of two parts or valves rather like that of the bivalves that we have already mentioned. The actual animal living inside its shell is not unlike a modern lobster. As it grows, the ostracod sheds its shell in a series of moult stages.

Ostracods all live in water, but it may be in stagnant fresh water or in rivers or in the sea. In fact, a single species can tolerate quite a wide range of conditions. They mostly live at the bed of the sea, river or pond and like the trilobites they are scavengers. The first ostracods can be found in rocks that are 550 million years old and representatives of the group can still be found today.

Another group of microscopic animals that are of special interest to the geologist are the *foraminiferids*. They are members of the Protozoa, which all consist of only one living cell, and they are important because they produce a skeleton which can be fossilized. They are all marine animals, but different types may have lived on the sea floor and some may have been free-floating. The skeletons were made in three different ways: there were some that were made of calcium carbonate, some of the material called chitin, and others which made the skeleton from tiny sand grains from the sea bed. Foraminiferids can be found from Ordovician to recent times, although it has been suggested that some forms may have existed in rocks of Cambrian age.

How long has man been walking the Earth?

Ever since the philosopher and naturalist, Charles Darwin and his contemporaries including Wallace, suggested that man had evolved from apes, there has been a continuous and almost frantic quest for evidence of our ancestors. Of course, where we come from has always been a fascinating question, but it is only comparatively recently that systematic searches have been made for traces of ancient men by such eminent scientists as L. S. B. Leakey and still more recently by his son, Richard. As you might imagine, the idea that man came from monkeys brought with it a great deal of public outcry, and in fact, modern research has shown that man did not descend directly from apes but that the ape and man evolved from a common ancestor.

Right:
A representation of the main groups of life forms that have appeared throughout the Earth's long history.

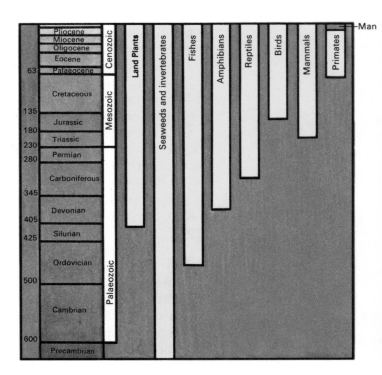

As you know the first thing that monkeys, apes, and man have in common is that they all have backbones, so that they are all vertebrates. Many characteristics in man have arisen from living in trees. We share them with other primates, as monkeys, apes and man are known. If you suddenly found that you had to live in a tree, what do you think the most useful adaptations would be? There would not be much point in having hoofs like a horse which help the horse to un fast. You would need to be able to hold on to the branches, however, as our hands are well able to do. If you wanted to jump from branch to branch, you would have to be able to judge distances. You would need stereoscopic vision, that is, two eyes positioned at the front of your head, not at the sides as in a fish. You are unable to smell the traces of scent that a dog can, but you do have a much enlarged brain. It is the growth of the brain that has enabled man to leave the comparative safety of the trees and compete with the other ground-dwelling animals that are stronger, have better hearing and sense of smell, can run faster and have warm coats to protect them from the extremes of climate.

As you might expect, because man and apes have developed from a common ancestor, it is not easy to tell when the remains of the primates that have been found are of men-like apes or ape-like men. But between ten and fifteen million years ago a creature which has been called a *Ramapithe-cus* lived in parts of Africa, Asia, and Europe. This may have been the ancestor of man and the other apes, though recent evidence suggests that our ancestor was another creature, the ancestor of the orang-utan. However, the groups became increasingly diverse until the first creature that could be called human arrived. This was around four million years ago.

Right:
It is estimated that *Homo habilis*, a primitive man able to use tools, lived a little less than two million years ago.

Below:
Peking-man, apparently able to use fire, probably lived between 400,000 and 500,000 years ago.

Homo habilis

Peking-man

Who were man's ancestors?

We have briefly looked at some of the developments which have occurred in man's evolution from the ape-like creatures of prehistory to the learned, technological *Homo sapiens* of today. But perhaps it is worth looking in more detail at some of the animals which have been proved by the investigators to be related in some way to ourselves.

The first creatures which have been identified as man's forebears were certainly not human. About four million years ago, ape-men known as Australopithecines – southern ape-men – inhabited parts of south and east Africa, as their remains indicate. Some of these ape-men lived in the open plains and were small, nimble creatures, well adapted to their life in these conditions. The other group lived in the forested regions, and consequently were much larger, stronger animals.

It has been suggested that these southern ape-men were among the first primates to use tools made of bones and teeth. It may be, however, that the remains of animal bones and teeth which have been found associated with the Australopithecines were just the leftovers from meals. But whether or not they used tools, the teeth of the plains' ape-men certainly suggest that they might have eaten meat and, of

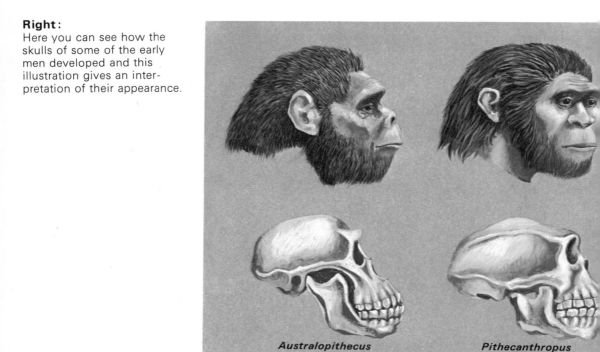

Australopithecus

Pithecanthropus

course, weapons would have been particularly useful in hunting and killing their victims. It is likely that their relatives living in the forests had a more vegetarian diet.

About one-and-three-quarter million years ago a primate existed, also in east Africa, which has been proved to belong to the genus *Homo,* that is, it was humanlike. There may yet be finds to come that will indicate an even older date for the origins of a true man, but as yet this is the first creature that has been proved to have made tools and weapons in definite shapes and sizes. The evidence provided by finds of bones from feet of these early men show that they probably walked on two feet like we do, rather than on four feet like an animal such as a dog. *Homo habilis,* as it is called, was probably the first primate to have been able to stand upright.

From this point onwards man seems to have made very rapid progress, and there is fossil evidence of a number of primitive men, but perhaps the most famous of all is the man whose bones have been found in eastern Europe particularly, *Homo sapiens neanderthalensis* – Neanderthal-man. This cave-dwelling creature is closely related to modern people, who are classed as *Homo sapiens sapiens,* but it is not our ancestor. The earliest known example of modern people is called Cro-Magnon man which emerged around 50,000 years ago. Its origins are still shrouded in mystery.

Above:
The skull and upper limb of a fossil ape, *Proconsul africanus*. This fossil ape may have lived as much as twenty-five million years ago.

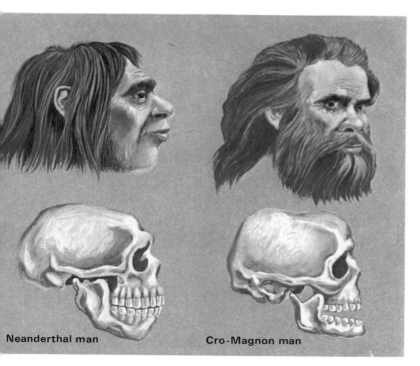

Neanderthal man   Cro-Magnon man

What kinds of tools did early man use?

Some animals and birds make use of tools. There are some good examples among the birds. For example, the song thrush commonly feeds on snails which it opens by flying up with the shell in its bill and dropping the snail on a convenient stone. The bird often uses the same stone on a number of occasions so that it may become littered with broken shells. The stone is often referred to as a thrush's anvil. The members of the shrike family often make use of thorns on which they impale their prey. But man more than any other animal has taken advantage of his large brain capacity to increase his power to hunt, kill, build his homes, and so on.

It is man's ability to hold things in his hand which has enabled him to make such use of tools, where other animals have had to rely on their strength and agility, their teeth and their claws. Man's first tools and weapons were stones which he had picked up. He chose stones that had been worn and sharpened by the weather into shapes that could be used as clubs or for cutting and scraping. As you might imagine the right shaped stones were not always easy to find, so that in time man learned to fashion primitive tools to a constant design that suited his purpose.

Many of the early men were carnivorous, that is, they fed largely on meat. This meant that a lot of the stones that have been positively identified as prehistoric implements were designed to kill animals, and then to scrape the flesh off the bones of the victim. Tools of prehistoric man could be made

Right:
Neanderthal-man. He is using a stone implement, like the one illustrated, to scrape a hide.

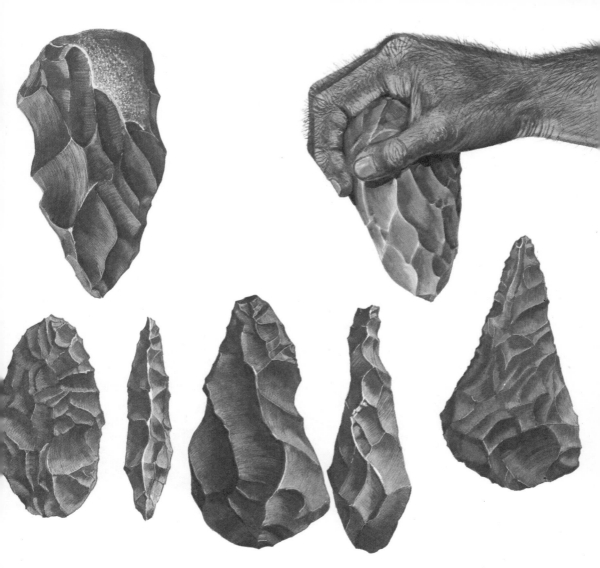

Above and right:
These are the kind of flint hand-axes that primitive man might have used about 400,000 years ago.

of bone, tooth, or more frequently stone, and in particular, flint. Flint was chosen because it breaks to give a flake with a very sharp, hard edge that could be used as, say, an axe. At first, these primitive weapons would be held directly in the hand. Eventually, however, man learned how to attach these axe-heads to a wooden shaft, and the power of the weapon was increased.

As he became more experienced in making stone tools, the tools became more and more advanced in their design so that soon he was making blades, scrapers, and even arrowheads. Arrowheads were a great advance because they meant that for the first time man could kill his prey without putting himself to the risk of approaching what could be a very dangerous animal. Of course, these weapons could also be used to wound and kill other men.

How should you collect fossils?

You have seen that during the long history of the Earth, there have been many species of animals and plants that have existed some which are still alive today, some long since extinct. Fortunately, the existence of most of these species has not gone unrecorded even though they may have vanished long before the appearance of man. We have fossils to thank for a comparatively clear picture of the life of the past.

Collecting fossils can be fun for all sorts of reasons. You may be interested in seeing at first hand the remains of creatures very different from those common today. You may want to collect fossils as an aid to other geological pursuits such as stratigraphy. You might just like the fascinating shapes that can be found. But whatever your reasons, it is important to go about fossil hunting in the right way, in the best places, using the most useful equipment.

As you know, some rocks are more likely to contain fossils than others. For example, it would be remarkable indeed to find a fossil in serpentine rock of the Lizard in Cornwall, but in Devonian limestones of Torquay not too far away, it would not be at all unusual. Before you begin your searches, consult a geological map of the area and the regional guide published by the Institute of Geological Sciences. A visit to the museum will also furnish valuable information. Then choose the best areas from what you have learned, bearing

take notes

first find the specimen

number the specimen

remove it carefully from the rock

in mind that cliffs, quarries, road and rail cuttings, river banks, and even the beach provide the best sites. Remember that these areas are dangerous, and for quarries it is usually necessary to obtain permission first. Make sure you are accompanied by someone who is experienced, and follow the country code.

For the best results you will need some equipment. For the most part, equipment is dealt with in another question, but other items should include newspaper to wrap your finds in, a pen with waterproof ink, and a notebook. You must remember always to mark the find with an identifying number which you have recorded in the notebook together with when and where it was found, including the rock it was found in and its exact location within that rock. It cannot be stressed too strongly that great care must be taken when removing any fossil from its containing rock. Many valuable specimens have been lost by over enthusiasm with a geologic hammer. Remember that a fossil can be very delicate. Think how long it has been resting there and think how quickly it could be destroyed. If you have difficulties, take home the whole rock so that you can remove it at home. If you are searching among clays or soft sands a trowel or a stout pocket knife will be more useful than a hammer, and for tiny fossils a selection of sieves will be valuable.

Left and above:
This young geologist is carefully removing a fossil specimen which will be taken home and catalogued.

Animals

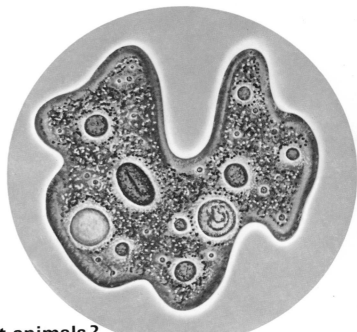

What are the simplest animals?

The protozoans are simple organisms that consist of only one cell. They make up the phylum Protozoa. It is difficult to refer to some of them as either animals or plants because although many are extremely active and catch and eat their food, others, like plants, use the energy of the sun to make their own food. A protozoan is made up of a single microscopic unit of protoplasm (the complex mixture of substances of which all animals and plants are made) enclosed by a membrane and controlled by a central nucleus.

Protozoans live in a remarkable variety of habitats. Although they are essentially aquatic they are found in all bodies of water from small muddy puddles of rainwater to all the oceans of the world. They can even exist in the thin film of moisture which surrounds soil particles and many are parasitic, living within the bodies of other plants and animals. They are very resistant and, if the pond or marsh in which they live dries up, they are able to secrete a protective skin around themselves. In this condition, the cyst, as the protozoan is then called, is able to survive and it returns to life again when favourable conditions occur.

Although extremely small in size and basic in structure, the protozoans are very significant to other members of the animal kingdom. They form the heads of food chains and so provide proteins and vitamins for other more advanced animals. They also play an important role in breaking down plant and animal remains. Parasitic forms cause diseases in man, for example, malaria.

An amoeba creeps slowly along changing its shape all the time.

Chlamydomonas is a protozoan that swims around by lashing the water with two flagellae.

How do these single-celled animals move?

Euglena has a single whip-like flagellum.

Protozoans move in a variety of ways. The amoeba has no characteristic shape, in contrast to the other protozoans, and moves along the substratum, or surface of objects, in a flowing movement, continually changing its form. The jelly-like protoplasm streams out into thin extensions called *pseudopodia* or 'false-feet' and the rest of the amoeba flows into them. In this way the amoeba slowly creeps about.

The majority of protozoans, however, are more active and lash the water with whip-like flagellae. *Chlamydomonas* and *Euglena* swim jerkily around.

A modification of the same method is seen in *Paramecium* in which the entire surface is covered with rows of short cilia. Their movements are co-ordinated and they beat rythmically in waves, propelling the animal smoothly through the water.

How does *Volvox* differ from other protozoans?

Volvox is a colony of protozoans. It is a group of several thousand individual protozoans arranged to form the wall of a jelly-filled sphere. Some of these individual cells have different functions and in this way *Volvox* and other similar colonies of protozoans are among the first examples of the arrangement of many-celled animals.

Each protozoan of the colony has a pair of flagellae which lash the water in a co-ordinated rythmic sequence. *Volvox* can be seen in pond water as a tiny green ball moving smoothly along in a rolling motion.

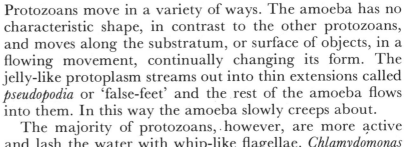

Paramecium has a characteristic 'slipper shape' and is covered with rows of short hairs called cilia.

Within this *Volvox* colony can be seen smaller daughter colonies which are released when they have grown large enough.

(*Right*) Some varieties of sponges encrusting a rock on the seashore.

(*Below*) Examples of the different types of spicules produced by sponges. Spicules are secreted by the sponge from salts in the water and form a single skeleton to support the soft body.

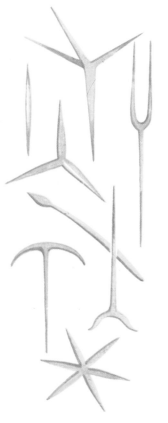

What are sponges?

Sponges are very primitive many-celled animals. They live in both fresh and sea water and encrust rocks and underwater objects in strange lumpy masses. Some spread over considerable areas, others hang in finger-like clusters, while others stand erect, branching irregularly up to 5 feet in height. Sponges are interesting because they represent a more advanced stage of development than the colony of protozoans. They belong to the phylum Porifera.

An individual sponge has a definite vase-like shape, and groups of the cells of which it is made are adapted to carry out special tasks. The cells of the wall of the sponge are called 'covering cells', and these protect it and help keep its shape. The inside layer of cells consists of cells bearing a whip-like flagellum to lash the water and make a current, as well as other cells which form pores on the outside of the sponge. Between the two, amoeba-like cells occur and these secrete strengthening rods called 'spicules' which make the sponge rigid.

How do sponges feed if they cannot move?

As the flagellae of the cells inside the sponge beat the water, a current is set up and water is drawn through the tiny pores into the centre of the sponge and then driven out through the hole at the top. Suspended particles of food in the water are caught on the flagellae of the cells and passed back to the amoeba-like cells. Another function of these cells is to absorb the food particles filtered from the water and to transport the digested food to the other parts of the sponge. The cells bearing flagellae can only deal with a certain size of food particle, and so no matter how large the sponge, it must feed on microscopic particles such as bacteria and protozoans suspended in the water.

This cut-away diagram shows the arrangement of the different types of cells within a single individual sponge.

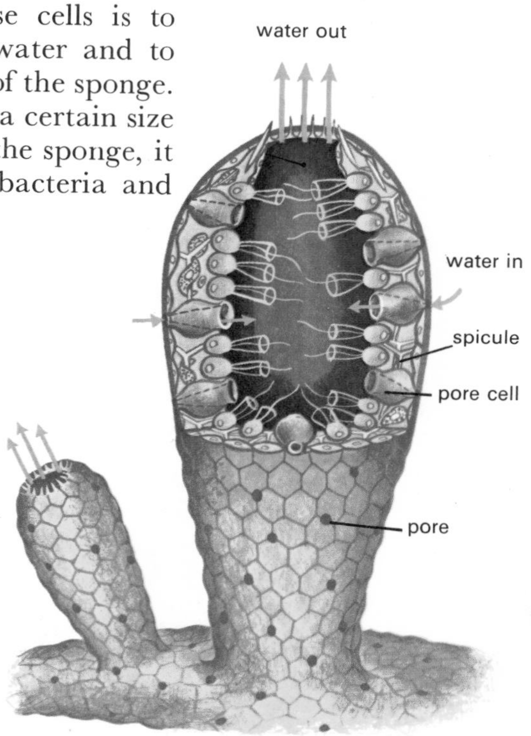

water out

water in

spicule

pore cell

pore

Three examples of commercial sponges in their natural state (before preparation as bathroom sponges). These are from the Mediterranean Sea.

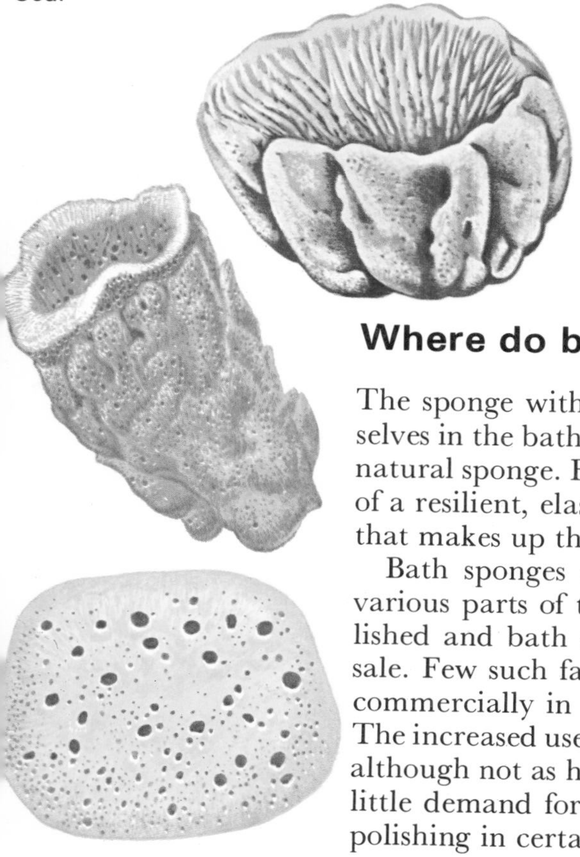

Where do bath sponges come from?

The sponge with which some people regularly soap themselves in the bath is really the skeleton of a particular type of natural sponge. Bath sponges are supported by a framework of a resilient, elastic material called 'spongin', and it is this that makes up the bathroom sponge.

Bath sponges are found in warm shallow seas, and in various parts of the world 'sponge farms' were once established and bath sponges grown from cuttings for eventual sale. Few such farms still exist, but sponges are still grown commercially in the Greek Islands and in the Philippines. The increased use of synthetic sponges – cheaper to produce, although not as hard wearing – has meant that there is now little demand for natural sponges, except for cleaning and polishing in certain industries.

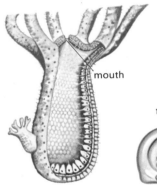

Are hydras more advanced than sponges?

You might easily overlook a hydra in a pond, lake or stream, because when disturbed, it contracts its body from the normal length of about half-an-inch to a tiny blob of jelly that you can only see if you look very carefully. Most people are more familiar with its marine relatives – the sea anemones, jellyfishes and corals – which are, of course, much larger and more colourful.

This group of animals belongs to the phylum Coelenterata which means simply 'hollow gut'. The hydra is basically a bag with a fringe of tentacles around the mouth at one end, and a disc at the other with which it sticks to a surface.

Instead of a loose arrangement of the cells into groups with different functions (as in the sponges), the body wall of a hydra consists of two definite layers. The cells act together in a much more organized way than those of the sponge. The hydra is also more responsive and active than the sponge and has a network of nerve cells which make up a primitive nervous system. It also has single muscle cells which enable it to bend and contract its body.

A group of hydras. The illustration below shows a hydra cut away to show the two layers of cells of the body wall and the mouth. A young hydra is growing on the wall.

mouth

(*Right*) The special stinging and holding cells which arm the tentacles. The cells are stimulated to fire when the trigger is touched by a passing animal.

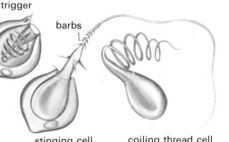

trigger

barbs

stinging cell   coiling thread cell

Hydra-like animals live in branching colonies such as *Obelia.* Some polyps of the colony are modified to produce free-swimming stages called medusae which bear the reproductive organs; the underneath view of one is shown.

How do hydras catch their prey?

The tentacles of the hydra, like those of the anemones and jellyfishes, are armed with special stinging cells which fire poisonous barbed threads into any unfortunate creature that happens to brush against them. Other cells of this type release long threads which coil around the prey and help hold it until it can be manoeuvred to the mouth and engulfed. Once inside the bag of the hydra the small water flea or worm is quickly digested and any remains are spat out from the mouth. It is an interesting fact that the hydra can catch and eat much larger animals than the sponge.

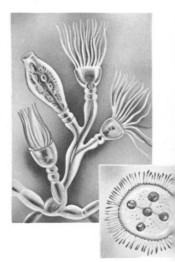

Velella, or the By-the-wind Sailor, is another animal which floats in the sea trailing its tentacles.

What is the Portuguese man-o'-war?

Although it looks very much like a jellyfish, the Portuguese man-o'-war is really a floating colony of hydra-like animals called polyps, clustered together under a gas-filled bladder. The bladder acts as a sail and the Portuguese man-o'-war is driven about the warm seas of the world completely at the mercy of the wind. (A jellyfish, of course, can actively swim.)

The animal itself is about 6 inches long, but the trailing tentacles of the polyps can extend up to 60 feet. The tentacles of some of the polyps bear stinging and holding cells similar to those of the hydra. They can catch and hold fishes as large as mackerel. Once overcome the prey is quickly drawn up within reach of other polyps which eat and digest it.

Sometimes storms drive masses of these animals on to the beaches of seaside towns where they become a serious menace. They are usually left stranded high up the beach and the bladders soon dry and shrivel. The tentacles can still give a nasty sting if touched, however, and bathing is often prevented until the Portuguese men-o'-war are removed.

The Portuguese man-o'-war is common in the warm seas of the world and particularly in the North Atlantic, and areas of the Indian and Pacific Oceans.

A Portuguese man-o'-war traps fishes in its deadly, trailing tentacles.

What are the 'flowers of the sea'?

Gaze into the rock pool at low tide and the gently waving tentacles of the beautifully coloured sea anemones will make it immediately apparent why these animals were once called 'plant-animals'. Anemones are not flowers, of course, and in fact they are greedy predators, catching and eating fishes, worms, crabs and any other creatures that touch their waving arms. Like the other members of the coelenterates, the tentacles of anemones bear stinging cells and their body plan is similar to that of the freshwater hydra. Anemones are more muscular, however, and have several rings of tentacles around the mouth. The stomach is divided by partitions to increase its surface area so that larger prey can be digested.

Anemones may look fairly static in the rock pool but if you could watch for long enough you would see that they are continually on the move, contracting and extending the body and slowly gliding about.

What is coral?

Coral, which people often collect as decoration, is the hard, dried skeleton composed mainly of calcium produced by colonies of small animals very similar to anemones. The polyps of living coral live in tiny cups in the skeleton and are continually adding to its mass. The coral grows into a variety of shapes. Some species produce numerous branches and in others the polyps are arranged in twisting rows on a rounded mass.

Coral thrives in warm, shallow water and it forms extensive reefs along tropical shores, particularly in the Pacific and Indian Oceans. The protection the reefs provide make them ideal habitats and they support crowded communities of fishes, many kinds of invertebrates and seaweeds.

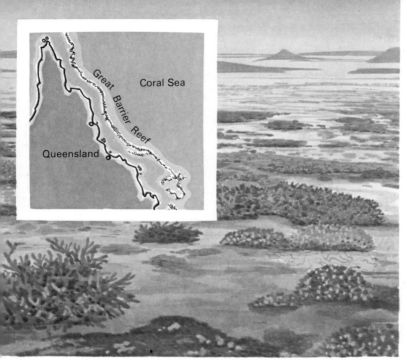

The Great Barrier Reef off the north-east coast of Australia stretches for 1,200 miles.

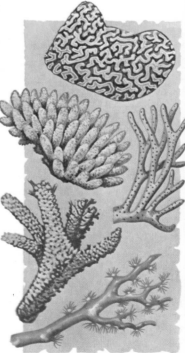

(*Below*) These examples of coral skeletons illustrate the enormous variety of shape and colour that can be found.

How are coral reefs formed?

There are three types of coral reef: fringing reefs grow close to the shore in shallow water; barrier reefs grow parallel to the shore but are separated from it by a deep channel which may be several miles wide; and atolls which are circular islands of coral enclosing a lagoon, often hundreds of miles from any other land.

There are numerous theories to explain the formation of these types of reefs. The most popular is that one type developed from another in a gradual transition so that all three are different stages of the same process. If a landmass with a fringing reef begins to sink into the sea, as long as the coral can grow at an equivalent rate to the subsidence, the reef will grow further and further from the coast. Eventually a barrier reef is formed some way from the shore. If the process continues and the landmass disappears altogether, a ring of coral will be left forming an atoll. This is the simplest explanation for the formation of reefs; the actual processes involved are more complex.

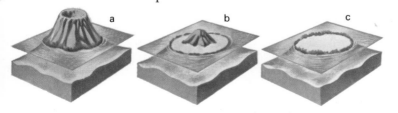

(*Left*) The three stages in reef formation showing (a) a fringing reef, (b) a barrier reef and (c) an atoll.

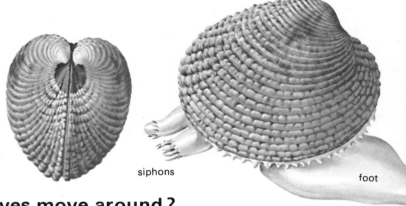

Two views of a typical bivalve mollusc. The left view shows the valves tightly shut while the right shows the siphons and foot extended.

siphons

foot

How do the bivalves move around?

A large group of molluscs have shells made up of two halves or valves, hence they are called the bivalves. A common feature of the bivalves is their large fleshy foot and this is used to move around in a way different from that of the chitons. The bivalves tend to be burrowers and they poke out the foot into the sandy or muddy bottom, the end swells to anchor the foot, and then the rest of the animal is drawn up and the foot extended again.

This is obviously a very slow process and not surprisingly the bivalves do not feed in the same way as the more mobile chitons. The mantle forms two siphons. Water is drawn through one into a large mantle cavity where it passes over the equally large gills before leaving by the other siphon. The gills not only extract oxygen from the water, they are modified to filter out suspended food particles which are then passed to the mouth and eaten. The bivalves have no head and no rasping radula.

Clusters of mussels are a common sight at low tide, clinging to pier supports, as well as to each other.

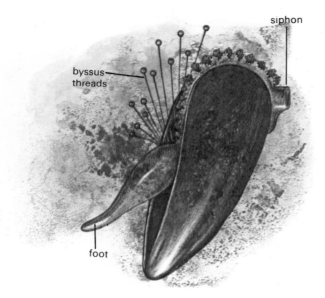

siphon

A mussel showing how it attaches itself to surfaces using its byssus threads.

byssus threads

foot

How do mussels fix themselves to surfaces high above the ground?

You may have wandered under a pier at low tide and glanced up to see masses and masses of mussels hanging high above you on the supports. In contrast to the chiton which 'sticks' itself to the rock surface, the mussels are actually hanging from surfaces of the pier on fine, strong threads. These are called byssus threads and are secreted by the foot. Mussels differ from burrowing bivalves in that they prefer to secure themselves in one place, 'hanging around' on rocks, piles and posts until the tide covers them again. Young mussels do move around a little by using the foot, but once they get older they settle down in one spot.

Many of the bivalves are of importance to us because we eat them in large quantities. Cockles, mussels, oysters and scallops are all popular as seafood.

A small green mussel from the Indian Ocean. A larger one (*below*) from Chile shows how attractive some shells become on polishing.

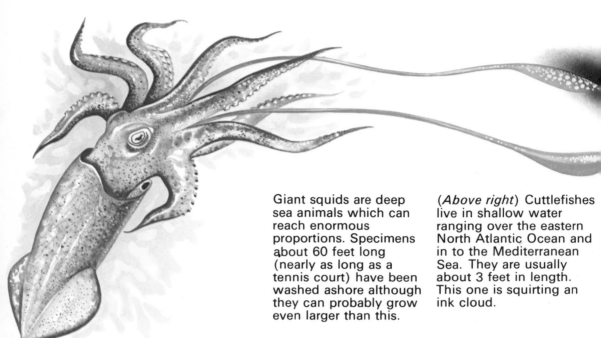

Giant squids are deep sea animals which can reach enormous proportions. Specimens about 60 feet long (nearly as long as a tennis court) have been washed ashore although they can probably grow even larger than this.

(*Above right*) Cuttlefishes live in shallow water ranging over the eastern North Atlantic Ocean and in to the Mediterranean Sea. They are usually about 3 feet in length. This one is squirting an ink cloud.

What is a cuttlefish?

You have probably noticed 'cuttlebone' pushed between the bars of a budgerigar's cage, or washed up on the beach. This 'bone' is not really bone at all but the shell of a cuttlefish, which is not a fish but a mollusc. The cuttlefishes, squids and octopuses belong to a group of molluscs called cephalopods and most are characterized by a very reduced shell or by not having one at all. The shell in the cuttlefish is completely enclosed by the mantle and, being very light, it helps to keep the animal buoyant.

The foot of all the cephalopods is modified to form either eight or ten tentacles which surround the head (cephalopod means head-footed). These bear suckers along their length and it is with them that the animals catch their prey. The edge of the mantle of the cuttlefish forms two flaps at the sides and by undulating these the animal swims about quite leisurely. In an emergency, greater speed is obtained by forcing out a jet of water from the mantle cavity through a funnel. The funnel can be directed in any direction and if suddenly attacked, the cuttlefish can shoot off out of danger.

Why does a squid squirt ink?

Another emergency tactic that can be adopted by cuttlefishes, squids and octopuses is the use of a smoke screen. All

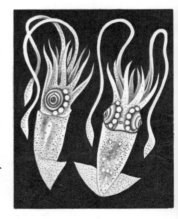

These are deep sea squids which are illuminated by light organs.

these animals can swim rapidly by the jet propulsion method. If, however, a hungry shark or penguin gets too close it may be surprised to discover that it is in fact chasing a cloud of black ink, the squid having quickly squirted this out while travelling at speed and, swivelling its funnel, darting off in another direction.

Is an octopus dangerous to man?

There are stories of people being attacked by an octopus and frantically trying to detach the suckers of the encircling arms. This may happen very rarely and when it does the octopus is really investigating a new moving shape rather than attacking it. If the person could manage to keep perfectly still the octopus would soon let him go.

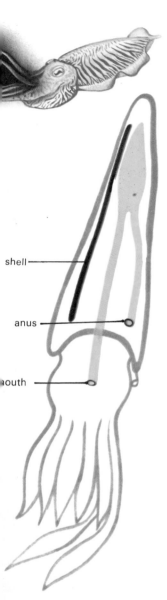

shell

anus

mouth

(*Above*) The body plan of a typical cephalopod.

(*Right*) Octopuses differ from cuttlefishes and squids in having eight arms rather than ten. They are also character- ized by the absence of an internal shell.

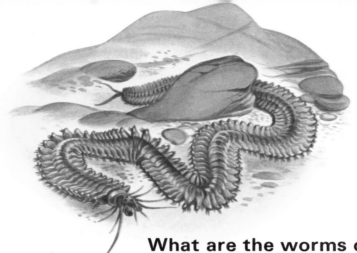

A ragworm showing the paddles and bristles which project from either side of each segment.

What are the worms of the seashore?

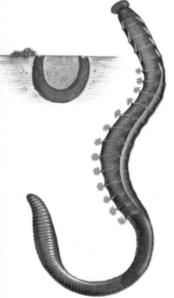

Two common worms that you can find on the shore are ragworms and lugworms. Ragworms can be found under stones but lugworms live in burrows in the sand and have to be dug out.

The ragworm is about 8 inches long and swims in a characteristic side to side motion. As the waves overtake the worm, the side extensions in every segment push back like paddles, propelling the worm along. The paddles also serve as gills, being well supplied with blood vessels, and the tuft of stiff bristles from each helps support it and provides some protection to the animal. Ragworms are carnivorous and can give a bad nip with strong jaws so handle them with care.

The little coiled casts of sand on the beach at low tide mark the openings to the U-shaped tubes in which lugworms live. In the bend of the tube about a foot down lies the

(*Above*) The red tufts on the lugworm are gills. The U-shaped tube and cast of the animal are also shown.

(*Right*) Fan worms extend their feathery crowns to trap food particles in the water.

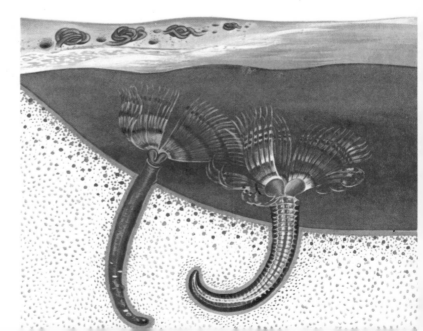

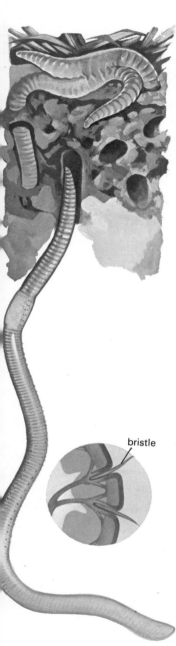

worm. By moving its head and swallowing sand the grains gradually sink above its head leaving a shallow pit on the surface. After feeding for about forty minutes the sand is passed from the worm at the open end of the tube to form the cast. By contracting its body the worm draws water into the tube from this end and this passes over its red gill tufts before flowing out of the other end. Both ragworms and lugworms are prized as bait by sea fishermen.

Other worms which live in tubes are the fan, or feather duster, worms. The tube projects from the sandy floor and from the end the worm spreads its beautiful crown of tentacles whenever it is covered by the tide. The tentacles sift out particles from the water, the smallest of which are eaten, those slightly bigger are used to extend the tube and the biggest are discarded. In some fanworms the tentacles act as gills.

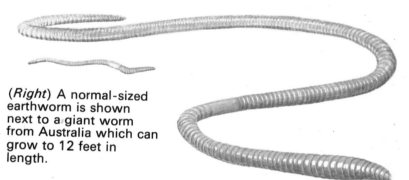

(*Right*) A normal-sized earthworm is shown next to a giant worm from Australia which can grow to 12 feet in length.

bristle

The bristles of the earthworm are shown in this section of the body wall, and can just be seen as two rows of paired dots along the length of the worm.

Why are earthworms good for the soil?

By their constant burrowing earthworms are forever turning over the soil, bringing fresh earth to the surface and covering it again. Their burrows allow air into the soil and water to drain from it. At night earthworms drag leaves and other plant remains into their burrows and perhaps eat only half, leaving the rest to decay in the soil. Humus mixed into the airy, well-drained earth makes it fertile and ideal for plant growth. Earthworms are adapted to an underground life by being streamlined; they have no projecting flaps or gills. However, if you listen to a worm crawling across a sheet of paper you will hear scratching noises. These are made by the short bristles (chaetae) projecting from each segment on either side. You can feel them by running your finger up the sides of the worm. It is these chaetae that help the worm crawl and prevent you from pulling it from its burrow head first. All the worms are characterized by their segmented bodies and they form the group called the phylum Annelida.

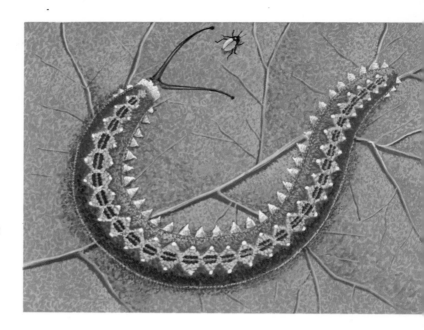

A typical peripatus about 3 inches long. These curious animals live in moist, dark places in the tropical forests of Australia, Africa and South America.

How does peripatus link the worms and the animals with jointed legs?

This insignificant looking creature excited zoologists in the nineteenth century when it was first discovered because it was unlike any other animal known at that time. It looks very much like a worm and yet it has rows of stumpy legs on either side and shows other features similar to animals of the phylum Arthropoda (animals with jointed legs).

The arthropods are the biggest and most diverse group of invertebrates and have successfully colonized the land and learnt how to fly. They include the crustaceans (barnacles, shrimps, lobsters and crabs), centipedes and millipedes, arachnids (spiders, scorpions, ticks and mites) and the insects. The feature that has been most responsible for the success of the arthropods is their tough external covering called an exoskeleton. This supports the animal's soft body on land and at the same time prevents it losing water by evaporation. It is light enough to allow easy movements and yet also provides good protection.

Another small freshwater crustacean related to the water fleas, called an ostracod.

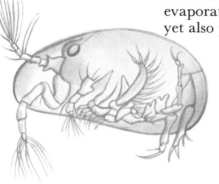

(*Right*) Water fleas are about $\frac{1}{10}$ of an inch long and seem to spend their lives trying to stay in one position in the water.

Because peripatus has features which are both worm-like (thin skin, eyes), and arthropod-like (claws, breathing system), it is thought to be descended almost unchanged from the animals that gave rise millions of years ago to the worms and arthropods.

Are water fleas really fleas?

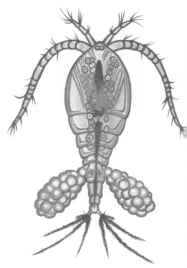

True fleas are parasitic insects. Water fleas are so called because of their erratic, flea-like swimming movements. The water fleas are common freshwater crustaceans and they are fascinating to watch in a pond or better still in an aquarium.

The folded shell which encloses the body is transparent and through it you can easily watch the workings of the water flea's body. The heart can be seen pumping away, and several pairs of feet are visible beating the water, filtering out single-celled algae and bacteria for food. You can even see the eggs and developing young on the back of the females. Watch how the water flea sinks a little and then frantically jerks its way back to its original position by thrashing the water with its two pairs of branched antennae.

A selection of copepods — small crustaceans which form the main food of fishes in the sea.

What are copepods?

Copepods are another group of small crustaceans which live in the sea. They are better swimmers than the freshwater water fleas and use their legs as well as their antennae to propel themselves through the water. Copepods drift in enormous numbers in the upper levels of the sea. Together with other minute creatures they form plankton on which all other higher animals feed, either directly or indirectly. Thus they are a very important link in the food chain that ends with man himself.

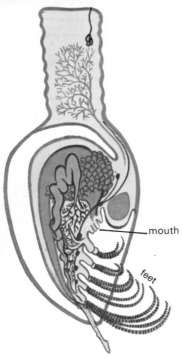

(*Left*) Goose or gooseneck barnacles often attach themselves by their long stalks to flotsam. Some even produce a bubble which acts as a float from which they can hang. Those shown here are attached to a piece of driftwood.

mouth

feet

The body plan of a goose barnacle.

Which animals live on their heads and kick food into their mouths?

The animals that live in this extraordinary position are the barnacles. You must have noticed barnacles encrusting large rocks at low tide on the shore and you might be forgiven for mistaking them for limpets or some other kind of mollusc. In fact they used to be called molluscs until it was noticed that the larvae hatching from the eggs have several features in common with crustaceans. The larva swims around for a while feeding and growing. It eventually changes into a shelled form and chooses a suitable place on a surface on which to settle head first. A special secretion sticks it in position and it quickly encloses itself in a shell made up of plates. When the tide exposes the barnacle the plates stay closed to prevent loss of water from the animal. When the tide returns, however, the top pair opens and the feathery feet are pushed out to comb the water for suspended food particles.

Barnacles vary in diameter from $\frac{1}{4}$ of an inch to a huge type in North America which can grow to 1 foot across. There are a number of species. The one *far left* is feeding with its feet.

Where do barnacles live?

Barnacles will encrust practically any suitable surface on the shore. These include piles, pier supports, old tin cans and crabs which do not move fast enough to avoid the settling larvae. At one time they caused ships to slow down by settling on their bottoms but special paints are now used which inhibit the larvae from settling.

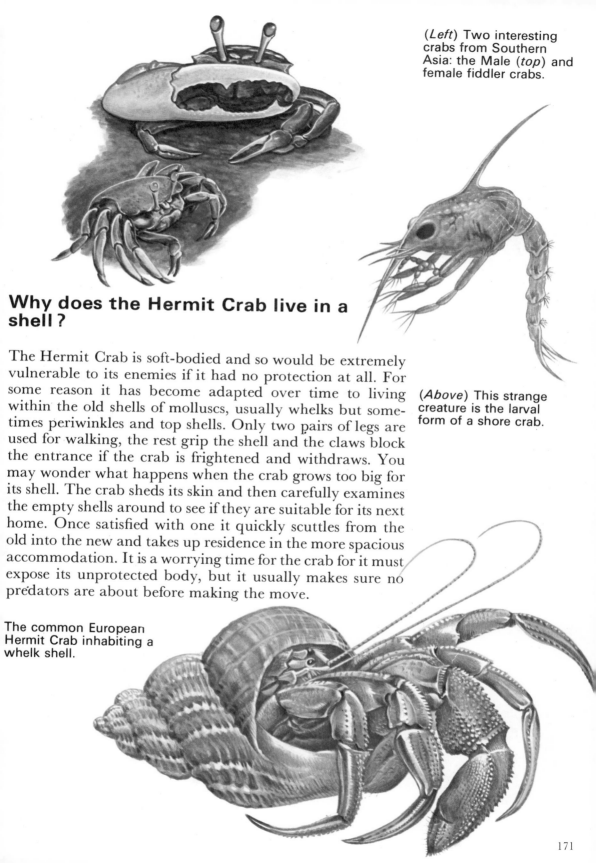

(*Left*) Two interesting crabs from Southern Asia: the Male (*top*) and female fiddler crabs.

Why does the Hermit Crab live in a shell?

The Hermit Crab is soft-bodied and so would be extremely vulnerable to its enemies if it had no protection at all. For some reason it has become adapted over time to living within the old shells of molluscs, usually whelks but sometimes periwinkles and top shells. Only two pairs of legs are used for walking, the rest grip the shell and the claws block the entrance if the crab is frightened and withdraws. You may wonder what happens when the crab grows too big for its shell. The crab sheds its skin and then carefully examines the empty shells around to see if they are suitable for its next home. Once satisfied with one it quickly scuttles from the old into the new and takes up residence in the more spacious accommodation. It is a worrying time for the crab for it must expose its unprotected body, but it usually makes sure no predators are about before making the move.

(*Above*) This strange creature is the larval form of a shore crab.

The common European Hermit Crab inhabiting a whelk shell.

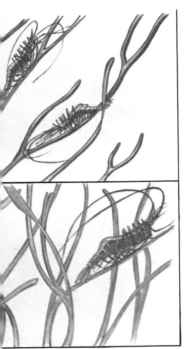

Can prawns change colour?

There is one prawn that is particularly good at changing its colour. This is the Aesop Prawn. Normally it is pink but it can vary its body colour to match that of its surroundings. This usually occurs in times of danger when a predator is lurking nearby. If it takes refuge on a brown seaweed it gradually turns brown and on a green seaweed it turns green. Strangely enough at night it always turns blue, no matter what colour its surroundings happen to be. The colour is produced by pigment cells all over the prawn's body.

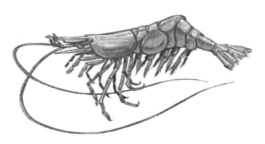

Can a lobster swim backwards?

If you look carefully at the rear end of a lobster you will see that it spreads out into a scoop-like structure called a tail-fan. Normally, of course, the lobster walks over the bottom or, if in a hurry, it can swim forwards using special swimming legs on its abdomen. If startled, however, it quickly bends its tail up underneath its body and paddles its way backwards out of danger at considerable speed. Shrimps, prawns and freshwater crayfishes also have a tail-fan and so all these crustaceans can swim backwards in this way. Another thing they have in common is that they are all enjoyed by man as food. Lobsters provide a lot of meat from the muscles in their large pincers and from the abdomen. The Spiny Lobster is found in both the southern Atlantic and Pacific Oceans. Europe produces the common European and the Norway Lobsters, the latter known as scampi.

(*Above left*) The Aesop Prawn matches its colour to brown and green seaweed. The normal colour is shown (*above*).

The European Lobster and the pot which is often used to catch it. Lobsters are scavengers and so the pot is baited with a choice piece of dead fish. The lobster climbs in easily enough but finds it practically impossible to find the narrow way out.

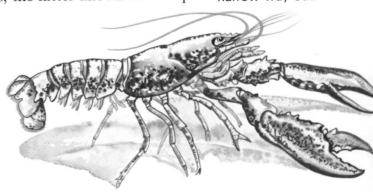

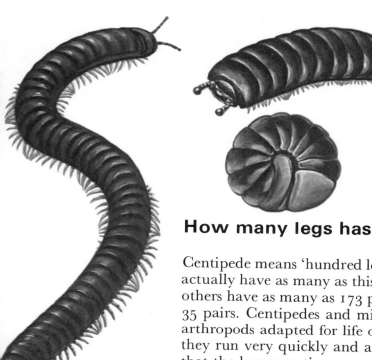

A giant millipede from Asia and a pill millipede walking and rolled up. Pill millipedes curl up when alarmed and some from the tropics are as large as ping-pong balls. Two centipedes are shown *below*.

How many legs has a centipede?

Centipede means 'hundred legged' but not many centipedes actually have as many as this. Some have as few as 15 pairs, others have as many as 173 pairs, but most sorts have about 35 pairs. Centipedes and millipedes form a small group of arthropods adapted for life on the land. With all these legs they run very quickly and although it has been discovered that the legs sometimes cross, the centipede never seems to trip up. Centipedes can sometimes be found in the home but usually live under the bark of fallen trees and under stones. They are generally about 1 or 2 inches long but species from North America can grow to 7 inches.

What is the difference between a centipede and a millipede?

A millipede does not have a million legs but it has twice as many as a centipede about the same length – two pairs to each segment. In spite of this the millipede moves more slowly than the centipede. It feeds on vegetation and often destroys valuable crops like potatoes, whereas the centipede is a carnivore and catches worms, spiders and insects, sometimes including flies.

Millipedes are interesting animals. At various times they have been known to swarm and once in France their seething numbers brought a train to a standstill. As they are blind their mating signals are highly developed. It has recently been reported that one type of millipede from Europe attracts a mate by banging its head on the ground.

Why are there so many insects?

The Cicada (*top*) and Bush Cricket are insects related to locusts well known for their strident 'singing' at night.

Of the animals with jointed legs, the insects form the largest and most diverse group and the group of animals that has had most success in adapting itself for life on the land. The first reason for this success is because they are small. On land their size is restricted for without the support of water their legs cannot bear the great weight of a large exoskeleton. Their muscles are generally well developed and so they are very active and do not have much difficulty in escaping from enemies. Another advantage of being small is that you do not have to grow much. Insects mature quickly and produce young several times a year. Large numbers of offspring have enabled insects to adapt to practically every sort of living condition and to practically every type of food.

 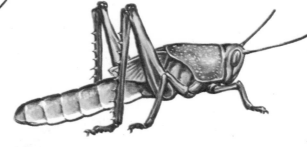

How do insects develop?

Primitive insects lay eggs from which hatch young which look like miniature versions of their parents. Restricted by their hard exoskeleton the offspring are forced to shed their skins in order to grow, and this happens several times before they reach maturity. In other higher insects a larva completely different from its parents hatches from the egg. The caterpillar larva of the butterfly, for example, lives on plants and eats large amounts of leaves while quickly growing. Eventually it forms a hard case around itself and from this pupa an adult butterfly emerges. The butterfly hardly feeds at all and after mating soon dies. This more advanced insect development enables the larva and adult to concentrate on different aspects of the life cycle. The larva is the passive feeding stage and the adult the active reproductive stage.

The two types of Desert Locust found in dry areas of Africa. The green type lives a solitary life but the yellow and black type wreaks havoc in agricultural areas by swarming.

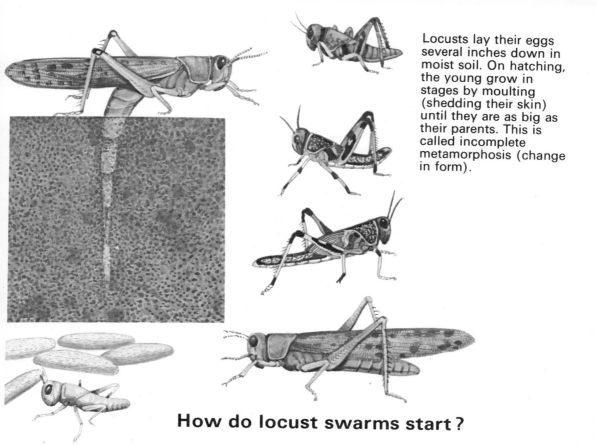

Locusts lay their eggs several inches down in moist soil. On hatching, the young grow in stages by moulting (shedding their skin) until they are as big as their parents. This is called incomplete metamorphosis (change in form).

How do locust swarms start?

One of the three types of locust that forms swarms in Africa is the Desert Locust. This locust usually lives like a grasshopper in what is called a solitary phase. Sometimes, however, all the solitary locusts from a wide area are driven together, perhaps by the weather, and they may find the conditions just right for feeding and mating. As locusts mate and lay eggs many times in a short period, enormous numbers of young locusts hatch and become stimulated by each other to form a swarm. They change colour and when all the available plants have been eaten they migrate in search of more.

The complete metamorphosis from larva to adult in the butterfly. The hard case from which the adult emerges is called the pupa.

How do these insects avoid detection?

The insects shown on these pages are mantids, a stick insect and a leaf insect. All live on vegetation and you will see that each has developed an appearance which blends perfectly with its surroundings. Mantids are usually coloured green or brown to match the colour of foliage and are often shaped to help the disguise, as well. Some are long and slender like twigs and others have a rough appearance to resemble bark. As they tend to keep very still for long periods during the day, these insects are very difficult to detect. The young stage of one species from Asia, the Flower Mantid, is even more adapted for concealment and bears a remarkable likeness to the pink flower of the plant on which it lives. It matches

The young Flower Mantid (*below*) is remarkably camouflaged among the flowers of the plant on which it lives. Once it matures, however, it loses its pink colour (*left*).

(*Above*) A mantid in its characteristic 'praying' attitude. It is waiting in readiness to pounce on an insect.

its colour perfectly and flattened extensions from its legs give the impression of petals. This mantid has the double advantage of attracting insects such as butterflies which it can then easily catch, while remaining perfectly hidden from its enemies. In the same way the other well-camouflaged mantids are able to pounce on unsuspecting insects that wander by without having to move an inch to hunt them.

The camouflage of stick insects and leaf insects probably serves only to hide them from their enemies as both feed on plants alone. However, their ability to avoid being seen is just as good as the mantids. The stick insect has an elongated body and spindly legs and assumes an attitude which is exactly that of an extension of the twig on which it is resting. Unless it moves it is difficult to believe it is really an insect.

The related leaf insect bears an incredible resemblance to

a leaf, even down to the ribs on the wings which look exactly like the veins of a leaf. Some even go to the length of having marks to give the impression of fungal growths and bird droppings.

How does the mantid catch its prey?

The mantid stands completely motionless in wait for unwary insects. The head and upper part of its body are held in an upright position and the large front legs are folded, almost as if the insect was praying. (This is why they are sometimes called Praying Mantids.) The legs have sharp spines along their length and are jointed so that they can snap closed in a vice-like grip. Once an unfortunate insect strays within the long reach of these specially adapted forelegs, they lash out and fix the prey in a terrible embrace. It is then rapidly devoured. Mantids are greedy carnivores and feed on most insects including other mantids.

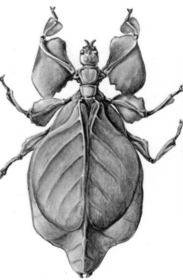

(*Above*) Leaf insects move slowly around on foliage in tropical forests. They bear an astonishing resemblance to the leaves on which they feed.

Where do mantids, stick insects and leaf insects come from?

Mantids are found in tropical and subtropical regions of the world. There is a European species which has been introduced into North America where it has become well established. The Flower Mantid of South-east Asia, sometimes called the Orchid Mantid, comes mainly from Malaysia and Indonesia, but species that. resemble flowers are also found in Africa.

There are about 2,000 stick insects and leaf insects and most come from tropical Oriental areas. However, some types are found in both northern Europe and North America. The stick insects you may keep in your classroom as pets are probably from the Orient and would not survive outdoors during a cold winter.

Some stick insects from Asia can grow to 1 foot in length. Not surprisingly they are the longest insects known. Most stick insects are much shorter than this.

How fast can a dragonfly fly?

It is very difficult to estimate the speed of insects in flight but it is thought that some dragonflies can reach 30 miles an hour. Dragonflies are easily the most skilled fliers of the insects. You may have seen them on a summer's evening along the river bank, flitting and darting in vivid flashes of beautiful iridescent colour. You can see from their shape that they are well adapted for strong flight and acrobatic manoeuvres to catch other flying insects. They are equipped with two pairs of powerful wings. The very elongated body streamlines the dragonfly and helps to stabilize it in flight.

The aquatic dragonfly nymph extending its mask to seize a small tadpole (*right*). After several months the nymph is fully grown and crawls up a plant stem above the surface. The adult emerges from the final moult. When its wings have expanded (*bottom right*) and hardened it flys off to begin the second stage of its life.

As you might expect, a predatory insect that weaves and dives after its prey in the air must have good eyesight. The dragonfly's head is dominated by an enormous pair of compound eyes.

The dragonfly is another insect that develops by incomplete metamorphosis. This is to say that, on hatching, the larva resembles its parent with only slight modifications so that it can lead a life in a different environment. The female dragonfly lays her eggs in water. The larvae, or nymphs, lead an underwater life for two years before they finally emerge to change into adults. The nymph is as much a greedy predator as its flying parent although not so active. It creeps stealthily among aquatic vegetation and catches the fry of fishes, tadpoles and other insects. It seizes its prey using a specially extendable jaw called a mask. At rest this is folded up under the head and partly covers the face. Once a young fish swims within range the mask is flashed out and a pair of claws closes on to the prey to secure it.

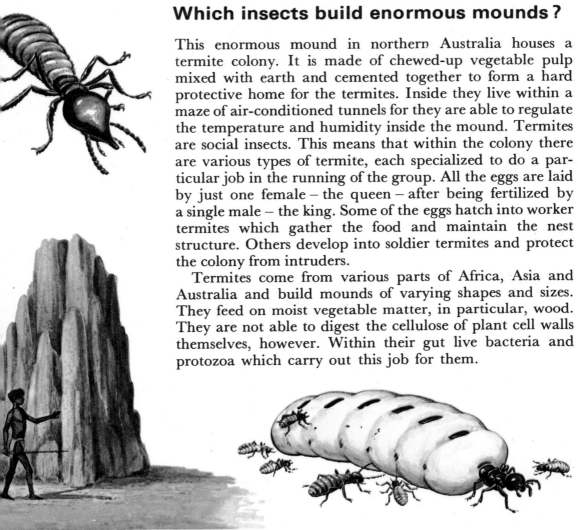

Which insects build enormous mounds?

This enormous mound in northern Australia houses a termite colony. It is made of chewed-up vegetable pulp mixed with earth and cemented together to form a hard protective home for the termites. Inside they live within a maze of air-conditioned tunnels for they are able to regulate the temperature and humidity inside the mound. Termites are social insects. This means that within the colony there are various types of termite, each specialized to do a particular job in the running of the group. All the eggs are laid by just one female – the queen – after being fertilized by a single male – the king. Some of the eggs hatch into worker termites which gather the food and maintain the nest structure. Others develop into soldier termites and protect the colony from intruders.

Termites come from various parts of Africa, Asia and Australia and build mounds of varying shapes and sizes. They feed on moist vegetable matter, in particular, wood. They are not able to digest the cellulose of plant cell walls themselves, however. Within their gut live bacteria and protozoa which carry out this job for them.

How does a termite colony start?

When conditions are right special fertile winged termites hatch within the mound. They suddenly leave the rest in a dense swarm and disperse. After travelling a short way they drop to the ground and break off their wings which they no longer need. A male and a female pair up, choose a suitable home, perhaps in an old rotten log, mate, and produce young. The offspring are the pioneer workers and soldiers of the new colony. As more and more eggs are laid and hatched, and a nest built, the colony gradually becomes established. The original pair – the king and queen – remains within the nest for years and years, simply producing a continuing supply of new termites.

(*Above*) The body of the queen termite becomes enormously enlarged so that her egg-laying capacity is increased. Two types of soldier termites are shown *top left* and *bottom right*.

How do aphids damage plants?

You probably know how upset gardeners are to see aphids on their prize roses. They have good cause for anxiety since aphids do a lot of damage to many plants. They also do considerable economic harm to farmers. Their activities affect crops in two ways. By sucking the sap aphids soon cause the plants to weaken and die, and by moving from one plant to another, they can be responsible for spreading virus infections among crops.

The mouthparts of the aphid are modified to form a needlesharp tube which is inserted into the sap-carrying cells of the plant. The sap is thus diverted to the aphid and because it has a low nutrient value the aphid drinks vast quantities. Most of the sugary sap passes straight through the aphid and is excreted as honeydew. It is this that is so favoured by ants and by stroking the aphids with their antennae they stimulate a faster flow of honeydew.

(*Above*) Female winged aphids settle on fresh plants and produce generation after generation of wingless females without mating. In a short time a heavy infestation results. A winged female is shown *below*.

Why does the scarab beetle roll dung?

A fairly common sight in the drier areas of southern Asia, the United States and Africa, is a medium-sized black beetle scurrying backwards rolling a ball of dung. This is often several times the size of the beetle and can be as big as a tennis ball. Often a beetle will be helped in its labours by another, but if it is not careful the newcomer will make off with the dung himself. Once a suitable spot is found the beetle digs a chamber and feeds on the dung underground. Later in the year the beetles pair up and as before bury some dung. This time, however, the dung is intended for their young. The female shreds it carefully and refashions it into a pearshape in which the egg is laid. On hatching, the larva has a readily available source of food which it quickly eats before changing into an adult.

The scarab beetle parents go to a lot of trouble to provide a handy food supply for their young. The larvae have no worries about setting out on dangerous feeding expeditions and they are very secure and well protected in their own underground larders. A lot of effort is involved in providing for the young in this way but the method is very successful. The female does not usually lay more than four eggs in a year.

A scarab beetle rolling a dung ball with its back legs. In the United States these beetles are called tumble bugs. A goliath beetle is also shown. In Africa this enormous insect can grow to 6 inches in length.

How does the ant lion larva catch ants?

In contrast to the graceful beauty of the adult insect, the larva of the ant lion bears a pair of cruel-looking jaws, and catches ants and small spiders in a most ingenious way. (It is the behaviour of the larva that gives the insect its name.) The small, fat creature carefully digs a steep-sided, conical pit in dry, sandy soil in a sheltered spot. The pit is about 3 inches in diameter and 2 inches deep and so forms quite a treacherous obstacle for any passing ant or other small insect. Alerted by dislodged grains of sand, the ant lion

(*Below left*) The larva of an ant lion successfully ambushes ants by digging pits in sandy soil. The beautiful adult is shown (*below*) and can be from 1 to 3 inches long.

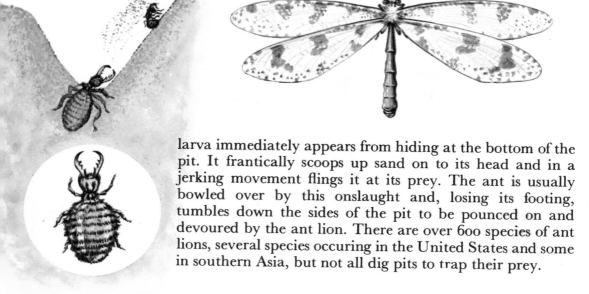

larva immediately appears from hiding at the bottom of the pit. It frantically scoops up sand on to its head and in a jerking movement flings it at its prey. The ant is usually bowled over by this onslaught and, losing its footing, tumbles down the sides of the pit to be pounced on and devoured by the ant lion. There are over 600 species of ant lions, several species occuring in the United States and some in southern Asia, but not all dig pits to trap their prey.

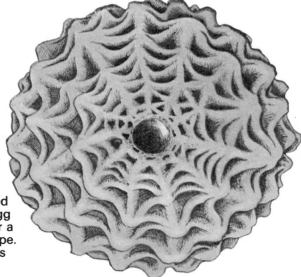

The Small Tortoiseshell Butterfly lays its eggs on the underside of nettle leaves. When the larvae hatch they will find themselves on a convenient food supply.

Where do butterflies lay their eggs?

Butterflies, and moths as well for that matter, are very particular about laying their eggs. Most butterflies leave them on only one sort of plant because this is the plant that the newly hatched larvae, called caterpillars, will feed on. So the female butterfly will spend some time finding the correct plant (the foodplant) before laying her eggs. You might think that for an insect this would be particular enough, but most butterflies even choose a particular place on the foodplant for the eggs and will leave them in no other. For example, one species of brimstone butterfly will only lay eggs on the topmost shoots of the buckthorn bush. You would never find them if you searched lower down the plant.

Further examples of butterflies' eggs magnified many times. Some butterflies lay their eggs on the undersides of leaves.

The attractive sculptured effect of a butterfly's egg as seen if viewed under a low-powered microscope. The hole in the centre is the micropyle.

What is the hole in the butterfly's egg for?

The hole in the butterfly's egg is called the micropyle. It is through this hole that the egg was fertilized in the female's body before it was laid. Once laid, it admits air to the developing larva inside, allowing it to breathe.

Some species of butterfly lay their eggs singly, others in small batches all over the foodplant, while yet others perhaps lay one large batch. All the eggs are varied in shape, size and colour, and viewed under a low-powered microscope, are beautiful to look at. They are so varied that it is usually possible to say from which group of butterflies a particular egg is from, if not the actual species.

A newly hatched caterpillar eating the egg shell it has just left.

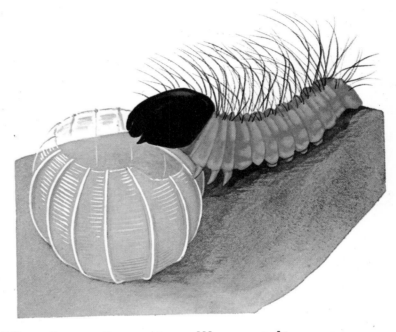

Why does the caterpillar eat its egg shell?

Some butterflies' eggs are transparent and it is interesting to watch the development from the time the egg is laid to the time the larva hatches. The egg at first looks as if it is full of liquid but gradually the larva grows to fill it. As this happens the egg often changes colour several times. The eggs of some species hatch in a few days but with others it may be between two and three weeks before the larvae emerge. Their first meal is generally the empty egg shell and it is thought that this contains certain essential food substances that the caterpillar must have in order to survive.

King crabs (*bottom right*) are found along the Atlantic coast of North America and on the coasts of China, Japan and the East Indies.

Two scorpions from southern Asia. Scorpions do not lay eggs but give birth to living young which promptly climb on to their mother's back.

What is the king crab?

The king crab, or horseshoe crab, is not really a crab at all. In fact it is not even a crustacean but a very primitive arthropod which belongs to a group of its own. From fossil evidence we know that king crabs were abundant in seas about 175 million years ago. The few species that survive today are virtually unchanged from those early ancestors and for this reason they are sometimes called 'living fossils'.

King crabs have some unusual features. They are about a foot across, have a heavy domed shell divided by a joint across the middle, four pairs of walking legs and a long spiky tail. The bony mouth extends between the bases of the legs which help in chewing up the food. These characteristics, together with their gills and mouthparts, tell us that the king crab is actually descended from the forerunners of another group of arthropods adapted for life on land – the arachnids. These include the scorpions, spiders, mites and ticks, and daddy longlegs or harvestmen.

Can a scorpion kill a man?

Scorpions are particularly ferocious animals, even to each other, and so they lead solitary lives. They live in dry, warm, areas of the world and in the wild hide themselves away in dark places, under logs or stones, for example, waiting for their prey. This normally consists of small insects and spiders. As scorpions cannot see very well they rely on these creatures brushing against them unawares. They are immediately pounced on when this happens, overpowered and torn apart by the scorpion's pair of large pincers. Only if resistance is met will the scorpion bring its deadly sting into action, usually held out of harm's way over its head.

The habits of scorpions make them particularly dangerous to man. They are attracted into homes and find ideal hiding places in shoes, beds and perhaps under carpets. Once disturbed they do not hesitate to use their sting over and over again. In the United States and Mexico it is said that more people die from scorpion stings than from snake bites.

Orb webs (*right*) of some spiders can be 8 feet in diameter and trap birds and bats. The enormous bird-eating spider (*far right*) from South America hunts its prey.

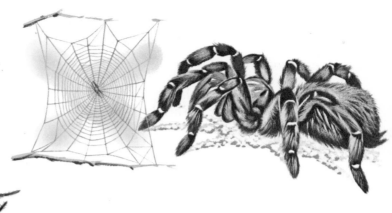

Do all spiders spin webs?

Most spiders spin webs of one sort or another but only some use the web to entangle their prey. The trapdoor spiders from tropical and subtropical countries are spiders that spin a tubular web in a hole in the ground. The hole the spider digs may be several inches deep and about an inch across. The web is spun to line the hole and once this is done the spider constructs a hinged trapdoor to fit the opening exactly. This is made from silk and small soil particles and is very often camouflaged with moss. This well-made retreat is a perfect home for the spider. If disturbed by its enemies it simply hangs on to the underside of the trapdoor, preventing it from opening. It is not fully known how the trapdoor spider catches its prey. It is thought that it peers out from the hole with the trapdoor ajar, and drags insects back into the hole as they pass by.

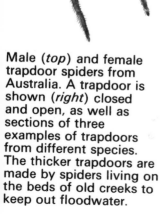

Male (*top*) and female trapdoor spiders from Australia. A trapdoor is shown (*right*) closed and open, as well as sections of three examples of trapdoors from different species. The thicker trapdoors are made by spiders living on the beds of old creeks to keep out floodwater.

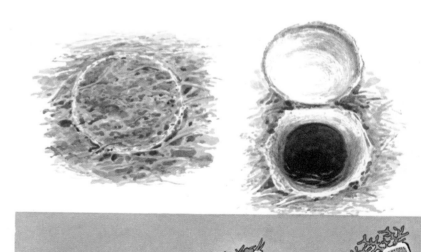

What are the echinoderms?

Starfishes, sea urchins, sea cucumbers and sea lilies all belong to the phylum Echinodermata. Echinoderm means spiny skinned and all these animals have a spiky or leathery appearance. The echinoderms have a skeleton made up of small plates. In the arthropods the skeleton is external, enclosing the body in a case, but in the echinoderms it is internal and lies just below the skin. The spines are extensions from the plates and echinoderms are able to move them slightly as they are hinged at the base. The member of this

Starfishes have remarkable powers of regeneration. A lost arm will soon be regrown and the arm itself will sometimes survive as a new individual. Angry keepers of mussel and oyster beds used to dredge up the starfish pests, break them up and fling them back. This only increased their numbers of course and made the problem worse.

group that you are probably most familiar with is the starfish. If you pick one up from the beach it will feel quite hard and rigid and this is because it is probably dead. The plates of the starfish's skeleton are not joined together and so when alive it can bend its body and move its arms easily.

How does a starfish move?

The starfishes and sea urchins creep slowly around on hundreds of hydraulically operated tube feet. If you flip a living starfish over you will see rows of these tiny feet running the length of each arm. (If you leave the starfish upside-down, time it to see how long it takes to turn itself the right way up again. Some can do it in two minutes, others take over an hour.) Each tube foot is connected to a muscular sac embedded inside the arm of the starfish. All the feet are joined up by a system of tubes which draws in water from the sea. The whole arrangement is called the water vascular system. The sac contracts and pushes out the foot under pressure. A suction disc at the end grips the sea floor, the foot contracts forcing the water back into the sac, and the starfish is drawn along a fraction of an inch. Each foot would have little effect on its own but when the feet are used in relays the starfish has a speed of 2 inches a minute.

A starfish creeping up on an oyster. Starfishes are particularly fond of bivalve molluscs and cause a lot of damage on mussel and oyster beds.

(*Below*) A starfish using its tube feet to prise apart a scallop.

Starfishes can have from between four and fifty arms and there are many beautifully coloured species. They live in all the shallow seas of the world.

How does a starfish open a mussel with its feet?

Have you ever tried to prise apart the shell of a mussel or an oyster? It is practically impossible to do by just pulling, so how does the starfish manage it using only its tiny feet? The secret is that the starfish again uses its feet in relays. It hunches itself over the tightly closed shell and attaches its tube feet to either side. By resting some feet and pulling with others the starfish is able to exert a strong pull over a long period, and gradually the bivalve weakens until it gives up the test of strength. Once the valves open a fraction the starfish turns its stomach inside out and pushes it into the shell to digest the contents.

Is the sea lily a flower?

(*Below*) There are many species of sea lily. In some the stalk may be up to 2 feet in length. Fossil sea lilies have been found, however, with stalks as long as 70 feet.

The sea lily certainly looks flower-like but it is in fact an animal. It is another echinoderm and so it belongs to the same group as the starfishes, sea urchins, and sea cucumbers, and has a basically similar body plan. The distinctive feature of the sea lily is its long stalk with which it fastens itself to the sea bottom, and the crown of feathery arms which arise from the top. In the depths of the oceans sea lilies spread these arms wide and catch food particles drifting down through the water from the upper levels. These are passed to the mouth and eaten. We do not know very much about sea lilies because most live only on the floors of very deep oceans and are therefore impossible to watch directly. They are very fragile animals and tend to break when dredged up from the sea bed, and will not survive in tanks. We do know that they belong to a very ancient group because many fossil lilies have been found which are 420 million years old.

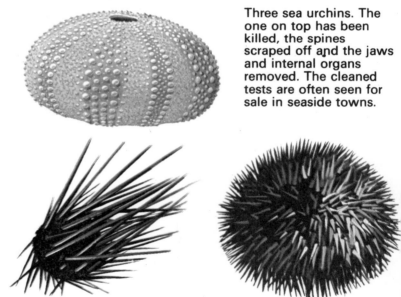

Three sea urchins. The one on top has been killed, the spines scraped off and the jaws and internal organs removed. The cleaned tests are often seen for sale in seaside towns.

Can you eat a sea urchin?

Many people do eat parts of these unappetizing spiny animals. They are popular in Mediterranean countries and the West Indies. It is the ripe ovaries that are roasted, fried or sometimes even eaten raw. Sea urchins are echinoderms with a box-like skeleton made up of tiny plates fused together. This 'test' as it is called, can be in many shapes: spherical, oval or flattened, and most have long moveable spines as extensions of the plates. Sea urchins have tube feet worked by the same system as the starfishes but they are generally longer, and project beyond the spines. The tube feet are arranged in five rows radiating from top to bottom of the test. Another feature in common with starfishes is the presence of tiny pincers on long stalks all over the sea urchin. These are gently waving all the time and pick off particles which settle on the urchin. This cleaning operation is important in slow-moving creatures that live on the sea floor because things are always dropping down on to them. Particles that are edible are passed round to the mouth in the middle of the underside. Urchins have particularly strong jaws to enable them to chew tough seaweeds.

A variety of sea cucumbers. On most can be seen the rows of tube feet that enable slow movements.

How does a sea cucumber avoid attack?

Sea cucumbers are echinoderms that have a tough leathery skin rather than a spiny one. Lying around on the sea floor in tropical and subtropical countries they look rather like long fat sausages with tentacles at one end. They feed by poking the sticky tentacles around and then placing them one by one into the mouth. All the food fragments are sucked off as the tentacle is removed, almost like licking marmalade from your fingers. To prevent being eaten by crabs, fishes and starfishes, many sea cucumbers produce a poison. Others when molested will eject long white sticky threads from the rear end to enmesh the attacker. More spectacular still are those species that partially turn themselves inside out when alarmed and rapidly shoot out their branched respiratory organs, reproductive organs and some intestine for good measure. This really confuses the attacker, allowing the cucumber to escape. It later grows a new set of everything that is missing.

How has life on the bottom changed the skates and rays?

The first obvious difference between skates and rays and more typical fishes is their shape. The skates and rays are bottom dwellers and they have developed this very characteristic flattened appearance. The pectoral fins, which in other fishes are situated just behind the gill cover on either side, are in rays enlarged to extend right round the head, rather like a pair of wings. By gently flapping these 'wings' up and down the skate or ray glides along very close to the bottom with the minimum of effort. The tail is hardly used at all and so it is very thin and trails behind, perhaps helping to steer.

Skates and rays, like the sharks, have a soft gristly skeleton made up of cartilage, unlike the more advanced bony fishes.

The skate's eyes are situated on top of its head as you might expect in a fish living on the bottom. This habit has also meant that the skate cannot breathe water through its mouth as other fishes do. If it did it would get a mouthful of mud and sand. Instead, water is drawn through two holes (spiracles) behind the eyes and passed out through the gills. Some rays that live in open water, however, breathe like other fishes.

The open spiracles behind the eyes of this ray are clearly visible.

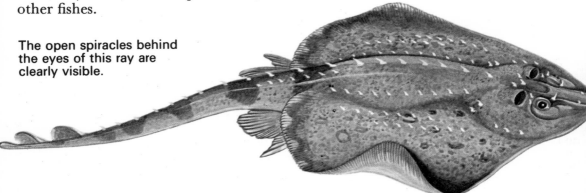

How dangerous is the stingray?

Natives from the Pacific region have been known to use the sharp spines of stingrays for the tips of spears and as knives. In Africa their tough skin has been used to make the heads of drums.

There are over one hundred kinds of stingray, widely distributed throughout the seas of the world. They all have longer and thinner tails than other rays and skates. Projecting from the top of the tail near the body end they have at least one but sometimes two sharp spines. These would be dangerous enough but the spines have poison glands, and stabs in the chest and abdomen have proved fatal on a number of occasions. When provoked the stingray can whip its tail round in a long, sideways thrust, or it can stab forwards over its head at its enemy.

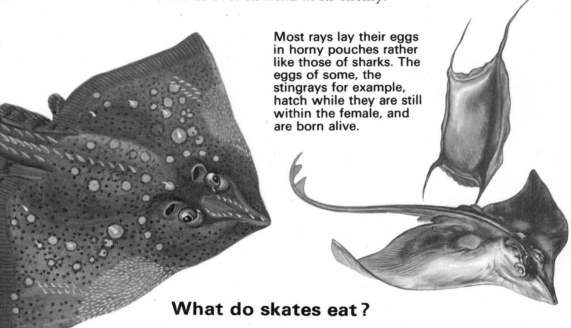

Most rays lay their eggs in horny pouches rather like those of sharks. The eggs of some, the stingrays for example, hatch while they are still within the female, and are born alive.

What do skates eat?

The Common Skate (*top right*) and the Thornback Ray (*above*). Both are sought after by sea fishermen.

Living on the bottom the skate naturally feeds on the other animals it finds there – crabs, lobsters and oysters and other molluscs. It has strong crushing teeth to deal with these shelled creatures. To get at choice molluscs buried in the sand the skate will flap away with its pectoral fins and gradually work its way under the surface. It will then often sit there with eyes and spiracles above the surface.

Why do salmon leap waterfalls?

You may have been lucky enough to watch salmon jumping from the churning mass of water below a waterfall, trying to leap over it to continue their journey upstream. It sometimes takes several attempts but the salmon usually manage it in the end. What drives them to swim upstream in rivers with obstacles such as this?

Both Pacific and Atlantic salmon are hatched in freshwater streams but live for most of their lives in the sea. After several years of feeding and growing fat in the sea, the salmon instinctively try to return to the stream of their birth to spawn. Although they may be hundreds of miles from the mouth of their home river, they somehow find their way back to it. Zoologists have discovered that salmon have a well-developed sense of taste and so they may be able to recognize the smell of the water from their own river. They swim upstream, leaping obstacles on the way, until they find a suitable gravel bottom for spawning. Once this is

The salmon (*below*) and the closely related trout (*left*) are probably the most popular fishes among anglers. They are sleek, powerful fishes which provide magnificent sport.

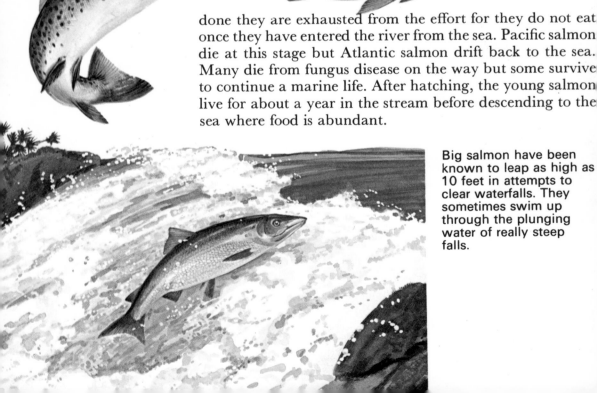

done they are exhausted from the effort for they do not eat once they have entered the river from the sea. Pacific salmon die at this stage but Atlantic salmon drift back to the sea. Many die from fungus disease on the way but some survive to continue a marine life. After hatching, the young salmon live for about a year in the stream before descending to the sea where food is abundant.

Big salmon have been known to leap as high as 10 feet in attempts to clear waterfalls. They sometimes swim up through the plunging water of really steep falls.

The marine hatchet fish (*right*) has a more striking appearance than the unrelated freshwater type (*left*).

To keep freshwater hatchet fishes in an aquarium you must have a cover to prevent them from flying out!

(*Below*) Arapaimas grow quickly to large sizes and have been known to live for eighteen years.

What are hatchet fishes?

It seems a strange name but some of these fishes really look like a hatchet or chopper. They are very thin fishes, flattened from side to side. The front half of their body is very deep and shaped like a blade. There are two groups of hatchet fishes, one that lives in the sea and one that lives in fresh water.

The marine hatchet fishes are small, ugly deep sea fishes. They have enormous eyes and flashing light organs along their sides. They hang motionless in the water and do not do much normal swimming. Instead they migrate to and from the surface each night to feed on plankton.

The freshwater hatchet fishes come from South America. They are said to be the only fishes that can truly fly. They leap from the water and propel themselves through the air for short distances by beating their enlarged pectoral fins.

What is the largest freshwater fish in the world?

The Arapaima from South America is generally thought to be one of the largest freshwater fishes in the world. The biggest one found is said to have been 15 feet in length with a weight of over 400 pounds. Most are between 7 and 8 feet long with a weight of 200 pounds, but even this is a colossal size for a freshwater fish.

Which fish is the freshwater shark?

This sequence shows the embryo pike inside the egg; the young pike, immediately after hatching, with its yolk sac which is slowly absorbed as food; and successive growth stages to the adult fish.

You have only to notice the long wide snout of the pike, bristling with razor sharp teeth, and its powerful long body, to realize how it came to be called the 'freshwater shark'. Pike are greedy, predatory fishes that ambush their prey. They stand motionless in the water, usually concealed in a weed bed, and wait until a shoal of smaller fishes flits by. Then the pike gives a tremendous thrust with its powerful tail and shoots from hiding into the shoal. The panic stricken fishes often explode from the surface in their efforts to escape the pike. The pike's jaws clamp shut on its victim and the fish is powerless to escape because the rows of teeth in the upper jaw point backwards. The fish is quickly swallowed head first.

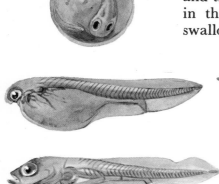

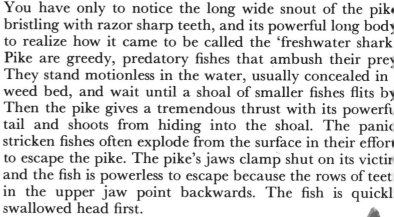

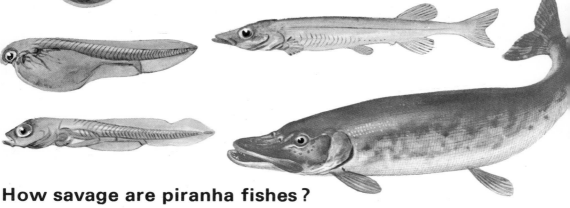

How savage are piranha fishes?

Piranhas are said to be savage enough to have once attacked a man on a horse fording a stream in South America, and killed them both. This is an old story and whether it is true or not is uncertain. What is certain is that these terrible fishes are feared through South America for their ferocity. They live in shoals – 'packs' is perhaps a better word – and they usually feed on other fishes. However, they will quickly strip the flesh from any animal falling into the water. They have been known to devour crocodiles and even cows in this way, leaving only the bones picked clean of any meat. There are about twenty species of piranha in South America but only four are really dangerous.

(*Below*) A piranha with a drawing of the head skeleton to show the powerful short jaws and razor sharp teeth. The teeth slice through flesh with ease.

Which fish keeps its eggs in its mouth?

The Wels Catfish grows to huge sizes in muddy-bottomed lakes in central Europe. Specimens grow to 9 feet in length and some compete with the Arapaima's claim to being the largest freshwater fish in the world.

The fish with this surprising habit is the Sea Catfish found in the Atlantic ocean off the east coast of America. Another surprising thing is that it is the male that takes on the job of looking after the future family, rather than the female. After the eggs have been laid and fertilized, the male quickly takes them up into his mouth. They form quite a mouthful as they can be the size of marbles and number up to fifty. They fill his mouth completely and prevent him from feeding. He carries them around for a month and all this time he is fasting, living off the stored food reserves he built up before spawning took place. His motherly role does not end when the eggs hatch. For another two weeks the youngsters swim into his mouth to hide when danger threatens.

All the catfishes have long fleshy extensions from around the mouth called barbels. It is because these faintly resemble whiskers that catfish were so-called. In fact they are used rather like whiskers. They are sensitive and they help the catfish feel its way around and find food in murky waters.

(*Below*) A male Sea Catfish displays a mouthful of eggs.

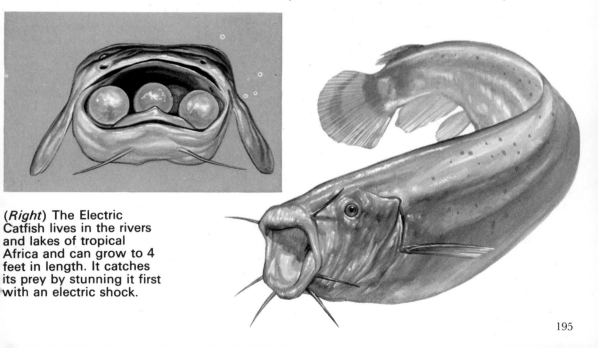

(*Right*) The Electric Catfish lives in the rivers and lakes of tropical Africa and can grow to 4 feet in length. It catches its prey by stunning it first with an electric shock.

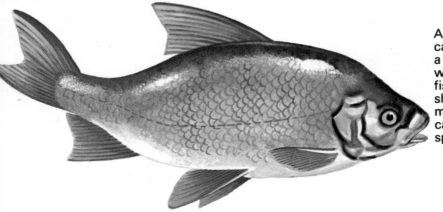

A common member of the carp family is the Roach, a silvery fish popular with freshwater fishermen. Roach live in shoals in still, or slowly moving water. A good catch is a 2 pound specimen.

Which are the fishes of the carp family?

In this enormous fish family there are about 1500 species of carp and carp-like fishes. They are all freshwater fishes most of which have one or more barbels around the mouth.

Such a large family naturally contains fishes of great variety in size and colour. Besides the carp themselves most of the fishes we are familiar with in rivers and ponds belong to the family: minnows, Bleak, Rudd, Roach, Tench, Gudgeon, Barbel, Chub and Dace. In America there are other species called shivers, suckers, as well as many other minnows. Among the smallest members are the minnows which are rarely more than 4 inches long. At the other end of the scale the Common Carp grows to about $3\frac{1}{2}$ feet and can weigh up to 60 pounds. Even bigger is the enormous Indian Mahseer growing to 9 feet in length.

(*Left*) The Common Carp prefers still water and feeds by rooting around the muddy bottom. It is an important food fish in central Europe where it is reared in carp ponds.

Which goldfishes are freaks?

The wild goldfish is a very common fish from China, usually green or brown in colour. About a thousand years ago the Chinese noticed that red forms of the wild goldfish occasionally appeared. They started to keep these more attractive forms in ponds and bowls and managed to breed them. Since then, goldfishes have always been popular as pets and many different varieties and forms have been produced. Some of these are so bizarre they barely resemble fishes at all. The Lionhead Goldfish for example, has a large head grossly

196

Goldfishes bred for their long flowing tails and fins (*left*) are popular. Other strange forms include the Lionhead Goldfish and the Eggfish (*below left*). Goldfishes looking more like their wild relatives are shown *bottom*.

swollen with warty bumps. Other varieties, equally grotesque, have bulging eyes so distorted that the fishes can only look upwards. We can safely refer to such creatures as fish freaks because if such creatures were released into the wild they would soon die. They can only survive if man looks after them in ponds and tanks so that they have no worries about finding food or avoiding enemies.

How big does the Tench grow?

The Tench is another placid fish that prefers still, weedy waters with a muddy bottom. It is popular with anglers in Europe and a good fish would weigh 7 pounds. Like the carp, the tench can survive in water that has a low oxygen content. For this reason, a variety called the Golden Tench is also popular as a pond and aquarium fish.

(*Right*) The Tench is a characteristically shaped member of the carp family. In Germany it is popular as a food fish but its flesh tends to have a muddy flavour.

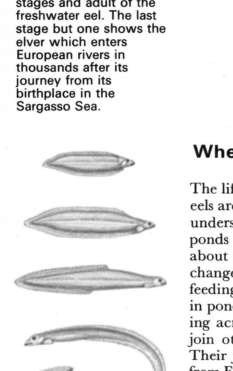

Where do eels go to breed and die?

The life histories of the European and American freshwater eels are remarkable, and even today they are not completely understood. After living in freshwater streams, rivers and ponds for about ten years in the case of the females, and about six years in the case of the males, the eels fatten up, change colour from a yellowy-green to silvery-grey, stop feeding and begin a long journey. Those that are confined in ponds and lakes begin their migration at night by slithering across wet grass until they reach a stream. There they join other mature eels travelling downstream to the sea. Their journey does not end there, however. Both the eels from Europe and those from America head for one particular area of floating weed in the western Atlantic Ocean, called the Sargasso Sea.

For American eels the journey is moderate but for European eels it is immense. It takes them about a year to swim the 3,000 miles to their spawning grounds. On arrival spawning takes place, the eggs are laid and the eels die. Tiny, transparent larvae, called leptocephali, hatch from the eggs. Those of American eels head back towards the United States, while those of European parents drift along in the Gulf Stream towards Europe. During this journey they pass through a number of stages until, three years later, they

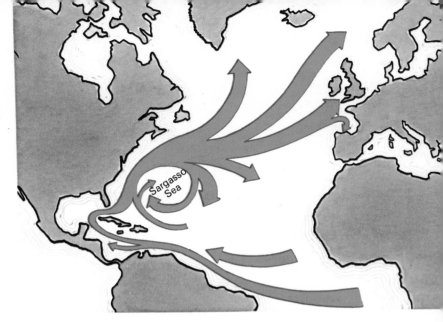

Left) The Conger Eel, a large marine eel from the Atlantic and Pacific Oceans, also journeys to the Sargasso Sea to breed and die. It has another spawning ground in the Mediterranean, however.

enter the estuaries of rivers as elvers, miniature versions of their parents. Swimming upstream they eventually reach the home streams, rivers and ponds which their parents deserted four years ago.

This map shows the routes taken by the leptocephali of freshwater eels from the Sargasso Sea.

Is the moray eel as fierce as it looks?

The moray eel certainly looks dangerous and there are many stories of people being seriously injured by attacks from these large, sinewy fishes. The moray eel, however, is a shy, retiring animal and spends the day hiding away in nooks and crannies in coral. If an underwater diver disturbs a resting eel, it will naturally resent this, and when cornered it will not hesitate to lunge and bite to escape. Unprovoked attacks on people collecting shells on coral reefs are probably cases of mistaken identity on the part of the eel. The moray eel is partial to octopuses and could easily imagine a person's fingers to be the succulent tentacles of one of its favourite foods. But it may grab at the molluscs the collector is holding rather than his hand.

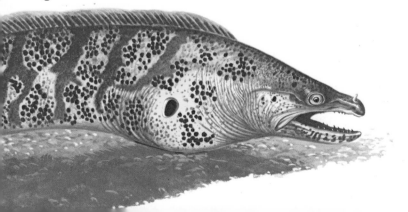

There are over 100 kinds of moray eel. They live in the shallows of tropical and subtropical seas and particularly on coral reefs. Some can grow to 10 feet in length.

The male dolphin fish ha[s] a blunt, square-shaped head. In the female the head is more rounded. Dolphin fishes are common in tropical seas and in some areas are popular as sport fishes.

Is the dolphin a fish or a mammal?

It is a confusing fact that there is both an air-breathing mammal called a dolphin that lives in the sea, and also a true fish of the same name. There are two kinds of dolphin fish. One is quite large and grows to about 5 feet in length, and the other is similar in looks but grows to only 2½ feet. The favourite food of the dolphin fish is flying fishes and they chase them at speeds of over 35 miles per hour under water.

The archerfish lives in brackish water estuaries in places where vegetation overhangs the water.

Which fish spits at insects?

The archerfish from South-east Asia has the remarkable ability of shooting down insects from overhanging vegetation with water pellets. Its aim is quite accurate and it can usually dislodge a beetle or a fly about four feet away, so that it falls in the water. The archer fish then pounces on the insect and eats it. It is interesting to discover how the fish is able to project accurately drops of water over such distances. The roof of the mouth forms a long groove. If the fish suddenly closes its gill covers, water is forced from the gill chamber into the mouth. At the same time the tongue is raised so the groove becomes a long tube from which water squirts in a line of drops.

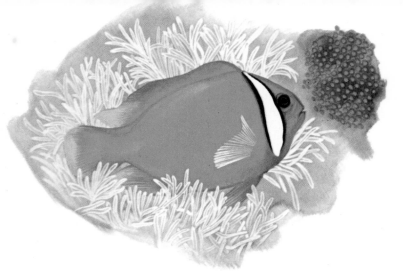

This Fire Clownfish has laid its eggs on a rock surface within easy reach of its sea anemone companion.

Why does the clownfish live among the dangerous tentacles of a sea anemone?

A beautiful and fascinating spectacle in a seawater aquarium is the vividly coloured common clownfish nestling in, and swimming among, the gently waving tentacles of a giant sea anemone. As we have seen, the arms of anemones are lined with thousands of stinging cells, and yet in some way the clownfishes seem unaffected by these. It is thought that the slimy secretion from the scales of the fishes probably helps to inhibit the effect of the stinging cells. The association between the clownfishes and the anemone is a symbiotic one, that is to say that both partners benefit from the arrangement. The fishes enjoy the luxury of a perfect hiding place from predators, which are probably occasionally lured into the anemone's arms, and the anemone also probably benefits from food brought to it by the fishes.

The Fire Clownfish is found throughout the central Pacific Ocean and usually lives in close association with a giant sea anemone.

Which fishes build bubble nests?

There is a whole group of fishes that constructs nests from bubbles. These are the labyrinth fishes from South-east Asia and Africa. Perhaps the most well known are the Siamese fighting fishes.

The male Siamese fighting fish blows bubbles, coated with a sticky secretion, just under the surface of the water. The bubbles cling together and eventually a nest several inches across and half an inch deep is formed. The female fighting fish joins the male under the nest and they spawn; the male twisting his body around the female to fertilize the eggs as they are laid. As each batch is laid the male retrieves the eggs from the bottom and blows them gently into the bubbles of the nest. When spawning is complete he drives the female away and tends the nest until the eggs hatch. He catches and replaces eggs that may fall from the nest and repairs any damage by blowing fresh bubbles. The eggs hatch within twenty-four hours.

Do fighting fishes fight?

Two male Siamese fighting fishes placed in the same aquarium instantly take up aggressive positions ready for a scrap. Their colours deepen, their long flowing fins become erect and they suddenly slash at one another at lightning speed. The fight is very dramatic and can last for up to an hour before one of the pair becomes too exhausted or injured to continue. The fight is such a spectacular sight that in Thailand contests are arranged before enthusiastic crowds and bets are placed on the outcome of the battle. For the aquarium market the fishes are bred for their beautiful flowing fins rather than for their fighting qualities. It is unwise to keep two males in a tank nevertheless.

(From top to bottom) The sequence of nest building, spawning and hatching of the fry of the Siamese fighting fish. The newly hatched 'fighter' is shown *bottom*.

(Above left) Only the male Siamese fighting fish has attractive long fins. Here a male and female are shown together.

What is dangerous about the scorpionfishes?

Their name may give you a clue as to why these fishes must be handled very carefully. These striking fishes are popular in marine aquariums. Drifting through the water with all their fins fully extended, they look wonderfully majestic. As you can see, the fins are composed of long, separate spines and it is eighteen of these that are potentially very dangerous. The spines have poison glands and if you are unlucky enough to be pricked, venom is injected in to the wound, causing great pain for several hours.

A Common Scorpionfish (above) and a Regal Scorpionfish. These fishes rarely use their spines in attack, merely for defence. There are several hundred types of these fishes including zebrafishes, dragonfishes, lionfishes and turkeyfishes. They all have tasty flesh and one species, the redfish, you may have eaten as 'fish fingers'.

How do frogs develop?

During the spring, probably in May, you may hear a noise rather like the quacking of ducks. If you investigate this strange sound, the chances are that you will discover a frog pond in which the males are croaking for all their worth to attract the females. A male clambers on to the back of a female and as she lays eggs in batches, he fertilizes them. A female can lay several thousand eggs in a season. A ball of protective jelly swells up around each egg as it is laid, sticking them all together into the familiar frogs' spawn. If you can find some frogs' spawn it is worth keeping a dozen eggs in an aquarium at home to watch their development. The eggs hatch in about ten days and the larvae hang from the leaves of water plants until their mouths open. They are active then and feed by scraping microscopic plants from the surfaces of plants and stones. Look carefully and you can see little tufts on either side of the head. These are the gills with which the tadpoles first breathe. As the

The male frog fertilizes the eggs as they are laid by the female *(above)*.

(Right) The circle shows the life cycle of the frog from spawn, to newly hatched tadpole, to the final stage of tadpole development, to adult. The cycle usually takes about three months.

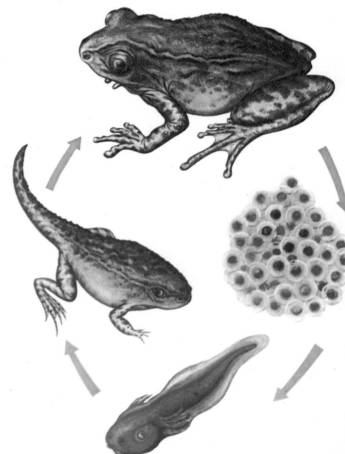

tadpoles develop, these gills shrivel up and a flap of skin grows over them. After about two months the legs appear, first the hind legs where the body joins the tail, and then the front legs. The tadpole gulps air from the surface into its newly formed lungs and starts to include meat in its diet. It is important to feed your tadpoles on small pieces of cooked meat dangled in the aquarium on cotton threads at this stage. The tail gradually shortens, the tadpoles stop feeding, and eventually emerge as miniature frogs ready to feed on small insects. At home, don't forget to provide a surface for your tadpoles to clamber on to. Once their lungs are fully formed they will soon drown if they cannot leave the water.

What are these frogs looking for?

Certain ponds and streams are used by frogs for breeding year after year. They travel overland from a wide area to these particular places during the breeding season, and meet up to find mates and lay their eggs. Sometimes these favourite spots are filled in and built over during the construction of housing developments. This is the reason hordes of frogs are occasionally seen entering new estates in the spring.

(Above) Some interesting frogs. *(From top to bottom)*: the African Hairy Frog develops rows of thin gill filaments along its body and thighs during the breeding season; a tiny frog known as the Glass Frog from South America; the Three-striped Arrow Poison Frog used by South American Indians to tip their arrows; and an African Arrow Poison Frog.

(Right) Frogs habitually seek out communal breeding places each spring.

The Water-holding Frogs survive droughts by storing water in their bodies. It is said that Aborigines dig them up and squeeze the water from them when they are thirsty.

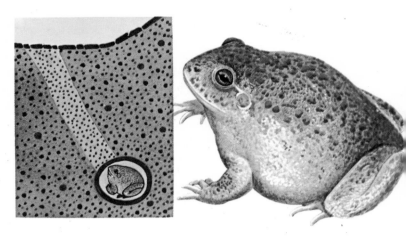

How can frogs live in the desert?

It is hard to imagine frogs living in the parched desert areas of central Australia. The rainfall in such regions is very light and every year the streams and ponds dry up completely in the periods of drought. This means that amphibians must not only be able to survive the drought, but must quickly lay their eggs and prepare themselves for the next dry period, too.

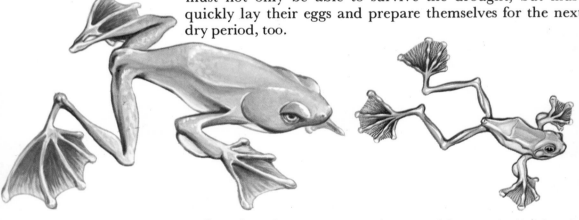

Wallace's Treefrog *(left)* from Malaya and another gliding frog *(right)* from Java.

One frog has overcome these problems admirably. As the pond dries up, the Water-holding Frog takes in water through its skin, swelling up to look very bloated indeed. It digs down into the mud while this is still soft, and lies dormant in a sealed cocoon for the period of the drought. When the rains soften the mud again the frog breaks out of its cocoon, replenishes its water supply and breeds. The eggs hatch quickly and the larvae turn into frogs in a couple of weeks while the water is still available. The young frogs grow rapidly, feeding on the insect life that also flourishes during the rainy period. At the onset of the next drought the young frogs also begin to store up a water supply to last them through the dry period. Water-holding Frogs also occur in the south-west United States.

Can frogs live in trees?

Another surprising place to find frogs is among the branches and foliage of bushes and trees. Frogs have been quite successful in adapting to these surroundings, and there are about 500 sorts of treefrogs widely distributed in the world. Some spend most of their time in water but others prefer to clamber and jump among branches and twigs in pursuit of insects, their favourite food. They are entertaining to watch while feeding for they are very agile and leap and swing in spectacular displays of aerial acrobatics. A modification of their feet gives them a good grip and helps them to hold on to branches after particularly long jumps from branch to branch. At the ends of the fingers and toes of the treefrog there is a small disc. These are tiny suction cups that enable the frogs to land and cling securely to the smooth surfaces of leaves and branches.

Many treefrogs are green in colour and this has an obvious value as camouflage among the foliage of their homes. Some treefrogs show startling patches of colour as they jump. These are not visible when the frog is crouching and the sudden flash of orange, red or yellow might temporarily distract an enemy to give the frog time to escape. These 'flash colours' as they are called are usually found on the inside of the frog's arms and legs.

Treefrogs *(from top to bottom)*: *Hylambates maculatus* from Africa; the Common European Treefrog; The Green Treefrog from North America; and the Smith Treefrog from South America.

Can frogs fly?

A species of treefrog from Malaya is even more adapted for scrambling and leaping after flying insects. This is Wallace's Treefrog and it has webbed feet with specially long fingers and toes. When the frog launches into a leap it stretches the fingers and toes wide apart, and the increase in surface area enables it to glide downwards for considerable distances. It does not fly so much as glide, but the advantage is that the frog can catch insects which it would otherwise be unable to reach by jumping normally.

The European Common Toad is a welcome visitor to gardens and may make its home in a broken flowerpot.

(Below) Toads' spawn is laid in long strings which stick to underwater plants. The larvae are not unlike frog tadpoles.

What is the difference between frogs and toads?

Most people recoil in horror at seeing a toad in the garden. Toads are certainly more ugly than frogs. They have large flattened bodies with dry, wrinkled and pimply skins. The head of a toad is blunter than a frog's and its arms and legs are shorter. The toad spends most of its time on land and it is a slow mover, unlike the active frog. It likes to establish a home for itself in some secluded spot to which it returns each evening after its leisurely feeding crawls. If you find a toad in your garden you might persuade it to stay by setting up a superior toad home – an old flowerpot is ideal. If it takes up residence your toad might stay for years. The flowers and vegetables should benefit by the toad's presence for it will feed on slugs, beetles and many other insect pests. It is often called the 'gardener's friend' for this reason. Don't worry about catching warts from your toad because this is just an 'old wives tale'.

(Right) The South American Toad grows to 7 inches in length and makes a splendid pet.

(Right) The male Midwife Toad takes care of the fertilized eggs. He carries them around on his back until the tadpoles hatch.

The Surinam Toad is another amphibian that sifts through mud to find its food. It has long, slender fingers for this purpose and each has a cluster of sensitive tentacles at the tip. These help the toad to detect its food by touch in thick mud or particularly muddy water.

Which toad hatches young on its back?

A Western Toad calls for over a minute using the air contained in its large vocal sac.

Another remarkable amphibian breeding habit is seen in the Surinam toad from South America. The female lays the eggs which are fertilized immediately by the male in the normal way. As the female lays them, however, he manoeuvres them up on to her back and presses them into her specially thickened skin. They sink in and after a short time the skin grows over them. The female then swims about her business quite unconcerned with the enormous lumpy load of about sixty eggs on her back. The eggs hatch and the tadpoles complete their development while still carried in the skin of their mother. A tiny lid on the top of each bump eventually pops open and each toadlet is released and swims up to the surface. As few eggs are laid the method is usually very successful.

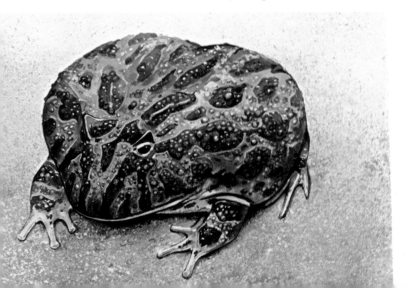

A fat, colourful toad from Brazil. The Brazilian Horned Toad is known for its aggressiveness and has sharp teeth in its upper jaw. It will even pounce on and devour a toad of its own kind if given the chance.

Is the Tuatara a prehistoric reptile?

The Tuatara certainly looks as if it stalked around the ancient landscapes of 200 million years ago. The long crest of spines running from its head along the length of its body gives it a very prehistoric appearance. Today the Tuatara is a very rare reptile and is found only on a few scattered islands lying off the New Zealand coast. It is another of those animals we call 'living fossils'. Creatures very much like the one species that exists today roamed around prehistoric landscapes millions of years ago. They formed a large and successful group called beak-heads and many fossil forms have been discovered widely distributed throughout the world. Together with many other successful reptile groups, such as the dinosaurs, the beak-heads suddenly declined in numbers. We still do not know why the age of reptiles suddenly ended but all Tuataras but one became extinct. Somehow this species managed to survive conditions that caused so many reptiles to disappear from the earth, and has lived unchanged up until the present day. It is a unique animal and represents a whole vanished order of reptiles. The other surviving remnants of the great prehistoric reptile disaster are the turtles, crocodiles, lizards and snakes.

Tuataras have lived for up to fifty years in captivity and it is claimed they may live up to 100 years in the wild. They are about 2 feet long.

The Leatherback Turtle is the largest reptile found today. It has discarded a bony shell and instead has a streamlined, smooth, leathery skin. It grows to $7\frac{1}{2}$ feet in length and weighs up to 1500 pounds.

When is a turtle a tortoise?

Turtles and tortoises form a large group of reptiles characterized by a heavily armoured shell. The protection this shell gives probably accounts for their survival, but it is not known exactly how this peculiar structure evolved.

Although the shell provides complete protection, it makes movement on land very slow and cumbersome, and most members of the group in fact live in the water. With the support of water the turtles have become good swimmers in both fresh and sea water. In America all members of this group are called turtles, whereas in Britain this name is reserved for those that live in the sea. Those that live in fresh water are usually called terrapins and those that live on land are called tortoises.

The Green Turtle *(right* and *below)* is the turtle we use to make soup. The eggs are also prized for food and the turtle has seriously declined in numbers recently due to heavy depredation by man. Attempts are being made to build up stocks again, however.

Why is this Green Turtle crying?

The Green Turtle hauls its enormous 300 pound bulk up out of the sea to above the high water mark and digs a large pit in which to lay its eggs. Its long powerful flippers, so efficient for swimming at sea, are not very suitable on land and the female has to drag the huge weight of her body along. Every few yards she stops for breath and with a huge sigh lifts the heavy shell from her body so that her lungs can fill with air. While on land her eyes are continually streaming and it has been suggested that she is reduced to tears by the exhausting task of laying her eggs! This is, of course, not true and the tears are actually a way of removing the extra salt the turtle takes in while feeding and drinking at sea. They are not seen until it comes ashore.

This ridiculous-looking South American turtle is called the Matamata. Its extended neck bears flaps of skin that wave in the water and attract fishes. The Matamata then quickly opens its enormous mouth and the fishes are swept in.

A large African Nile Crocodile about to enter the water. Crocodiles are protected by a thick, scaly skin which is prized for making items such as handbags and shoes. Nile Crocodiles are now rare as a result of hunting for this trade and the sale of crocodile products is discouraged.

What is the difference between alligators and crocodiles?

The crocodiles, alligators, caimans and the gavial make up a group of about twenty reptiles. They all have the same basic appearance and, like the turtles and terrapins, they are all amphibious. The alligator differs from the crocodile in having a shorter and broader snout although there is yet another, more definite difference. In both animals the fourth tooth of the lower jaw is enlarged. The teeth in the narrower upper and lower jaws of a crocodile are in line and so this tooth fits into a groove of the upper jaw, and can be seen when the crocodile closes its mouth. The teeth in the broader, upper jaw of an alligator overlap those in the lower. The enlarged tooth this time fits into a pocket in the upper jaw and cannot be seen when the mouth is closed.

(Below) The ugly snout of the man-eating Salt-water Crocodile. This species comes from India, the Philippines and northern Australia, and is notorious for attacking man.

The long, powerful tail of the crocodile indicates that it is a good swimmer. The ears, eyes and nostrils are all in line on top of the head so that it can lie practically submerged waiting for its prey. It is also quite agile on land and leaves the water to breed and bask in the sun.

(Left) The American Alligator is another animal that has become rare due to hunting for its skin and for sale to tourists. Alligators do not make good pets, however, because they soon grow to an unmanageable size.

How dangerous are crocodiles?

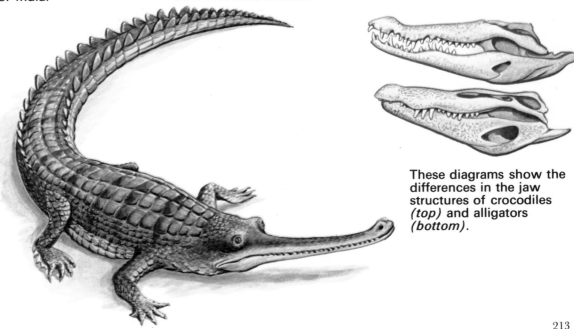

A baby caiman hatching from its egg. Crocodiles from South and Central America are generally called caimans.

All crocodiles are meat eaters and feed in water. They are particularly successful in catching smaller animals because they can float up very close to their prey without being seen. They catch animals at water holes in this way and, holding them under water, they back off into deeper water until the prey drowns. Crocodiles tear pieces from their victims by gripping with the teeth and turning over and over. Crocodiles mysteriously attack man in only some areas of Africa. They are probably more aggressive when protecting a nest or when the water is drying up. Older 'rogue' specimens perhaps become used to catching domestic animals in a particular locality and eventually attack the men who tend them.

Why does this crocodile have a long snout?

If you take a stick and sweep it through water you may be surprised to find that little effort is needed to part the water. The stick does not offer much resistance and so slices through very easily. The gavial is unlike other crocodiles in that it feeds almost exclusively on fishes. You may be beginning to realize why it has such a long, narrow snout. Powerful strokes of its strong tail propel it quickly through the water after its prey, and long sideways slashes of its mouth soon render the fishes helpless. The gavial is a shy crocodile and does not attack man.

(Below) The Gavial lives in the rivers and estuaries of India.

These diagrams show the differences in the jaw structures of crocodiles *(top)* and alligators *(bottom)*.

How can a gecko run up the wall?

(Above) These geckos show the curiously shaped toes that enable them to cling to surfaces in impossible positions. Geckos belong to the enormous lizard and snake group of reptiles.

Visitors to tropical countries are usually introduced to the acrobatic antics of geckos on their first evening. As the lights go on and insects begin to cluster around them, the geckos appear from their daytime hiding places. To reach the insects they think nothing of scampering up the wall and sometimes even across the ceiling. A close examination of the gecko's foot reveals how it is able to carry out these gravity defying movements. The toes are fat and flattened and the underneath of each consists of rows of soft, folded skin bearing thousands of tiny hooks. These catch in any irregularity, however small, in the wall or ceiling, and support the animal's weight.

What use is the Frilled Lizard's frill?

As the Australian Frilled Lizard bounds away from danger *(above)* its frill lies folded along its neck. When cornered, however, it turns and opens its frill at its enemy in a dramatic bluff display *(above right)*.

The Frilled Lizard grows to 3 feet in length in dry and sandy areas of north-eastern Australia. It lives in trees but often comes down to feed on the ground. If you come across one in the open and chase it you will soon discover why it has a frill. When disturbed the Frilled Lizard at first takes to its heels, sprinting across the ground on its hind legs, with its long tail acting as a stabilizer. If there is no tree to climb and it finds itself cornered, it turns and tries to frighten its enemy away. The long frill is suddenly erected around its neck and the mouth opens wide in a defiant, aggressive gesture. The sudden flash of colours from the frill and inside the mouth, together with angry hissing noises, usually changes the attacker's mind. If you were chasing a lizard that suddenly turned on you with a head several times bigger than it was a moment ago, wouldn't you have second thoughts about catching it?

How can a chameleon look at two things at once?

If you see a chameleon in the zoo you may notice that although it sits on a branch with one bulging eye on you, the other eye may be looking in a completely different direction. The eyes are very curious. Each has a thick conical lid which covers nearly all the eye apart from a small peephole at the tip. Each of these lids can revolve independently of the other and they look very much like

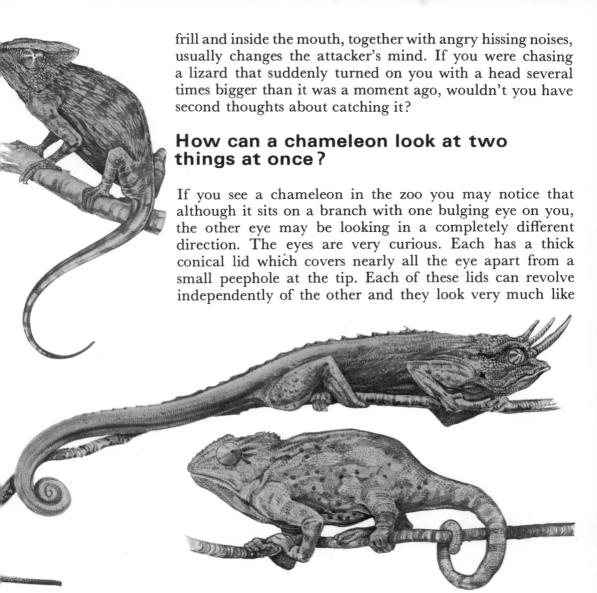

(From top to bottom) The Indian Dwarf Chameleon, Jackson's Chameleon and the Common Chameleon. Chameleons are well adapted for living among foliage. Their toes are joined into two groups so that their feet grip the branches like pairs of tongs. The tail is also used for gripping and, of course, Chameleons can change their colour and usually match their surroundings.

turrets as they swivel around focusing on objects. The objects they focus on most are insects. Chameleons live in trees and their roving eyes probably give them a better chance of spotting their prey among the foliage without being seen themselves. They are very stealthy creatures and stalk along the branches after insects extremely slowly. They can look all round them on either side, without turning their heads. Once an eye sees an insect, the other swivels round to focus on it as well. After carefully judging the range, the chameleon suddenly darts out its tongue and snatches the insect into its mouth. This happens more quickly than we can see but the chameleon's aim is deadly and it rarely misses.

What is the American Chameleon?

The American Chameleon is really an anole lizard. The anoles are a large group of tree-lizards that come from North and South America and the West Indies. The American Chameleon became so called because it can change its colour – a well-known characteristic of chameleons. There are no chameleons in the New World and so the anole lizard is the creature that most resembles them. Anoles change their colour a lot more slowly than chameleons and in response to more than just their surroundings. The temperature, light intensity and how the anole is feeling at the time, all affect its final colour.

The female American Chameleon *(below)* is drab compared to the splendid throat sac of the male *(right)*. He can expand this to show off its bright colours either to attract a mate or warn off a rival.

Which lizard squirts blood from its eyes?

The horned toads come from desert areas of North America and Mexico. They are insect eaters and bury themselves in the warm sand each evening as night falls. They can grow up to 5 inches long.

Nobody knows quite how or why the Horned Toad (which is really another lizard) squirts blood from its eyes, but we know for certain that it does happen on occasions. Naturally there are a number of theories to explain this strange phenomenon. Somehow the lizard is able to increase the blood pressure in its head, rupture the membranes of tiny blood vessels in its eyes, and squirt drops of blood for several inches. It is said that this action is usually defensive and that when squirted into the eyes of an attacker, the blood of the Horned Toad acts as an irritant.

Which big lizards eat seaweed and cacti ?

The Marine Iguana and the Land Iguana come from the Galapagos Islands in the Pacific Ocean. They are both enormous lizards. The Marine Iguana grows to 4 feet in length and the Land Iguana to $3\frac{1}{2}$ feet.

The Marine Iguana is the only lizard to have adapted to life in, or at least next to, the sea. It lives on the cliffs and rocks of the coast in large colonies and feeds on the beds of seaweed exposed at low tide. It can swim well, however, using its long, vertically flattened tail, and sometimes dives under the surface to feed.

The Marine Iguana *(left)* and the Land Iguana *(below)* are large lizards of the Galapagos Islands.

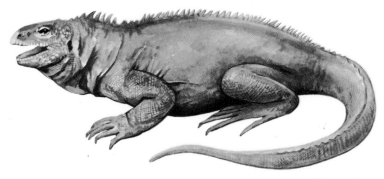

The Land Iguana, as its name suggests, lives inland from the coast and leads a more conventional lizard life. It is also mainly a vegetarian but, instead of seaweed, feeds on a variety of plants including shoots and fruits, but particularly cacti, spines and all. Larger Land Iguanas have been known to eat small mice and rats.

The large iguanas of the Galapagos were once very abundant. When man settled on these islands, however, he brought with him many domestic animal competitors for the iguana habitat, and today the iguanas are very reduced in numbers.

How can skinks see with their eyes closed?

The skinks make up a large family of fairly small lizards found in all the warm countries of the world. There are about 600 species and many of them come from Africa where they are the most common lizard. Despite their abundance most people are not at all familiar with skinks and this is probably because they are shy and retiring. If you did see one you would not think it a particularly remarkable lizard, for skinks have no fancy frills or striking coloration.

The majority of skinks live on or actually in the ground. They crawl among stones, fallen logs and leaf litter. They are not fast movers on the ground but many are very accomplished at burrowing. They are well adapted for this sort of movement being slender, smooth-skinned and having a small, pointed head. Another skink characteristic which is designed to help this worming, squirming movement through the soil is the reduction in size of the limbs. In some skinks the feet look ridiculously small for the body and in others they have disappeared altogether.

In addition to their streamlined appearance some skinks have another adaptation to their subterranean way of life. To protect its eyes when burrowing or grubbing through ground debris, the skink will close its eyes. In lizards the lower lid closes over the eye. The lid of some skinks has a small, more or less clear 'window', so that its vision is not completely cut off.

A group of skinks: *(top left)* the Western Greater Skink, *(bottom left)* the European Skink, and *(top right)* the Five-lined Skink.

Which is the most beautiful reptile?

The reptile awarded this title is the European Green Lizard. It is the second largest lizard to be found in Europe, the male reaching a length of 16 inches, 10 inches of which is its tail. (The largest European Lizard is the Eyed Lizard which reaches 2 feet in length.) Green lizards are found widely throughout Europe although they do not occur naturally in Great Britain. Attempts have been made to establish colonies but it is believed that the climate is not really warm enough for them.

Two members of a large lizard family which is found across Europe and Africa: *(top)* the European Sand Lizard and *(left)* the European Green lizard. The Uta Lizard *(right)* is from the New World.

You may find a Green Lizard for sale in a pet shop, for their elegant reptile shape and vivid colouring make them popular as pets. They are not difficult to look after but do need proper conditions, so take advice before you buy one. You can feed them on insects, spiders and worms.

Why do lizards shed their tails?

Confronted by an enemy many lizards snap off their tails to distract the attacker while they scamper to safety. In some skinks the brightly coloured tail twitches and jumps for a time to add to the confusion. The lizard soon grows a replacement.

What is the largest lizard in the world?

Can you imagine a lizard 10 feet long and weighing 300 pounds? There is a monster lizard of this size called the Komodo Dragon. It is easy to see how it came to be called a dragon. Its long neck supports a large head with cruel-looking jaws and its powerful, thick tail accounts for half its length. Short legs with clawed feet and a stout body complete the picture, but the final dragon-like touch is the forked tongue which the Komodo Dragon flicks out as it trundles along.

Altogether this is a thoroughly frightening lizard. It is said that the tail is fairly ineffective against man, but the terrible jaws would make a serious wound if they clamped on to an arm or leg. The Komodo Dragon is a ferocious carnivore and will kill and eat any smaller animal it can catch. Some have even been reported eating small deer and pigs.

Some lizards are very snake-like in appearance. The skink *(above right)* has a slim body with small limbs and the Slow-worm *(below right)* has lost its legs altogether.

Differences between lizards and snakes: *(below)* lizards have several rows of belly scales *(left)*, whereas snakes have only one *(right)*; and *(far right)* lizards usually have eyelids and a visible ear drum *(above)* whereas snakes' eyes are protected by a transparent scale *(below)*.

Are snakes really modified lizards?

Several features of the monitor lizards are not found in other lizards but are found in snakes. For example, the monitor lizards are the only lizards to swallow their prey whole, or if it is too big, pieces of it. Other lizards chew and crush their food before eating. Another snake-like characteristic is the monitor lizard's forked tongue, again unknown in other lizards. Finally, monitor lizards are unable to shed their tails, a typical lizard characteristic unknown in snakes. These clues indicate that monitors and snakes probably descended from the same ancestor way back in prehistoric time.

Other lizard families also have snake-like features and we have already seen that the burrowing skinks have long, streamlined bodies with reduced limbs. One lizard often mistaken for a snake is the Slow-worm. You can tell the Slow-worm is a legless lizard, however, by the several rows of scales along its belly (snakes have only one row), by the presence of eyelids (snakes have none), and by its notched tongue (snakes have forked tongues).

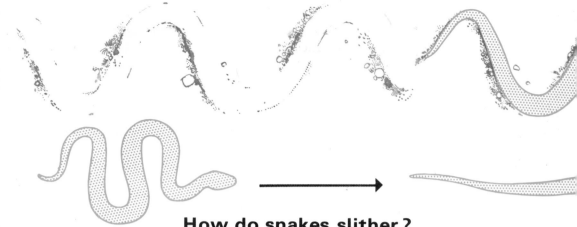

How do snakes slither?

You might think that, without legs, snakes would have difficulty in moving. However, snakes have developed the art of slithering to a fine degree and grass snakes, for example, can slither as fast as a man can walk. They move along sending waves of contractions alternately along the muscle of either side of the body. This results in horizontal curves or waves passing from the head of the snake down to the tail. The rear edge of each wave pushes backwards, and so if the passage of waves down the snake is checked by bumps and stones on the ground, the snake moves forward. A snake crossing a sandy patch leaves a trail with sand heaped up at the rear of each wave, showing where the thrust was made.

Some snakes move by a variation of this method called 'concertina locomotion'. The snake throws the front half of its body into waves, grips the ground and draws up the rear half. The rear half then forms waves which push the straightened front half forward.

Heavy, fat snakes tend to creep forward in a straight line. They do this by sending a wave of contraction down the narrow row of overlapping scales on their belly. These scales move forward slightly and then back, and their continued action along the snake push it forward slowly.

How does a sidewinder move?

If you place a snake on a very smooth surface, the waves passing down its body will not grip and the snake will not move forward. Loose, shifting sand has much the same effect on conventional snake slithering, and so we find a different method of movement in desert snakes. A side-winding snake throws its head into a sideways loop. It places its neck on the sand and twists the rest of its body off the sand and through the same spot, pushing downwards and

the same time. As the body spirals through this point the head makes a new loop and again touches down in front and to the side. These actions leave a line of parallel 'J' shapes in the sand. The curved bottom of the 'J' is made by the head touching down, the stem by the body looping through and forwards, and the cross by the tail thrusting off. A sidewinder travels forward even though it is spiralling sideways.

How does a snake shed its skin?

Slithering along the ground tends to wear out the snake's skin so it replaces it from time to time with a new one. The new skin grows underneath the old and when it is fully formed, fluid is secreted between the two to keep them apart and lubricated. The fluid behind the transparent eye scale clouds the eye and prevents the snake from seeing for a few days. It hides away and then splits the old skin at its lips by rubbing its head. The old skin is turned inside out as the snake wriggles out.

(Above) The normal slithering action of a snake leaves a characteristic trail with sand heaped up at the edge of each wave *(top)* The 'concertina' method of movement is shown bottom.

(Far left) The sidewinding action of snakes in deserts leaves a series of 'J' shapes in the sand.

(Above) A snake turns pale and its eyes go cloudy when it is about to moult. The old skin is pushed back from the head and turns inside out as the snake emerges *(right)*.

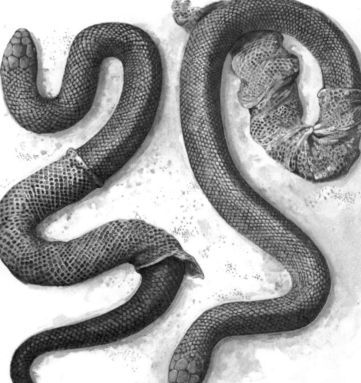

Why is this snake seeking the shade?

If you feel chilly you begin to shiver and if you feel warm you begin to perspire. Both these actions result in you controlling the temperature of your body independently of the temperature of the air. Birds can also do this but reptiles cannot. This is why birds and mammals are spoken of as warm blooded and reptiles as cold blooded. A snake's blood is not always cold, however. It is true that a snake has no insulating fur or feathers to prevent heat loss from its body but it does have a limited amount of control over its temperature. Its method of control is simple: in the morning it warms up its body by basking in the sun. Once it is warmed up it can begin the day's activities. If the snake then becomes overheated it will seek the shadow of a rock or bush in which to cool off. The body temperature of a snake is therefore always more or less that of its surroundings.

What is a hibernaculum?

In temperate countries the temperature in the winter months remains low over a long period. Snakes and other reptiles would soon die if they were exposed to such cold and so they hibernate. By hiding themselves away in underground holes and burrows made by other animals they escape the low temperatures and pass the winter in a torpid state. This means that all their bodily actions are slowed down so that hardly any energy is used up. Some snakes hibernate on their own but others return each autumn to a communal hole or hibernaculum. Forty snakes have been found sharing the same winter quarters, and a popular hole is often used by more than one species.

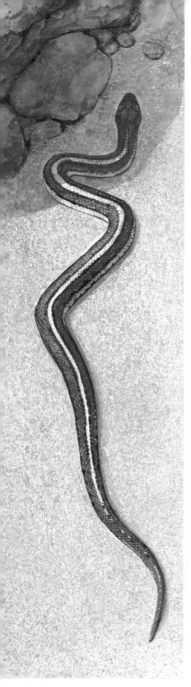

(Above) A snake cannot control its body temperature as well as birds and mammals. If it becomes too warm it must seek the shade. *(Right)* In a hibernaculum several snakes will share the same winter quarters.

How does a snake swallow its prey?

Snakes catch live animals and eat them whole. They can swallow prey several times larger than their head. This is made possible by very loosely jointed jaws which enable the mouth to be opened wide. Backward pointing teeth grip the prey while the mouth is worked over the animal. Lots of saliva helps the meal to slip down the snake's throat.

A snake can catch and swallow whole an animal several times wider than its head. The jaws of a snake are especially mobile and its skin is capable of being stretched taut over bulky bodies.

(Left) The Tree Boa is a particularly attractive boa from tropical South America. When resting it stacks up the loops of its body along a branch, with its head inside the outer coils. Its coloration makes it difficult to see among the foliage.

Does a Boa Constrictor crush its prey?

The boas and pythons are giant constricting snakes. Many people imagine this means they coil themselves around their prey, and squeeze and squeeze until the victim is crushed to death. This is, in fact, not so. A Boa Constrictor, or any other boa or python, strikes at its prey with an open mouth. Backward-pointing teeth grip the animal while the snake quickly throws loops of its body around its prey. The snake may secure itself by coiling its tail around a fixed object, such as a tree, and then tightens two or three of the coils around its victim. This prevents the animal's ribs from moving so that it stops breathing and quickly suffocates. As soon as the victim ceases struggling the boa unwinds itself and starts to swallow it. Boa Constrictors eat reptiles, birds and small mammals.

The Royal Python (above) and the Rubber Boa (below) both curl up into balls when threatened.

The Boa Constrictor is found in Central and Southern America and can grow to 15 feet in length.

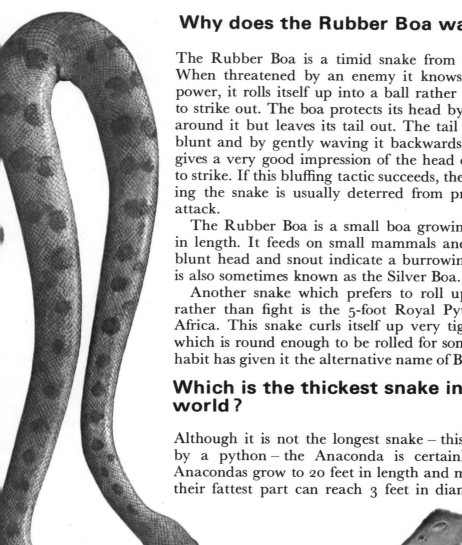

Why does the Rubber Boa wave its tail?

The Rubber Boa is a timid snake from North America. When threatened by an enemy it knows it cannot overpower, it rolls itself up into a ball rather than attempting to strike out. The boa protects its head by coiling its body around it but leaves its tail out. The tail is both stiff and blunt and by gently waving it backwards and forwards it gives a very good impression of the head of a snake about to strike. If this bluffing tactic succeeds, the animal disturbing the snake is usually deterred from pressing home an attack.

The Rubber Boa is a small boa growing to only 2 feet in length. It feeds on small mammals and lizards and its blunt head and snout indicate a burrowing way of life. It is also sometimes known as the Silver Boa.

Another snake which prefers to roll up out of danger rather than fight is the 5-foot Royal Python from West Africa. This snake curls itself up very tightly into a ball which is round enough to be rolled for some distance. The habit has given it the alternative name of Ball Python.

Which is the thickest snake in the world?

Although it is not the longest snake – this title is claimed by a python – the Anaconda is certainly the thickest. Anacondas grow to 20 feet in length and measured around their fattest part can reach 3 feet in diameter. Naturally

By lying in wait near water, the Anaconda surprises and overcomes mammals as large as the Agouti *above right,* shown to scale.

such a colossal snake (weighing about 17 stone) cannot move swiftly and so the Anaconda relies on lying in wait for its prey. One favourite place is in the trees that overhang river banks and swamps, and another is in the shallows of the water itself. As animals come down to the water to drink the Anaconda pounces from its hiding place and overpowers its startled prey. The Anaconda is sluggish on land, but it can swim and it can climb up the branches of trees to rest and sunbathe during the day. Although there are stories of it being a man-eater, these are doubtful, no reliable evidence ever having been produced to prove them.

The 3-foot Flying Snake from South-east Asia, India and Ceylon flattens its body and glides from tree to tree. Both the tree-snakes illustrated here are venomous, killing their prey with poison injected through their fangs.

Do snakes live in trees?

(Above) The African Vine Snake puffs out its throat when alarmed to reveal the more brightly coloured skin of its throat.

Many snakes live in trees. One in particular, the African Vine Snake, shows most of the tree-snake characteristics. It is only about 4 feet in length and nearly half of this is the snake's long and slender tail. The slim shape of the Vine Snake is ideal for climbing quickly through the branches of trees, and its mottled colouring provides a perfect camouflage among the foliage. The Vine Snake

lies along branches with about one third of its body extended into space. It remains like this for long periods, carefully scanning the area for birds, frogs, chameleons and geckos. It has very good eyesight for a snake. Its eyes are situated on the front of the head and grooves along the snake's nose give uninterrupted vision. The tongue of the Vine Snake is brightly coloured. The constant flicking in and out is thought to attract prey.

Can snakes fly?

Snakes cannot fly but one or two have become very good at gliding. A snake with this ability launches itself into space from high up in a tree. As it falls it flattens its body and draws itself in underneath to an almost concave shape. The increased surface area cushions the snake's fall and enables it to prolong its descent through the air. It either glides into another tree in this way, or all the way to the ground. One flying snake is also good at leaping across wide gaps in the branches. It coils itself up, then suddenly unwinds, shooting itself across the gap in a stiff, upright position.

Do snakes eat snakes?

King snakes are particularly fond of eating other snakes although they do not go out of their way to track them down. A chance encounter with another species usually results in the king snake overcoming the other by constriction. King snakes are immune to the venom of poisonous snakes and so even such deadly species as rattlesnakes and copperheads are not safe from them. King snakes are protected in some areas, for their snake-eating habits are considered useful.

A king snake *(right)* constricting a copperhead snake. King snakes are common in the southern United States.

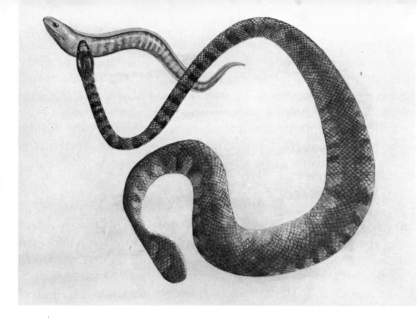

Seasnakes are found in the warm, coastal waters of the Indian and Pacific Oceans. Most are about 4 or 5 feet long.

The drawings *below* are of the large venom glands and fangs of a viper. The fangs are shown folded into the mouth and then erected just before striking a victim.

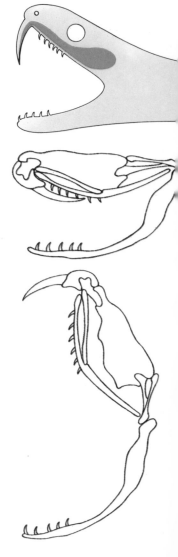

Which snakes live in the sea?

There is one group of snakes that is so well adapted for life in the sea that most of them never leave it. If you caught a seasnake and placed it on the ground it would flop around and show no sign of the efficient slithering of its land relatives. In the water, however, seasnakes are excellent swimmers. Their bodies are flattened from side to side towards the rear end, and the tail is often paddle-shaped to help drive the snake forward. Other adaptations of the seasnakes include nostrils on the top of the head and valves in the nostrils which prevent the entry of water when the snake is diving.

Seasnakes are extremely venomous but surprisingly they are among the least aggressive of poisonous snakes. They are particularly fond of eels which succumb within seconds to their venom. The quick-acting venom presumably prevents the prey escaping into awkward holes and crevices once it has been bitten. Seasnakes rarely bite man and fishermen disentangle them from their nets by hand with little fear.

Which snakes have folding fangs?

The snakes with the most advanced venom injection system are those with folding fangs – the vipers and rattlesnakes. These snakes have large venom glands and long fangs which are folded into the mouth when not in use. When about to strike, the snake erects its fangs and then plunges them deep into its victim. Unlike other venomous snakes which hang

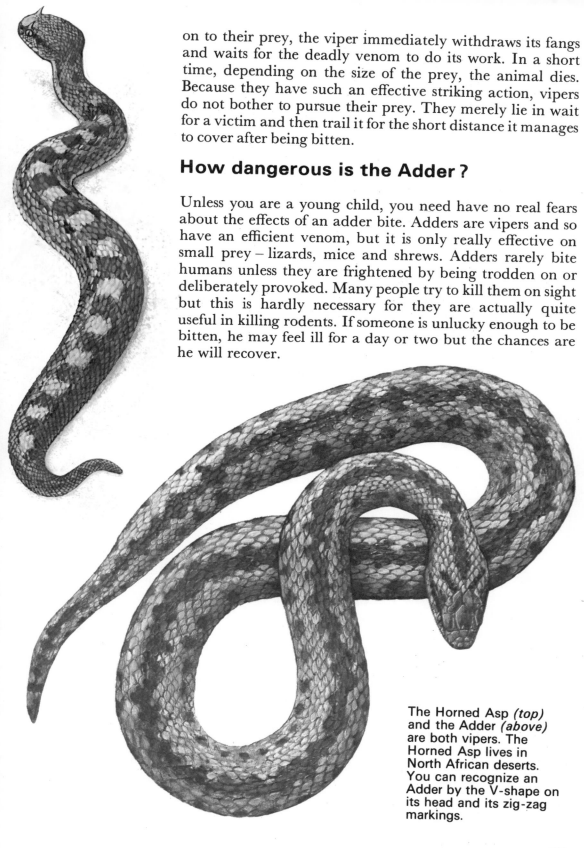

on to their prey, the viper immediately withdraws its fangs and waits for the deadly venom to do its work. In a short time, depending on the size of the prey, the animal dies. Because they have such an effective striking action, vipers do not bother to pursue their prey. They merely lie in wait for a victim and then trail it for the short distance it manages to cover after being bitten.

How dangerous is the Adder?

Unless you are a young child, you need have no real fears about the effects of an adder bite. Adders are vipers and so have an efficient venom, but it is only really effective on small prey – lizards, mice and shrews. Adders rarely bite humans unless they are frightened by being trodden on or deliberately provoked. Many people try to kill them on sight but this is hardly necessary for they are actually quite useful in killing rodents. If someone is unlucky enough to be bitten, he may feel ill for a day or two but the chances are he will recover.

The Horned Asp *(top)* and the Adder *(above)* are both vipers. The Horned Asp lives in North African deserts. You can recognize an Adder by the V-shape on its head and its zig-zag markings.

Which are the modern running birds?

The flightless Australian Cassowary *(below)* is built like a bird battering ram, in contrast to the chicken-sized kiwi *(right)* which probes the ground for earthworms and grubs.

There are several groups of birds alive today that are unable to fly. These are the ostriches, rheas, emus, cassowaries, kiwis and penguins, and it is worthwhile considering why they cannot fly. You might think that enormous birds like the cassowary, emu and ostrich are too heavy to lift themselves into the air. This is, of course, a factor, but it is not the real reason why these birds have tiny wings and are unable to take to the air. It was at one time thought that the modern flightless birds evolved separately from the animals that eventually gave rise to the flying birds. The flightless birds were assumed to have not yet developed the power of flight

because their wings are still evolving. This view is no longer held. It is now realized that the modern running birds did have flying ancestors, but that they lost the power of flight through disuse of their wings. Living in areas free from predatory enemies, the running birds have had no need to fly away from danger, and so have developed powerful legs and bodies for running about instead.

Why does the cassowary have a bony crest?

At 5 to 6 feet high the emu is the second largest bird in the world. It lives in most undeveloped areas of Australia.

The bone 'helmet' of the Australian cassowary can be directly related to its habit of charging through dense undergrowth at speeds of up to 30 miles an hour. This stocky, flightless bird comes from northern Australia and New Guinea and may be up to 5 feet high. It is rarely seen for it prefers to live in the middle of impenetrable rain forests and so not much is known about its habits in the wild. It is fairly obvious, however, that with its protective horny crest, powerful, wedge-shaped body, and long, flexible feathers, the cassowary is well equipped for forcing its way through thick jungle at speed. A cassowary in a zoo once charged through the netting of its cage, leaving a clear outline of its body in the wire.

What is the largest living bird?

Standing 8 feet high and weighing 300 pounds, the ostrich is easily the largest bird in the world. On African grasslands it has adopted the habits of a grazing animal and groups roam about feeding in the company of zebras and gazelles. It is well adapted to this sort of habitat. Good eyesight and a long neck enable it to spot danger from a long way off. Powerful thighs and long legs can carry it at 40 miles an hour out of harm's way. It is the only bird with two toes, another feature which enables it to run that much faster over the grassy plains.

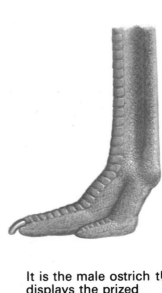

It is the male ostrich that displays the prized plumage of long white feathers on the wings and tail. An ostrich has only two toes *(above)*, an extreme adaptation for running at speed.

A Ringed Penguin *(top)* and a Gentoo Penguin *(below)* chasing fishes. Penguins use their wings as paddles and their feet as a rudder to manoeuvre themselves expertly after their prey.

Which birds 'fly' underwater?

In contrast to the powerful running birds we have already seen, there is one group of flightless birds that at best can only waddle on land. These are the penguins, but what they lack in walking ability they certainly make up for in skill at swimming. Their flipper-like wings are useless for flying but are ideal for propelling the streamlined penguin through the water at speed. Penguins waddle on land because their feet are set so far back on the body. This is just the right position for a rudder, however, and this is how the penguin steers underwater. Penguins are so agile in the sea they can be described as 'flying' underwater.

The King Penguin incubates the single egg on its feet, under an insulating flap of skin.

(Left) Adelie Penguins congregate in their noisy thousands at nesting grounds called rookeries. The nest is a pile of pebbles on which the eggs are laid.

How do penguins cope with the cold?

Some penguins breed during the Antarctic winter and often have to stand around in freezing blizzards of driving snow for hours on end. They withstand such conditions by having a very dense plumage all over the body (unlike the plumage of other birds). Underneath this thick coat of closely packed feathers there is an insulating layer of blubber. This helps maintain the body warmth, and stores food and water as well. If the temperature drops too low, penguins resort to huddling together in an attempt to conserve body heat.

(Right) The Emperor Penguin is the largest penguin at 4 feet, and is shown here next to an Adelie Penguin, as a comparison of their sizes. Both have chicks in attendance.

An Emperor Penguin parent fussing over its chick.

What are these grebes doing?

If you are a bird watcher you may have been lucky enough to watch the spring courtship displays of Great Crested Grebes. The birds face each other and shake their heads in opposite directions, or they may dive and surface with weed in their beaks, rear up breast to breast and sway from side to side. These displays are very exciting to watch. Both male and female grebes have strikingly coloured plumes and ear tufts which emphasize the head movements.

The Great Crested Grebe is a water bird, of course, and you can often see it on gravel pits, reservoirs and large lakes. It is in its element in the water and rarely leaves it, building a nest of floating vegetation in which to lay the eggs. The nest is abandoned as soon as the eggs hatch and the young grebes climb on to the backs of the parents for journeys around the lake. They are even carried underwater when the parent bird dives for food, although sometimes they are dislodged and can be seen to bob up to surface, none the worse for the experience.

The Great Crested Grebes *above* and *below* are displaying to each other prior to mating. The displays are very elaborate and a number of characteristic movements can be recognized.

(Below) The toes of the Great Crested Grebe have flaps along their length. As the feet thrust through the water the flaps are spread and act like paddles to propel the bird along.

Why are albatrosses ringed?

A small metal ring clipped to the leg of an albatross provides valuable information about the extent of the bird's travels if it can be recovered.

This man is carefully placing a metal ring or band on the leg of an albatross. Many species are ringed in this way by bird organizations in order to study bird movements. Many birds migrate – albatrosses travel enormous distances – and much is learnt about this phenomenon by analysis of the information the recovery of the rings provides. The rings are stamped with the name of the organization carrying out the research, and numbers which indicate the place of ringing, the date, and other relevant information. If you ever find a bird with a ring, send the ring to the appropriate people, for you will be helping them to carry out their valuable work.

The slender, long wings of the albatross enable it to soar effortlessly over the ocean for miles and miles. Albatrosses feed on fishes, squids and crustaceans that they can catch on the surface of the sea. They will follow a ship for miles to feed on the refuse dumped overboard.

Does the bill of a pelican 'hold more than its belly can'?

The pouch of a White Pelican from south-east Europe, Asia and Africa holds three gallons, more than twice the capacity of its stomach. This gives the impression that the pelican uses its enormous pouch to store food. Indeed it is often said that when full the food in the beak lasts the pelican for a week. However, the pouch is used not for storage but for fishing and all the fishes caught are eaten immediately. Pelicans sometimes fish together in line and drive the fishes into shoals. They all dip their beaks in together and scoop out the fishes.

The Chilean Pelican *(above left)* and the Spotted-billed Pelican *(above)*. In spite of their size and awkward shape pelicans are graceful fliers. They fly in formation with wing beats synchronized.

(Right) The strong webbed foot of a pelican.

(Left) The Shag is a cormorant found along the shores of Europe.

How do cormorants fish for man?

In China and Japan the ancient art of cormorant fishing dates back for hundreds and hundreds of years. The cormorants are trained to fish tied to a long lead and with a leather thong around their necks. This prevents the birds from swallowing their catches which they disgorge into the boat when the owner pulls them in. At the end of the night's fishing the owner unties the thong and gives the cormorants their share of the catch to eat. Modern methods have made cormorant fishing uneconomic in Asia but it is still demonstrated as a tourist attraction.

Cormorant fishing is carried out at night. Large flares in the boats attract fishes to the fishing area.

Why is the frigate bird the 'pirate of the seas'?

The piratical behaviour of buccaneers of old has been compared to the way a frigate bird obtains food at certain times of the year. By flying alongside another bird and pecking at it until it realizes it cannot escape, the frigate bird obtains a meal for nothing. If the victim has just fed, its crop will be full of half-digested mush. In fear, or to lighten its load so that it can escape the frigate bird, the bird will disgorge the contents of its crop. This the frigate bird pounces on as it falls and scoops it into its beak before it hits the water. You will realize from this that the frigate birds are superb fliers.

The Magnificent Frigate Bird inflates its colourful throat pouch in the breeding season to attract a mate.

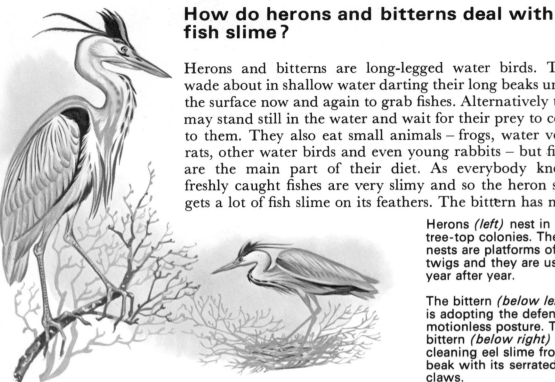

How do herons and bitterns deal with fish slime?

Herons and bitterns are long-legged water birds. They wade about in shallow water darting their long beaks under the surface now and again to grab fishes. Alternatively they may stand still in the water and wait for their prey to come to them. They also eat small animals – frogs, water voles, rats, other water birds and even young rabbits – but fishes are the main part of their diet. As everybody knows, freshly caught fishes are very slimy and so the heron soon gets a lot of fish slime on its feathers. The bittern has more

Herons *(left)* nest in tree-top colonies. The nests are platforms of twigs and they are used year after year.

The bittern *(below left)* is adopting the defensive motionless posture. The bittern *(below right)* is cleaning eel slime from its beak with its serrated claws.

of a problem. It is partial to eels which are covered with even more slime than fishes and which wriggle a great deal more when caught.

Herons and bitterns remove the slime by dusting themselves down with a fine powder produced from patches of special feathers. These feathers never fall out and are continually fraying at their ends to form the powder. Herons distribute the powder over their feathers using the beak. Bitterns rub their slimy heads in the powder patch. After a short time the powder absorbs the slime and the birds clean their plumage by combing it out with a specially serrated claw on the middle toe.

Why does a bittern freeze when startled?

Rather than run away when disturbed, a bittern will thrust its head and neck into the air and stand motionless. This bird lives in the dense reed beds of marshes and it relies on its remarkable camouflage to escape detection. The striped plumage of its breast blends perfectly with a background of reeds. By squinting under its beak in this position, the bittern can accurately judge the range of the intruder, and decide whether or not to fly off.

Why were the egret's feathers nearly its downfall?

In the breeding season many egrets display beautiful long feathery plumes which grow from the head, breast and back. At the turn of the century, these plumes, called aigrettes, became very popular for decorating hats. The millinery trade demanded enormous numbers of aigrettes and thousands and thousands of birds were killed at a time of year when they were most vulnerable. Nests were deserted and chicks left to die to increase the disastrous effect of the slaughter. In the end, due to the efforts of conservation bodies publicizing the plight of the egrets, public opinion was turned against the use of aigrettes in hats and the demand slumped. The birds are now protected in many parts of their range.

These Little Egrets at nest from southern Europe and Asia, Africa and Australia show the fine, trailing plumes that were so prized for decorating hats.

Where do spoonbills and ibises live?

Spoonbills and ibises are wading birds of the same bird family. They live in flocks and fly with the head held straight out in front and the legs trailing behind. Both groups fly slowly, but whereas spoonbills fly with regular wingbeats, all the ibises in a group alternate flapping with gliding so that they fly in unison. The Common Spoonbill breeds in northern and southern Europe, southern Asia and Africa. The Roseate Spoonbill is found in the southern United States and through much of South America. The Scarlet Ibis lives in tropical America from Venezuela to Brazil.

The bill of an ibis is downcurved for probing along the lake shore, while that of a spoonbill is spoon-shaped for sifting small organisms from mud and water. Roseate Spoonbills *(below left)* and Scarlet Ibises *(top right)* are shown.

(Above) The strange-looking beak of the flamingo is unique in the bird world.

Why do flamingos have bent beaks?

The beak of a flamingo looks as if it has been broken in half and the halves bent downwards and rejoined. As you might expect there is a very good reason for this peculiar shape. Flamingos like to live in shallow lagoons and lakes. Despite their large size and their large beaks flamingos feed on the smallest of organisms in the water. The flamingo stalks along with its head bent right down to dip the beak in the water. In this position the upper half is underneath and the beak is now an ideal scooping organ. The flamingo sweeps its head from side to side through the water to collect tiny molluscs, crustaceans and single-celled algae. As the tongue pumps water through the beak, this food is caught on a sieve-like structure inside and passed down the throat.

(Below) Greater Flamingos looking after a group of youngsters.

Two beautiful flamingos from high altitude lakes in South America: the rare James' Flamingo (left) and the Andean Flamingo (right).

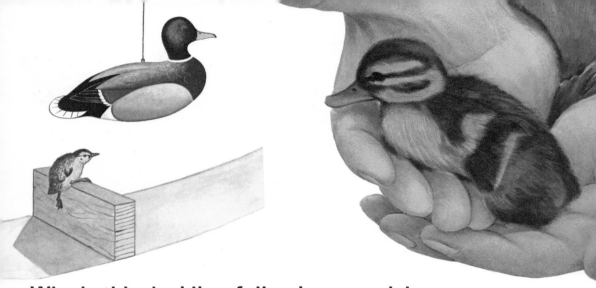

Why is this duckling following a model mother?

It has been known for a long time that the young of ducks, geese and chickens sometimes behave very strangely after hatching. If the parent duck, for example, is absent for some reason, ducklings will form an attachment with any object or person that comes close to them. To them the new object or person becomes their 'mother' and they will trail behind if the 'mother' moves. It seems that the strong attachment is made at a particular time after hatching and if the parent bird should appear later it will be ignored by the duckling. Some very strange friendships indeed have been made by young birds. One became firmly attached to a ping-pong ball, imagining it to be its mother, and others have adopted a person as their parent, following him everywhere. When the ducklings hatch normally they form this strong attachment to their natural mother, of course. This ensures that when she leaves the nest and waddles to the comparative safety of the water, they will all waddle closely behind. They realize at this time that they are ducks and not ping-pong balls or people, and so will be able to recognize their own kind later in life.

The newly hatched duckling *(above)* will adopt an artificial 'mother' in the absence of its real mother. It will even climb obstacles to follow a model duck *(above left)*.

All these red-faced ducks are Muscovy Ducks although they have quite different colouring.

Where do ugly muscovies come from?

You may be feeding the ducks one day when a scruffy fat duck with a red knobbly face and black and white plumage swims on the scene. This is a Muscovy Duck and others will probably soon appear although all will have slightly different plumage. Muscovies originally came from the forests of Central and South America. There the wild birds are much more attractive with glossy green feathers. Centuries of domestication have resulted in the muscovies having a rather drab appearance and varied colouring.

The male Mallard *(left)* loses its colourful plumage at the end of the breeding season. The Mallard's feet *(above)* are strongly webbed like all ducks'.

Which duck provides eiderdown?

As you snuggle under your soft and beautifully warm eiderdown, spare a thought for the Eider Ducks from whose nests the down is collected. Eider ducks are northern sea ducks and breed in colonies on the coast. Man soon realized the value of the down which the birds pluck from their breasts to line their nest. In Scandinavia and Iceland the birds are encouraged to breed in specially prepared and protected areas. The down is harvested from these eiderdown farms twice in each breeding season.

The down from the Eider Duck *(right)* is also used in sleeping bags.

Trumpeter Swans have completely black beaks. These large North American swans were reduced to near extinction by overshooting only forty years ago. Fortunately, vigorous protection measures and breeding programmes have re-established the Trumpeter Swans in North America.

Is the Mute Swan really mute?

It is easy to understand how the Mute Swan came to be so called. Gliding gracefully along with head held high, it looks too gentle to be a noisy bird. It is not altogether a silent bird, however. A party of swans moving up a stream will often make small grunting noises to each other, for example. Other 'conversational' sounds made by Mute Swans include growls and short yaps, and all these sounds probably serve to keep the group together. A more sinister sound is made when the Mute Swan is angry. It arches its neck and half raises its wings before lunging at an intruder with fierce hissing sounds. (It is well known among anglers that you can usually deter a swan from coming too close by hissing loudly at it.)

The Mute Swan *(below)* occasionally gives its cygnets a ride on its back.

What is swan-upping?

The Mute Swan has been a domesticated bird in England for over 800 years. It is sometimes called the 'royal' bird and in fact by the thirteenth century all the swans in England belonged to the Crown. People were allowed to keep swans on open water as long as the birds were prevented from flying away, and they carried their owner's mark. Hundreds of swan marks were developed. Birds usually had a series of notches or a symbol on the orange part of their beak. One man, the Royal Swanherd, was responsible for registering all the marks and for actually marking the birds. Each year he would set out on swan-upping expeditions to gather all the year's cygnets for marking. This ancient practice is still carried out each year on the River Thames where all the swans belong to the Queen.

Which are the black swans?

Not all swans have pure white plumage. Two species, one from Australia and New Zealand and one from South America, have black plumage. The Black Swan must have been an amazing sight to the seventeenth century explorers of Australia who had previously seen only white birds. Black Swans soon arrived in England and America and were popular as decorative curiosities on the lakes and ponds of stately homes. The other black swan, with less black in its plumage, is the Black-necked Swan from South America. It has a black head and neck, a white eye stripe and a red bill. It occurs from southern Brazil to Patagonia and also breeds in the Falkland Islands.

The Black Swan of Australia (left and top) is not entirely black. It is not apparent from the bird at rest but the trailing edges of the wings are white. The Black-necked Swan (above) has a curious, red knobbly bump on its beak.

(Right) Falcons hunt their prey by rushing at it from a great height and stunning it with a tremendous blow from their talons.

(Below) These two birds illustrate the range in size of birds of prey. The smaller is a falconet, about 6 inches in length, and the larger is an Indian Vulture about 30 inches in length. Other vultures are even longer than this.

What is a bird of prey?

Birds of prey are birds which feed on other animals. They catch and eat animals that are usually smaller than themselves, on the ground, in the air, or in water. Not all bother to chase their prey. Some prefer feeding on the flesh of animals already dead. Birds of prey have strong wings and are powerful fliers: some – the vultures – have mastered

(Right) The feet are the main killing weapons of birds of prey and owls. They often suffer damage through injury from constant use. It is interesting to notice that these feet are an owl's and that they are feathered. Owls swallow their prey whole and so do not feed as messily as birds of prey.

(Above) A Kestrel hunts by hovering over open ground and then plunging down on to its prey before it can escape.

the art of soaring flight. They all have curved talons for grabbing and holding their prey, and large hooked beaks for tearing at flesh.

There are several different methods of hunting. Where there is sufficient cover, some eagles hide in a tree and wait for their prey to wander into a clearing. Where the ground is more open, Kestrels and other birds of prey hover over likely places, scouring the ground for the slightest tell-tale movement of a mouse or vole. Over undulating country a slow gliding flight at low level may be used by harriers to cover a wide area with the minimum effort. Carrion eaters soar on outstretched wings at considerable heights for hours on end, peering down for animals already dead, or one about to die. In contrast, small birds of prey like the Sparrowhawk dash at high speed through trees and along hedgerows, hoping to surprise a smaller creature. Buzzards, eagles, falcons, harriers, hawks and vultures comprise the birds of prey; owls also catch smaller animals but they are usually treated separately.

Why do birds of prey have bare feet?

Birds of prey kill with their feet. Some also use the beak but the sharp curved talons of the feet are the main killing weapon. The rear and inside talons are usually larger than the middle and outer talons, and with these the bird exerts a strong pincer grip on the prey. The neck of the creature is dislocated or it is fatally pierced or crushed, but however it dies it is soon torn to pieces by the beak. This is a messy way of feeding and if the feet of a bird of prey were feathered they would soon become matted and bloodstained. Most have bare feet since these are much easier to keep clean.

(Above) A selection of feet of birds of prey illustrating the variety in size and strength. Each type of foot suits each bird for its particular diet and method of hunting.

(Left) A number of Old World vultures clustered on the carcass of a zebra.

The colourful King Vulture (below) from Mexico and Argentina is the third largest of the New World vultures.

How do vultures find their prey?

Any animal that has just died in an area frequented by vultures is soon picked over by a horde of these ugly birds. How can they all arrive at one spot so quickly from the huge areas they patrol? Vultures, of course, are the soaring birds of prey mentioned earlier. They have excellent eyesight but they examine not only the ground as they glide high in the sky. They also closely watch each other and the descent of any one bird is always noticed by at least one other. All the vultures from a wide area soon swoop down to see what it was that interested the first bird.

Vultures have weak beaks and feet adapted for running rather than killing. They have bald faces for the same reason that other birds of prey have naked feet. The Sociable Vulture (top) is one of the first to arrive at a carcase and tears off large pieces of flesh. The Egyptian Vulture (bottom) arrives later and its narrower beak is more suitable for picking the bones left by the larger birds.

How big is the Andean Condor?

The grotesque-looking Andean Condor is one of the two largest flying birds found today. Almost 4 feet in length, with a wingspan of 10 feet, it weighs up to 28 pounds. The California Condor is similar in size. A bird as big as this requires a lot of food and the Andean Condor has to eat at least a pound of meat a day. Condors spend hour after hour gliding effortlessly over enormous areas in search of carrion, although if this is scarce the Andean Condor will attack and kill lambs and calves. It will also come down to feed on stranded animals on the shore, including whales if it is lucky enough to find one.

There are two unrelated groups of vultures, one from the Old World (Europe, Africa and Asia) and one from the New World (North, Central and South America). The New World group includes the condors.

(Below) Large vultures spend hours wheeling and soaring in thermals of warm air rising from the ground.

(Right) The naked head of the Andean Condor is suited to poking around a decomposing carcase.

Golden Eagles will return year after year to the same eyrie. Sites include cliff ledges and caves, trees and sometimes hollows in the ground.

Where do Golden Eagles nest?

In Asia, Golden Eagles have been trained by tribes to hunt wolves.

The Golden Eagle is probably the best known of all the birds of prey. It is a magnificent bird, up to 3 feet in length and with a wingspan of up to 8 feet. Golden Eagles patrol enormous areas of remote mountainous country throughout the northern hemisphere. They are long-lived birds which pair up for life, usually returning to the same nesting site each year. A predatory bird as large as this obviously cannot nest anywhere. The most favoured place for an eagle to build its eyrie is on an inaccessible ledge of a steep cliff, commanding a good view of the surrounding countryside. Here the eagle cannot be approached unawares. In North America eagles seem to prefer to nest in trees. As the eyrie is added to year after year, the weight of sticks sometimes becomes too great, and the nest may overbalance the tree.

This is the underside view of a Golden Eagle gliding directly overhead.

How many young are reared?

Two eggs are usually laid by the Golden Eagles, the second within a few days of the first. One eaglet is therefore slightly bigger than the other. If food is scarce the stronger will bully the weaker of the two to the extent that it eventually dies. The stronger bird therefore has a better chance of survival during the periods when its parents are unable to find much food. If food is plentiful, both eaglets survive.

(Right) This sequence shows the development of a Golden Eagle from the newly hatched eaglet *(top)* through the half-grown stage *(middle)*, to the immature bird *(bottom)*. Eaglets leave the eyrie after ten weeks but usually stay nearby to learn the skills of hunting from their parents.

(Above) The white-bellied Sea Eagle lives along the coasts of South-east Asia and feeds on fishes, corals and sea snakes.

How does the Osprey catch fishes?

The Osprey is a bird of prey that specializes in catching fishes. You can see this by looking at its feet. Instead of the usual bird of prey arrangement of three front toes and one rear, the Osprey has two at the front and two at the rear, all of equal length. Each toe bears a razor-sharp talon curved downwards, and underneath a patch of special spine-like scales. Both these features enable the Osprey to grasp fishes securely, however slippery. The Osprey circles slowly over water looking out for fishes just below the surface. Once the prey is spotted, the Osprey hovers for a moment, and then plunges downwards. Just before hitting the water it swings its feet forwards to grab the fish. It struggles for a moment to rise again and then flaps up from the surface with its prey held firmly in a vice-like grip.

The feet of an Osprey are adapted for holding fishes. One foot is placed in front of the other on the fish's back, so that the four toes on either side have a very secure hold. The Osprey sometimes disappears from view when it hits the water. In the United States this bird is called the Fish Hawk.

How does the Secretary bird catch snakes?

The Secretary bird prefers to walk around looking for its prey rather than to fly. As a result its feet are less adapted for killing. The Secretary bird strides around African grasslands on its long legs hoping to disturb its prey. It catches insects, small mammals and lizards, but it is best known for eating snakes. It attacks a snake by shielding itself with open wings and trampling and battering the snake with its feet. Its long scaly legs give it good protection and eventually the snake is beaten to death.

(Right) South African farmers sometimes keep pet Secretary birds to control the snakes and rats on their land.

(Above) The falconer ties a bell around the foot of his bird so that if it flies out of sight he is still able to follow it.

What is falconry?

Falconry is the ancient practice of training birds of prey to kill for man. It dates back thousands of years, the earliest falconers probably using the birds as a means of obtaining food. It soon developed into a sport for kings and queens and the well-to-do, and became very fashionable during the Middle Ages in Europe. Today it is much less widely practised, but small groups of dedicated enthusiasts still train birds for this exciting sport. It is not a sport that anyone can take up, however. For a start, in most countries birds of prey are protected species and in Britain you need a licence to take one from the wild. Immense patience and understanding are needed to train the young birds to fly after prey, kill, and then return to the falconer. It is something you cannot teach yourself and for this reason the sport is exclusive.

The falconer's arm is protected from the bird's claws by a leather gauntlet. He holds the bird by leather straps called jesses which are attached to its feet.

(Left) A made-to-measure leather hood fits snugly over the heads of the falconer's birds, to prevent them being distracted before the moment of flight.

Are these birds really injured?

Some birds become very angry if their nesting sites are disturbed. Owls and terns, for example, show little fear and will not hesitate to attack an intruder. Other birds have developed more unusual ways of preventing the discovery of their nest. Pratincoles nest on the ground in regions of Asia, Africa, Australia and southern Europe. If you happen to stumble into a nesting area the birds would probably 'freeze' on their nests in the hope that you wouldn't notice them. If you show no sign of going away the pratincoles begin their distraction display. A group of about twenty birds flutters and crawls about, trailing wings and making plaintive cries. They look as if they are mortally injured. This display is very convincing and the intruder usually follows the birds, which look such easy game, and is skilfully led away from the eggs and chicks.

Male Ruffs develop a collar or ruff of brightly coloured feathers in the breeding season. In America Greater Prairie Chickens put on similar displays to attract females.

Why does a gull have a red spot on its beak?

You may have noticed a red, or sometimes a black spot near the end of a gull's beak. When the parent bird arrives at its nest the spot catches the eye of the newly hatched chick and it instinctively pecks at it. This action stimulates the parent bird to regurgitate some food from its crop and, of course, the chick promptly eats it. This form of communication between young and parent birds has been studied intensively in the Herring Gull. A series of cardboard models of bird heads were presented to chicks to test the pecking reaction. It was discovered that the chick would peck at more or less any shape, as long as the red spot was present. It seems that the red spot is all important in this curious 'begging' behaviour in young gulls.

In tests young gulls pecked at odd cardboard shapes with red spots but not at those without the spot.

A parent Herring Gull is stimulated to disgorge food from its crop by the pecking action of its young.

What are these Ruffs doing?

These birds are also putting on a display, but for a different reason. Whereas most birds pair up in the spring to build a nest and raise a family, male and female Ruffs come together only very briefly at this time. The male birds develop an elaborate head and neck plumage and they strut around in a special area of open ground called the 'lek'. Each defends his own small patch and all this showing-off activity attracts the females to the lek. After selecting the males of their choice, they mate and then go off to build the nest and lay the eggs.

What is the difference between pigeons and doves?

There is no real difference between pigeons and doves. In the pigeon family there are about three hundred species. Some of these are larger and plumper than the others and have square tails – these are often called pigeons. Others are smaller, sleeker and have pointed tails – these are usually called doves.

Pigeons have been kept by man since Roman times. In those days they were fattened for food. Later on they were used for carrying messages back to their roost and today they are used for racing. Special fancy varieties are also bred for showing, like these two *right*.

Of the many sorts of pigeons there are, you are probably familiar with at least one type depending on whether you live in the town or in the country. If you live in a town you probably know the feral pigeon only too well. These pigeons are descended from domesticated birds. They gather in enormous flocks in public places where people like to feed them. They usually make a nuisance of themselves by fouling pavements and buildings. If you live in the country you probably know the Wood Pigeon best. This pigeon is also considered a pest for it loves to feed on the farmer's crops, so that he has to wage continual war on it.

Two fancy pigeons, the fantail *(top)* and the pouter *(middle)*. The Rockdove *(above)* is the original pigeon from which the fancy varieties are bred.

What do macaws feed on?

The macaws are a group of large and vividly coloured parrots from tropical America. They are popular in zoos and also make good pets. They are quite easy to keep on a T-shaped perch and will often amuse their owner by learning to talk or mimic everyday sounds. It is not known for certain exactly what the macaw's diet is in the wild. It undoubtedly eats fruits, seeds and nuts – the powerful bill cracks open the hard shells of Brazil nuts with ease – but it also probably eats insects and their larvae. In captivity it is quite happy to accept peanuts, various types of seeds, fruit and meat.

Where do budgerigars live in the wild?

The parakeets are a widespread group of small Old World parrots. Best known is the Grass Parakeet or Budgerigar which is popular as a cage bird in so many homes. Budgerigars come from Australia. Large, chattering flocks feed among the grasses of the wide, inland plains. They eat the seeds of a variety of grasses, the fresh shoots of plants and any small insects they may discover while foraging. If you keep a budgie, do not be surprised if it snaps at a fly or other insect, for it is merely supplementing its diet like its wild relatives. Wild budgerigars are predominantly grass green in colour with yellow heads and blue tails. They make a spectacular sight as they flock each morning and evening to drink at a waterhole.

The Scarlet Macaw (above) from Mexico and Central America is the largest of the group at 3 feet in length. Two feet of this consists of the tail.

(Right) The name Budgerigar is derived from an aboriginal word 'betcherrygah' which means 'good food'.

What is the Laughing Jackass?

The Laughing Jackass or Kookaburra of Australia is a member of the kingfisher family of birds. Not all kingfishers live near streams and catch fishes. One group lives far from water and feeds on a variety of animals. The Laughing Jackass, 17 inches long, is the largest of this group and is probably best known for its raucous, cackling cry, which can sound almost human.

The Laughing Jackass *(above)* is a large kingfisher, valued in Australia for its preference for eating poisonous snakes. It either batters them to death, or flies up and drops them to the ground.

There are over three hundred types of hummingbirds found in the New World. All are small birds with beautiful, iridescent plumage. The Sword-billed Hummingbird is shown *above right.*

How do hummingbirds hover?

Hummingbirds have developed the most amazing powers of flight. They can fly straight up and down, forwards, sideways and backwards, and even hover stationary in front of a flower while probing with their bills. To be as manoeuvrable as this in the air, the hummingbird's wings have to beat at a very high speed. A definite hum is produced as these beautiful birds dart from flower to flower sipping sugary nectar, and their wings disappear into a faint blur. The secret of the hovering flight lies in the attachment of the hummingbird's wings to its shoulder. This is a swivel joint and instead of beating up and down, the wings swivel round to beat backwards and forwards in a figure of eight motion. At each stroke forwards and backwards air is forced downwards so that the hummingbird is able to 'hang' in the air. Hummingbirds use up an enormous amount of energy in this high-powered flight and are continually feeding on nectar rich in energy-giving sugars, and insects.

Which bird imprisons its mate?

Hornbills tend to nest in tree-holes, either natural or perhaps those left by woodpeckers. When the female is about to lay she is walled up in the hole by the male using a mixture of mud, regurgitated food and saliva. He leaves a small hole through which to feed his mate, who remains within the well-protected nest until the eggs have hatched.

The female hornbill may be confined for up to six weeks within the nest. Her mate is faithful to her all this time and gathers food to regurgitate through the hole for her to eat. Two hornbills from southern Asia are shown *left*.

(Left) A honeyguide leading the way through the African forest to a wild bees' nest. The bird usually enlists the help of a honey badger but has been known to lead Africans to a nest for the same purpose.

Which bird leads the way to honey?

Honeyguides are a small group of African birds that feed mainly on insects. They are particularly fond of bees and wasps and some will even enter bees' nests to snap up the insects and their larvae. One or two honeyguides are actually known to eat the beeswax of which the nests are constructed. This is a very rare habit among birds. Even more interesting is the way the birds enlist the help of a honey badger to break open the nest so that they can get at the beeswax. Once a honeyguide discovers an occupied nest it flies off for a short distance and then chatters loudly from a low bush. A honey badger attracted by the urgent

The beautifully coloured bill of the Sulphur Toucan.

The toucan's bill is very useful for fruit picking.

calling moves towards the bird which promptly flies off a few yards and chatters again. When the badger has caught up, off goes the bird again until the badger eventually finds the nest. The honeyguide waits patiently while the nest is broken open. As soon as the honey badger has eaten its fill of honey and has moved away, the bird flies down for its share.

Why do toucans have such large bills?

The enormous, gaily coloured bills of toucans look heavy and ungainly but in fact the birds manage very well with them. The bill is not as heavy as it looks. A network of bony fibres is covered with a hard, horny sheath making the bill remarkably strong and light. It is not known exactly why toucans have such large bills. As fruit-eaters they must find the length useful for reaching out to pluck berries from branches that would not support their weight. They pick berries with the very tip and have to toss them into the air and catch them in their throats to eat them. It is unlikely that the bill evolved as an offensive weapon, but its impressive size may have had some value in frightening off would-be attackers. Another suggestion is that the distinctive colours and prominence of the bill may help the toucans with similar body colouring to recognize each other in the forest. Alternatively, the bright colours may act as signals between the birds either in aggressive displays or in courtship behaviour.

How long is the woodpecker's tongue?

Drilling the bark of trees with a chisel-like bill, the woodpecker exposes the tunnels of wood-boring insect larvae. It flicks in its tongue (up to 6 inches long in the Green Woodpecker) and stabs the grubs with the barbed tip to withdraw them.

Special bones and elastic tissues support the woodpecker's long tongue coiled up within its head (right).

How does the bowerbird attract a mate?

Most male birds advertise their presence to the females in the breeding season by bright plumage. The male bowerbird, however, displays no impressive finery and so must resort to alternative means of attracting a mate. Instead, he builds her an elaborate bower and decorates it with brightly coloured objects in order to impress her. There are seventeen species in the bowerbird group and four types of courting activity are shown. The first group does not bother with a bower at all. The second group, called 'stage-makers', clears an area of ground and lays freshly picked leaves on it. Other bowerbirds, 'maypole-builders', heap twigs around the base of a sapling until the pile is several feet high. Another heap around a neighbouring tree is joined to the first to form a tent-like bower, often with an associated 'garden'. The bird decorates the walls and floor with fresh flowers, mosses, bright berries and snails' shells. The most elaborate bowers are those of the 'avenue-builders'. The bird first lays down a floor of twigs. Then two walls of interwoven twigs are erected, arched at the top, and also decorated with objects such as pebbles, feathers and flowers. Two species even daub the walls with colouring using leaves or bark as a 'brush'.

(Above) The Golden Bowerbird builds a less elaborate maypole bower. Once the birds have mated, the female goes off alone to build a nest and lay the eggs, and the bower is abandoned.

Bowerbirds come from New Guinea and Australia. They are among the few groups of birds known to use a tool (see page 196). The bowerbird, *left*, from New Guinea has built a maypole bower and garden.

Which birds have the most attractive displays?

Of all the birds, the bird of paradise develops the most varied of spectacular plumage during the breeding season. The tails of the males are usually elaborated into beautiful fans with a pair of extra-long feathers trailing down behind. Some birds are adorned with long neck feathers which can be erected in colourful ruffs around their heads. Others hang upside-down from branches and their long plumage hangs around them, creating elegant displays.

Naturally such beautiful birds did not go unnoticed when their home, the island of New Guinea, was first explored in the sixteenth century. A tremendous trade in the birds' skins grew up to satisfy the fashion demands of the nineteenth century. Many birds became endangered. Fortunately the trade in bird of paradise feathers is now controlled and so the birds have a chance to recover their numbers.

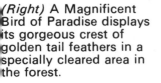

(Right) A Magnificent Bird of Paradise displays its gorgeous crest of golden tail feathers in a specially cleared area in the forest.

(Below) The Jay is called a 'passive anter' because it allows ants to run all over it while standing still.

Why is this Jay covered in ants?

The Jay is deliberately letting the wood ants run all over its wings and body by standing near their nest with its wings spread. This is called 'anting' and many birds have been seen doing it, although others actually rub the ants into their feathers. It is thought that the formic acid from the ants (which makes the sting when the ant bites) stimulates the birds' plumage, and may perhaps act as an insecticide.

What is the Australian teddy bear?

Practically everyone has owned a teddy bear as a child, but not everyone realizes that the animal it is modelled on is not a bear at all. Bears are placental mammals whereas the Koala, which is often called the Australian teddy bear, is another marsupial mammal grouped with the phalanger family. It is interesting that a number of the marsupials restricted to the Australian region look and act like placental mammals found in other continents. The gliding phalanger is very much like the flying squirrel for example. Why is this?

Two more Australian marsupials from the phalanger family: the monkey-like Spotted Cuscus *(top)* and the Brush-tailed Phalanger *(above)*.

About fifty million years ago Australia became cut off from the other continents as the mammals evolved. This allowed the marsupials to adapt themselves to live in every kind of habitat, free from competition from the more advanced placental mammals. In every other continent the placentals flourished and replaced the marsupials so that apart from Australia (and America where some opossums have somehow managed to survive), marsupials are found nowhere else in the world. So, in separate continents, representatives from two unrelated groups of mammals became adapted to live in all the available habitats. Where particular conditions were the same in either continent, the animals which evolved to suit them bear similarities in shape and behaviour. This phenomenon is called *parallel* or *convergent evolution*.

(Left) The young Koala stays with its mother for six months after leaving the pouch and often rides pick-a-back.

What does the Koala eat?

The Koala is a very specialized eater. It feeds only on the leaves of the eucalyptus tree. It will not eat any eucalyptus leaves, however, but only those that are young and tender, and even then it will eat only the very tips. Added to these preferences, some races or varieties of Koala will eat only the leaves from particular types of eucalyptus tree. The fussy feeding habits of the Koala and its inability to adapt to alternative foods make the animal particularly vulnerable. The felling of eucalyptus forests, forest fires and, in the past, the shooting of Koalas for their skins, have sadly reduced their numbers.

(Above) The tiny embryo kangaroo crawls up its mother's fur to the safety of the pouch.

(Right) Once there it quickly finds a nipple and starts to suckle.

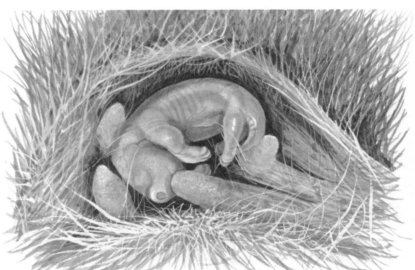

(Below) The baby kangaroo is suckled for eight months within the pouch. After leaving its mother it still frequently returns to her for milk for another six months.

How is a baby kangaroo born?

Until about twenty years ago nobody was really sure how baby kangaroos were born. As in all marsupials, the kangaroo is born prematurely and completes its development within the pouch of its mother. What was not known, however, was how the tiny embryo managed to get into the pouch. Some people maintained the mother placed it there with her mouth, others denied this. We now know that before giving birth the mother squats down and licks her pouch and the fur down to her birth opening. The tiny inch-long embryo appears and crawls slowly up her wet fur towards the pouch. In three minutes it has climbed in and quickly closed its mouth over one of the nipples. The tip swells inside its mouth and holds it securely within the pouch while it is being suckled.

What are solenodons?

Solenodons are curious rat-sized creatures with long snouts. They were once found in North America but the only survivors of this ancient group are found on two islands of the West Indies, one species on Cuba and another on Haiti. Solenodons are members of a primitive group of mammals called insectivores. These were the first placental mammals and in general the representatives we know today are small creatures (shrew-like, mole-like or hedgehog-like) which feed on a variety of invertebrates. Solenodons are shy creatures, sleeping during the day and appearing at night to feed. They run clumsily on their toes in a zig-zag course and if chased are likely to trip over.

(Below left) Solenodons have managed to survive on two West Indian islands. Competition from man and introduced higher mammals (dogs and cats for example) has made them rare animals and they seem doomed to extinction.

In many insect-eating bats the nose is obscured by highly folded flaps of skin. Two examples are shown *above* and *below*. It is thought that this 'nose-leaf' concentrates the high-pitched squeaks emitted from the bats' nostrils, and even possibly directs them.

Which mammals really fly?

True flapping flight, almost as proficient as that of the birds, has been achieved by only one group of mammals, the bats. Bats probably evolved from a group of early insectivores that fed by leaping from the branches of trees to catch passing insects. It is interesting that bats fly by cupping their wings in front of the body and dragging this air behind them, rather than flapping their wings up and down.

Bats can be arranged into two large groups: fruit-eaters and insect-eaters. In general the fruit-eaters are large, can see well and fly in dim light. Insect-eaters are usually smaller, have poor eyesight and have developed a good system of

echo-location to enable them to fly in pitch blackness. By sending out series of ultrasonic squeaks and listening for the returning echoes with very efficient ears, the bats can navigate their way around obstacles and catch their insect prey in darkness.

Which mole has a star on its nose?

Moles, also members of the insectivore group of primitive mammals, are burrowing creatures completely adapted for an underground life. A mole on the surface can hardly move forwards at all but once burrowing it quickly disappears from sight. Short but powerful clawed limbs stick out sideways and shovel the soil behind the mole as it tunnels forwards. Moles cannot see very well, some are blind, but they have very highly developed senses of hearing and touch. To perfect its sense of touch, the North American Star-nosed Mole has a remarkable bunch of twenty-two tentacles on the end of its nose. These are highly sensitive and mobile and are brought into use when the mole is searching for food, usually under water.

(Above) The Star-nosed Mole lives near water and dives for its food which it detects with the sensitive feelers on its nose.

The hearing of insect-eating bats is well developed. The Mouse-eared Bat *(above)* is appropriately named. The fruit bats *(right)* feed on dates, figs and bananas.

How advanced are the primates?

You would think that a group of mammals that included man would be the most advanced in the animal kingdom. This is not so, however. Of course, as a single species man has become the most intelligent and successful animal, but the group to which he belongs is quite primitive. The primate group branched off from the insectivores, the first placental mammals to appear. They did this by taking to the trees, becoming more active, developing grasping hands and feet and good eyesight. However, other primate features are still quite primitive when compared to further developments in other mammal groups. Primates still have five fingers and toes, for example, and simple teeth.

Indrises are found only on Madagascar. The two shown *below* are Verreaux's Sifaka *(left)* and the Indris *(right)*. Both are fond of basking in the sun among the treetops, turning over when one side is 'done'.

(Below) The Aye-Aye is another strange primate restricted to Madagascar. Its middle finger is very long and by tapping it along a branch it can detect the presence of grubs in the wood. These are quickly hooked out with the same long finger and eaten.

What are the main primate groups?

The primates are a large group of very varied animals ranging from the small, squirrel-like treeshrews to man himself. The first major division is into less advanced primates and more advanced primates. The former (prosimians) includes treeshrews, lemurs, bushbabies, indrises, the Aye-Aye, lorises and tarsiers. The more advanced primates (anthropoids) include monkeys from both the Old and New Worlds, the apes and man himself. The anthropoids have more expressive faces than the prosimians and are more intelligent. They are active during the day whereas a number of the prosimians are active only at night.

How did the Indris get its name?

Not many people have seen an Indris. It lives only in small groups on the island of Madagascar in the tree-tops of dense mountain forests. It is an odd-looking primate and at first glance could be mistaken for a long-legged man with a foxy face, crouching up a tree, wearing woolly gloves. The European to discover this primate called it an Indris because it was first pointed out to him by a native jumping up and down shouting '*indris izy*!' All the observant man was really saying in his own language was, 'There it is!' Indrises have the interesting habit of sunbathing holding their hands out to the sun to warm them.

(Below) Galagos or bushbabies are prosimian primates usually grouped with the lorises. They have long bushy tails and sleep in communal 'dormitories' during the day. The Fat-tailed Galago *(left)* is shown with a bushbaby *(right)*.

Which are the strangest-looking primates?

(Above) There are three species of tarsier from the Philippines, Sumatra and Borneo and the Celebes. The disc-like pads on the fingers increase the tarsier's grip. Treefrogs possess a similar feature (see page 105).

The tiny tarsiers have a strong claim to this title with their large ears and enormous staring eyes. The eyes are perhaps the most fascinating feature of these curious creatures. They are completely circular, set quite close together and stare straight forwards. If your eyes were in the same proportion to the size of your face as the tarsier's are, they would be at least as big as dinner plates. Tarsiers are nocturnal, as you might expect with eyes this big, and they spring from branch to branch catching insects, lizards and spiders. They are very agile, easily leaping distances of 6 feet, balanced by the long tail trailing out behind.

(Left) The gibbons are the smallest of the apes but the most agile of all the mammals. Their very long arms are ideal for swinging along under the branches, and gibbons fling themselves across gaps of up to 30 feet.

What is the difference between monkeys and apes?

All the primates on these pages are apes. The apes are divided into three groups: the gibbons, the great apes, and man. Apes differ from monkeys by being tailless, having arms longer than legs and by being more intelligent.

Chimpanzees spend most of their time on the ground in the wild but climb trees to 'make their beds'.

Where do chimpanzees sleep?

Every night the chimpanzee spends five minutes making its bed for the night. It bends two or three leafy branches together to make a platform quite high up in the trees. It curls up on its side with legs drawn up and soon falls asleep.

Who is the 'old man of the woods'?

The remarkable human features of the elderly Orang-utan led to it being referred to by this name. As it grows old the male Orang grows a moustache and beard, the rest of the face remaining hairless. It often develops a pot belly, its skin becomes wrinkled, and its cheeks and throat grow flabby as flaps of loose skin develop. Orangs usually live in trees, but old, fat males find they no longer have the strength to swing through the branches and so sit around on the ground instead. Like the chimpanzees, Orang-utans make a tree platform to serve as a bed for the night. The Orang's bed is improved, however, by the addition of a shelter to keep the rain off the animal while it is asleep.

There are two varieties of Orang-utan, one from Sumatra and one from Borneo. A female *(left)* and male *(right)* Borneo Orang are shown *below*. The males grow to twice the size of the females and may weigh as much as a man.

The largest of the primates, the Gorilla *(below)*, is in fact a gentle giant and prefers to avoid any contact with man.

Why do Gorillas beat their chests?

Everybody has been impressed by the size of the male Gorilla at the zoo. He can stand over $5\frac{1}{2}$ feet tall, weigh 28 stone, with an arm span of 8 feet. In the wild he gives a terrifying, angry display if he is suddenly disturbed. He rises up on his hind legs, roars loudly and runs sideways, beating his chest and throwing plants into the air. In spite of all these threats, a Gorilla has never, in fact, been known to attack a man face to face. All gorillas beat their chests and in females and youngsters it is thought that this is a way of releasing tension in the animal.

Sloths are either called two-toed *(below)* or three-toed *(left)* but this really refers to the number of fingers on the front feet. Both kinds have three toes on the hind feet.

Which animal spends its life upside-down?

In contrast to the acrobatic antics of the monkeys and apes, sloths move about the tree-tops in very slow motion. They hang underneath the branches from hooked claws of both the fingers and toes, and spend most of their lives in this upside-down position. They eat, sleep, mate and even give birth to their young upside-down. There are two interesting features of a sloth related to its upside-down way of life. The first is its ability to turn its head almost right round to compensate for its reversed position. The second is the way its hair lies in the opposite direction to that of most animals. The sloth's hair runs from its belly round to its back, and this ensures that heavy tropical showers run straight off.

Some people claim that the Giant Anteater *(left)* uses its long bushy tail to sweep ants into piles before licking them up.

Why does the anteater walk on its knuckles?

If you look closely at the feet of the Giant Anteater at the bottom of the opposite page, you will notice that they look slightly odd. The anteaters are animals with a specialized diet, feeding on termites, ants and their larvae. Specialized feeders usually have special features. The anteaters have strong claws on the front feet to break open termite nests, and a long narrow mouth with an equally long sticky tongue, to probe around and lick up the insects. It seems that the anteater walks on the knuckles of its front feet to protect the curved claws and to keep them sharp.

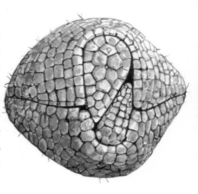

Most armadillos can curl up a little to protect themselves from predators. The Three-banded Armadillo rolls up completely to avoid attack.

Which animals are armoured?

The armadillos are well protected by a shell of bony plates covering the back and sides of the body. The skin of the head, tail and legs is also thickened and scaly so that the animals have an impressive, heavily armoured look. The main shell is divided across the back into a number of bands allowing some degree of movement. The number of bands varies in the different species of armadillo. Armadillos are strong burrowers and can soon disappear from sight into the ground if alarmed. One species is able to roll itself up completely into a ball.

Sloths, anteaters and armadillos comprise a group of primitive but specialized animals called the edentates. They are all found in South and Central America. These armadillos *(left)* are Nine-banded.

275

All the animals on this page are rodents. Rodents make up an enormous group of gnawing mammals which are grouped into squirrel-like, mouse-like and porcupine-like animals.

How far can a jerboa jump?

The long tail of the jerboa *(below)* balances it in a long hop and props it up when the animal is resting.

Jerboas are small rodents that look rather like miniatur kangaroos. Their back legs are four times as long as the front legs, and the tail is longer than the head and body pu together. Like kangaroos they travel by leaps and bound and at top speed can cover 10 feet in a single jump. The ta trails behind and helps to balance the jerboa as it shoot through the air, often faster than the eye can see. Jerboa live in desert areas of Asia and Africa and escape the fierc heat of the day by hiding in cool underground burrows.

Can a porcupine shoot out its quills?

Porcupines of the Old World are burrowers whereas thos of the New World climb trees. Both have thousands c needle-sharp quills which are erected and rattled as a warn ing if the animal is attacked. The porcupine turns its bac and either runs backwards to drive the quills into the in truder or angrily lashes its tail causing loose quills to fly ou In neither case are the quills actually fired.

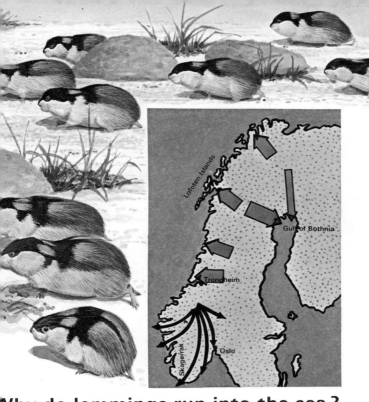

When numbers of lemmings become too great for a particular area they stream away in all directions in search of fresh food. Only some arrive at the coast and attempt to swim the ocean. The map shows the migration routes of two kinds of lemmings from Scandinavia.

Why do lemmings run into the sea?

You may have heard stories about lemmings flinging themselves from cliffs in their thousands to perish in the sea. This is only part of the whole story. The Norwegian Lemming lives high up on the mountainside and normally produces several litters of young each year. If conditions for breeding are particularly favourable over two or three years, exceptional numbers of lemmings are produced. This is called a population explosion. The available food is quickly eaten and then large numbers of lemmings migrate in all directions in search of fresh areas. They seem to panic and rush headlong down the mountains streaming through rivers, over walls and other obstacles. Usually these migrations die out inconspicuously but where a stream of lemmings reaches a cliff-top the result is spectacular.

Two species of Old World porcupine are shown *below*. They need to be treated with care for it is very difficult and painful to remove a quill which has pierced the skin.

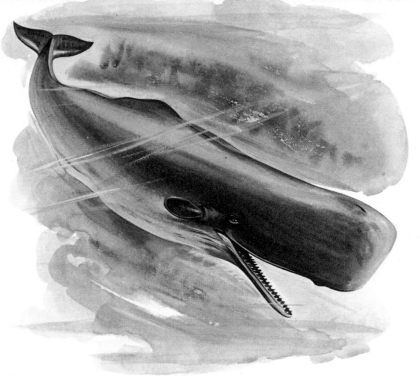

Dolphins *(above)* differ from porpoises *(below)* by having a beak, a narrower head and a different shape of the dorsal fin.

(Above) The Sperm Whale is a toothed whale which appears to be all head. It is a valuable whale and has been ruthlessly hunted by man for centuries.

(Below) The Killer Whale is reputed to be the most ferocious animal of the sea. It hunts in packs and will feed on anything including seals, sealions, penguins and even other whales.

What makes whales mammals?

The whales are a large group of aquatic animals that var in size from about 4 feet in length to nearly 100 feet. Durin the evolution of mammals tens of millions of years ago on group returned to live in water. These mammals becam streamlined in shape, developed a powerful tail and fron limbs for use as steering fins, and lost the use of the bac limbs. Whales, descendants of this group, are mamma because they breathe air, are warm-blooded and suckle thei young with milk. They have lost the mammalian coat o hair in order to help them swim, but they have replaced with an insulating coat of thick blubber.

In America the Common Porpoise *(below)* is called the Harbor Porpoise.

How do whales feed?

We all know that the whales are huge mammals (the Blue Whale is probably the largest animal that has ever lived on the earth) but it may surprise you to learn that the biggest whales feed on the tiny organisms that make up plankton. There are two sorts of whales; the toothed whales and the baleen whales. The toothed whales have rows of large but quite ordinary teeth and catch crustaceans, squids, fishes and some smaller marine mammals. Instead of teeth, the baleen whales grow thin plates of horny outgrowths (whale-bone) from the roof of the mouth, which hang down on both sides of the mouth. These plates filter out tons of plankton from the water as the whale cruises along with its mouth gaping. As the mouth closes, water is forced out through the plates, and the whale's huge tongue licks off the plankton and pushes it down its throat.

(Below left) The red arrow in this drawing shows the flow of water out through the sieve of baleen plates of a baleen whale. Some plates have been removed to make this clearer. (Rub your tongue over the roof of your mouth and you will feel the ridges similar to those from which the plates of the baleen whale have been developed.)

(Below) The dimensions of the Blue Whale are breathtaking. A 100-ton specimen and a cart-horse are shown here drawn to the same scale.

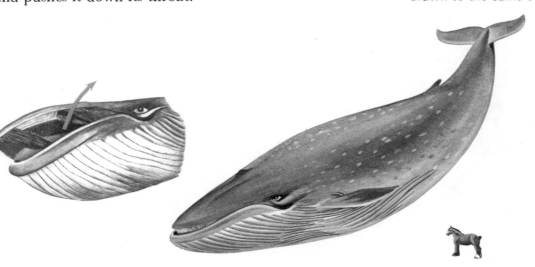

Do whales spout water?

You have no doubt seen films or photographs of whales sending up impressive plumes of what looks very much like water. The usual cry of whalers is 'Thar she blows!' for this was and occasionally still is the way the whales are spotted. However, the spout is not so much water as steam. After a dive lasting perhaps up to an hour, the used air in the whale's lungs becomes hot and laden with moisture. As it rolls on the surface the whale opens its single nostril, the blowhole, and blasts this warm humid air into air which is often freezing cold. The moisture in the whale's breath immediately condenses and it is this that pin-points its position as a spout visible from a considerable distance.

Which dog cannot bark?

The Dingo is one of the very few dogs in the world that is unable to bark. It is not a silent dog, however, as it makes up for not barking by howling and whining very loudly indeed. Dingoes are a very ancient breed of wild dog from Australia. They are probably quite closely related to the primitive dogs from which our domestic dogs of today evolved. Dingoes must have arrived in Australia with the first Aborigines to settle there from Asia. They soon went wild although the Aborigines of today still rear pups and train them for hunting. Dingoes are considered a pest in Australia because of the large number of sheep and cattle they kill every year.

The dog family belongs to a large group of mammals called the carnivores. This name means flesh-eater and apart from one or two exceptions they all have strong jaws and sharp teeth for killing and tearing the flesh from their prey.

Apart from its inability to bark, the Dingo differs from other dogs by not being able to lower its ears. A Dingo is shown living in an Aborigine camp *(left)*.

(Below) These Asiatic, or Golden, Jackals also belong to the dog family and generally live by scavenging near towns and cities.

Which dog looks like a fox on stilts?

This strange description has been used for the Maned Wolf, and if you have been lucky enough to see one in a zoo, you would understand why. The dog's fox-like body is balanced on extremely long, slender legs which give the animal a rather elegant look. As you might expect, the Maned Wolf is a good runner and ranges widely in search of prey over

The Maned Wolf is said to run faster than any other member of the dog family.

open country and small areas of forest in South America. It is rarely seen because it hunts at night and is a very wary animal.

How many wolves are there in a wolf-pack?

Each autumn the cubs born to a pair of wolves join their parents in hunting as a family group. A typical wolf-pack like this may have five members, but if the winter is particularly hard, family packs join up to form a larger pack. A large wolf-pack rarely has more than thirty wolves, however.

(Below) By hunting in packs, wolves are able to attack and kill large animals such as the moose.

Which is the biggest bear?

Imagine a bear 10 feet long, standing 4 feet tall at the shoulder and weighing nearly a ton. This is the size of the largest bear (and therefore the largest carnivore) there is, the Kodiak Bear from Alaska. You might wonder how dangerous such an enormous bear would be if you suddenly disturbed it in a clearing. Bears tend to be unpredictable creatures and often attack with no warning at all. The chances are that your encounter would be very dangerous indeed. Do not be misled by the bear's slow, lumbering movements. It is a very powerful animal and can quickly move in range to deliver deadly blows from its huge front paws. Bears do not kill by hugging but by swiping their paws, armed with sharp claws, at their prey.

Grizzly Bears and Kodiak Bears are thought to be of the same family as the Brown Bear. Brown Bears *(right)* are widely distributed and vary a lot in appearance over their range.

Which bears wear 'glasses'?

A small bear from tropical South America has rather odd face markings. The bear has a creamy yellow snout, and fur of the same colour runs from its nose in various patterns. Sometimes the lines of lighter fur encircle the eyes and cross the nose, giving the bear the comical appearance of wearing a pair of glasses. Not surprisingly the bear has come to be called the Spectacled Bear although the markings are never the same in any two bears. Some Spectacled Bears may have only the bottom half of their 'glasses', whereas in others the eye rings are so thick they completely fill the face.

All bears can climb trees but the Spectacled Bear is particularly expert at clambering among the branches to feed on leaves, fruit and nuts.

Which is the smallest bear?

The Sun Bear from southern Asia is not much bigger than a large dog, in contrast to the mighty size of the Kodiak Bear. The little Sun Bear is about 4 feet long with a 2-inch tail, and stands 2 feet tall at the shoulder. It is another bear with an odd marking, this time on the chest. Some individuals have a crescent shape in lighter fur on their front which, in the East, is said to represent the rising sun – hence the bear's name. The Sun Bear spends most of its time clambering through the tree tops in search of food. It will eat any small animals it can catch, lizards and baby birds for example, honey from wild bees' nests and some fruit.

(Above) Another excellent climber, the Sun Bear displays its characteristic chest markings from the fork of a tree.

Polar bears *(right)* are also very fast movers on ice, and can lumber along at speeds of up to 18 mph. Hair on the soles of their feet prevents them from slipping.

How well can the Polar Bear swim?

It is difficult to imagine a large, bulky animal like a bear being able to swim very far. The Polar Bear is a remarkable swimmer and has been reported swimming strongly out at sea more than 200 miles from the nearest land. The Polar Bear has a long neck and by thrusting its head out of the water and paddling with its wide front paws alone, it is able to swim steadily for long periods (actually much faster than you can walk). These bears live among the shifting pack-ice and freezing waters of the Arctic Ocean. A less inviting place for a swim would be difficult to imagine. The Polar Bear is well insulated from the cold by a thick layer of blubber and a long, thick coat of fur. Polar Bears have a varied diet but prey mainly on seals.

Although Giant Pandas are particularly partial to the tender young shoots of bamboo, they have been known to eat other food. Grasses, roots, irises and crocuses and small rodents, birds and fishes are all eaten from time to time by Giant Pandas.

What does the Giant Panda eat?

The Giant Panda has been adopted by the World Wildlife Fund to symbolize the plight of rare and endangered animals throughout the world.

Practically everyone must remember the publicity that accompanied the attempts at persuading Chi-chi and An-an to mate at the London and Moscow Zoos. However, did you know that although the Giant Panda looks very bear-like, it is in fact more closely related to the raccoons? We don't know all that much about the Giant Panda, but we do know that it is a specialized feeder. Its particular preference is for tender, young bamboo shoots, and so naturally its distribution in the wild is restricted to bamboo forests. These tend to occur in inaccessible mountainous areas of Central China, and the Giant Panda has not yet been properly studied in its natural habitat. Only a very small number of animals are kept in zoos outside China and little is known about the animal's breeding behaviour. Great excitement was shown when An-an was twice introduced to Chi-chi in the hope that he would mate with her. Alas, Chi-chi refused all his approaches.

Sea Otters even sleep floating on their backs and often wrap long strands of seaweed around their bodies to prevent themselves from drifting away. They were once abundant along the Pacific coasts but are now rare, and a protected species.

Why is this Sea Otter carrying a stone?

Otters are long, slim creatures with short paddle-like webbed feet. They are excellent swimmers. Some species live in the fresh waters of rivers and lakes while others are marine animals and live in the shallow waters of rocky coasts and islands. The Sea Otter rarely leaves the water and a lot of its time is spent floating idly on its back. It feeds on hard-shelled marine invertebrates and deals with them in a characteristic way. It dives down to collect molluscs and crabs together with a flat stone from the bottom. While floating on its back it rests the stone on its chest and smashes the shells of the animals on it, eating only their soft bodies. The Sea Otter is one of the very few mammals to use a tool.

How big are the largest otters?

The biggest otters live in the slow-moving rivers of South America. These Giant Otters are, incredibly, 6 feet long on average, some specimens reaching 7 feet. They are stream-lined animals and rarely leave the water. When they do, their stumpy legs are of little use and they have to resort to sliding along on their bellies.

(Left) A Giant Otter standing, propped up by its tail. These enormous otters are rarely seen on dry land.

Palm civets from southern Asia are smaller than most civets, and spend more time in trees. *(From top to bottom):* the Common Palm Civet; the Masked Palm Civet; and the large Indian Civet.

Why do civets smell?

The characteristic odour of a civet is enough to make your nose wrinkle. The smell comes from a liquid called musk secreted from glands near the civet's reproductive organs. The musk is a valuable substance and in parts of Africa civets are kept on farms and the musk collected from them several times a week. You must be wondering what possible use such a strange liquid could have. The clear, yellow liquid is collected in very small amounts and sent all over the world to the makers of the most expensive perfumes. Musk is used as a fixative in perfume making because it contains certain important oils and fats. A fixative is a substance that helps to bring out and preserve the scents of other ingredients of the perfume. Although the musk smells awful when it is secreted by the civet, once it is diluted, it begins to smell quite pleasant. The strange thing is that it is the male civets which have the more powerful smell in order to attract the females. The scent that women wear today has the opposite effect of course, by attracting men. Civets are cat-like carnivores with long bodies and tails and pointed noses.

How does a Mongoose kill a snake?

The Mongoose is best known for being able to attack and kill large poisonous snakes such as cobras. It is a slender, weasel-like animal, and the secret of its success against

(Left) The 5-foot Binturong, or Bear Cat, is the largest of all the civets. It is the only Old World Mammal to have a prehensile tail.

snakes lies in its wonderful agility. At a confrontation, the cobra rears up and faces the mongoose. The mongoose entices the snake to strike but at the same instant nimbly sidesteps the lunging fangs and crushes the snake's head in its jaws.

There are over forty species of mongooses from southern Asia, Africa and Madagascar. They all look very much alike and have similar habits. An Indian Mongoose is shown *above*.

Are hyenas cowardly?

Hyenas seem to have gained a reputation for cowardice. They are well-adapted for killing their own prey, however, but although strong, cannot run at high speeds for any distance. Instead of being active predators themselves, their role in life seems to be clearing up after other animals. They feed on carrion and scavenge the remains of carcases left by lions, tigers and other big cats. Short, powerful jaws crunch through bones of any size and hyenas leave hardly a scrap of waste from such meat. If driven by hunger they will kill for themselves but even then will, more often than not, only attack a young or defenceless animal offering no resistance. Hyenas have been known to hunt in packs, however, harrying a zebra until it could be overcome by cooperative effort.

There are two well-known species of hyena: the Striped and the Spotted *(right)*, and a third, rare, Brown Hyena, all of which come from Africa.

The African Elephant *(left)* spends more time in the open and the large surface area of its ears speeds the loss of heat from its body. This is why African Elephants flap their ears to keep cool.

What is the largest living land mammal?

The largest land mammal living today is the African Elephant. A fully grown male measures 11 feet high at the shoulders and may weigh over 6 tons. It eats 700 pounds of vegetation and drinks over 50 gallons of water in a day, its trunk having a capacity of $1\frac{1}{2}$ gallons. It can walk at 4 miles an hour, which is about as fast as a man can walk, but it can run at an impressive 30 miles an hour but is unable to jump the smallest of obstacles. There is another species of elephant found today. The Indian Elephant has smaller ears, a more rounded back, a trunk with one 'finger' at the end (rather than two), a domed forehead and a smaller overall size.

The Indian Elephant *(below)* spends most of its time in dense shade.

The Indian Elephant *(right)* is found in dense forests of Sri Lanka (Ceylon), Burma, Thailand and Malaya. The African Elephant is found in most parts of Africa south of the Sahara.

Can an elephant drink through its trunk?

This is the equivalent of asking, 'Can you drink through your nose?' and of course the answer is no. The elephant's trunk is an extension of its nose and upper lip. It does not just hang limply but can be operated to carry out a vast range of tasks. The most important of these is food gathering. The sensitive finger (or fingers) at the tip of the trunk enables the elephant to pluck foliage and pass it into the mouth. The trunk is also used as a hose pipe. It can squirt water or dust over the elephant, and can also squirt over a gallon of water straight in to the mouth when the elephant is drinking. Other uses are as a snorkel or breathing tube when the elephant is swimming, as a lifting device, as a weapon for defence and lastly, for smelling, of course.

Rock Hyraxes *(below)* live on mountain slopes and among rocky outcrops. They are very active and can jump directly upwards and balance well.

Why are the hyraxes a puzzle?

Both Rock Hyraxes and Tree Hyraxes *(above)* have padded feet which act as suction cups to increase their grip. They are kept moist by sweat glands on the soles.

This small group of rabbit-sized animals from Africa has confused zoologists for a long time. Nobody has been really sure how the hyraxes are related to other larger mammals because they show an odd mixture of features. Some have teeth like rhinoceroses, others like hippopotamuses. The bone structure of their front legs and feet is like that of an elephant, as is the shape of their brain. Their back legs and feet resemble those of an ancestor of the horse and their stomach is also horse-like. Other features are intermediate between rodents and hoofed animals. It is now thought that hyraxes may have descended from a group of animals that eventually gave rise to the elephants, rhinoceroses, hippopotamuses and horses as we know them today.

What are sea-cows?

If cows lived in the sea what would they be like? They would probably be large, slow-moving mammals living in herds and feeding by grazing across beds of seaweeds. There is a group of animals that fits this description, and not surprisingly, they are called sea-cows. After the whales, sea-cows are the group of mammals most adapted to an aquatic life. Like the whales they have lost their back limbs and instead have a horizontally flattened tail. The front limbs are flippers and they have practically no hair on the skin. The two groups are unrelated, however, for the whale's ancestors were carnivores whereas those of the sea-cows were herbivorous. There are four species of sea-cows. One is the Dugong and the other three are called manatees. The Dugong has a notched tail, while that of the manatee is more rounded and paddle-shaped.

Who thought sea-cows were mermaids?

Imagine you had been a sailor on an early sailing ship passing through shallow coastal waters in the tropics. You might have been at sea for many months, and heard all sorts of seamen's yarns and tales. Suddenly a strange animal reared up out of the water to watch the ship pass. It had a fish-like tail and a face that could be vaguely human. As you look closer at this strange creature you discover that it is suckling a baby by holding it to its breast. What would you think it was? Without knowing all about sea-cows you might be excused for imagining that you had seen a mermaid, and it is thought that this is how many mermaid stories arose hundreds of years ago. Today, looking at the bald head and the wrinkled and hairy face of the Dugong, it is difficult to imagine mistaking it for a beautiful mermaid.

The Dugong *(left and above)* is found from the Indian Ocean to the northern coasts of Australia. It reaches a length of about 8 or 9 feet.

Manatees *(left)* grow up to 15 feet in length and can weigh 500 pounds.

How do sea-cows graze?

The Dugong and the manatees have slightly different methods of grazing the lush beds of vegetation that grow in the sheltered waters of tropical coasts and estuaries. The Dugong has an enormous upper lip which curls over the seaweed, pressing it against the lower lip so that it can be plucked. The manatees have a notched upper lip divided into two lobes which work against one another. These make a very good gripping organ. The manatees pluck enormous quantities of seaweed (up to 100 pounds a day), and the front flippers help by cramming the greenstuff into the mouth while it is chewed. As sea-cows are grazers, their teeth are continually wearing down. Instead of each tooth growing to replace wear, the old teeth drop out at the front of the mouth, and new ones appear at the back on a conveyor system.

The three species of manatee are the North American from the Caribbean area, the South American *(right)* and the West African.

Which hoofed mammals are odd-toed?

It seems strange to refer to animals as either odd-toed or even-toed but that is how the two groups of mammals that are hoofed – the ungulates – are distinguished. The herbivorous ungulates evolved on firm grassy plains – ideal places for running at high speed. The fewer fingers and toes an animal has the faster it can run. This is why you run on the very tips of your toes when you sprint for a bus, to give you more spring forwards. The fingers and toes of the ungulates became reduced, their remaining claws developed into hooves and their legs lengthened to allow fast galloping across the plains. If you draw a straight line down the middle of an ungulate's foot (this is called an axis), in some it will pass through the middle finger or toe. During the evolution of these ungulates this finger or toe has become lengthened and developed into the hoof, while the toes on either side have become lost or reduced. So the hoof is either made up of just one toe or of three in these ungulates, and they are therefore called odd-toed. Today's representatives of this group are horses, asses and zebras, and tapirs and rhinoceroses.

It is not known exactly how the domestic horse *(above)* was derived from wild horses and so it is regarded as a separate species. It is interesting to compare its appearance with the wild horse *(above left)*.

The rare Asiatic Wild Ass is now a protected species in remote areas of Asia. It is thought that the domestic donkey was derived from the African Wild Ass, now believed to be on the verge of extinction.

Are there any truly wild horses?

Apart from the zebras, which also belong to the horse family, the only really wild horse found today is Przewalski's Wild Horse and the Asiatic and African Wild Ass. Another wild horse, the Tarpan from the Ukraine, became extinct only recently (in 1919), and Przewalski's Horse is precariously near extinction. Wild horses of many species were once common in Europe and Asia, and from one or two of these man developed the domestic horse. Domestic breeds of horses and donkeys are now found all over the world and in many places they have gone back to the wild. These semi-wild horses readily breed with the remaining small numbers of truly wild horses, so that the pure species are gradually diminishing and will eventually disappear.

Zebras *(right* and *below)* are sometimes referred to as striped horses but their long ears, stiff manes and tufted tails make them more similar to asses.

Why are zebras striped?

This is the most obvious question to ask about zebras but unfortunately nobody really knows the answer. Looking at zebras in the zoo, the striped patterning seems very conspicuous and could hardly be thought of as protective. One theory, however, claims that this is, in fact, so. The bold stripes may serve to break up the shape of the zebra. From a distance, across the shimmering grassy plains on which the zebra lives, the blurred collection of stripes that the lion or tiger sees may not be instantly recognizable as an animal. The patterning is variable and no two zebras are exactly alike. It is interesting that African people think of zebras as black animals with white stripes whereas we think of them as white animals with black stripes.

Several odd-toed ungulates are shown on these pages. The coloration of the young Malayan Tapir bears little resemblance to that of its parent.

Why does the tapir have a white back?

Seen in the zoo, the coloration of a Malayan Tapir looks slightly absurd. It looks very much as if it is wearing a closely fitting white coat similar to the dog coats you sometimes see worn by the pampered pets of old ladies. To understand why such an odd-looking animal has such an odd-looking coloration we must consider the sort of places the tapir lives in and the sort of life that it leads. When we do this the tapir's appearance doesn't seem so odd after all. Tapirs are secretive, nocturnal animals living near water, in dense tropical forests. They are quite large, about as big as donkeys although with shorter legs, and being herbivorous tend to graze all night in order to find sufficient food. By moonlight their shadowy black and white outline blends well with the background so that the tapirs are perfectly camouflaged during their nocturnal wanderings. Patterning which breaks up an animal's shape like this is called *disruptive coloration*.

The head of the White Rhinoceros showing its broad square lips.

How many sorts of rhinoceros are there?

There are five species of rhinoceros living today, two from Africa and three from Asia. The two African rhinoceroses and one from Asia, the Sumatran, all have two horns whereas the other two Asian species have only one.

The largest of them all is the White Rhinoceros from Africa. It stands 6 feet high at the shoulder and can weigh over 3 tons. An interesting difference between this rhino and the Black Rhinoceros, also from Africa, lies in the shape of the lips. The White Rhinoceros has a wider, square

The Black Rhinoceros
head-on *(above)* and
from the side *(right)*.

The three Asiatic
rhinoceroses: the
Sumatran *(above)* the
Javan *(below)* and the
Great Indian *(below
right)*.

mouth, very suitable for cropping grass as it grazes across the savannah. The Black Rhinoceros is more of a browser and has a pointed upper lip for grazing and plucking leaves and shoots from shrubs and bushes. The other two-horned species, the Sumatran Rhinoceros, is the smallest of them all, standing only about 4½ feet at the shoulder.

Both the Javan and the Great Indian Rhinoceros look as if they are wearing heavy armour plating held together with rivets. This effect is given by thick skin hanging in deep folds and hard raised knobs on the front and back ends of the animals. The Great Indian Rhinoceros may weigh up to 2 tons and so is a formidable beast, but like most rhinoceroses, it is usually anxious to avoid any confrontation with man.

All the rhinoceroses are unfortunately rare animals. They have been hunted by man for their horns for years because of the belief that magical properties are imparted to the owner.

The camels shown *above* are two-humped or Bactrian Camels. The only other species is the one-humped Arabian Camel which is no longer found wild.

What does a camel store in its humps?

You have no doubt heard stories about the wonderful endurance of camels plodding through the desert for days without a drink, living on the water stored in their humps. The claims for the camel's endurance are often exaggerated but it is true that this animal can survive for several days without taking water. However, the camel does not fill its hump with water before it starts such a journey, rather as you might fill a car's tank with petrol. The humps are composed of fatty tissues which break down to give energy during periods when the camel is without sufficient food. Water is stored by the camel in its tissues and it draws on this supply as it plods along. After a long journey the camel is usually very thin and dried up and it takes an enormous drink as soon as it can, to make up the loss. It drinks over 20 gallons of water in ten minutes.

The South American owner of a herd of Llamas *(left)* can make rugs and clothing from their fur, sandals from their hides, candles from their fat and fuel from their droppings.

Do all camels have humps?

Apart from the two species of camel already mentioned, there are four other members of the camel family which do not possess humps. These are the Llama, Guanaco, Alpaca and Vicuna, all from South America. From the time of the Inca civilization these animals have been domesticated by man, and to this day they are invaluable to Indians living at high altitudes. They are used mainly as beasts of burden and will happily bear loads of up to 100 pounds in weight if properly handled. A Llama that is annoyed will spit in the face of the offender with great accuracy.

What use are antlers?

The male of most species of deer bears antlers. As these are grown throughout the year only to be shed soon after the breeding season they seem to be rather pointless. During the breeding season males spar by clashing antlers together but these are more trials of strength than serious fights. A recent, most interesting theory on the purpose of antlers is that they help to keep the deer cool during the summer months. As they grow, they are covered in skin richly supplied with blood vessels. In warm weather body heat would quickly be lost from such surfaces. As the time for breeding approaches, the skin (velvet) falls off. Many of the even-toed ungulates bear paired bony outgrowths from their skulls. Some are skin covered and either drop off each year (for example, in deer) or are permanent (for example, in the giraffe). Others are covered in horn (for example, in cattle).

The deer shown here are the Pampas Deer from the plains of South America *(left)* and the Red Deer *(above)* from the woodlands of Europe and Asia.

Male Okapis have a pair of short, skin-covered bony horns which they keep all the year round. The females usually have a pair of bumps on the head.

What is the Okapi?

The Okapi looks as if it is a cross between a zebra, a donkey and a giraffe. It is a very recognizable animal and is quite large, as big as a horse, and yet it was first discovered only about seventy years ago. It is very shy and retiring, living in the densest tropical forests of the Zaire basin. The Okapi is the only living relative of the Giraffe. It has a giraffe-like supple neck and a long tongue for plucking the leaves from trees.

Why is the Pronghorn so called?

Often misleadingly called an antelope (antelopes come from Africa and Asia), the North American Pronghorn derives its popular name from the forward-pointing branch of its horns. The Pronghorn's horns are extremely interesting. They are composed of two parts: a bony central cone

Once near extinction but now a successfully conserved species, Pronghorns inhabit dry areas of western North America and Canada.

which is permanent like those of the true antelopes, and a sheath of fused hairs supplying the horny covering. The branched horny covering splits each year and is shed revealing a new growth of horn underneath.

How long is the Giraffe's tongue?

The Giraffe is easily the tallest of the mammals at 18 feet. Apart from its legs and neck another long feature of the Giraffe is its tongue. When fully extended to pluck a distant leaf or twig, the Giraffe's tongue is 17 inches long. The Giraffe feeds on the foliage of acacia trees on the savannahs of South Africa, and because it usually browses around the trees at a constant height, they often end up with an hourglass shape. The long neck is ideal for reaching up into trees but is not as convenient for drinking. The Giraffe has to splay its front legs or bend its knees in order to reach the ground to drink.

There is only one species of Giraffe, but a number of races with slightly different colouring are recognized.

The North American Bison was slaughtered by the thousand throughout the nineteenth century during the exploration of the American West. Numbers have been built up from a few hundred to the 20,000 animals of today.

How many sorts of bison are there?

Most people know that there is a North American Bison, sometimes called the Buffalo, but there is another species which comes from eastern Europe, the European Bison or Wisent. Both are enormous shaggy animals with humped backs. The American species is an animal of the open plains whereas the European prefers thick woodland and forest. Both have come close to extinction in the past but are now protected in parks and reserves in their respective countries.

What are the true buffalos?

The best known true buffalo is the Asiatic Water Buffalo, of the cattle group of mammals. This buffalo has been domesticated for hundreds of years and is the 'work-horse' of all tropical Asia, being used for a whole range of tasks on the land. It is an immensely strong beast with impressive horns over 6 feet in length..There are two African Wild Buffalos,

The Gaur (far left) is the largest of the wild cattle and small herds are found in mountainous forest areas of southern Asia. Although domesticated, the Asiatic Water Buffalo (left) will attack anyone without provocation and can do great damage with its enormous horns.

Rocky Mountain Goats are found in the North American Rockies. Their coats and beards of long white hair are particularly striking.

the common form and a smaller and rarer forest form. The African Buffalo also carries massive curved horns and lives in herds in moist swampy areas. The Dwarf Forest Buffalo is more retiring and large herds move through thick forest without drawing much attention to themselves.

What are rock-goats?

There are four species of goat that are true rock-dwellers. The Goral, Serow, Chamois and Rocky Mountain Goat are known for their remarkable ability to bound up and down steep mountainsides and cliffs. All goats are sure-footed but rock-goats are particularly skilful climbers. They seem to defy gravity by walking along vertical cliff faces using footholds only half-an-inch wide.

Throughout history the domesticated even-toed ungulates have provided man with food, drink, clothing and transport. Pigs, camels, llamas, deer, cattle, goats and sheep all belong to this important group of mammals.

There are a number of sure-footed wild goats called Ibexes, living in mountainous areas. Their horns are particularly strong with large, evenly spaced ridges along their length.

Exploration and Discovery

Who were the first explorers?

The first real explorers of the Ancient World were the Phoenicians.
They were a people who had settled on a coastal strip of land at
the eastern end of the Mediterranean, now known as the Lebanon,
who had many colonies, the most important being Tyre and Sidon.
Phoenician wealth originally came from a dye made from a small

A single-masted Phoenician trading vessel

shellfish found on their shores which was called *murex*. It produced
the colour known as 'royal purple', favoured by kings and the
nobility. No other country had this dye, but as the supply of *murex*
dwindled, the Phoenicians were forced to search for other sources of
wealth. Their courageous seamen took their single-masted galleys
along the shores of the Mediterranean and then, some time after
900 B.C. they struck out into the unknown. Sailing their ships into
the Red Sea, they eventually crossed the Indian Ocean to India.

The Phoenicians also ventured northwards and traded with
Europe and the countries on the Baltic. They were frequent visitors
to Devon and Cornwall on the south coast of England, which they
called the 'Tin Islands', exchanging cloth and jewellery for tin,
copper and skins.

Captain Cook shoots
the sun with a con-
temporary sextant (1731)

How did the early mariners navigate?

The early seamen sailed by the sun and stars, rarely venturing out of sight of the land. Then the Chinese discovered the lode-stone or guiding stone, and the fact that it always pointed to the magnetic north. It was first used in Europe in the twelfth century, and the idea of attaching it to a compass card is credited to Flavia Gioia of Amalfi in 1302. Latitude was worked out by observing the sun with a 'cross-staff', a wooden T-square with a sliding cross-piece which was moved until one end was in line with the sun and the other with the horizon. The 'back-staff' and astrolabe were also used to estimate latitude. Accurate longitude was impossible to determine until a Yorkshireman, John Harrison, invented a reliable time-keeper in the eighteenth century.

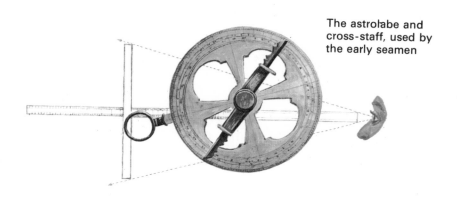

The astrolabe and cross-staff, used by the early seamen

Marco Polo on one of his remarkable overland journeys

Who was Marco Polo?

In 1260, two Venetian brothers, Niccolo and Maffeo Polo, set off on an amazing journey. They had travelled as far as Russia and were on their way home by way of the Caspian Sea when they met some envoys from the court of Kublai Khan, the emperor of China. Instead of returning to Italy, the two brothers decided to accompany the envoys to the Khan's palace in Peking. They were well received and did not return to Venice until 1269.

Two years later they set out for the Khan's court once more. This time Marco, Niccolo's 17-year old son, travelled with them. The three went on and on, across arid deserts and over high mountains and finally arrived in Peking. The Khan was greatly taken by young Marco and began to send him on special missions throughout his vast empire. Marco served the Khan for seventeen years and kept detailed notes of everything he saw. He visited nearly every part of the Chinese empire about which Europeans knew very little. He finally returned home at the age of forty-one and wrote a book about his strange and wonderful adventures. Unfortunately the Italians, who had no idea of what the Far East was like, mistrusted his book and believed it to be full of lies. It was not until many years after his death that other explorers confirmed the truth of what Marco had written.

Who first sailed from Europe to India?

In 1497, Vasco da Gama, a young Portuguese sea captain, was summoned to the court of King Manuel I. The king informed him that, as one of the most notable navigators of his day, he had been chosen to lead an expedition in an attempt to find a sea route from Portugal to the Indies, round the southern tip of Africa. He was given a flotilla of four vessels, one of which was commanded by his brother, Paolo.

Four months after leaving Lisbon, on 22 November, despite hurricanes and mutinies, the ships rounded the Cape of Good Hope. Da Gama, in his flagship the *San Gabriel*, led the small fleet farther north along the African coast than any other European had ever ventured before. After calling at Mozambique and Mombasa, he sailed north-east across the Arabian Gulf, with a Hindu pilot on board. Three weeks later the ships reached Calicut in India. Da Gama's voyage proved more immediately valuable to the world than Columbus's discoveries in the New World, for it opened up a trade route by which the great riches of the East could be carried by sea to Europe.

Vasco da Gama from a contemporary picture

Above: Columbus
lands on Hispaniola

Why did Columbus sail westwards?

Christopher Columbus was an Italian from
Genoa living in Portugal. Although in the
fifteenth century most people still believed that
the world was flat, others, including Columbus,
had come to believe it was round. If this was
so, he argued, a ship could sail around the globe
and return to its original starting point. Thus
the shortest route to the Spice Islands of the
East Indies would be by sailing *westwards*.
He sought support for his theory but it was
rejected again and again. Finally, after years
of disappointment, he gained the help of
Ferdinand and Isabella, the king and queen
of Spain. In August 1492, three small ships set
sail from Spain, their bows pointing westwards
across the wide, unknown Atlantic. They were
the *Santa Maria*, the *Niña* and the *Pinta*. On
12 October land was sighted. Columbus was
convinced that it was an island off the coast of
India. When other islands came into view he
named them the 'Indies'. His 'mistake' was
nevertheless a vitally important event in the
discovery and exploration of the West.

Why is Prince Henry of Portugal called 'The Navigator'?

Prince Henry was the fifth son of King John I of Portugal and of Queen Philippa, grand-daughter of Edward III of England. In his youth he had proved himself to be a brave warrior, but his one desire in life was to extend the sea-routes of the world and to make his country rich by trade. He set up an academy at Sagres on Cape St Vincent and began to study astronomy, chart-making and mathematics. At his command, mariners set off on voyages of exploration that steadily pushed back the borders of the unknown. When his captains returned, they gave him charts of their voyages from which

Prince Henry the Navigator

he was able to prepare surprisingly accurate maps. His men, both Portuguese and Italian, ventured further and further into uncharted waters. One, Diego Cam, not only reached the mouth of the Congo (now Zaire) River, but sailed south for another 800 km before turning back. Other explorers discovered Madeira and the Canary Islands. Because of Prince Henry's great interest and encouragement, geography became a science and navigation was much improved. Prince Henry died in 1460 but not before his mariners had reached Sierra Leone on the west coast of Africa. He had certainly justified the proud title of 'The Navigator'.

Who were the first Australians?

About 20,000 years ago a race of dark-skinned, curly-haired natives, known as Tasmanoids, paddled their canoes from New Guinea and settled in what is now Australia. At the same time, another race, the Australoids, arrived from southern India. These two races began a desperate fight for the land, which ended with the Tasmanoids being driven from the mainland and settling in what is now known as Tasmania. The Australoids remained to become the ancestors of the Australian aborigines.

Which Europeans first landed in Australia?

During the sixteenth century, the Portuguese were the principal traders in the East Indies. By 1600, however, their place had been taken by the Dutch who, sailing via the Cape of Good Hope, set up a powerful base on the island of Batavia. Soon their ships were seeking new lands in order to open up more trade. In 1606 a Dutch ship called the *Duyfken*, 'the Dove', anchored off northern Australia and some of the crew went ashore – the first Europeans to do so. They were refilling their water casks when they were driven off by fierce natives. The *Duyfken* sailed away again without exploring any other part of the vast Australian continent.

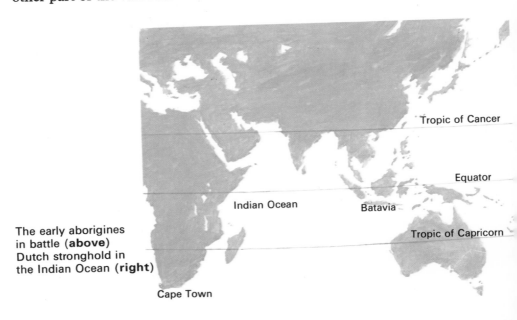

The early aborigines in battle (**above**)
Dutch stronghold in the Indian Ocean (**right**)

Tropic of Cancer

Equator

Indian Ocean

Batavia

Tropic of Capricorn

Cape Town

Which ship first sailed around the world?

On 20 September 1519, five small ships set sail from Spain. Their combined tonnage was less than 500 tons. In command was Ferdinand Magellan, a Portuguese sailing under the Spanish flag. The ships battled across the Atlantic in the face of fierce gales and, on reaching Brazil, turned southwards, seeking a passage from west to east. Eventually they discovered a strait at the tip of South America and the three remaining ships – *Victoria, Concepcion* and *Trinidad* – sailed through it and entered the Pacific Ocean. They

The *Victoria* in the
Magellan Straits

continued to sail westwards until they reached the Philippines. Here Magellan was killed by natives in a skirmish and Sebastian del Cano took command. The *Concepción* proved unseaworthy and had to be burned, and the *Trinidad* returned to Panama leaving only the *Victoria* to complete the voyage. Del Cano continued sailing westwards until, with a crew of thirteen Europeans, the *Victoria* finally anchored off Seville in September 1522. In three years the gallant little *Victoria* had sailed right around the world – the first ship to do so.

Who was the first explorer known by name?

Herodotus, the Greek historian of the fifth century B.C., tells in his *History* of an expedition made by Phoenicians at the orders of the Egyptian pharaoh, Necho. He mentions its importance but fails to give the names of any of those who took part. About a century later another expedition set sail under a Phoenician called Hanno, and one of its members wrote an exciting account of the voyage.

The journey began about 500 B.C., when Hanno sailed from his home in Carthage as the leader of a fleet of nearly 70 galleys carrying 30,000 men and women. The object of the expedition was to set up new colonies along the west coast of Africa. The fleet sailed west-

Hanno's men meet the 'Gorillas'

wards through the Straits of Gibraltar, into the Atlantic, and then turned southwards. A number of colonies were formed, but often attempts to land on the African coast were unsuccessful, for the would-be settlers were met by 'wild men, clad in the skins of beasts who cast stones and drove us off, preventing us from landing'. They sailed on, recording many strange sights including a huge 'mountain of fire', possibly Mount Cameroon, and also fierce, shaggy-haired creatures which interpreters on board their ships called 'Gorillas'. Supplies ran low as Hanno's fleet neared the Equator and he was forced to turn and head for home.

A Greek galley of the type used by Pytheas on his amazing voyage

Who was the first explorer to visit Britain?

In about 325 B.C. a young man called Pytheas decided to leave home and see what lay over the horizon. He left the Greek colony of Massilia (now Marseilles in France) and sailed westwards. When he reached the Atlantic, Pytheas turned north, hugging the Spanish and French coasts until he came at last to Britain. He was very interested in all he saw, especially the Cornish tin industry about which he wrote in detail, explaining how tin was extracted, smelted and taken by wagon to St Michael's Mount for shipment to France. And this was more than 2,000 years ago! Having covered most of Britain on foot, Pytheas then set sail again, heading northwards. He visited Scotland, the Shetland Isles and, it is believed, Iceland. Being used to the warm, tideless Mediterranean, he marvelled at the rise and fall of the tides, especially in the Orkneys, and the drifting ice he saw on the surface of the northern seas. When he returned home he wrote of the wonders he had seen, but like so many explorers that were to follow him, many of his readers refused to believe a word of what he had written.

What was Tasmania originally called?

During the early part of the seventeenth century, Dutch ships sailed from their base in Batavia, searching for fresh markets for trade. A number of Dutch captains landed on the Australian coast but were not attracted by what they saw. The place seemed empty and barren whilst the natives were 'wild, black and barbarous' as well as 'cruel, poor and brutal'. Nevertheless, the new governor of Batavia, Anthony van Diemen, was anxious to discover new sources of wealth and sent out Abel Tasman (above) to find them. Tasman was ordered to sail to Mauritius in the south, and then east-wards into the Indian Ocean. Tasman, a very experienced seaman, set off with two ships, the *Heemskerck* and *Zeekaen*. They reached Mauritius in October 1642 but on putting out to sea again they ran into a series of storms which forced Tasman to alter course to the east so as to gain the steady westerly winds. These drove him straight to a huge land mass which, in honour of the governor, he named Van Diemen's Land. Later, to mark his own great ability as a navigator this name was changed to include his own – Tasmania.

Who discovered Newfoundland?

John Cabot (below) was an Italian and a native of Venice. When he sailed westwards in the little *Matthew*, in 1497, however, he flew the banner of St George at his masthead, for he had been sent on a voyage of discovery by England's King Henry VII. After a crossing of six weeks, land was sighted. Cabot went ashore to claim what he called 'Prima Vista' – 'First Seen' – for England. It later became known as Nova Scotia. He then sailed northwards along the southern coast of 'New Found Land' naming capes, bays and islands as he went. He was particularly impressed by how rich the seas were in salmon, sole ('about a yard in length') and cod. He returned to England on 6 August to a great welcome and a gift of £10 from the not over-generous king.

Who divided the world in two?

With the discovery of the New World, Spain and Portugal became great rivals. Before this rivalry led to war, Pope Alexander VI divided the world, in 1494, into two parts by drawing a line from the south of Greenland to the mouth of the Amazon. All lands to the west of this line belonged to Spain, all to the east to Portugal. Unfortunately this left out England, France and Holland who were also searching for new territories. In consequence, this impractical division – known as the Treaty of Tordesillas – was to lead in time to arguments and much bloodshed.

The world divided
into two by
Pope Alexander VI

Which European first sighted the Pacific Ocean?

Vasco Nuñez de Balboa was a Spanish soldier of fortune. To escape his debts he fled to South America and became the leader of a group of settlers. He was surprised to learn from an Indian chief, one day, that a vast sea existed 72 km away, and set out to find it. The Spaniards had to hack their way through forests and swamps full of Indians waiting to kill any stragglers. At last Balboa reached a mountain top and, alone, stared out over the great Pacific Ocean.

Balboa wades into the
Pacific Ocean and
claims it for Castile

The first settlement at the Cape was established by the Dutch in 1652

Why is the Cape of Good Hope so called?

In 1486, Bartholomew Diaz, a Portuguese nobleman set sail from Lisbon, determined to follow the African coast further than anyone had before. After he had passed the mouth of the Congo (now Zaire) River, a fierce storm sent his ship reeling out to sea. When the gales had blown themselves out, he tacked back to the coast and found to his surprise that it now lay to the *west*. The storm had blown his ship right around the Cape. On his return to Portugal, Diaz told King John II that he had named the great promontory the 'Cape of Storms'. But the king, realizing this discovery might open a route to greater wealth, suggested that it be renamed the Cape of Good Hope.

How did America get its name?

America is named after Amerigo Vespucci (right), an Italian mariner who sailed under the Portuguese flag. He charted the American coastline from what is now Chesapeake Bay to Honduras a few years after Columbus's discovery of the New World. On his return, Vespucci wrote of his discoveries and people began to realize that the great land mass was not Asia or India, as Columbus had thought, but a separate continent. In 1507 a German cartographer suggested that this unnamed continent should be called 'America' after the explorer Amerigo, and so it was.

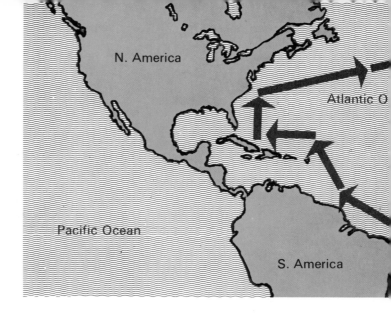

What was The Great Circuit?

When Portugal began to trade with the native towns on the West African coast her captains sought gold, ivory and pepper. At the beginning of the thirteenth century, however, a new source of wealth in the form of slaves suddenly presented itself. Brazil was discovered by Portugal in 1500 and to provide additional labour, Africans began to be imported to work on the vast sugar plantations. Thus the terrible slave trade began. England's seamen soon realized the wealth that lay in this trade and they began to fill the holds of their ships with living – or barely living – cargo.

The first English captain to embark on the wicked trade of carrying slaves to the New World was John Hawkins, who came from Plymouth. King James I of England officially granted a charter to the 'Company of Adventurers of London Trading into Parts of Africa'. The trade grew, and by 1713 England had the monopoly for the supply of slaves to South America. Thus the 'Great Circuit' came into being (above). This was a triangular course taken by the slave ships. They sailed from Channel ports with cargoes of gaudy jewellery and bales of cheap cotton cloth for the coast of Africa. The 'cargoes' were exchanged and, packed with Negroes, the ships headed westwards across the Atlantic to the West Indies and America. The slaves were then sold and sugar bought with the proceeds. Brought back on the third leg of the 'Great Circuit', the sugar was sold in Europe. This trading played a great part in the growth of the Lancashire cotton mills which produced most of the goods for barter in Africa.

Where was the Roanoke colony?

One of the great Elizabethans was Sir Walter Raleigh who wanted to see a large English settlement established in the New World. In 1583 his half-brother, Sir Humphrey Gilbert, had unsuccessfully tried to set up a colony in Newfoundland. The following year Raleigh decided to try again further south. He sent out two ships which touched at Roanoke Island, off the coast of what is now North Carolina, and then returned to England with the news that the land was suitable for settlement.

In 1585, a further expedition was organized by Raleigh. It consisted of seven ships, under the command of Sir Richard Grenville, carrying settlers to Roanoke Island. The would-be colonists went ashore, the seamen from the fleet helped them build huts and a stockade and then, satisfied that the colony would flourish, Grenville sailed away. But trouble began when the colonists antagonized the once friendly Indians, and before long they did not dare venture outside their stockades. The survivors were glad to abandon their settlement when Francis Drake called at the island, and to return to England with him.

Part of a very early map of the 'Virginia Coast', now the coast of North Carolina

Who was the first explorer of the Sahara?

In 1822, Hugh Clapperton, a young naval lieutenant, agreed to go with Walter Oudney and Dixon Denham to try and discover the source of the River Niger in North Africa. They journeyed south across the Sahara from Tripoli to Lake Chad, the first white men to visit the region. Oudney died at Murner, and the other two separated, Clapperton going on alone to Kano, a great trading city west of Lake Chad. He then travelled to Sokoto, where he became friendly with the sultan who ruled the vast area, returning to meet up with Denham again in Kuka. Having established that none of the rivers flowing into Lake Chad was associated with the Niger, Clapperton returned to England and wrote a book of his adventures. In order to solve the problem of the Niger he returned to Africa in 1825, and set out on another journey starting from the Bight of Benin. Nine months later Clapperton arrived in Sokoto, where his detention by the sultan, added to the hardships of the journey, so affected his health that he died soon afterwards, at the age of thirty-nine, and was buried outside the walls of Sokoto.

Hugh Clapperton, one of Africa's first explorers

Captain James Cook,
Britain's greatest
explorer

What did Captain Cook prove in the Southern Hemisphere?

As a result of Tasman's discoveries, Australia, Tasmania and New Zealand were thought to be part of one enormous continental island. It was shown on maps of the time as *Terra Australis Cognita* (or Southern Known Land) separated from another to the south shown as *Terra Australis Incognita* (or Unknown). Captain Cook, however, proved that the former was not one but a number of huge islands. He charted the coastline of New Zealand and found it to be two islands separated from Australia by 2,400 km. He also searched for the great 'unknown' southern continent but finally decided that no such place existed, only a huge land mass of ice and snow which extended into both the Atlantic and Indian Oceans and which is now known as Antarctica.

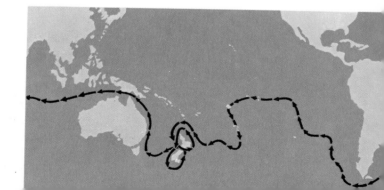

Cook charted New
Zealand and the east
coast of Australia

Which European discovered the Victoria Falls ?

Although David Livingstone had trained to be a doctor, he decided to go to Africa as a missionary. He sailed for what was then called the Dark Continent on 20 November 1840 and soon found that his work took him into areas that were virtually unknown. In time he crossed the great Kalahari Desert and later reached the bank of the mighty Zambezi River, where no white man had ever been before. He spent many months exploring this river, discovering and naming the magnificent Victoria Falls. In 1865 he went to Zanzibar and while journeying around Lake Nyasa (now Malawi) witnessed the extensive and brutal slave trade existing in that area, against

Livingstone names the
Falls after his queen

which he was to campaign vigorously for the rest of his life. He was later to describe slavery as the 'open sore of the world'. On the shores of Lake Tanganyika in 1871, when no news of him had reached the outside world for some time, he was 'found' by an American Newspaperman, Henry Stanley. Although ill and exhausted, he continued his work, until, on 1 May 1873, he died amongst the natives he had served so well.

Orellana and his men
are attacked by fierce
'Amazons'

Why is the Amazon River so called?

In 1539 a large Spanish force set out from the town of Quito, in Ecuador, to find out what could be discovered to the east. As their supplies were running out, Gonzalo Pizarro, a brother of the conqueror of Peru, ordered a small party to retrace their route by boat and return with fresh supplies. Commanded by Francisco de Orellana, the fifty men set off. However, a strong current swung their boat around, forcing them eastwards in the opposite direction. After several exhausting days, Orellana decided to let the current carry them where it would. Luckily they soon reached a village where they found food. Setting off again, the strong current carried them past hot, steamy jungles where trees fringed the water's edge. On one occasion they were attacked by more than 2,000 natives and had to fight them off, using cross-bows, for their powder was damp. Shortly after they met a fleet of canoes filled with tall, fair-haired women who shot arrows at them, killing seven of their number. Because of this incident, Orellana called the river the 'Amazon' after a race of legendary women warriors. Finally, after a voyage of nearly 4,000 miles, they came at last to the Atlantic Ocean—the first men to cross South America at its widest part.

Far right: In this ransom room, gold was stacked 2 m high.
Right: Atahualpa is garotted on the orders of Pizarro

Who conquered the Incas?

Long before the first Spaniards arrived in the New World, a great empire existed in the Andes Mountains. The borders of this empire spread into what is now Peru, Bolivia, Ecuador and parts of Chile and Argentina. This was the Inca Empire, with its capital at Cuzco, the Sacred City of the Sun. It had a civilization in some ways more advanced than that of Europe, with magnificent buildings, paved roads and a population of many millions, everyone of whom had a place within the state. About 1523 the Inca ruler died and a pretender, Atahualpa, seized the true heir and claimed the throne. The country was in a state of confusion when news came of an army of white men that was advancing from the coast commanded by a Spanish adventurer, Francisco Pizarro. He led an army of only 108 men with 62 horses, but with this tiny force he eventually overthrew the great Inca empire. He captured Atahualpa by a trick and said he would be released only if a large room was filled with gold. Although this was done, Pizarro did not keep his word and the Inca was garotted. Without their leader, Indian resistance virtually collapsed, Pizarro claimed control and won enormous wealth.

Spanish soldiers in the Inca city of Cajamarca

Who discovered the 'Silver Mountains'?

In 1516, one of three Spanish ships which were exploring the coast of what is now southern Brazil, ran aground on the incredibly beautiful island of Santa Catarina. Most of the crew were able to reach the shore and they made a settlement under their leader, Alejo García. They were visited by natives who told them of mountains to the east which were rich in silver. García immediately decided to go and look for these mountains. He set out with four companions on a fantastically difficult journey. After crossing the unexplored Parana plateau, struggling across the rivers of the Parana and Paraguay and warding off hostile Indians, they found they had covered 3,200 km to the Andes. García allied himself with a tribe of Indians who were deadly enemies of another tribe which lived in the area of the silver mountains. An attack was made and García and his comrades made off with sacks full of articles made from solid silver. They managed to reach the River Paraguay again but García got no further. He was murdered by his Indian 'allies'.

Shipwrecked Spaniards
on Santa Catarina

Who was Australia's most famous explorer?

In 1800, Matthew Flinders was a young naval lieutenant with a passion for exploring. He sailed around the Australian coast with a friend called George Bass in a small boat they named 'Tom Thumb'. Once, on going ashore, they were menaced by hostile natives but Flinders won them over by trimming their hair and beards! Later, in 1801, Flinders sailed in HMS *Investigator*, sounding and charting the Australian coast and filling in many of the gaps left by Captain

Flinders makes friends
with the help of a pair
of scissors

Cook. Eventually his ship became unseaworthy and had to be broken up, so the crew was divided between HMS *Porpoise* and the *Cato*. The ships sailed for Sydney but both were wrecked on a reef off the coast of Queensland. Only three men were drowned and the remainder were rescued after two months' existence on a small sandbank. On his return to England, Flinders wrote *A Voyage to Terra Australis* which became a classic of exploration.

Where was the Spanish Main?

The Caribbean Sea, named after the Carib Indians who once lived on its shores, is separated from the Atlantic and the Gulf of Mexico by a chain of beautiful islands. Columbus discovered the sea in 1492 and claimed it for Spain. Although Spain tried to keep all other nations out, English and French adventurers settled on several islands. There they cured meat for their voyages by a process known as 'boucanning'. In time these 'buccaneers' were strong enough to fight against the Spaniards, notorious for their cruelty. Gradually they developed into professional pirates who plundered Spanish towns and shipping in an area known as the Spanish Main.

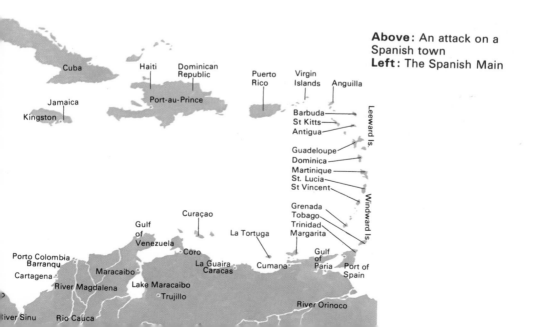

Above: An attack on a Spanish town
Left: The Spanish Main

How did New England come into being?

All attempts to colonize Roanoke Island and the surrounding territory of Virginia in the sixteenth century had proved unsuccessful. It seemed as if no one from England would ever enjoy the fine climate and rich soil of this huge, unspoiled area. But although Queen Elizabeth I died in 1603 the adventurous spirit of the Elizabethans lived on and a number of 'gentlemen and traders' formed two separate companies – the London Virginia and the Plymouth Virginia Companies – obtaining a Charter from James I which allowed

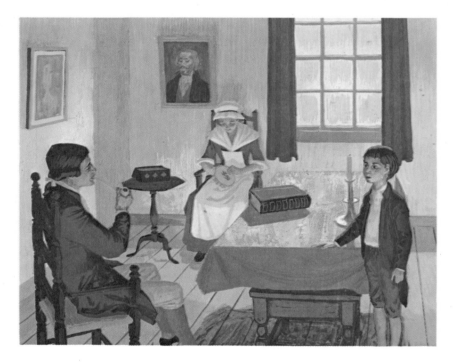

The interior of a typical New England home of the late eighteenth century

them to make further attempts at colonization. In 1607, when the former company settled on a site on the North Atlantic coast, one of the members, Captain John Smith, went exploring in an area then known as North Virginia. He renamed it New England and later described it in a pamphlet called *A Description of New England*. At this time there was hardly one Englishman in the whole area which, in fact, seemed likely to be taken over by French and Dutch settlers. The arrival of the Pilgrim Fathers a few years later, however, resulted in the territory being soundly established under the English flag.

Right: Samuel de Champlain
Below: A sketch by Champlain
of a fight with Iroquois Indians

Who were the first Europeans to explore Canada?

In A.D. 1000, Leif Ericsson, a Norseman, sailed from Greenland to North America but only landed for a brief period. Five centuries later, John Cabot also sailed along the coast but no explorer actually ventured into the interior of Canada until 1524, when François I of France sent an Italian, Giovanni da Verrazano, to search for a northern sea route to the Indies. He was unsuccessful but mapped much of the coast from Newfoundland to North Carolina. In 1534 a Frenchman, Jacques Cartier, ventured into the interior and during his travels he spoke to the natives. Hearing them use the word 'Canada' (meaning 'village') he thought it was their name for the whole country, and so officially called it this. The greatest pioneer sent out by France was Samuel de Champlain, who not only explored much of Canada, but also founded many settlements.

An ancient Egyptian drawing symbolizing the universe

How was the secret of Egyptian picture writing discovered?

For centuries men had tried to make sense of the long inscriptions that were to be found on the ancient temples and tombs in Egypt. All had failed. Some even believed that the drawings of men, plants, birds and so on were not even words, but some kind of magical writing that was not meant to be read like ordinary words.

Then a soldier's spade unearthed the key. In 1798 Napoleon invaded Egypt and his army included many scholars and scientists. As they were carrying out building operations at a small town called Rosetta, a French soldier dug out a slab of black stone. A scholar who inspected the slab noted that one side was covered with lines of neat carving. He became excited when he saw that it was in three languages, Greek, demotic (a form of long-hand Egyptian) and hieroglyphics. When Napoleon was forced to abandon Egypt after his defeat by the English the stone came to London and was housed in the British Museum, yet it was a French scholar, Jean-François Champollion, who finally unravelled the mystery. When he was a boy of nine he saw his first hieroglyphic inscriptions and on learning that no one could read them said, firmly, 'In a few years, when I am big, I will be able to.' The task was to take him many years, but because of his knowledge of many of the 'dead' languages and his own personal genius, he managed to solve the mystery by 1828, before his early death at the age of forty-one.

Why is Botany Bay so called?

When Captain James Cook sailed for the South Seas in HMS
Endeavour, his ship also carried a number of scientists. One of these
was Joseph (later Sir Joseph) Banks, a wealthy botanist who went
with the expedition to draw and collect botanical specimens. The
Endeavour reached the Australian coast on 28 April 1769 and dropped anchor in a large and sheltered bay. Cook's first attempt at
landing was met by a hostile reception from the Aborigines, but the
crew frightened them away with a few shots and Cook and Banks
went ashore and named it Sting Ray Bay. During the next few days,
however, Banks and his assistants collected such a vast variety of
exotic plants that it was renamed Botany Bay.

Aborigines watch Cook
and Banks come ashore

After many attempts to cross the Great Stony Desert Sturt admits himself defeated

How did the Sturt Desert get its name?

The first explorer to venture deep into the barren heart of Australia was an Englishman, Charles Sturt. He was an army captain when, in 1826, he was sent to New South Wales with a shipload of convicts. He became military secretary to the governor, but his real interest lay in leading expeditions into the interior, during which he discovered and named the Darling and Murray Rivers. In 1844, he set out with fifteen men in an attempt to reach an inland sea which he believed, mistakenly, lay at the centre of the continent. He fought against terrible hardships but was defeated at last by the impassable stony desert which now bears his name.

What was the *Fram?*

A Norwegian, Fritdjof Nansen, had the idea of building a ship that would be lifted up by the pressure of ice forming around it. It would then drift northwards with the floes, where no ship had ever been before. His famous ship the *Fram* was the result. He sailed it to northern Siberia and it drifted exactly as he had planned. In the spring of 1895 he left the ship to try and reach the Pole overland, but was unsuccessful. Incredibly, he met another expedition and returned to Norway in their ship, the *Windward.* A week later he learned that the *Fram,* as strong as ever, had, in fact, managed to break free of the ice which had imprisoned her for nearly three years and was homeward bound.

Darwin at Tierra del Fuego, where he studied 'man in his lowest and most savage state'. In his book he wrote, 'from so'simple a beginning, endless forms most beautiful and wonderful have been, and are being evolved.'

Darwin stated that apes and men have a common ancestor

Who explained the evolution of man ?

In December 1831, HMS *Beagle* was sent by the British Government on a surveying expedition. Attached to this mission as naturalist was a young man, Charles Darwin. Born in Shrewsbury in 1809, he had disappointed his father by refusing to become a doctor or a clergyman. It was feared he would be a failure in life but he became interested in natural history and the five years he spent in the *Beagle* helped him understand the relationship between all living things. The ship visited the South American coast and the Galapagos, then sailed on to Australia, New Zealand, Tasmania and places which, at the time, were hardly known. On his return Darwin wrote *The Origin of Species*. Twelve years later another book, *The Descent of Man*, caused a sensation, for it suggested, for the first time, a new theory of evolution: that man was descended from strange, ape-like creatures – an incredible theory for those days but one which has since been proved correct.

What strange animals were discovered in Australia?

Joseph Banks, the naturalist, who went with Cook to the South Seas in the 1760s was busy collecting botanical specimens when he saw a very unusual creature. It was large, brown and hopped along on strong hind legs. He learned from the natives that it was called a 'Kangaroo'. This was but one of the many strange animals and birds that the early explorers discovered in Australia and which did not exist in any other country. The most attractive of these is the Koala. Indeed, there was a time when Koalas had nearly become extinct, but the species is now protected. Another animal that nearly suffered a similar fate is one of nature's jokes – the Duck-billed Platypus. This has the beak of a duck, a

Above: Kangaroo
Left: Pygmy Glider

beaver's tail and lays eggs! It was hunted for a long time for its beautiful fur, but now, like the Koala, it is fully protected. More strange animals belong to the Possum family. Some of these have skin between their front and hind legs which enables them to take gliding leaps from branch to branch. Wombats, Wallabies and Bandicoots are other unusual animals that startled and delighted the first white men who saw them, as did Australia's unique birds, including the Emu, Cassowary and the Lyrebird.

Below: The Duck-billed Platypus

How did New York get its name?

An Englishman, Henry Hudson, employed by Holland, was one of the many explorers who tried to find a route to the Indies via America. Although he sailed far up the river which later bore his name, he did not succeed in discovering a route. Nevertheless, the Dutch claimed all the land on either side of the Hudson despite the fact that it drove a wedge through English possessions. In 1626 they bought Manhattan Island from the Indians, built a settlement there and called it New Amsterdam. A governor was appointed, a one-legged Dutchman called Peter Stuyvesant. This was too much provocation for the English settlers. A fleet sent by James, Duke of York, sailed from England and anchored off New Amsterdam. The town gave in without firing a shot although the governor did all he could to make his men fight. Later its name was changed from 'New Amsterdam' to 'New York' to honour the royal duke who had financed the invasion.

Left: Peter Stuyvesant
Below: Settlers
trading with Indians

Who first explored America's Far West?

In 1803 the United States purchased from France a huge area known as Louisiana which gave the U.S. twice as much territory as it had previously owned. Much of it was unexplored, however, and President Jefferson ordered Captain Meriwether Lewis (top) and Lieutenant William Clark (below) to explore this 'wild' western area as thoroughly as possible. They set off up the Missouri River in May 1804, leading an expedition of forty-five people, and wintered in an Indian village. Starting out again in the spring, they surveyed and charted rivers as they went, as well as hills and other landmarks, and made notes on the location and customs of the Indian tribes. By July they had reached the Rocky Mountains, and their difficulties began. Food ran short and the expedition had to exist on dried fish, roots and berries. In November they sighted the Pacific. On the return journey Lewis and Clark split up, travelling by different routes to explore further the mysterious and hitherto unknown 'Far West'.

Who first traced the route of the Mississippi River?

Below: Jolliet and Marquette, a Jesuit priest, on the banks of the Mississippi

The Spanish explorer Hernando de Soto was, in 1541, the first white man to see the Mississippi, but it was not until June 1673 that two Frenchmen, Louis Jolliet and Jacques Marquette, actually explored the river in canoes. They travelled far enough south to prove that it emptied into the Gulf of Mexico and could not, therefore, be the hoped-for North-west Passage.

How was coffee brought to Brazil?

Although coffee was drunk centuries ago in Ethiopia it did not come to Europe until the seventeenth century. Soon 'coffee houses' were to be seen in every city, the first in London being opened in 1652. These coffee houses became fashionable places where people met, and the famous Lloyd's insurance association started in one in about 1688. Until the end of the seventeenth century coffee came from the region of the Yemen in Arabia. Other countries, however, wished to see if they, too, could grow the plant. Several trees were taken to French Guiana where they flourished, and soon the country was making a great deal of money by exporting coffee beans to South America. The plants were well guarded, however, and several people who tried to smuggle cuttings from the country were arrested. Usually the distinctive smell of the coffee flowers gave the officials an indication of what was happening. Brazil was one of the countries that wanted to grow coffee and a handsome officer in her army was sent to French Guiana with orders to bring back a plant, at any cost. The officer proceeded to flatter the governor's wife and through her obtained a cutting. Hiding this in a bouquet of flowers to mask its aroma, he sailed for home. Today about one-third of the entire world's production of coffee comes from Brazil.

The handsome Brazilian officer charms the wife of the Governor of French Guiana in order to obtain a coffee plant to smuggle out

Who discovered the St Lawrence River?

The first French explorer in the New World was Jacques Cartier (right). On 20 April 1534 he sailed westwards with two ships, seeking a short route to the Indies. Having reached Newfoundland, he waited until the winter ice had cleared, and then sailed through a strait and explored a great bay, claiming the territory in the name of France. On a second journey Cartier returned to the bay on 10 August – the feast of St Lawrence – and named it after the saint. He then explored the river beyond, and before returning to France named it, too, after St Lawrence.

Who discovered the Mississippi River?

One of the many who went on a vain search for El Dorado was a Spaniard, Hernando de Soto. He set off with a few mounted companions from Florida in 1539 on a journey that was to last for three years. De Soto and his party pushed their way through unexplored territory and in 1541 came to the banks of a huge river, the longest in the world, which the Indians called the 'Mississippi'. A year later De Sotoa died, wounded in a skirmish with Indians on the banks of the river he had discovered.

Who discovered the source of the Nile?

For thousands of years the world had speculated about the origin of the River Nile, but it was not until Richard Burton and John Hanning Speke, two experienced explorers, led an expedition to Africa in 1857 that a real attempt was made to solve the problem. The entire journey was complicated from the start by the fact that neither of the two men could stand each other, and argued violently the whole time. They both became extremely ill, and the expedition

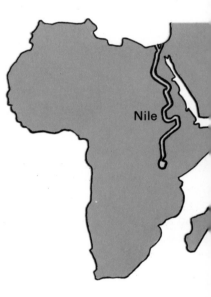

John Hanning Speke, one of the great explorers of Central Africa

achieved little more than the discovery of Lake Tanganyika. On the return journey, Speke reached Lake Victoria which he thought might be the source of the Nile, although Burton strongly disagreed. In 1860 Speke set out on another expedition, this time with James Grant. They followed the previous route as far as Tabora, but from there headed towards the country west of Lake Victoria. Continuing around the lake, Speke finally reached the Ripon Falls (1860), at which point he was certain that he had found the source of the Nile, and indeed his theory was proved right.

The type of Anglo-Saxon long-ship found in the barrow.

What was found at Sutton Hoo?

Near the River Deben in Suffolk, at Sutton Hoo, are eleven mounds or 'barrows' dating back to the 7th century. In 1938 it was decided to open the largest of these to find out what it contained. The result was the greatest archaeological discovery ever made in Britain. Within the barrow was a king's ship, 25 metres long, and, inside this, a royal treasure which included gold and silver buckles, silver dishes and bowls, and a king's helmet.

Who rediscovered Cretan civilization?

Whilst shopping in Athens, Arthur Evans saw some small stones on which was an unusual style of writing. Learning that these stones came from Crete he went to the island and, in 1893, began digging. In time he unearthed a great city that had been ruled by the legendary King Minos. Evans had, in fact, discovered the remains of a brilliant civilization that was more than 3,500 years old.

Examples of Cretan jewellery

How was Tutankhamen's tomb discovered?

In November 1922 an English archaeologist, Howard Carter, found in Egypt the tomb of a pharaoh that was filled with wonderful, exciting treasure. Newspapers were full of stories of golden thrones, beds and chariots, of jewelled caskets, even of flowers still preserved in

the dry, airless tomb. Carter, who was working for Lord Carnarvon, had been busy in the royal burial site at Thebes, known as the Valley of the Kings. He knew that nearly every royal tomb had been found and that a pharaoh called Tutankhamen, still in his teens when he died, was almost the only one undiscovered. He narrowed the area of search down to one small part of the Valley, and a stairway and top of a doorway were soon revealed. The door bore some seals, two of which were those of Tutankhamen! By the end of November the door was fully uncovered and Carter made a small hole in it through which he shone a torch. The light winked back from the golden riches of a pharaoh who had died nearly 3,300 years before. It was one of the most important archaeological finds in history. The treasures from the tomb are now in the Cairo Museum. (Above) Jewellery worn by Tutankhamen.

Macarthur and the flock
of sheep that started
Australia's great industry

How did Australia's sheep industry begin?

At the end of the eighteenth century, Australia was going through a difficult time. Food was scarce and only storeships from England staved off actual famine. Things were so bad that officers in the army were importing rum and using it instead of money. However, John Macarthur, one of these officers, was convinced that money could be made out of fine-wool sheep, and he left the army to breed Merino sheep. Today there are 150 million of them in Australia.

Who first explored central Australia?

Even by the 1830s, central Australia was still a great mystery. Several people had tried to explore the interior but had been defeated by desert, lack of water and hostile natives. One of these was Edward Eyre, who had failed twice. His third attempt also seemed hopeless but finally, after an appalling journey of 2,000 km, Eyre and Wylie, his faithful aborigine servant, reached the south-west coast at Albany (below).

Why are Australians called 'Diggers'?

Early in the 1800s, gold was discovered in Australia. Most of the 'strikes' were in the vicinity of the Blue Mountains near Bathurst. In 1851, a prospector named Hargraves – who had been in California during the gold-rush two years earlier – discovered rich traces of gold in Summer Hill Creek. The news spread rapidly and within two months the whole area was swarming with prospectors. The fact that there was gold to be had sent men digging in other areas, especially around Melbourne. In time the cities were deserted and ships lay

Edward Hargraves and
gold prospectors on
the Turon River

empty in the harbours, for everyone seemed bitten by the lust for gold. Towns sprang up overnight and were soon the scenes of rioting and bloodshed. The army had to be called in and a battle took place between soldiers and diggers. The incident became known as the battle of Eureka Stockade. By 1856, however, the day of the 'amateur' digger was almost over. Deep shafts had to be sunk to reach the gold and such mines had to be run by companies. But, in memory of the gold-rush days, Australians are still sometimes called 'Diggers'.

What was 'The Island of the Blessed'?

For many centuries, there were tales of islands lying somewhere out in the Atlantic. One of these was the 'Island of the Blessed', an earthly paradise just over the horizon. Several Irish monks decided to look for it but although they braved many dangers, they took fright at last when they saw an Icelandic volcano. Because of this voyage, 'St Brendan's Isle' was talked about for years. Another mysterious island was the island of the Seven Cities. It was said that seven bishops, driven from Spain by the Moors, arrived at this unknown island and built seven cities – one for each. There was also a legend of the lost island of Atlantis which was supposed to have been engulfed by the sea. This was heard of again later under the name of Antilha, but was never found.

How did Rhode Island come into being?

An early English settler in North America was a clergyman, Roger Williams. He disagreed with the Puritan form of religion, and eventually was ordered back to England. Instead of obeying, he slipped away, bought some land from an Indian tribe and founded his own colony in 1636. Others seeking religious freedom joined him and soon four communities were thriving. Williams went to England and obtained a Charter which enabled him to join the four settlements together into a loose federation which came to be known as 'Rhode Island'.

Which pirate was also an explorer?

William Dampier was a Somerset man who turned pirate, although the ships and towns he plundered were usually Spanish. In January 1688 he was second-in-command of a ship called the *Cygnet* when the coast of New Holland – as Australia was then called – came in sight. The ship was run into a bay to be careened, and Dampier went ashore with some of the crew. He was therefore in the first group of Englishmen to step on to Australian soil. He met some Aborigines and was to describe them later as 'the miserablest people in the world'. The party explored a little of the coast before sailing away to the north. On returning to England, Dampier wrote the story of his adventures, calling the book *A New Voyage Round the World*. It

William Dampier and his unusual memorial

made him famous, and his readers conveniently forgot his past as a pirate. The Admiralty did the same, for in 1699 he was appointed to command the *Roebuck*. He returned to New Holland and charted much of the coast, including a group of islands now known as Dampier's Archipelago. His ship foundered on the way home, destroying many of his notes and papers, and Dampier and his crew, struggling ashore, were forced to live on turtles and goats until they were rescued, five weeks later.

Who was the first Englishman to sail around the world?

In 1570, Francis Drake, a Devon seaman, sailed to South America and sacked the Spanish town of Nombre de Dios. Later he climbed a tree on the Isthmus of Panama and saw, away in the distance, the shimmer of the Pacific Ocean. He swore that one day he would return and sail an English ship on that great ocean. It was seven years before he achieved this aim. Five ships, led by his flagship, the *Pelican*, sailed from Plymouth on 8 December 1577. They called at the Cape Verde Islands, then set sail again for the coast of South America. The three largest ships – for the others had been emptied of stores and set adrift – then turned southwards. They reached the Magellan Straits and sailed through to the great expanse of the Pacific Ocean. To celebrate the fact that his dream had come true, Drake decided to change his flagship's name, renaming it the *Golden Hind*. Alone now, for the other ships had turned back, the *Golden Hind* began to plunder Spanish settlements on the west coast of South America. Finally, heavy with treasure, the ship turned away from the coast and again headed westwards. On 3 November 1580, nearly three years after leaving England, Drake sighted Plymouth again, having sailed right around the world. He was not only the first Englishman but the very first sea captain to circumnavigate the globe.

Above: Drake's ship, the *Golden Hind*, was a vessel of about 100 tons. She had a crew of over eighty
Below: Francis Drake

With which Indian tribes did the American settlers come in contact?

When Christopher Columbus made his first landfall in the Bahamas he was so certain that he had reached the East Indies that he called the natives 'Indians', the name by which they are still known today. He found them a friendly, peaceful people. Spaniards who explored what is now the southwestern United States found the natives equally friendly. They lived in permanent settlements, growing crops. The tribes on the eastern sea-board, however, spent much of their lives hunting and fishing in the deep forests where they made their homes. One of the tribes in the east was the Iroquois, another a group which included the Seminoles, Choctaw, Chickasaw, Natchez and Creeks.

At first Indians and white men lived and traded in harmony but as time went on the former, seeing that their lands and food supplies were threatened, began to fight for their very existence. Soon there was continuous small-scale fighting. One of the most powerful tribes, the Blackfeet, killed every white man, woman and child who entered their territory, although the whites, in their turn, took a terrible revenge. The early pioneers moving westwards in their lumbering 'prairie schooners' and the men laying the Union Pacific railroad were always in danger of surprise attacks from Indians. This was especially likely in the south where the Crow and Cheyenne hunting grounds were, as well as those of the Kiowa, Navaho, Comanche and Apache further south still. Finally, these skirmishes flared into open warfare in 1866 when the great Sioux nation resolved to throw the white man out of their lands. After a few initial victories they wiped out a strong American force under General George Custer at the Battle of the Little Big Horn. That was their last great victory however. By 1890 treaties were signed and an uneasy peace existed at last between Indians and 'Palefaces'.

A brave, a squaw and her papoose, members of the Seminole Indian tribe

Who gave the colony of Virginia its name?

Two relatively obscure captains, Arthur Barlow and Philip Amada, were sent by Sir Walter Raleigh to explore the New World. They sailed along the coast between Chesapeake Bay and Florida and claimed the whole area in the name of Queen Elizabeth I. When they returned to England in 1584 they reported to Raleigh that the land they had found was ideal for settlement. It had good soil, plenty of water and game in abundance. The Indians, too, were peaceful and friendly. Most of them were fishermen who sailed far out from the

shore in canoes made from tree-trunks which they hollowed out with burning brands (above). A skilful artist named John White had gone with the expedition and he showed Raleigh paintings of the green and pleasant country, and of the Indians who lived there. The queen also saw these paintings, as well as the two Indians who had been brought back to England. Raleigh was anxious to send a further expedition to colonize this new territory and Elizabeth suggested that it be called by that name which referred to her unmarried state – 'the Virgin Queen'. And 'Virginia' it became.

Left: Animal pelts
Below: A trader with produce from the New World: potatoes, tobacco and maize

What were the first products brought back from the New World?

When John Cabot's ship reached the Newfoundland coast in 1497 he was amazed at the fantastic amount of fish existing in those waters. His account of the vast quantities of cod that could be caught simply by lowering a bucket over the side and scooping them up soon brought fishermen of other countries to the area. When Jacques Cartier explored Canada he was similarly impressed by the richness of the country and particularly mentioned the maize, or Indian corn. Early settlers sent back timber and rich pelts, but the two most important products brought to the Old World from the New were potatoes and tobacco. Both were introduced into Europe by the Spanish: potatoes from Peru and tobacco from Mexico. They were later brought to Queen Elizabeth's court by Sir Walter Raleigh.

What was the North-west Passage?

In the sixteenth century, every seafaring nation was looking for a sea route to the East Indies either by way of the New World or around Africa. Because Spain commanded the Cape Horn route and Portugal the one around Africa, the rest of Europe had to seek a third alternative. Their seamen hoped to find a passage north-west through or around North America. Frobisher, Davis, de Verrazano, Cartier and Hudson all tried without success. After 1616 the search was abandoned for nearly two centuries. Then others took up the challenge, but it was not until 1906 that it was discovered by a Norwegian, Roald Amundsen, in the *Gjöa*.

Who gave Maryland its name?

George Calvert was a favourite courtier of King James I, who made him Lord Baltimore and promised him a grant of land in the region of Newfoundland. Baltimore sailed for his new territory but decided that the place was too cold and barren for him. He complained, and the new king, Charles I, agreed to give him part of Virginia instead. The Charter was accepted by the second Lord Baltimore, his father having died. He was delighted, for he had been given a vast estate, with freedom to make his own laws and coin his own money. He informed the king that he would call the colony 'Crescentia' but the king insisted that it be called *Maryland*, in honour of his queen, Henrietta Maria. In fact, the second Lord Baltimore never went to America, the colony being governed on his behalf by his brother, Leonard Calvert.

Which early settler's life was saved by an Indian girl?

The first successful English settlement in North America was founded in 1607 by Captain Christopher Newport. It was situated on an island and named Jamestown in honour of the king, James I, who had given the settlers their Charter. Newport later returned to England and Captain John Smith became the new leader. Early in 1608 he was exploring the Chickahominy River when he was captured by Indians. The chief of the tribe sentenced him to be killed but just as the executioner raised his club, Pocahontas, the chief's daughter, ran forward. Taking the Englishman's head in her arms, she begged for his life to be spared. Her father, Powhatan, was moved by her plea and agreed to let Smith go free. Later she was persuaded to go to Jamestown, and there she married John Rolfe, a Norfolk man. Three years later, Pocahontas and her husband sailed to England. She was received at the court of James I, where her beauty was highly praised. Pocahontas fell ill in England and died in 1617, before being able to return to Jamestown.

Above: A portrait of Pocahontas shown in English costume of the time. Her grave is in a church in Gravesend.
Left: John Smith

Who first traced the course of the Congo?

Henry Stanley (right) is usually remembered as the American news-paperman who, on first meeting the Scottish explorer, Livingstone, deep in the African interior, greeted him with 'Dr Livingstone, I presume?' Yet Stanley was a distinguished explorer in his own right. In 1874 he returned to Africa to explore the Luabala River which Livingstone believed formed the headwaters of the Nile. He followed the course of this river, forcing his way through thickly wooded country west of Lake Tanganyika to prove that it was, in fact, the headwaters of the Congo (now Zaire). In August 1876 he began to follow the river as it flowed to the Atlantic. It was to prove a fantastic journey. Day after day he was attacked by unfriendly tribes. On one occasion his own few craft were attacked by a fleet of fifty-four war canoes. It was led by a huge canoe with forty paddlers on either side, and altogether there were two thousand Africans. Stanley's men opened fire with their muskets and the attackers were forced to break off the action and retreat. Finally, after losing his European companions and 170 native followers, Stanley reached the trading station of Boma and three days later gazed out over the Atlantic Ocean. He had solved the mystery of the Congo after 4,800 km of exploration.

Where did the French first settle in America?

One of the reasons why the French wished to establish colonies in the New World was because some of them wanted to escape religious persecution at home. In 1562, a group of thirty French Protestants, led by Jean Ribault, landed at the mouth of the St John's River in the Spanish territory of Florida (left). However, the Indians were hostile, and when the colonists weren't defending themselves, they were looking for gold instead of cultivating food, and so were soon starving. On their way home to France they were even reduced to cannibalism, and the final disaster came when the remaining survivors were captured by an English ship.

Spaniards struggle through rivers, swamps and jungle in their search for El Dorado

What was 'El Dorado'?

An old South American legend told of a strange coronation ceremony. It took place high in the Andes on the shore of Lake
Guatavita. Every new king had his body anointed with oil and then
covered with gold dust. Glittering with this golden skin he plunged
into the lake whilst his subjects cast in further gold and jewels as
offerings to their god. When this legend reached the first Spanish
settlers they called the king 'El Dorado' – The Gilded Man – and
the city, Manoa. With this knowledge came a great desire to find
the legendary king and his golden city. Many expeditions were
undertaken in search of fabulous treasure, but all, in fact, failed.
One of the first expeditions was headed by Gonzalo de Quesada
who, in 1569, led an army of eight hundred men into the remote
fastnesses of the Andes. After a year of incredible difficulties
Quesada reached a city where he discovered a certain amount of
gold and silver articles, a relatively small prize for all the hardships
he and his men had endured. This city was named New Granada
(now Bogotá). Others after him continued the search for El Dorado
and many died in the attempt. Sir Walter Raleigh led two expeditions
from England, both of which were unsuccessful.

Who were the Pilgrim Fathers?

In Tudor times a number of Puritans lived in Lincolnshire in England, where they were often badly treated because of their faith. At last they could stand the situation no longer. They decided to sail for Holland where other Puritans had already settled. Living in Amsterdam to start with, they moved to Leyden where they were warmly received by the friendly Dutch. They never forgot that they were English, however, and finally came to a great decision. They would sail to England's settlement in North America where they would have freedom to worship as they wished. About thirty-five of them arrived in England and with sixty-seven others – men, women and children – they sailed from Plymouth in 1620 in the *Mayflower*. After a voyage of two months during which the ship was blown off course, they anchored in Cape Cod Bay, Massachusetts. They had hoped to settle in Virginia but their captain would not take them further. Some of the men went ashore to search for a suitable place for a settlement and found one with plenty of wood and water. They named it Plymouth because that city had been their last link with the Old World. Their first winter was a hard one and by the spring of 1621 half of them had died. Even so, none wanted to return to England. Things slowly improved, especially when they made friends with their Indian neighbours. Other people joined them from England and the colony set an example of faith and courage to all future settlers who, in time, were to become Americans.

Above: The first boatload of the 'Pilgrim Fathers' – the elders of the new community – go ashore under their leader John Carver, who later became governor of Plymouth Colony.
Right: The *Mayflower*

grande Templo de Mexico

Left: The temple of Tenochtitlan. At the dedication of a single temple in 1487, 20,000 human hearts were offered to the gods.
Below: Two forms of human sacrifice. These are from original Aztec paintings.

Who were the Aztecs?

During the twelfth or thirteenth centuries the third and greatest of the Mexican civilizations arose – the Aztecs. They were a warlike race which gradually grew in power, becoming the strongest nation in Mexico. Their capital, Tenochtitlan, was built on islands in a marshy area where Mexico City stands today. They worshipped a blood-thirsty pantheon of gods, led by Huitzilopochtli, the sun god. These gods had to be pacified by the sacrifices of hearts torn from the living bodies of human victims. The Aztecs had reached the height of their power when, in 1519, they were invaded by a Spanish army of five hundred men led by an adventurer, Hernán Cortez. Although the Aztec king, Montezuma, could call upon an army of thousands of warriors, he was convinced that Cortez was a god called Quetzalcoatl returning in human form to avenge himself, and so he did virtually nothing to save his people. The Spaniards easily conquered the Aztecs and within a few years the Aztec civilization had been completely destroyed.

What part did Captain Bligh play in the history of Australia?

William Bligh is best known to history as the captain of HMS *Bounty* whose crew mutinied and set him adrift in a small boat. His voyage in this boat of 6,500 km reveals what a skilful seaman and navigator he must have been. He was also second-in-command to Nelson at the Battle of Copenhagen. Because of his distinguished services he was appointed Governor of Australia and sailed to take up his new post in August 1806. On arrival he found that a number of army officers had taken over control of the country and were also making personal fortunes out of the sale of rum. Bligh, well known for his strict discipline and short temper, tried to curb their powers. He even had their leader arrested and accused of sedition. But the officers turned on him and marched to Government House to take him prisoner in turn. His daughter tried to bar the way but they pushed past her and found Bligh hiding beneath his bed. He was put under arrest for a year but made so much trouble that everyone was relieved when he voluntarily left Australia for England in 1810.

Above: Captain Bligh
Left: Bligh's daughter, Mary, defies the rebels at Government House

Who first reached the North and South Poles?

Men began to explore the Arctic as early as 1553, but it was not until 6 April 1909 that the Pole itself was reached. Three and a half centuries of effort and courage ended with an American, Robert E. Peary 'nailing the Stars and Stripes to the North Pole'. The quest for the South Pole began much later, the first landing in Antarctica being as late as 1895. In 1910 a Norwegian, Roald Amundsen, sailed for the Arctic in Nansen's ship the *Fram*. Hardly had he started, however, than he heard of Peary's success. He at once put his ship about and sailed south. On 20 October 1911, from his base in the Antarctic, he set off for the South Pole. The going was difficult; fog and blizzards slowed the men down. They reached their goal on 14 December and raised the Norwegian flag over the estimated position of the Pole (above). It was still flying when a month later Captain Robert Scott arrived with four other Englishmen, only to discover that they had been beaten by Amundsen. On their return to base, Scott and his men perished in a blizzard.

Who first sailed north of the Magnetic North Pole?

In 1819, Edward Parry, a young naval officer, was given command of two ships, the *Hecla* and *Gripper*, with instructions to find a sea route to the Pole. He was defeated by the ice but his ships, nevertheless, were the first to sail north of the Magnetic Pole – then 71°N. 96°W. (right). As they did so Parry was delighted to see his compass needle pointing *south*, for this meant that a prize of £5,000 had been won by the two ships. After two more voyages to the Arctic, Parry put

forward an exceptionally daring plan to try and reach the North Pole by travelling overland – something that had never been tried before. He sailed for the Arctic in the *Hecla* and after anchoring in Spitsbergen, he and some of his men set off in two amphibious sledges that had been specially built for the venture. They were called *Enterprise* and *Endeavour* and were drawn by reindeer. The ground became so broken, however, that the animals were abandoned and the party had to drag the sledges. They failed in their attempt to reach the Pole but managed to get closer to it than anyone else had succeeded in doing up to that time. Parry also proved that it was possible to winter in the Arctic regions and return with a crew in robust health and good spirits.

Byrd's tri-motor Fokker,
first over the North Pole

Who first reached the Poles by aircraft?

As early as 1897, the first attempt was made to reach the North Pole by aircraft, when a Swedish explorer and three others set off in a balloon. Thirty years later their bodies were found near where the balloon had crashed. By then the North Pole had been crossed by a three-engined Fokker monoplane, the *Josephine Ford*. It carried Lt. Commander (later Rear-Admiral) R. E. Byrd with Floyd Bennett as pilot. The plane left Spitsbergen on 8 May 1926 and after twice circling around the Pole, returned to base after having flown 2,500 km. Four days later on 12 May, the Pole was crossed again, this time by an airship, the *Norge*, commanded by the veteran explorer, Roald Amundsen. A year later an airship, the *Italia*, crashed on yet another Arctic flight and whilst searching for survivors Amundsen lost his life. In 1927 Byrd set up a base at Little America in the Antarctic. He was now ready to set out on an attempt to cross the South Pole. From four aircraft available he selected a three-engined Ford and, with Bernt Balchen as pilot and two other companions, took off on 28 November 1929. The plane circled the Pole, then, after being airborne for nineteen hours, touched down again at the base. Byrd thus had the honour of being the first man to fly over both Poles.

Byrd's Ford Tri-motor,
first over the South Pole

How is man exploring outer space?

From earliest times men have dreamed of travelling in space, exploring new worlds, reaching for the stars—an apparently impossible dream. Then rocket research which took place during World War II gave a great impetus to space travel for which rocket propulsion is essential. After many experiments the first major

break-through came in April 1961 when a Russian, Yuri Gagarin, spent 108 breath-taking minutes in space. Three weeks later Commander Alan Shephard of the U.S. Navy also journeyed into outer space. The greatest milestone so far passed was in July 1969 when two more Americans, Neil Armstrong and Edwin J. Aldrin Jr. stepped on to the moon (above).

The Past

Who were the Incas?

The Incas were an Indian people who lived in the Andean region of South America. The first Inca ruler, Manco Capan (c. A.D. 1200) was believed to have been descended from the sun god.

The Incas thirsted for power. They warred against and defeated their neighbours, and soon their empire extended from central Chile to the present Colombia-Ecuador border. Having a highly developed agricultural system, they grew maize, beans, tomatoes, chillis, peppers, cotton – almost all then completely unknown in Europe.

Most of the Inca people were farmers. Nobody paid taxes, but every man was periodically called to service in the army, or on building roads and temples, or mining. The Incas built suspension bridges, hillside terraces, long irrigation canals and immense fortresses. Medicine and surgery were highly developed.

The Incas were conquered by a Spanish adventurer, Francisco Pizarro, in 1532.

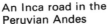

An Inca road in the Peruvian Andes

What is the secret of Stonehenge?

The great stones stand gaunt against the sky in the countryside of Wiltshire, England. What is their origin? There are many theories. One of the earliest recorders of this stone system was Henry of Huntingdon, who died in 1154. But the stones are older than that. Some people thought that Boadicea, a queen of the ancient Britons was buried there. Another legend, as related by Geoffrey of Monmouth (c. A.D. 1136) was that the Wizard Merlin magically transported the stones from Ireland and rebuilt them on Salisbury Plain. Wizard Extraordinary he must have been, for investigation in more recent years has indicated that some of the great stones were taken from the Prescelly Mountains in Dyfed, in south-western Wales.

A further opinion was that Stonehenge was Danish. The architect and surveyor, Inigo Jones, who made a plan of it for James I, said it was Roman. Another expert said: 'the Druids'. Was it a Sun Temple? Some astronomers, working on this assumption, put its date as 1680 B.C. Almost certainly, Stonehenge was built in three stages during Late Neolithic to Early Bronze Age (1800–1400 B.C.). Almost equally certainly it was constructed as a place of worship. But Stonehenge keeps its secret. The mystery remains.

What is an aqueduct?

An aqueduct is an artificial channel, usually an elevated one, for carrying water. The ancient Romans and Greeks were enthusiastic builders of aqueducts. Before the end of the first century A.D., Rome was supplied by nine aqueducts with a total length of more than 386 km, of which about 56 km were raised above ground.

When were bricks first used?

Since the very early days of their history men have been making bricks of clay or other materials for use in building. The Tower of Babel, for which, according to the Old Testament, 'they had brick for stone', was probably a brick temple. People who lived in ancient Egypt built their houses from both sun-dried and kiln-baked bricks.

In an early brickworks men are seen at work digging the clay, moulding it and firing the bricks in the kilns

What is a 'motte and bailey' castle?

A simple fortification consisted of two parts: a natural or artificial mound (motte) with a wooden tower or keep on top, and a larger area at the foot of the mound enclosed by palisades, (and later by walls and towers of masonry), called a bailey. The bailey was used for stores and huts. This outer walled space sometimes had a ditch in front of it which might be flooded to make a moat.

These 'motte and bailey' castles were built mostly in France during the tenth century, but the building of this type of private fortress spread over western Europe in the following century. In the Middle Ages land was owned under the feudal system. Princes and

Typical Norman 'motte and bailey' castle with wooden walls

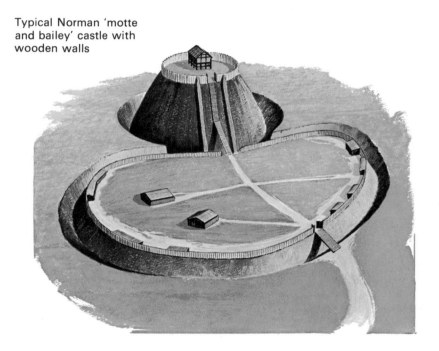

nobles kept private armies to enforce power over their own domains. War was constantly breaking out between local lords, and a fortified dwelling was essential. These castles were simple but effective. They could withstand a siege. Gunpowder had not yet been invented and success was achieved by starvation – or treachery. They offered a refuge for neighbouring villagers and their flocks.

Little trace remains today of the wooden 'motte and bailey' castles, but many with stone keeps are still standing. They were tall, square buildings, with a single room on each floor. Sometimes, for greater protection, an outside stair led to an entrance on the first floor.

This ancient bronze statue of Romulus and Remus with the wolf is in Rome

Who were Romulus and Remus?

According to Roman legend Romulus and Remus were grandsons of Numitor, King of Alba, who was deposed by his brother, Amulius. Numitor's daughter was forced to become a Vestal Virgin, but Mars, the god of war, fell in love with her and she gave birth to twin sons. Amulius commanded that the infants be drowned and they were thrown into the River Tiber in a basket of reeds. However, the basket was eventually washed ashore, and the babies were suckled by a she-wolf. They were later discovered by the king's shepherd who took them home and brought them up as his own sons.

When Romulus and Remus were grown up they rose against the king, killed him and restored the throne to their grandfather. They decided to found a town and Romulus began to build a city on the Palatine Hill. His brother jeered at him, and in the ensuing quarrel Remus was killed. Romulus built the city and named it Roma (Rome).

What is a cameo?

The Emperor Augustus shown on a famous cameo

A cameo is an engraved gem on which the subject or figure is carved in relief on a stone or other material which provides two layers of colour, such as chalcedony, onyx and shell. One colour forms the background while the design is cut out of the other. Finished cameos are often mounted as brooches. Favourite subjects are portraits and mythological scenes. Among the portraits are valuable representations of Roman emperors and princes.

What are mosaics?

A mosaic is a picture or pattern made by placing, or fixing, small different-coloured pieces of stone or glass side by side.

The art was an invention of the Mediterranean peoples and flowered between c. 300–31 B.C. In the Roman period, or about the first five hundred years of the Christian era, mosaics of great beauty and variety were designed all over the empire spreading from

Byzantine mosaic of the
Empress Theodora at Ravenna

Syria to Spain, and from Africa to Britain. The most brilliant mosaics in the world adorn walls and ceilings of sacred buildings in Rome, Ravenna and Salonika. Mosaics which have been discovered dating from the pre-Christian era were for the most part laid on the floor.

The legionary carried a *scutum* (shield), a *pilum* (throwing spear), and a *gladius* (short sword). Helmets, with face masks, were used for triumphal parades

What were the Roman Legions?

Legion is a military term that has been used since ancient times. In early Rome the 'legion' was a levy of citizens marching to war, or, in other words, a citizen army. As conquests grew, Rome needed more men and *Legio* came to denote a force of four to six thousand heavy infantry supported by a cavalry contingent and light infantry. The light infantry were armed with darts, slings and other missile weapons. The military system of the legions enabled the Romans to conquer and rule the ancient world. This was the way the men of the legions fought: they were arranged in three lines, the Hastati in front, followed by Principes and lastly by the Triarii. The Hastati engaged the enemy but, if beaten, retired, leaving the Principes, highly experienced troops, to continue the battle. The Triarii knelt and positioned their spears to form a defensive line. Each legion had its proud traditions. Renowned was the 10th – the favourite of Julius Caesar. About the period 200 B.C. every Roman from the age of seventeen to forty-six was liable to be called to serve as a soldier in one of the legions.

Did the Romans use flags?

The answer, in the modern use of the word flag, is 'no'. The word is of Germanic origin and was used in the fifteenth and sixteenth centuries to mean a piece of cloth, or other material, displaying the insignia of a community or armed force, an office, or an individual. They were used originally mainly in warfare, and were signs of leadership. They also served to identify friend and foe and were useful as rallying points. Flags of various forms are known as colours, standards, banners, ensigns, pennons, guidons and burgees. The earliest insignia used in battle were not flags. They can be more correctly described as standards. The ancient standard, such as the Roman legions carried into battle, consisted of some solid object fixed on a bracket at the top of a pole.

Cities of ancient Greece had distinctive signs such as a sphinx or a pegasus. The Romans followed this example, at first using effigies of gods, of generals or of animals – wolves, horses and bears – until it was decreed that the Roman legions should have only the eagle (*aquila*) as a standard. This eagle effigy was revived in France by Napoleon I and later in Fascist Italy. The *vexillum* or Roman cavalry flag was nearer to a flag in the modern sense of the word. It was a square piece of cloth fastened to a bar fixed crosswise to a spearhead, and is still used in ecclesiastical ceremony in both Roman Catholic and Eastern Orthodox religious processions.

This was the earliest sort of standard carried by Roman centurions. They used them so that the men of the Roman legions should have a rallying point

What is the significance of the date 2 June 1953?

In London a moment of historic pageantry was celebrated on this day – the Coronation of Queen Elizabeth II. It was also the day when London heard the news of the conquest of Mount Everest's 9,608 m by Edmund Hillary, a New Zealander, and Tensing, the famous Sherpa porter from Nepal. The London *Times* wrote:

'Seldom since Francis Drake brought the *Golden Hind* to anchor in Plymouth Sound has a British explorer offered to his Sovereign such a tribute of glory as Colonel John Hunt (leader of the expedition) and his men are able to lay at the feet of Queen Elizabeth for her Coronation day.' The queen sent a message to the Everest expedition expressing her 'warmest congratulations on [their] great achievement'.

The flags of the United Nations, Great Britain, Nepal and India, fly on top of the world at the ascent of Everest in 1953. Ten previous attempts on Everest had failed

Mountain climbing was popularized by Horace de Saussure, who was the first to bring the words 'geology' and 'geologist' into general use

Who popularized mountain climbing?

Mountaineers of today owe a good deal to a Swiss scientist called Horace Bénédict de Saussure, who was born at Conches, near Geneva, in 1740. He changed the general attitude to mountains from one of superstition and dread to one of inspiration. De Saussure was professor of physics and philosophy at the University of Geneva and a pioneer of geology, mineralogy and meteorology, plant anatomy and alpine botany.

He was the first traveller to reach the summit of Mont Blanc (1787) and to measure its height by barometric pressure.

Who were the 'Bird Men'?

The story of man's attempt to rival the birds is as old as the human race. From Greek mythology we have the story of Icarus who had wings of feathers sewn on with threads and fastened with wax. He flew too near the sun, and the wax melted. Icarus fell into the sea and was drowned. Oliver of Malmesbury, an English monk, tower-jumped with wings in 1020 and survived – with injuries. Leonardo da Vinci (1452–1519) gave the world plans for a flying machine and a parachute. In 1678 Besnier, a French locksmith, created a glider-type machine, an arrangement of rods and planes worked by his hands and feet, and claimed to have flown over a barn.

Who first flew the Atlantic non-stop?

The year was 1919. On 14 and 15 June the first non-stop trans-Atlantic flight was made by John Alcock and Arthur Whitten Brown. Alcock was the pilot, Whitten Brown the navigator. Their aircraft was an adapted Vickers Vimy bomber fitted with two Rolls-Royce Eagle VIII engines. They took off from St John's, Newfoundland, and landed, sixteen hours, twenty-seven minutes later, in a bog at Clifden, Co. Galway, Ireland. Average speed: about 193 km.p.h. Distance: approximately 3,040 km. A week later Alcock was killed in an air crash in France.

When was history made in twelve seconds?

The date was 17 December 1903; the scene: the cold windy hills of North Carolina; the name of the place which was to go down in history: Kitty Hawk; the occasion: man's first powered flight. The aeroplane had arrived. Orville Wright (one of the two aviation pioneer brothers, Orville and Wilbur) was at the controls. The aircraft, powered by a four cylinder engine, careered through space for twelve seconds at 48 km.p.h. airspeed, swept down and landed in soft sand. Orville wrote: 'This flight lasted only twelve seconds but it was, nevertheless, the first in the history of the world in

which a machine, carrying a man, had raised itself by its own power into the air in full flight, had sailed forward without reduction of speed and had finally landed at a point as high as that from which it started.' The Wrights' aircraft was called *Flyer*. Only five people were there to watch it make history. One photograph recorded the scene. It was not until three years after Kitty Hawk that the *Scientific American* wrote: 'In all the history of invention there is probably no parallel to the unostentatious manner in which the Wright Brothers of Dayton, Ohio, ushered into the world their epoch-making invention of the first successful aeroplane flying machine.'

When was a sea captain treated like a god?

On 17 January 1779 two ships of Captain James Cook anchored in Kealakekua Bay, Hawaii. The natives believed that in ancient times Lono, god of fertility and cultivated foods, came down from the sky. Lono was honoured in the Makahiki festivities that lasted from October to February. When Cook landed, the people greeted him as Lono. Priests brought offerings, and the inhabitants prostrated

themselves. The king, Kalaniopu, took off the feather cloak (opposite page) he was wearing and put it around Cook's shoulders – a sign of awe and reverence. Finally, the season of plenty drew to a close, and Cook set sail. A few days later he put back to repair a damaged ship, but by now the islanders had changed their ideas about the divinity of the Englishman. A dispute arose about a ship's boat which had been stolen. On 14 February a skirmish took place, and the British sailors retreated to their boats. Cook, the last to withdraw, was struck down from behind and killed.

Tsiolkovski, Soviet space pioneer

Who led the way to the stars?

Konstantin Eduardovich Tsiolkovski was born in Russia in 1857. He spent his life teaching in school and doing practical and theoretical research work in the fields of aeronautics and astronautics. In 1883, long before the first aeroplane had been built, he began to consider the many different factors involved if man were to journey into space. In so doing, he developed an important theory – the theory of mass ratio: that is, the ratio between the mass of a rocket with its fuel and the mass of the rocket after the fuel has been used up. Tsiolkovski worked out the principle of staging in booster rockets, and came to the conclusion that only a multi-stage rocket could overcome the pull of the earth's gravity. His design for 'a passenger rocker-train of the year 2017' was over 90m long and and made up of twenty stages. He demonstrated that liquid propellants would be efficient rocket fuel.

Tsiolkovski led the way to the stars – but he did not live to see his dreams come true. He died in 1935.

HMS *Ark Royal*, the aircraft carrier that bears a famous name

A torpedo being fired from a 24 m motor torpedo boat of a type in service at the outbreak of the Second World War

Where is the *Ark Royal*?

The name *Ark Royal* goes back a long way in the annals of the British Navy. Sir Walter Raleigh, that famed Elizabethan seaman, had a great ship built which he called after himself, *Ark Raleigh*. She was launched in 1587. When the menace of the Spanish Armada loomed, the Crown bought her and she became *Ark Royal*. Probably the most

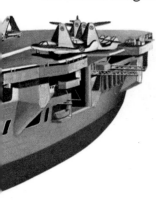

famous bearer of the name was the Second World War aircraft carrier. She was launched in 1937 and was the centre of many actions. William Joyce ('Lord Haw Haw'), broadcasting from Germany, repeated time and again a question meant to worry the British: 'Where is the *Ark Royal*?' It was the ship the Germans most wanted to sink. The *Ark Royal* hunted the German *Graf Spee* and helped trap the *Bismarck*. The end of the *Ark Royal* came in 1941. On 14 November the Admiralty announced that she had sunk after being torpedoed by a German submarine. Of her 1,541 men only one was lost. *Ark Royal*'s name lives on, borne by another aircraft carrier. Joyce was executed for treason in 1946.

Which missile is nicknamed 'tin fish'?

The British Navy's nickname for a torpedo is 'tin fish'. It is an underwater powered projectile which can be launched from a ship, submarine or aeroplane to explode against a hostile ship. Robert Whitehead, a British engineer, designed the first self-propelled torpedo over a hundred years ago. Torpedoes strike their target below water. When a shell or bomb explodes above the water line, much of its power is wasted on air, which is compressible. But water is inelastic and the full impact of the explosion blasts the ship's hull.

What is a dhow?

The word 'dhow' is used to describe any kind of Arab sailing vessel.
They are the regular Arab trading craft, and make long voyages from
the Red Sea and Persian Gulf down to the African coast. The com-
monest are the small, square-sterned dhows known as 'sambuks'.
Then there are the smart 'booms', and the short, wide 'bedeni' from
Muscat in the Persian Gulf. The largest are the 'baghla' (above).
These have carved, ornamental, square sterns copied from European
ships trading with India in the seventeenth and eighteenth centuries,
overhanging bows, and two or three short, heavy, masts carrying the
tall, triangular (or lateen) sail common in the Mediterranean.

Which was the largest battleship ever built?

The greatest of the fighting giants of the sea was the Japanese
Yamato. She gave her name to a class of four battleships designed
to be invincible. *Yamato* displaced 72,000 tons. Her main armament
consisted of nine 45.9 cm guns in triple turrets – overwhelmingly
superior to any other battleship in the world. The *Yamato* was
completed soon after the Japanese attack on the U.S. base at

What were the Pillars of Hercules?

This is the name by which ancient people knew the Strait of Gibraltar, the narrow body of water which connects the Mediterranean Sea and the Atlantic Ocean. One of the pillars is Gibraltar. The other massive promontory lies across the Strait on the African coast (probably Mount Acho, just east of Ceuta). The Strait is about 58 km long, and at its narrowest point only 14 km wide. The width between the ancient Pillars of Hercules is 22 km. Legend claimed that the pillars were rocks torn asunder by the Greek hero Hercules, in order to open the Atlantic Ocean into the Mediterranean. Other myths related how Hercules once joined them to make a bridge, or fixed them to narrow the Strait, so as to keep out the monsters of the deep.

Pearl Harbor on 7 December 1941. Her last mission was to Okinawa, with enough fuel for a one-way trip. The object was to act as a diversion, and to give the Japanese 'suicide' pilots a better chance against American aircraft carriers in action there. On 7 April 1945 she survived seven heavy bomb hits by U.S. aircraft, and at least twelve torpedo strikes, before blowing up.

Japanese giant
Yamato: each of her
45.9 cm shells
weighed 1,451 kgm

What is a 'longship'?

From about A.D. 800 the Norse sailors raided the coasts of north-west Europe, and the craft they used were the broad and shallow 'longships'. The Vikings, as the Norsemen are commonly called today, set out from their creeks or fiords in Scandinavia and Denmark in early spring and late summer, and sailed away on long, bold searches for plunder. These explorers were merchants and colonizers as well as warriors. We know they reached places on the coast of North America, but these have not been precisely identified. Monks of the Scottish islands felt their might; they chanted: 'From the fury of the Northmen deliver us, O Lord!'

Some of the Viking ships have been preserved because of their habit of burying a dead chief in his longship, and covering it with earth in a burial mound. One such ship, found at Gokstad in Norway, dates from about A.D. 900. She is built of oak, and is 24 m long, and 5 m broad. The longship has sixteen oars a side. From the end of her keel the stem and stern posts rise in beautiful curves.

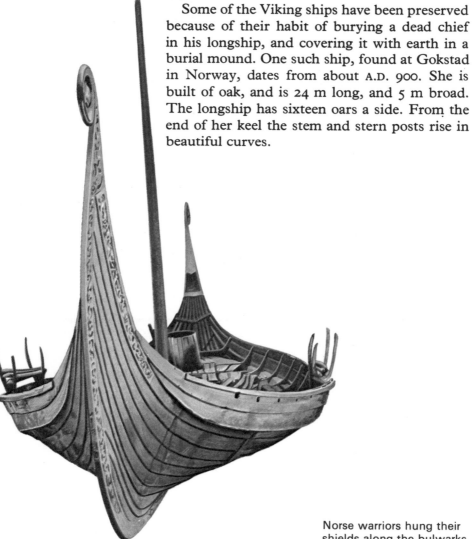

Norse warriors hung their
shields along the bulwarks
of their longships to
form a protective wall

What happened to the men of the *Mary Celeste* ?

The mystery of the *Mary Celeste* has occupied men's minds for a hundred years. She was a ship of 282 tons and she sailed from New York on 7 November 1872 bound for Genoa, with a cargo of alcohol. Her master was Benjamin Briggs, and with him sailed his wife, their

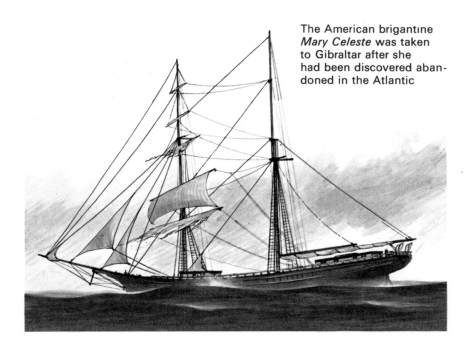

The American brigantine *Mary Celeste* was taken to Gibraltar after she had been discovered abandoned in the Atlantic

two-year old daughter, two mates and five seamen. On 5 December, between the Azores and Portugal, she was sighted by another vessel, which sent a boarding party on to her. They found no one on board. Some sails were set, the wheel was free. One version of the discovery said that in the cabin the table was laid for a meal. In the crew's quarters were pipes and tobacco. Cups of tea were still warm, so was the galley stove. The chronometer and ship's papers were missing. But the log was there and the last entry gave her position ten days earlier as 36° latitude north and 27° longitude west.

Sitting on a locker was the only living thing aboard the ship – a fat cat, asleep. In the cabin was discovered a cutlass. It was bloodstained. One of the ship's boats was missing and one of the hatchcovers was open. Theories came in profusion, but from that day to this no one has ever been able to establish with certainty what happened to the crew of the *Mary Celeste*.

Top: Model in a bottle of the famous tea clipper *Cutty Sark*

How did the *Cutty Sark* get her name?

The *Cutty Sark* was one of the last of the clipper ships specially built for the tea trade between China and Britain. Her unusual name was taken from the witch in Robert Burns's poem 'Tam O Shanter', and her figurehead represented a witch.

She carried a great spread of canvas and it was said of her that in her day no ship could outdistance her in a steady breeze abeam. She could average fifteen knots for long periods. The opening of the Suez Canal in 1869 spelt the end of the days of the famous racing tea clippers. But the *Cutty Sark* stayed in the trade until 1880 when her tall masts were shortened. She sailed to Australia and raced home with a cargo of wool. In 1895 she was sold to the Portuguese. In 1922 she arrived in the Thames and not long afterwards was bought back into British ownership. Thirty-five years later, after a complete restoration, the *Cutty Sark* was placed in a dry berth at Greenwich. There she now is – a fascinating memorial to a hard and heroic period of the British Merchant Navy.

The *Cutty Sark*, designed by Hercules Linton and built at Dumbarton, Scotland, in 1869. She was 921 tons, 64 m long, with a beam of 11 m

What was the Boston Tea Party?

One of the immediate causes of the American War of Independence (1775–83) was a conflict between the British Government and the American colonists over taxes imposed by the British. Tea was one of the things taxed. On 16 December 1773 Samuel Adams, a political leader of the colonists, presided over a mass meeting of Boston townsfolk. 'This meeting', he announced, 'can do nothing more to save the country.' At this signal fifty to a hundred men disguised as Red Indians boarded ships carrying tea from Britain and hurled their cargoes into the harbour. This was known as the Boston Tea Party. Retaliation followed. The port of Boston was closed, and the colony of Massachusetts was deprived of many of its rights of government. The colonists banded together. Agitation was whipped up. Volunteers began to arm and drill. On 19 April 1775 British troops, sent to seize a store of muskets, were attacked at Lexington, and this was the signal for the outbreak of war.

Where is tea-drinking a time-honoured ritual?

The ceremonial drinking of tea has long been a time-honoured institution in Japan. The central idea of the ceremony is the appreciation of the beautiful in life's daily routine such as preparing a meal and tea, cleaning the house, working in the garden and so on. The ceremony is called in Japanese *cha-no-yu* (which can be interpreted as 'hot water tea'). It is a way of entertaining guests, who after they have been served a meal are given thick, weak tea made of pulverized tea leaf stirred in hot water. The entertaining is done in a small room. It may be 2.7 m square or even smaller. Much thought is given to the construction of the little room. There is an alcove in which ornaments may be placed and there is a small sunken fireplace. This is used for heating the kettle during winter. In summer a brazier with a charcoal fire is used. The way the guests enter the room is designed to demonstrate humility. Their way in is through an opening less than 1 m square. The tea room is called *chaseki*. Before entering the *chaseki* each guest is required to wash his hands and rinse his mouth. This is a symbolic gesture of cleansing himself externally and internally and is one of the four qualities which the tea ceremony emphasizes. There are three other qualities which are part of the ceremony. One is harmony between the guests and the utensils used in the ritual. Another is respect not only among those taking part, but also for the utensils. Yet another is tranquillity, which suggests the quality of mellowness given to things by long and fond use.

Implements used in the Japanese tea ceremony, invented by Sen Rikyu (1521–91)

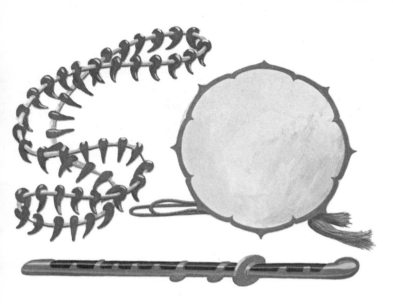

What are the three sacred treasures of Japan?

Japanese legend says that the Sun-goddess Amaterasu ruled over the Plain of High Heaven, and her Storm brother's empire was the Sea Plain. But Susanowo, her brother, was so violent that Amaterasu hid in a cave and plunged the world into darkness. She peeped out when the gods hung a necklace and mirror in a tree, and light returned. Susanowo was banished to the earth. He killed a monster, and found a sword in one of its eight tails. This he gave to his sister as a peace offering. So the Imperial Regalia of Japan consists of a sword, mirror and necklace.

What is Ikebana?

Ikebana is the general term applied to any style of Japanese floral art or flower arranging. The arrangement of flowers in Japan is an elaborate and unique form with highly developed conventions and complex symbolism. The art stems from the custom of offering flowers to Buddha. It was introduced to Japan in the seventh century by the Japanese Ambassador to China. Buddhist priests, warriors and noblemen practised the art. But after the beginning of the twentieth century it was also taken up by women.

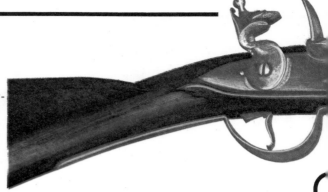

English coaching blunder-
buss made about 1780.
Barrels were usually
made of iron or brass,
the stocks of plain beech
or walnut

Why is a blunderbuss so called ?

Blunderbuss probably derives its name from the
German *donder buchse*, 'thunder gun'. The gun
was built with a bell-shaped barrel – wider at
the muzzle than the breech. This amplified the
noise of the explosion. The weapon was loaded
with a number of small balls and it was thought
that the bell-mouth would cause the shot to
spread. But it was later discovered that this did
not in fact increase the spread of the pellets on
leaving the barrel. There is mention of the
weapon in England as early as the seventeenth
century. In 1654 'a hundred brass blunder
bushes' were ordered as equipment for the Hispaniola expedition. It would seem that the period
of the blunderbuss's greatest popularity was the
last quarter of the eighteenth century. Blunder-
busses were in demand as personal protection
weapons, and were carried by the guards on
Royal Mail coaches and on the old stage coaches
in the United States, before the day of the
double-barrelled shot gun. The big gaping
muzzle no doubt was reckoned to have a frightening effect on robbers. It was a sea-going weapon,
too, being used to repel boarders – or to shatter
a ship's rigging. Some types of blunderbuss were
fitted with a bayonet.

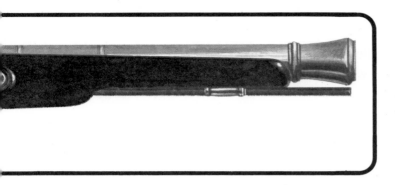

What was 'Mons Meg'?

This famous old cannon can be seen at Edinburgh Castle, Scotland. It is known to have been used at a siege in 1479. In 1489 an account recorded eighteen shillings being paid for drinks for its gunners, when they 'cartit Monss by the King's Command'. In 1650 there appears a mention – by Oliver Cromwell – of the 'great Iron Murderer, called Muckle Meg'. Another account of the origin of the gun's name suggests that as Flanders was the chief place for making early cannon, the gun was named after the town of Mons in about 1449, and was sent as a gift to Scotland by the Duke of Burgundy. It split its side when firing a birthday salute in honour of James II when he was Duke of York.

Mons Meg was later removed to the Tower of London. Sir Walter Scott, in patriotic zeal, campaigned to have it sent back to Scotland, and in 1829 King George IV ordered its return to Edinburgh. Pipers played as it made the last stage of its journey when it was accompanied by the 73rd Regiment of Foot and three troops of cavalry.

Mons Meg, in Edinburgh,
weighs five tons

What was chain mail?

An important development in the story of armour was the introduction of flexible garments made of numerous small metal rings which interlocked like chains, known as 'mail'. The coat of mail remained in favour for five centuries.

A complete tunic of armour made of mail contained up to 200,000 iron rings. During the Crusades in the twelfth century, knights wore a linen surcoat over the mail to reduce the effect of the sun's rays beating down on the metal.

What was a 'lobster-tail pot'?

The 'capelin' or 'lobster-tail pot' was a helmet worn in the cavalry for a hundred years or so from around 1630. It was oriental in origin. The hemispherical skull piece was fitted with a vizor made up of cheek pieces, an adjustable rod to protect the nose, and overlapping plates connected with joints to guard the neck.

Right: Typical three-barred 'pot'

What was a gorget?

One of the last pieces of armour to survive in the British Army was the gorget. It was a kind of collar, originally worn to protect the throat. Discoveries made in Egypt show that warriors wore armour as long ago as 1500 B.C., and by the sixteenth century both horse and rider were encased in steel from head to foot. But during the seventeenth century the main body armour was dispensed with. Some gorgets were retained as decoration. Although abolished in the British Army in 1830, gorgets continued to be worn elsewhere in Europe, and during the Third Reich the Germans revived the practice.

What was the Indian Mutiny?

This was a revolt by Indian soldiers, or sepoys, against their British officers and rulers in 1857. One of the immediate causes was the issue of new cartridges. These were believed to contain the fat of cows, sacred to Hindus, and of pigs, which Moslems regarded as defiling. In May eighty-five sepoys at Meerut were court-martialled for refusing to use the cartridges. The sepoy garrison mutinied, captured and killed officers and marched on Delhi. There, too, the sepoys rose. Others joined them, and many Europeans were killed. The mutineers acclaimed a new ruler – a descendant of one of the old Mogul emperors.

Rebellion spread like fire through the state of Oudh, with its capital Lucknow, and into Bengal and central India. But in northern India the Punjab was held firmly in the grip of its chief commissioner, John Lawrence. In September, Delhi was retaken. The garrison at Lucknow held out, and after British reinforcements had reached Calcutta, the rebel armies were finally defeated at Lucknow in March, and in central India in June 1858.

The East India Company (whose sepoys had helped to conquer India) was abolished. The number of British soldiers in India was increased, and British rule went on for another ninety years.

Who were the 'Noble Six Hundred'?

Alfred, Lord Tennyson immortalized these six hundred British soldiers in his famous poem 'The Charge of the Light Brigade'. This commemorated the Battle of Balaclava during the Crimean War (1864–66), in which Russia, Turkey, Britain and France were involved.

The Light Brigade (the six hundred) was told, in a confusion of orders, to charge strong Russian batteries. They suffered heavy losses and fewer than one-third survived. Tennyson recounted the heroic story and his poem ended with the words:

'When can their glory fade?
Oh, the wild charge they made!
   All the world wonder'd.
Honour the charge they made!
Honour the Light Brigade
   Noble six hundred!'

The Crimean War was chiefly caused by Russia's ambition to control Constantinople. Turkey declared war in 1853 and Britain entered the war with France as an ally. An outstanding figure of the war was Florence Nightingale who revolutionized the nursing of the wounded. Balaclava was one of the great battles of the campaign which finally forced Russia to abandon her claims.

Who is Tommy Atkins?

Tommy was (and still is) the nickname of the British soldier—the typical private. The custom began with the use of the name in specimen forms laid down in Army Regulations after the Napoleonic Wars, to show how forms should be filled in with the soldier's name and other details about him. As Rudyard Kipling wrote:

'Oh, it's Tommy this, an' Tommy that, an' Tommy go away;

But it's 'Thank you, Mr Atkins', when the band begins to play.'

When Tommy went off to fight in the First World War (1914–18) he wore a khaki field service dress with web equipment, and he was armed with the famous Lee Enfield rifle.

Was there ever a real Tommy Atkins? One theory is that a soldier of that name was mortally wounded under Wellington in Holland, and that many years later Wellington, when Secretary of State, adopted the name in the army form.

A British private soldier of the First World War, affectionately known as 'Tommy'. The Scots equivalent is 'Jock'

What was the secret of the Trojan horse?

The story of the battle of Troy is told in Homer's poem the *Iliad*. About 1200 B.C. a huge, hollow, wooden horse was left outside the great walls of the mighty city of Troy. Inside, a group of armed men lay hidden. For nine years Troy had been besieged by the Greeks. It appeared they had now abandoned the siege, and sailed away, leaving the horse behind them. The Trojans dragged it within the walls. Night fell, and the city slept. From the horse's trapdoor the Greeks slid, killed the Trojan sentries, opened the city gates, and signalled to the waiting fleet. The Trojans were soon defeated and their city reduced to a smoking ruin.

What was the legend of the flying horse?

6th century Corinthian coin bearing the device of Pegasus, inspiration of many a flight of fancy in poets and writers

Pegasus was the winged horse of Greek mythology – the steed ridden by Bellerophon when he killed the Chimaera, a fearsome, fire-breathing animal. When Bellerophon tried to fly to heaven, Pegasus threw him and he was killed. Pegasus became a constellation. Another legend about Pegasus concerns a song contest held by the Muses. The music made Mount Helicon start to grow higher. Pegasus struck it with his hoof to stop it and a fountain sprang forth. Its water inspired the poets and now a poet is said to 'mount his Pegasus' when he begins to write.

What is the Spanish Riding School ?

There is only one place where the horse is ridden according to traditional rites which have come down from the days of chivalry – the Spanish Riding School in Vienna. Its beginnings can be traced from 1572. The art of *haute école* has hardly changed since it was developed by Louis XIII's Master of the Horse.

The Riding Hall was built in 1735. Its lofty ceiling, unsupported by pillars, is at its loveliest at night when two vast chandeliers each blaze with a hundred lights. In this stately setting the horses go through the classical movements of an equestrian ballet, a display of strength and grace which is the ultimate expression of breeding and training. The world-famous white Lipizzaner stallions take their name from the village of Lipizza, near Trieste, where the original stud was founded in 1580 by Archduke Charles, with Spanish horses. Now the stud is at Piber in Styria. Only stallions go through the schooling. In *haute école* the horse's natural movements are developed to perfection. Movements include the *pirouette*, the *piaffe*, the *passage*, the *courbette*, the *capriole* and the *levade*.

What was the Pony Express?

The year 1860 is memorable in the United States as the year that saw the birth of the Pony Express. The opening up of the West brought the need for faster and faster communications, and the Pony Express riders carried the mail at breakneck speed. They were young men chosen for their light weight, horsemanship and powers of endurance. They had light saddles and their mailbag was known as a 'mochila' – a leather blanket with four pockets, which fitted over the saddle. The pockets were lined with oilskin. They carried letters weighing not more than half an ounce, each bearing a ten cent U.S. stamp and a $5 Pony Express stamp.

The riders rode from relay station to relay station where fresh horses were waiting. These 'home stations' were 120–160 km apart. The service undertook to deliver letters from east to west in thirteen days. The speed for the route of just under 3,200 km covered by the Pony Express, which more or less followed the Oregon-California Trail, had to average 14 km an hour whatever the hazards.

Among the famous Pony Express riders were William 'Buffalo Bill' Cody and 'Pony Bob' Haslam. The Pony Express, one of the legends of the West, lasted only eighteen months. It could not compete with the transcontinental telegraph line, completed in October 1861, and was discontinued.

Pony Express riders who provided a fast mail service between St Joseph, Missouri, and Sacramento, California

The time is 1830 — a mail coach with ostlers tending the horses stands in the yard of a galleried inn

When did mail coaches operate?

Regular mail coaches began to run in England in the 1780s. Armed guards travelled on them to protect them from highwaymen. By 1800 regular stage coach services were running between all the big towns and those carrying mails ran to a fast timetable. 'Fast' meant an average of 8 km an hour.

What was a knifeboard?

The London bus of the 1880s, drawn by two horses, was nicknamed 'knifeboard'. Those adventurous passengers, usually agile and male, who climbed to its top deck had to sit back-to-back on a long narrow board. The accommodation was rough and some wag soon named the bus 'the knifeboard' after the rough emery boards on which cutlery was cleaned until the invention of stainless steel. The knifeboard was one of the first of the double deckers. 'Garden' seats, or transverse seats, each seating two, were introduced in 1881.

Why was Africa the centre of the slave trade ?

Trade in human slaves began in the earliest times and went on until the nineteenth century. But it was in the sixteenth century, after the discovery of America when the need grew for labour on the new plantations, that the slave trade began to increase. Its centre was Africa. Millions of slaves were transported from that continent. The British, French, Dutch, Portuguese and Spanish all engaged in the trade. There was also a trade by the Arabs across the Sahara and from East Africa to Asia. The Arabs had a long history of slavery, and their African traffic in human merchandise was only suppressed towards the end of the nineteenth century. After the trade had been made illegal by western nations, Arab dealers in Africa continued to buy and sell people. They took them from the interior of Africa in caravans to the shores of the Mediterranean, the Red Sea, the Persian Gulf and the Indian Ocean. Some were sold at the coast but most were shipped on to Turkey, Arabia, Iran and other eastern lands. The biggest slave market in those days was in Zanzibar. In 1845 the British reached an agreement with the Sultan of Zanzibar by which his territory ceased to be the centre of the traffic, but it persisted on the African mainland and was abolished only gradually.

An armed Arab stands guard over Africans on their way to be sold

What was a treadmill?

A treadmill was an apparatus of punishment used in prisons. It was a large hollow cylinder, rather like the wheel of a water mill, with twenty-four steps. Each prisoner held on to a bar in front of him and kept on treading on the steps, thus making the cylinder revolve. The machines were used for pumping or grinding, or simply as a punishment. The treadmill was introduced in the early 1800s but fell into disuse long ago.

Bottom: Early horse locomotive with the horse turning a form of treadmill

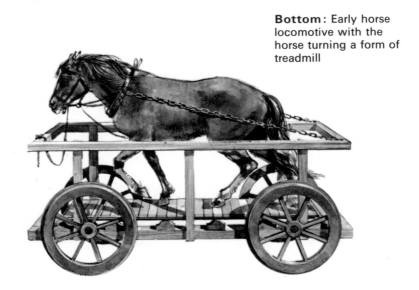

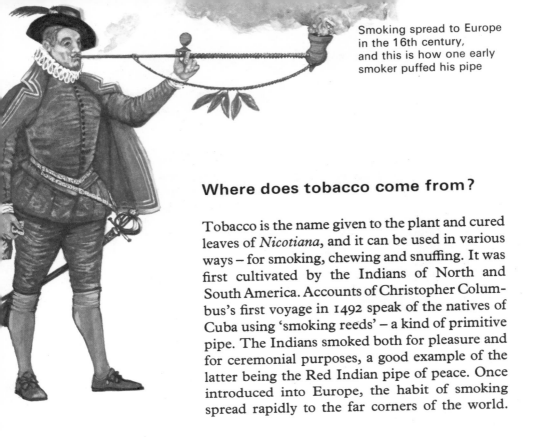

Smoking spread to Europe in the 16th century, and this is how one early smoker puffed his pipe

Where does tobacco come from?

Tobacco is the name given to the plant and cured leaves of *Nicotiana*, and it can be used in various ways – for smoking, chewing and snuffing. It was first cultivated by the Indians of North and South America. Accounts of Christopher Columbus's first voyage in 1492 speak of the natives of Cuba using 'smoking reeds' – a kind of primitive pipe. The Indians smoked both for pleasure and for ceremonial purposes, a good example of the latter being the Red Indian pipe of peace. Once introduced into Europe, the habit of smoking spread rapidly to the far corners of the world.

Who were the Green Mountain Boys?

A private of the American Green Mountain Boys

The Green Mountain Boys had their origins in a dispute over land in America. In 1749 Governor Benning of New Hampshire began to grant lands west of the Connecticut River (which today is Vermont), even though New York put in a strong claim. In 1770 the New York Supreme Court held that all Hampshire patents were invalid. But the people of New Hampshire west of the Green Mountains were determined to fight. They formed military companies. They terrorized the New York settlers. They tore up fences, burned down cabins and drove off New York sheriffs. The Green Mountain Boys fought in the War of Independence. They took the British post at Ticonderoga and helped defeat the British at the Battle of Bennington. In 1791 the Green Mountain State was admitted into the Union.

The American flag still flies over Fort McHenry after the British attack — an event which inspired Francis Scott Key to write 'The Star-spangled Banner'

Who wrote the American national anthem ?

When the British retreated from Washington during the war of 1812 they took prisoner a Dr William Beanes and held him aboard a warship in Chesapeake Bay. Francis Scott Key, an American lawyer, obtained permission to intercede for the release of his friend as the British fleet was preparing to bombard Fort McHenry, which protected Baltimore. The British agreed to release Beanes but held both Americans until the battle ended. So from the midst of the enemy, Key watched the British shelling his countrymen. The captives knew Fort McHenry had little defence, but as the smoke and haze of battle cleared they saw the American flag still flying. Key wrote down the words of a poem, 'The Star-spangled Banner'. Set to music it became the national anthem of the United States in 1931.

'. . . the star-spangled banner in triumph shall wave
O'er the land of the free and the home of the brave.'

Where did east meet west in the United States?

One of the great dates in the opening up of the American West was 10 May 1869, for it was then that the transcontinental railway became a reality. In 1862 President Abraham Lincoln took the decision to build the railway despite the civil war between North and South. An Act of Congress created the Union Pacific, a company which received a subsidy of 45,000 dollars for every mile of track completed. The Union Pacific's job was to build a railway from Omaha, a railhead on the Nebraska prairie, to Great Salt Lake Basin, there to join up with the Central Pacific, a company constituted under similar arrangements a few months before. Their line was to run from Sacramento, California, to Salt Lake. A start was made from both ends in 1864. Irish labourers were recruited by the Union Pacific. The Central Pacific imported Chinese labour. The line built by these men met at Promontory, Utah, during the month of May, 1869 and a golden spike was driven in. A month later America could be spanned from coast to coast in about six days.

East meets west. The Union Pacific and Central Pacific met at Promontory, Utah, in 1869

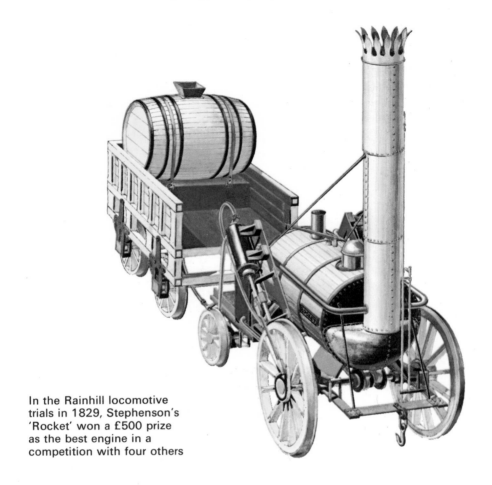

In the Rainhill locomotive trials in 1829, Stephenson's 'Rocket' won a £500 prize as the best engine in a competition with four others

Which was the first public railway worked entirely by steam locomotive?

On 15 September 1830 a train steamed slowly away from Liverpool along the new 'iron road' to Manchester – the first in a procession of eight locomotives. The occasion was the opening of the Liverpool and Manchester Railway, the first railway in the world to carry goods and passengers. Cheering crowds greeted the Duke of Wellington as his luxurious coach was drawn along by the Northumbrian engine.

The day was one of triumph for George Stephenson, for he had initiated the 'railway age'. But it was to bring tragedy. When the trains halted to take on more water several people, among them William Huskisson, M.P. for Liverpool, stepped down from the Director's coach. As they stood talking, another locomotive, the 'Rocket', approached on the parallel track. In the general panic, Huskisson tried to mount a step and so get back into a carriage; but he was hit by a door, thrown in front of the oncoming train and killed. The railway had claimed its first victim.

Early railway sailing car on the Baltimore and Ohio Railroad, which opened on 24 May 1830

Who sailed a train?

In 1827 a railroad was built from Baltimore to Ohio to counteract the prosperity that canals were bringing to Philadelphia and New York. It was originally intended to use horse power. But in 1830 a cheap, though not very reliable, method of propelling trains was tried out. The Baltimore and Ohio's sailing car 'Aeolus' made its maiden voyage in the charge of a sailing-master from Chesapeake Bay. Four days later she set off again carrying this time an eminent engineer. With a good breeze she glided along at a spanking pace, but when they came to the end of the track the sailing master forgot to apply the brakes and charged a bank of earth. The South Carolina Railroad tried a sailing car later. Loaded with three tons of iron ballast and fifteen people, its mast was broken by a gust of wind when making nearly twelve knots.

Why was the 'penny-farthing' so called?

Bicycles of many shapes and sizes have led up to the bicycle we know today. The 'penny-farthing' bicycle was first seen on the roads of England in 1871. It was invented by James Starley, who later became known as the 'father of the cycle industry'. It had a large front wheel which varied between 100–150 cm in diameter, and a smaller rear wheel of 35–45 cm in diameter. One revolution of the pedals caused one revolution of the wheel – so the larger the wheel the greater the distance covered with each push. These large driving wheels were hard to turn, and long-legged men soon found they were able to cycle faster than short-legged men!

Lightness was combined with strength when the solid steel frames were replaced by tubular steel frames. 'Penny-farthings' were very unstable and uncomfortable to ride, but they were very popular and continued in use for some years after the first chain-driven 'safety' bicycle appeared.

The first one-hour cycle record was set up by F. L. Dodds on 25 March 1876 in the grounds of Cambridge University. Riding a solid-tyred 'penny-farthing' he covered a distance of 25 km.

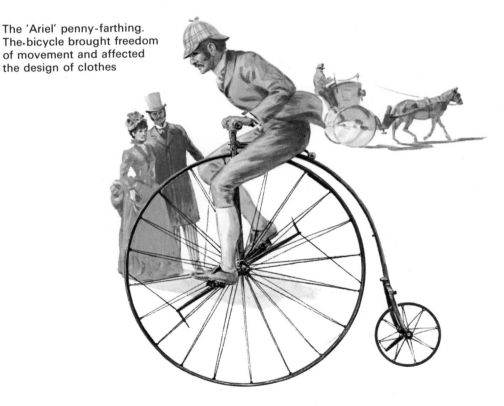

The 'Ariel' penny-farthing. The bicycle brought freedom of movement and affected the design of clothes

What was motoring's Emancipation Day?

Efforts to ease the restrictions on the motor car culminated in an Act of Parliament which became effective on 14 November 1896. It laid down that 'locomotives' of less than three tons, unladen, were regarded as 'light' and were exempted from the need for an attendant to walk in front. At one time the attendant had to carry a red flag. The Act raised the speed limit to 19 km.p.h.

Those enthusiasts who had been pressing for reform of the laws governing motor cars then decided to celebrate by arranging a procession of 'horseless carriages' from London to Brighton on 14 November. This was the Emancipation Run. There were not many motor cars in Britain at that time, so some were brought over from France to join the procession. The day seems to have been marked by some chaos and confusion. There were thirty-three starters. Only ten were recorded officially as finishing. Among the entrants was a vehicle described as a steam bicycle. Some vehicles, it was said, did most or part of the journey by rail. The start of the Emancipation Run was marked by a ceremony at which the Earl of Winchilsea tore up a red flag.

Various mishaps marked the day – the bursting of an 'unpuncturable' tyre was one of them. Overheating was another. One driver, getting out of the way of a frightened horse, ran his car into a ditch. According to the official return the first man home covered the whole 90 km of the run in three hours forty-four minutes and thirty-five seconds.

What was the original home of motor racing?

In 1907 a concrete track for testing and racing motor cars was opened at Brooklands, near Weybridge in Surrey. It was built by Hugh Locke-King, a motoring enthusiast, at a cost of nearly £250,000. It was the first to be constructed in the world. The track was almost 5 km long, averaged 30 m in width and was banked at the sides to prevent cars from over-running the edge. Many records were set up at Brooklands, probably the most famous being established by Percy 'Pearley' Lambert. Driving a 25 h.p. Talbot of 4,531 cc he covered a distance of 164 km, 1,320 m in one hour in 1913.

Brooklands was also used by early pioneers for testing aircraft.

What is a 'tester'?

A 'tester' is a canopy over a bed, which is supported on the posts of the bedstead or suspended from the ceiling. Formerly the word was used to describe the vertical post at the head of the bed which rose to, and sometimes supported the canopy or the framework on which the canopy and curtains rested. The term 'testour' occurs constantly in medieval accounts and inventories, together with the word 'celour' or 'celure' (a 'canopy covering'). By the sixteenth century tester was generally understood to imply a canopy.

After the fourteenth century, 'testours' and 'celours' were made of velvets, satins and silks. Curtains, designed to offer privacy and keep out draughts, were suspended from the tester by rings.

Early in the reign of Elizabeth I, the four corners of the tester were usually surmounted by vase-shaped 'cups' or 'finials', covered with the same material as the valances and holding large bunches of ostrich plumes. An inventory of 1600 refers to 'fower guilt topps for the iiii corners of ye bed teaster'.

A hundred years or so later, beds of the 'Angel' or half-tester' type were made. The half-tester was a kind of open bed without posts – the canopy or tester usually extending only over part of the bed and screening only the head and shoulders of the person reclining.

A half-tester or 'Angel' bed. The iron frame is decorated with papier-mâché, that is, paper which has been repulped with paste or glue so that it can be moulded

The St George cabinet,
painted by William Morris

Who was William Morris?

William Morris was an eminent Victorian, born in 1834. He had a many-sided career as poet, artist, manufacturer and socialist. At Oxford he began a life-long friendship with Edward Burne-Jones, the painter and designer, who subsequently introduced him to Dante Gabriel Rossetti, the poet and painter, and a leader of the Pre-Raphaelites.

At one time Morris intended to enter the church, then began to write poems and prose romances, decided (under Rossetti's influence) to become an artist – and eventually became an architect. Jane Burden, whom he married in 1859, was painted many times by Rossetti. In furnishing his red brick house at Upton, Kent, Morris found his true vocation as artist and designer. He founded a firm in Bloomsbury where, with the help of Rossetti, Burne-Jones and others, he produced furniture of simple shapes and solid workmanship, and fabrics, hangings and carpets which did much to change the heavy Victorian outlook on interior decoration.

Throughout his life William Morris took an active interest in social reform. He preached socialism in writing, in lectures and at meetings. He was arrested twice – once in 1885 and again in 1887, after the 'Bloody Sunday' meeting in Trafalgar Square on 13 November. His interest in early printed books led to the foundation of the Kelmscott Press (1890) – a landmark in the history of printing which revived the art of fine book production.

Who was the first prime minister of the Commonwealth of Australia?

Australia, like the United States, is a federal union. The six Australian states – Queensland, New South Wales, Victoria, Western Australia, South Australia and Tasmania – joined themselves together in 1901 to form one country. The first prime minister of the Commonwealth of Australia was a barrister, Edmund Barton. During the 1800s the Australian states were separate self-governing colonies of England. But customs and policies differed and a union was proposed. Federation became a fact on 1 January 1901. The Duke of York opened the first Federal parliament. Barton was a superb orator and risked his political career by becoming leader of the federal movement. He did a great deal to shape the actual form of the Commonwealth constitution, and was a member of the delegation which went to England with the bill in 1900.

Edmund Barton was knighted in 1902, when he resigned the premiership. He became a judge of the high court of Australia the following year, and died, aged seventy-one, in 1920.

Where is 'the biggest pebble in the world'?

The largest single block of stone in the world is in Mount Olga National Park, Northern Territory, Australia. It is Ayers Rock. This huge monolith is over 2.5 km long and rises 348 m above the sand and gravel plains of the Great Plateau. It is oval-shaped and is built

Ayers Rock was named after the premier of South Australia, Sir Henry Ayers, in 1873

of water-worn pebbles of granite cemented by finer sands. Aboriginal tribes regard the rock as of great religious and magical importance, and aboriginal rock carvings and paintings can be seen in shallow caves near its base. The colour of the rock varies from mauve to fiery red, depending on the time of day.

What story does the Bayeux Tapestry tell?

The Bayeux Tapestry represents scenes of the conquest of England by William the Conqueror in 1066, culminating in the Battle of Hastings. The scenes number seventy-two and over each is a short description in Latin. It is embroidered in coloured wool on linen, and is more than 60 m long and about 50 cm wide. The tapestry,

What is sanskrit?

Sanskrit is the name given to the ancient classical language of the Hindu inhabitants of India. It was introduced into India probably about 1500 B.C. and was for a time the spoken language as well as

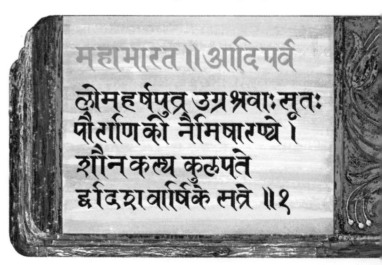

recorded in an inventory of Bayeux Cathedral in 1476, was exhibited in the Church for eight days every year at the feast of St John, but it was practically unknown outside the town until early in the eighteenth century. Traditionally, the tapestry is supposed to be the work of William the Conqueror's wife Matilda, but it is more probable that it was commissioned by his half-brother, Odo, Bishop of Bayeux. The tapestry belongs to the town of Bayeux in Normandy.

the literary language. The sacred Hindu books – the Vedas – were written in Old Sanskrit, but the name really applies only to the form of the language defined by the Indian grammarian Panini about 400 B.C. He wished to teach the correct form of speech of the learned men of his day and to protect the language from popular corruptions.

What is the legend of the Golden Fleece?

The Greek legend of Jason and the Golden Fleece is believed by some scholars to be founded on fact. The story begins in Thessaly when King Aeson was deposed from the throne by his step-brother, Pelias. When his son Jason grew up he demanded his father's kingdom back. Pelias promised to surrender the kingdom if Jason would bring back from Colchis the golden fleece of a ram which hung in an oak grove there, which was guarded night and day by a serpent.

Jason set sail in his ship *Argo* which means 'the swift', with fifty or more other heroes, among them Castor and Pollux, Hercules and Orpheus. After many adventures they reached Aea, the capital of

Late Roman relief shows
Jason stealing the fleece

Colchis. The king refused to let Jason have the golden fleece until he had carried out a number of seemingly impossible tasks. He yoked a pair of fire-breathing bulls with brass feet to a plough, sowed a field with the teeth of a dragon which then grew immediately into armed warriors. Then he fought and overcame the warriors. All these tasks Jason accomplished with the help of Medea, the king's daughter, who had fallen in love with him. Medea gave him the means to resist fire and steel, and a drug which charmed the serpent guarding the golden fleece.

Jason and his companions escaped in the *Argo* taking the golden fleece and Medea with them. The Argonauts survived many dangers and disasters before they finally reached Thessaly in safety.

What is an Achilles heel?

Achilles was a legendary Greek hero. Before he was born the Fates had told his mother Thetis (who was a sea nymph) that he would die young. So when he was a baby she tried to make him immortal by plunging him into the River Styx, whose magic properties were supposed to give protection from all harm. But the heel by which she held him did not get wet – and this remained mortal.

Years later when the Trojan war broke out, Thetis dressed Achilles

An ancient vase painting depicting Achilles, one of the bravest warriors of Greek mythology, slaying the Amazon, Penthesilea

up as a girl and hid him among the women at the court of the king of Scyros so that he would not have to go to fight. But he was discovered by the Greek warrior Odysseus, also known as Ulysses. Achilles fought on the Greek side in the Trojan war, about which Homer wrote in the *Iliad*. He soon became famous for his heroic adventures, such as his slaying of the Trojan hero, Hector. But his own end was near. Hector's brother, Paris, shot a poisoned arrow at him. The god Apollo guided it to pierce Achilles in the foot, and he died from the wound. So the phrase 'an Achilles heel' has come to mean a weak or vulnerable spot.

The Achilles tendon attaches the muscles of the calf of the leg to the heel-bone. It is frequently strained by athletes.

The great seal of Richard I. The lions on the crest on top of the helmet and on the shield provide an early example of true heraldry

Who was 'The Lion Heart'?

Coeur de Lion, the Lion Heart, was the nickname of King Richard I of England (1157–99). From his youth he was engaged in almost constant war against his father, his brothers, or the king of France. Richard became king on his father's death in 1189. He went off on the Third Crusade, and, captured on his way home, was imprisoned and ransomed. He spent the rest of his reign fighting Philip Augustus of France, and was killed while besieging the castle of Chaluz.

What is heraldry?

Armorial bearings were at first a simple way of identifying individuals on the field or at the tourney. Part of the knight's armour was a shield, on which was depicted a distinguishing pattern. This pattern, which remained the same, was the personal property of its owner and passed on to his descendants. The science of heraldry dates from the second half of the twelfth century. Rules were framed for the ordering, regulation and composition of armorial bearings.

The heraldic shields shown are: (*top*) the baton sinister, a symbol denoting illegitimacy; (*centre*) the fess, which occupies the centre third of the shield: (*bottom*) the saltire, usually called a St Andrew's cross.

The most honoured
and exclusive English
Order of the Garter

Which Order 'exceeds in majesty, honour and fame all Chivalrous Orders of the World'?

The Most Noble Order of the Garter, the highest British Order of Knighthood, is as sought-after and honoured now as it was over six hundred years ago. The exact date of the foundation of the order, which John Selden, the historian, described as exceeding 'in majesty, honour and fame all Chivalrous Orders of the World', is uncertain. One version tells of a ball held by King Edward III at his court near Calais to celebrate his victories in France. The Countess of Salisbury's garter broke and dropped to the floor. The king picked it up and, noting the lady's embarrassment, rebuked onlookers with the words '*Honi soit qui mal y pense*' ('Dishonoured be he who think evil of it'). He then tied the garter round his knee, saying: 'I will make of it ere long the most honourable garter that ever was worn'.

The insignia comprises the garter itself, made of dark blue velvet edged with gold, and bearing the motto '*Honi soit qui mal y pense*' in gold letters; the star, with St George's Cross; and a collar of gold, with a badge. King Henry VII introduced a collar for the order. This was of gold and enamel and represented St. George (patron saint of England) in armour on horseback, slaying the dragon with his spear. This badge came to be known as the George.

The Order of the Garter has, since 28 June 1831, consisted of the Sovereign and twenty-four Knights Companions, such lineal descendants of King George I as may have been elected and, finally, of those Sovereigns and Extra Knights who have been admitted by special statutes.

The World
Around Us

The nuclear-powered
USS *Enterprise*

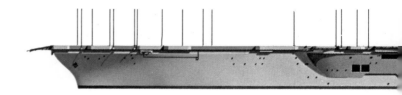

What are aircraft carriers?

Aircraft carriers are warships which are like floating airfields. They are built so that the top deck is almost free from any kind of super-structure and can act as a runway for aircraft. This is called the flight deck. The aircraft belonging to the carrier are stored and repaired in hangars inside the ship, and raised and lowered to and from the flight deck by giant lifts.

The first true aircraft carriers were built just after the First World War. During the Second World War great naval battles were fought between fleets of aircraft carriers, each fleet sending its aircraft to attack the other. Since the Second World War fewer aircraft carriers have been built. However, one famous carrier of today is the American USS *Enterprise*. She is nuclear powered, and one of the largest warships now afloat. Modern jet fighter aircraft can land and take off from her 240 m twin-runway flight deck, and she has her own guided missile defence system.

Aircraft with folded wings being lowered from the flight deck

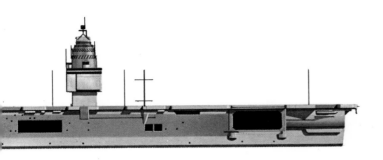

How does a magnet work?

When you bring a magnet close to another metal object such as a nail, the nail will be attracted towards it. This power of attraction is created by lines of force which surround the magnet. They cannot be seen, but if you place a thin sheet of paper over a magnet, and scatter iron filings on the upper side of the paper, the filings will fall into place according to the lines of force. They will reveal what is known as a magnetic field.

Most of the filings on the paper will be attracted to the two ends of the magnet. These ends are the magnet's poles. The earth itself is like a giant magnet, with its opposite ends at the North and South Poles. This is why the metal needle of a compass will swing round until it is in line with the earth's magnetic field and points towards the North Pole.

The earth's magnetic field

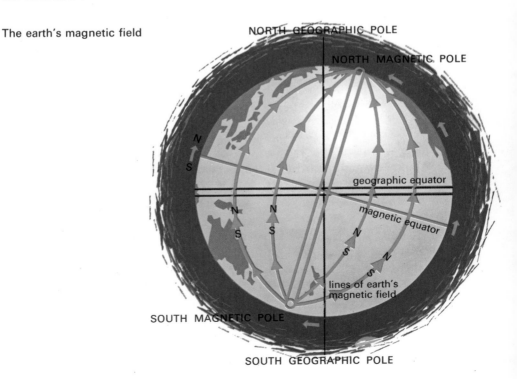

Left: A harbour lighthouse
Below: The interior of
a lighthouse, showing
the arrangement of
living and work areas

Why do we need lighthouses?

Along many stretches of coast, lighthouses have
been built to warn ships of special dangers such
as rocks, or to indicate a harbour entrance.
During the day lighthouses can be clearly seen,
because they are usually tall, narrow structures,
often painted in broad bands of black and white.
It is at night that they are especially valuable
to shipping, because at the top of their structure
they house a powerful electric lamp, very much
like a searchlight, which swings round and sends
great beams of light out to sea. When ships'
captains or navigators see this beam they can
tell their exact position, and steer clear of whatever dangers the lighthouse is indicating. In
foggy weather lighthouse keepers used to warn
approaching shipping by ringing a bell. Today
lighthouses are equipped with electric horns or
sirens.

The first lighthouse in the world was the
Pharos of Alexandria – one of the Seven Wonders
of the World. It was built in about 300 B.C. and
was 119 m high, with a fire burning at the top.
One of today's most famous lighthouses is the
Bishop Rock lighthouse off the Scilly Isles, which
is the first sight of land for many ships approaching Europe from the Atlantic.

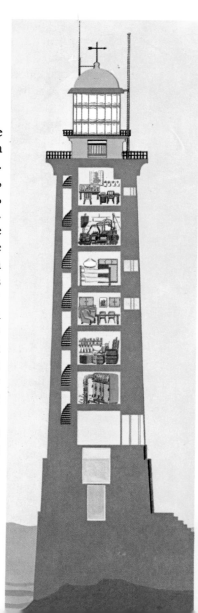

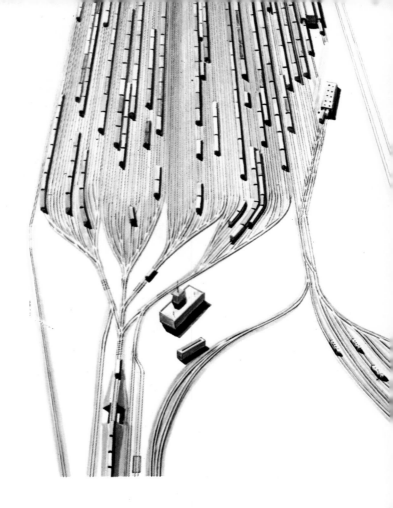

A railway marshalling yard. Note the 'hump' at the bottom of the picture

What is a marshalling yard?

On railways, freight is loaded on to wagons at depots or factories. Some of it will be going to docks for export. Some of it will be going to other factories. Some of it will be going to towns for distribution. All of it must be sorted out and assembled into different goods trains to make sure that the right goods go to the right places. This is what happens at a marshalling yard. Freight trains arrive from various starting points. They are then split up and their wagons re-grouped to form new trains, each intended for a different destination.

A big marshalling yard can handle over 10,000 wagons at a time. An important feature is the 'hump'. Wagons are pushed up a slope. At the top of this slope they are uncoupled to run down the other side and into the correct set of tracks where new freight trains are forming up.

A Cossack horseman

Who are the Cossacks?

Many hundreds of years ago, Russia was full of different tribes and races of people who had made their way from the great plains, or steppes, and mountain ranges of Asia. One of these races – the Cossacks – settled along the banks of the River Don which flows into the Sea of Azov, near the Black Sea. At the same time, they bred a special kind of horse which was noted for its great strength and stamina, and they became splendid horsemen. Their reputation as riders and warriors grew over the years, and they came to be looked upon as some of the finest cavalry soldiers in the world.

Sometimes the former Russian rulers, the tsars, used the Cossack cavalry to crush rebellions among the peasants. At other times the Cossacks were the pride of the Russian army, and could always be relied upon to strike fear into the hearts of the enemy. They were especially effective during Napoleon's invasion of Russia in 1812, attacking his lines of communication and pursuing his armies during the terrible winter retreat. The German army also came to fear the Cossack regiments during the Second World War.

Today the Cossacks are as famous as ever. They give exciting riding displays. They have also formed a choir which gives concerts all over the world.

What is show-jumping?

Show-jumping is a competition to see which horse and rider can best jump a series of walls, fences and other obstacles. Points are won and lost as the horses, one after the other, attempt each obstacle on a specially prepared course. Sometimes extra points are awarded to the horse which completes the course successfully in the fastest time.

Some of the special walls on a show-jumping course are made of bricks, and if the horse kicks any of the bricks off the wall as it goes over the top it will lose its rider points. Fences are often made of wooden poles, and again, none of the poles must be kicked out of place by the horse if its rider is to score full points. Also, there are often ditches filled with water, which the horses must be able to clear. If a horse refuses to jump a fence, it will mean a serious loss of points. And if a horse throws its rider out of the saddle, this is worse still.

Show-jumping is popular with millions of people today who can see such contests on television. Some show-jumping horse riders are now as famous as racing jockeys.

A show-jumping horse in action

What is a mosque?

The Moslem religion was founded by the prophet Mohammed, just as Christianity was founded by Jesus Christ. A mosque is a church for Moslems. Most mosques are found in the countries of North Africa and the Middle East, where Islam – another name for

A mosque with its minaret

the Moslem faith – is the official religion, although there are also mosques in big cities like London and New York.

Inside a mosque there are prayer mats on which the faithful can bow down and pray, facing in the direction of Mecca, the holy city of Islam in Arabia. The walls are usually covered with beautiful examples of Arabic script, called arabesques. This is because the Moslem religion forbids the drawing or painting of people and animals, and above all, of Mohammed himself.

Another interesting feature of mosques is the tall, narrow tower seen from the outside. This is called a 'minaret', and by tradition the priest, or 'muezzin', climbs to the top of the tower to call the faithful to prayer.

One of the most famous mosques in the world is the Santa Sophia mosque in Istanbul. This was built as a Christian church as long ago as A.D. 537, but was changed into a mosque when the armies of Islam conquered the city in 1482.

Where is the Doge's Palace?

Five hundred years ago Venice was one of the most prosperous and important cities in the world. It was not a part of Italy or of any other country. It was an independent city-state, which meant that it had its own rulers and made its own laws. It was immensely prosperous because of the trade which it handled. Christians and Moslems often fought each other in holy wars, but there was an enormous amount of trading, not only between Christians, Arabs and Turks but also between Europe and countries as far distant as China. Metal goods, timber, spices, silk, perfumes and many other valuable goods and materials made up this great trade, and a large part of it was handled by the merchants of Venice.

As the wealth and influence of Venice increased, so the city merchants and bankers built themselves more elaborate palaces and houses to live in. One of the most beautiful of all these buildings is the Palace of the Doges. The word 'doge' comes from the Latin word *dux*, meaning leader, and the Doges were the rulers of Venice. They were elected from among the city's richest and most influential citizens.

The Doge's Palace is among the most famous buildings in the world. It stands on one side of the equally renowned St Mark's Square, and faces on to the Grand Canal. It took over two hundred years to complete, and is also of great interest because it contains several different styles of architecture.

The Doge's Palace and
St. Mark's Square. Note
the gondolas

How do rockets work?

Rockets and jet engines work according to an extremely simple scientific principle discovered by Sir Isaac Newton, the English mathematician and scientist. He found that 'to every action there is an equal and opposite reaction', and on this he based his experiments.

What this means can be shown with the aid of a toy balloon. If we blow up a balloon and then grip the end, the air inside will push with equal force against every part of the balloon's surface. If we then release the end of the balloon, the air will rush out. This escaping air is thus the 'action'. At the same moment that we release the air from one end, the balloon will rush forward in the opposite direction with an equivalent force. This demonstrates the 'reaction' part of Newton's theory.

Rocket and jet propulsion basically works in this way. In the case of a real rocket or jet engine, however, filling it with air would be of little use. The air would be used up far too quickly. Instead, a fuel is burnt. The hot, expanding gases produced by this fierce burning escape through the exhaust at one end of the engine, making it move forward in the opposite direction. The principle is the same as that demonstrated by the experiment with the balloon. A firework rocket uses a fuel like gunpowder, which will propel it several hundred metres into the air. Giant space rockets, weighing nearly a thousand tons, use fuels like liquid hydrogen and oxygen. These burn so fiercely that they produce enough 'thrust' to carry the rocket hundreds of kilometres into space at a speed of over four kilometres per second.

With all jet engines and rockets, flying through air is a distinct hindrance rather than a help. But Newton's discovery about 'action' and 'reaction' applies just as well in a vacuum and, in fact, rockets travel most easily in outer space where there is no air at all to offer resistance to their flight.

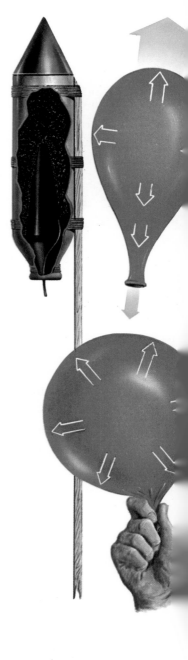

A balloon can be used to demonstrate the principle of rocket and jet propulsion

What is an electron microscope?

An ordinary magnifying glass with a single lens can magnify something two or three times. In an optical microscope a series of lenses and mirrors is arranged to produce a much greater degree of magnification. Such a microscope is called 'optical' because the eye still looks at the object under observation through the system of lenses. The best optical microscopes can magnify an object nearly 2,000 times. They cannot improve on this, because the details revealed at this degree of magnification are already so small that ordinary light cannot show up anything smaller.

However, electrons can reveal much greater details still. Electrons are themselves some of the smallest particles of matter. They are like tiny electrical charges, and in an electron microscope a beam of them is used instead of ordinary light. This beam is focused, not by a lens, but by a magnetic field, on to the object to be observed. When the electron beam passes through the object the pattern the electrons then make can be recorded by special processes on to a fluorescent screen for observation. This pattern can reveal details of an object magnified one hundred thousand times. At this magnification, the actual atoms and molecules of which all matter is composed will begin to show up.

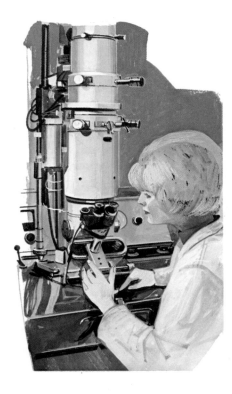

An electron microscope can reveal atoms and molecules — the smallest objects of all

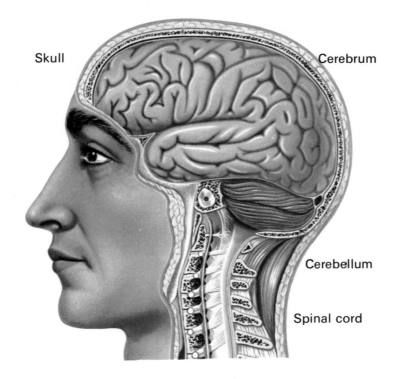

Skull

Cerebrum

Cerebellum

Spinal cord

What happens in our brain?

Our brain controls the entire life of our body. People often say 'use your brain', meaning 'think'. The truth is we are using our brain every moment of our lives. Every single movement of our limbs and the organic functions inside our bodies are controlled by the brain.

The brain itself is made up of millions of cells, between which thousands of electrical impulses are constantly passing. It is connected with every other part of the body by nerves, and messages to and from the brain pass along these nerves, much as thousands of telephone conversations are carried along telephone wires to and from a central exchange. The largest group of nerves comes out at the base of the brain and runs down inside the spine.

The brain is divided into two parts: the cerebellum and the cerebrum. The cerebellum is the smaller part, tucked under the cerebrum, and, together with the passages of the inner ear, controls the body's general movement and balance. The cerebrum is the main part of the brain. Different areas of it are responsible for different bodily activities. One part deals with our sense of sight, another with hearing, another with taste and smell, and so on. The very important front part of the brain is responsible for our emotions, memory and reasoning.

What is a snake charmer?

Most snake charmers live in India and other countries of the Far East, where they attract large crowds at bazaars and fairs with their strange and daring performances.

A snake charmer carries his snake – usually a cobra – in a large basket. He places the basket on the ground, takes off the lid and then starts to play a special kind of tune on his pipe. The snake slowly uncoils itself, rears up from the basket and sways to and fro in front of the charmer. Most people assume that the snake is charmed by the music. In fact, although a snake does have ears it cannot hear sounds in the air. It can only 'hear' vibrations on the ground as they are transmitted to its ears through the bones in its head. Therefore what probably happens is that the snake is mesmerized in some way by the charmer's movements as he plays.

A snake charmer is certainly a brave man, because if he makes a false move during the performance he could be seriously hurt or even killed by a bite from his dangerous pet.

A snake charmer

What is our blood made of?

Our blood is made up of three basic substances: red cells, white cells and a liquid called plasma.

The red cells contain oxygen which enters the blood stream in the lungs. Oxygen is essential to the conversion of food energy into bodily movement, so the red cells really carry energy to whatever part of the body requires it. They also carry away from different parts of the body such waste products as carbon dioxide. New red cells are produced in the bone marrow.

The white cells are the body's defence against infection. If we cut ourselves, white cells will be carried in the blood to the region of the cut. They will then attack whatever harmful bacteria are trying to enter the body and which might otherwise cause infection.

The plasma of the blood carries the red and white cells about in it. Plasma also contains an important substance called fibrinogen. This begins to congeal when exposed to air and will form a clot over a wound. Clotting stops the loss of further blood and allows the wound to heal beneath it.

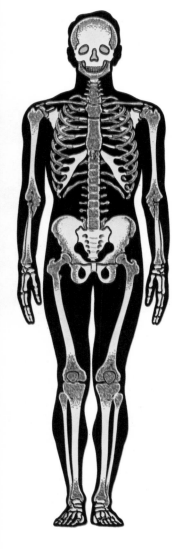

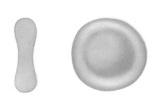

Far left: New red cells are produced in the bone marrow
Left: Top and side view of a red cell
Below: Red and white cells highly magnified

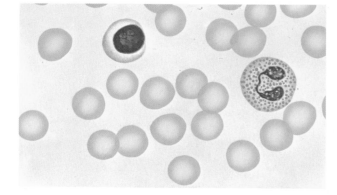

What are calories?

Calories are a measurement of heat. They do not record actual temperatures like the degrees on a thermometer, but they are a means of measuring how much heat a substance will create if it is used in some way.

All food can be measured in calories, because food is the fuel the body digests and uses to produce its own heat and energy. Every time we eat something we are adding to our intake of calories. On the other hand, just to stay alive we are using up the heat and energy

We use up calories at different rates depending on what we are doing

Exercise and leisure

Sleep

Sedentary work

Travelling

produced by our food. So a constant balance in our bodies has to be kept between the number of calories we produce from our food and the amount of heat and energy we use up. Heavy physical exercise uses up many more calories than sitting quietly in a chair, which is why we usually feel much hungrier after running or swimming than we do just staying indoors and reading a book. The extra calories we have used need to be replaced by more food. If we create more calories in our bodies than we use up, then these extra calories of heat and energy turn into fat.

What is radioactivity?

The word 'nuclear' means to do with the central part, or *nucleus*, of an atom. The atoms of some chemical elements have a nucleus which scientists call unstable because they release tiny fragments of themselves. These fragments fly off in beams, or rays, of nuclear particles. Substances containing atoms which produce such particles are said to be radioactive. The sun even produces radioactivity in the form of cosmic rays, though most of these are absorbed by the earth's atmosphere. A few minerals found in the earth are also radioactive.

Some radioactive rays are fairly harmless. However, gamma rays – similar to X-rays – can be extremely dangerous to plant and animal life. Atomic bombs of all kinds produce a deadly cloud of radioactive particles called 'fall-out'. Nuclear power stations produce quantities of harmful radioactive waste which has to be disposed of. Radioactive substances can also be of great value to scientific and medical research. But scientists have to take special precautions when handling radioactive materials, and they need to receive frequent checks to make sure they have absorbed no harmful doses of nuclear radiation.

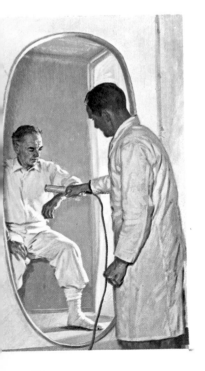

Above and below:
Cleaning and checking
for radioactivity
Bottom right: A
scientist works on
radioactive material
from behind a
protective wall

Where is the world's oldest underground railway?

The first city to build an underground railway was London. Once the route was planned, a great trench was cut along the streets, the railway tracks were laid and the trench was covered over again, to restore the road and create a railway tunnel underneath. This method of tunnel making is called 'cut and cover'.

The original route of the London Underground was nearly four miles long and ran from Paddington Station to Farringdon Street in the City of London. It was opened in 1863. The first trains were hauled by steam engines, and the smoke in the tunnels made the

journey very unpleasant. But as the world's first underground railway it was a cause of great excitement and regularly carried 30,000 passengers a day.

Further sections of steam operated underground railway soon followed. Then in 1890 the first really deep-tunnel, or 'tube' railway was built in London. For this new tube railway, electric locomotives were built. The first trains they hauled had no windows, because windows were thought to be unnecessary if the train was only to travel through a tunnel deep under the ground. The train guard called out the name of each station as the train arrived at it.

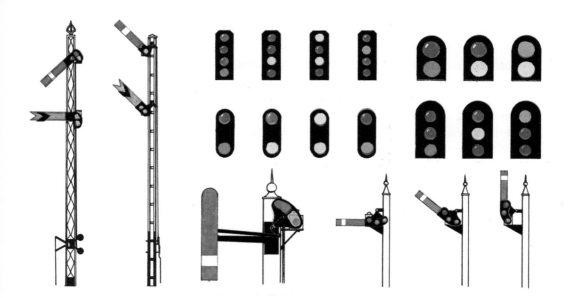

How do railway signals work?

Modern semaphore and colour-light signals. The busy sections of almost all railways have colour-light signals, but many semaphore signals are still in use

In the early days of railways, men stood beside the track with a flag and either signalled the train driver to stop or waved him on. As trains were developed, their speed and numbers increased, so mechanical signals were invented. The most common type, called semaphore signals, swung up or down on a tall wooden or metal pole next to the track. They were operated by a signalman in a cabin who pulled levers to make them swing into the 'stop' or 'go' position, according to the messages he received from other signalmen down the line telling him whether the track was clear or not.

In a modern signal cabin, signalmen watch an illuminated plan of the track showing the position of every train

Nearly all railway signals today are colour-light signals, and are controlled electrically. Like traffic lights, red means 'stop', green means 'go', and yellow, or amber, means 'caution', or 'prepare to stop'.

What is electric arc welding?

An electric arc is a charge of electricity passing across a space from one point to another. A flash of lightning is an example of an enormous electric arc. An electric arc welder's apparatus consists of a welding rod connected to an electric current. When the current is switched on an electric arc can be made to form between the welding rod and the metal object to be worked. The heat of this

An electric arc welder working on a metal pipe

arc is intense, and by moving the welding rod the arc can be made to move over the metal, temporarily melting it and allowing it to be re-shaped or welded to another piece of metal. In addition to the heat, the arc gives off a blinding light, which is extremely harmful to the eyes and skin, so an electric arc welder must wear special protective clothing.

A beautiful aviary in
an Indian market place

What is an aviary?

An aviary is a house or very large cage for birds. For thousands of
years, birds have been kept in aviaries to be enjoyed for their beautiful plumage or to be sold as pets. In the great markets and bazaars
of India, whole buildings, resembling palaces, were built as aviaries.
Most zoos have an aviary, which is often a large, glass domed building, built so that the birds have plenty of light and space to fly
about in. A small aviary can be quite easily built on to a simple
garden shed by removing some of the wooden wall and fitting wire
netting, or by adding to the shed a framework of wood or metal
covered with netting.

A garden aviary built
on to a shed

Who are the Bedouins?

The Bedouins are a nomadic Arab tribe whose name is derived from *badawi* meaning 'desert-dweller'. They make up about one-tenth of the population of the Middle East, but cover in their wanderings nearly nine-tenths of its land area. Their pattern of life is determined by the grazing needs of their flocks which they follow all the year round, living in black goats' hair tents. Traditionally they despise agricultural or manual work, and are happiest tending their herds of sheep, camels and highly-bred horses.

What is a lightship?

A lightship is like a floating lighthouse. It anchors in one spot to warn other shipping of such nearby dangers as sand banks or dangerous currents. At night it projects a powerful beam of light. The lamp is fitted in such a way that the beam stays steady, even if the ship is being tossed about by waves. Lightships also have their name painted on each side, so that during daylight hours ships can use them to check their own positions.

A lightship anchored at her position. Lightships are marked on navigational charts in the same way as lighthouses and important buoys

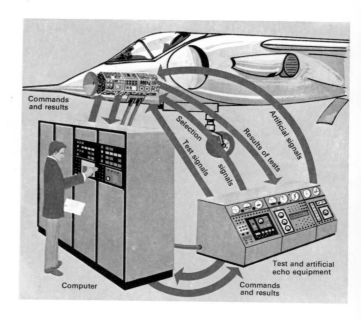

A computer designed to test radar equipment and report its findings The test equipment can simulate, or artificially imitate, actual radar signals to find out whether the radar equipment is responding properly

Commands and results

Selection signals

Test signals

Artificial signals

Results of tests

Test and artificial echo equipment

Computer

Commands and results

What are computers?

Computers are machines, although they do not work like other kinds of machines. They are more like mechanical brains. By means of complicated electrical circuits, they can store information and then supply it again when needed. Some types of computer can calculate mathematical problems far more quickly than we could do it ourselves. Others are designed to check and control other machinery. To operate them they have to be supplied with a specially coded set of instructions called a programme, devised by programmers.

Today, computers are to be found in all branches of industry and commerce. From banking to space travel, they play a vital role.

Computers can control television transmissions and teaching machines

Right: The first electric locomotive was so small that the driver sat on top of it, straddling it like a horse.
Below: Volk's Electric Railway at Brighton

When did the first electric train appear?

The world's first electric locomotive was designed by the German scientist Werner von Siemens. It was shown at an international trade exhibition in Berlin in 1879. A special track was built for the locomotive, which hauled up to thirty visitors at a time around the exhibition. One of the earliest electric railways in England was Volk's Electric Railway, built along the sea-front at Brighton. This railway was opened in 1883. It was a marvellous holiday attraction at that time, and is still very popular with visitors to the seaside town. The first electric trains to be used as a serious means of transport appeared on the London Underground in 1890, and the building of longer distance electric railways began after the First World War.

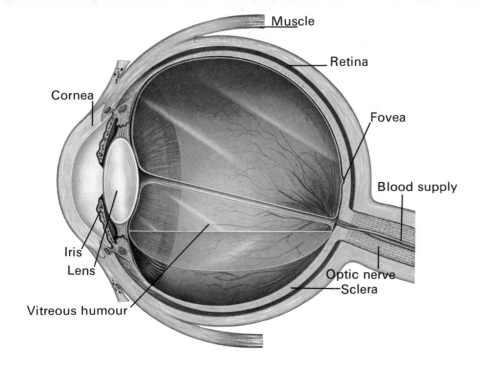

Muscle

Retina

Cornea

Fovea

Blood supply

Iris

Lens

Optic nerve

Sclera

Vitreous humour

How do our eyes work?

Only a small part of our own eyes and those of other people is visible. The complete eye is ball shaped, and it works very much like a camera. In the front part of the eye there is the equivalent of a camera lens. This focuses the image of what we are looking at on to the retina, a delicate membrane stretching across the back of the eye, which may be compared to a photographic film. Nerve cells in the retina then pass the image to the brain in the form of nerve impulses, so that we may become aware of what the eye has seen. The iris in front of the lens opens or closes according to how much light the eye needs to obtain a clear image.

Above: Cutaway side of the eye
Right: We become short-sighted or long-sighted when the lens of the eye does not focus correctly on the retina

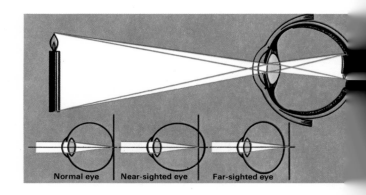

Normal eye   Near-sighted eye   Far-sighted eye

What is an electrocardiograph?

When a doctor takes a pulse he is feeling the patient's heart-beat. If the heart is beating faster than normal it may be a sign – like a rise in temperature – of illness somewhere in the body. For signs of illness in the heart itself a more careful check is usually needed.

The working of the heart is controlled by electrical impulses, and each part of it – the various valves where blood flows in and out – produces its own electrical wave pattern. By attaching electrical

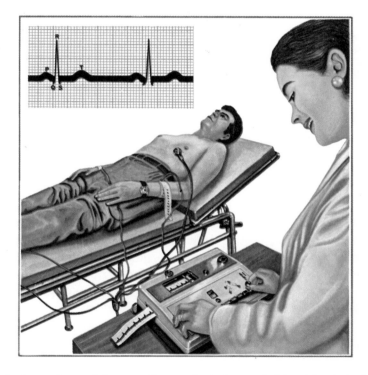

An electrocardiograph in operation, and what recorded heart beats look like

terminal points to the outside of the chest and connecting these to an electrocardiograph, these wave patterns can be observed. For when the electrocardiograph is switched on, an automatic device like a pen moves up and down over a special sheet of graph paper, recording each wave impulse. This shows exactly the pattern of each complete heart beat. If anything is wrong with the heart, it will be shown by irregularities in these patterns. The pattern sheets, or electrocardiograms, can then be kept by doctors and compared over a period of time, which is extremely useful in the treatment of heart illness.

What are totems?

Among the so-called primitive races of people, animals, plants and even lifeless objects such as rocks are regarded seriously. They are often believed to be the spirits of dead people, or of gods. One particular animal or plant is usually believed to be the most important of all, and a whole family or tribe will feel themselves connected with it in some special way. This animal or plant then becomes the totem of that family or tribe. In many tribes, men and women belonging to the same totem, like close relations in any family, are not allowed to marry each other. And often the tribe will be forbidden to kill or eat whatever animal or plant their special totem represents.

The idea of having totems is common to races and tribes in very different parts of the world – among the aborigines of Australia, the ancient races of India, and tribes of various parts of Africa. The people most famous for their totems are the American Indians. They take great tree trunks and make them into tall poles with the emblem of their totem – often a bird like an eagle – carved out of the top. Beneath the emblem of the totem itself the Indians carve images to represent their ideas of the creation and history of their tribe. They sometimes believe that they are descended from whatever animal is their totem.

An American Indian
totem pole

What is a fetish?

Some of the first European people to explore the west coast of Africa were the Portuguese. One of the things they soon noticed about the native tribes and races with which they came into contact was their fondness for making small carved images of people or animals. So impressed were the explorers by the number and variety of these objects that they gave them a special

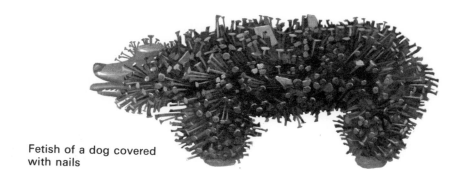

Fetish of a dog covered
with nails

name – fetish – which comes from the Portuguese *feitiço*, meaning
'something made'.

For the people of West Africa and the Congo region, fetishes
were magic charms. They believed that a person's fetish would
protect him from danger and bring him good fortune. Naturally,
these fetishes, which figured so importantly in their lives, were
made with loving care and were often elaborately decorated as well.
One very interesting kind of fetish was covered with nails which
were hammered into it, one by one. Each nail was meant as an
offering to the gods.

Two fetishes of human
figures. The one on
the left is decorated
with beads

A cutaway view of a Polaris submarine, showing how the missiles are stored. On the right is a drawing of the Polaris A3

How was the Polaris missile developed?

The first modern type of rocket to be used as a weapon was the German V-2 rocket of the Second World War. From sites in France and Holland, V-2 rockets carrying a powerful explosive charge were launched against London.

Soon after the Second World War, the United States and the Soviet Union started to build much bigger and more efficient rockets which could travel thousands of kilometres. These were called I.C.B.M.s, which stands for 'Inter-Continental Ballistic Missiles'. They were designed to carry atomic and hydrogen bombs, and both countries installed them in launching sites, ready to be fired against the other side if war started. The trouble was that these sites could themselves be hit and destroyed by the other side's I.C.B.M.s. To avoid this danger, the United States had built a fleet of submarines designed to carry and launch missile weapons from deep under water. Each missile is fired from the submarine, and the rocket that propels it takes over as it leaves the water. The missile is called Polaris, and the largest has a range of nearly five thousand kilometres. The advantage of Polaris submarines is that the enemy can never know where they are at any given moment. They could be in almost any of the world's oceans and still be able to launch their missiles against enemy targets.

The Soviet Union, Great Britain and France also have submarines which are armed with missiles similar to the American Polaris.

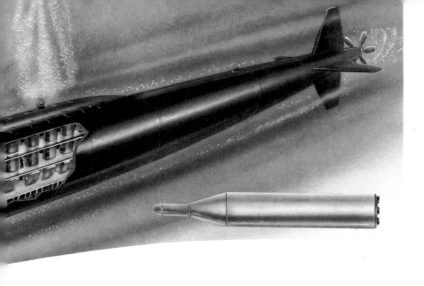

What is a funicular railway?

Funicular railways run up and down very steep slopes. The coaches that run on them are built so that the part of the coach which carries the passengers remains level with the ground however steep the gradient. These coaches are usually connected to a very strong steel cable. The cable is operated by stationary engines at each end of the track, and as it is wound and unwound between the engines so it pulls the coach up and down the track with it.

The famous Montmartre church of Sacré-Coeur in Paris can be reached by funicular railway

What do guide-dogs do?

Dogs are what we call domesticated animals, meaning that for thousands of years they have played a very close and important part in men's lives. One of the most valuable jobs a dog can be trained for is to act as a guide-dog. These dogs are owned by blind people and lead the way when they want to go out. Such

A guide-dog wearing its special harness

dogs are selected for this job when they are about two years old, and it takes four or five months to train them. They are trained to lead their blind master down a street so that he won't bump into other people or walk into buildings or lamp posts. They are also taught to stop at the curb and not lead their master across the road until the traffic has stopped or is a safe distance away. As they are highly intelligent animals, they can even help their masters safely in and out of buses and trains.

What are snake farms?

In hot countries some of the snakes have such poisonous bites that anybody bitten by them can easily die if he is not given proper treatment immediately. The best way to protect people against the bite of a poisonous snake, or to help them recover from the effects of an actual bite, is to inject them with special serums. These serums – called antivenins – are based on the poison itself, and laboratories need constant supplies in order to keep up the manufacture of the antivenins. Snakes are bred for this particular purpose on special kinds of farms, where the poison can be extracted from them. The men who work on these farms are not only skilful but also very brave.

When they want to extract poison from a snake they have to grab it by the neck and, holding it correctly behind the head, catch the drops of poison in a cup as they fall from its fangs. One false move and they may be bitten themselves.

Top: Poison being collected from a snake's fangs
Left: Snakes are kept in small domed huts on a farm

449

How do our lungs work?

Our lungs are like two spongy bags. Just as a sponge can be filled with water and then squeezed dry again, so our lungs fill with air when we breathe in and then release most of the air again when we breathe out. As air enters the lungs it passes down a series of smaller and smaller tubes, which are known as the bronchial tubes, until it ends up in thousands of tiny air sacs. At this point oxygen from the air passes through the lining of the lung and into the blood. This oxygen is vital to the blood stream, as it helps to carry food energy to every other part of the body. Oxygen passes into the blood stream through the lungs, and so, in a similar way, waste products, such as carbon dioxide, pass out of the blood and are removed from the body as we breathe out again.

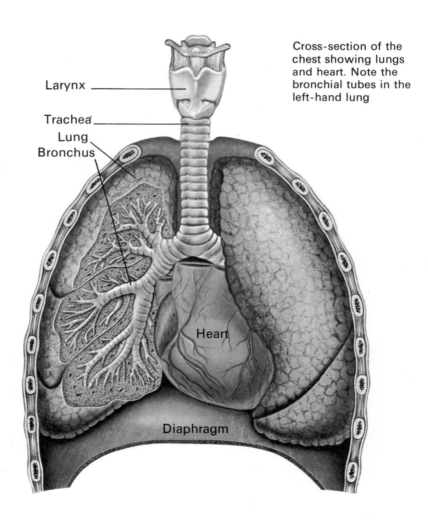

Larynx

Trachea

Lung
Bronchus

Cross-section of the chest showing lungs and heart. Note the bronchial tubes in the left-hand lung

Heart

Diaphragm

How is paper made?

Paper is made from wood, and many of the world's paper mills are found in those countries which have great forests – Canada, Sweden and Finland.

The newly cut trees are usually stripped of their bark, branches and foliage where they have fallen, so that by the time they arrive at the paper mill they are ready for processing. The tree trunks are first

Above: A pulping plant below a Canadian forest of conifers
Right: The final stage of processing the paper inside the plant

cut into thin strips, mixed with water, and ground to a heavy, sticky pulp. This wood pulp is then cleaned of dirt and other impurities, and also chemically bleached to remove the original brownish colour of the wood. The cleaned and bleached pulp next passes through special kinds of rollers which flatten it and draw it out until, at last, it begins to look like sheets of rather soggy paper. These sheets are finally dried and refined until the finished paper is produced.

High quality paper is further 'coated' with clay and other materials to give it a specially smooth, white surface.

What are atoms and molecules?

Atoms are the smallest particles of true matter. It is difficult for us to realize how small they really are. They are about a hundred-millionth of a centimetre across. Even something as small to our eyes as a pin head contains millions of them.

Everything is made up of atoms: every solid, liquid and gas. In a natural state they do not exist singly. They are joined to other atoms to form molecules. A simple molecule could contain as few as two atoms. Complex molecules contain many thousands.

In an atom, the protons in the nucleus and the electrons in orbit, or in 'shells', are balanced electrically. In an aluminium atom there are thirteen of each

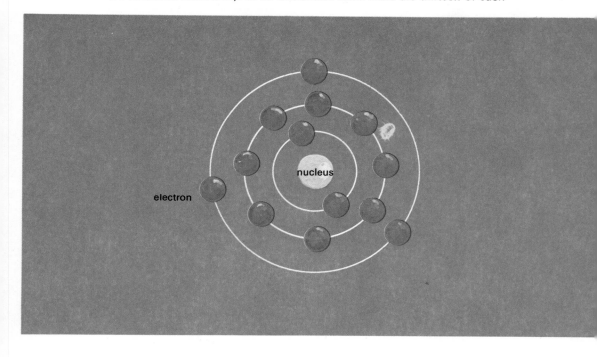

Atoms, and molecules of the same type, make up the elements – chemical substances like nitrogen and sulphur which cannot be split up into any further substances. The elements, in turn, combine in thousands of different ways to form compounds and mixtures. Oxygen and hydrogen are elements. Molecules of each of them join together in a special way to form water, which is a compound. Air, on the other hand, is a mixture. It contains oxygen, nitrogen and various other gases, none of which is in an exactly fixed proportion to the rest.

Do animals generate electricity?

All living creatures have electricity inside them. Our own brains work by means of electrical impulses, and messages or instructions to and from the brain and all other parts of the body pass along the individual nerve fibres of the nervous system. These nerve fibres are very like miniature electric cables and electrical impulses can pass along them as fast as 100 m per second.

Some animals use electricity in other ways, too. The electric eel uses its electrical supply as a means of attack or defence. This creature can build up electricity inside itself to an amazing extent. It can deliver a pulse, or shock, of 600 volts, which is enough to kill most other fish and could stun a human being so badly that he might drown.

Another well-known example of animal electricity is found in the firefly. This little creature produces what is known as 'electro-luminescence'. Chemicals in its body react with oxygen in the air to produce a glow of light around its body.

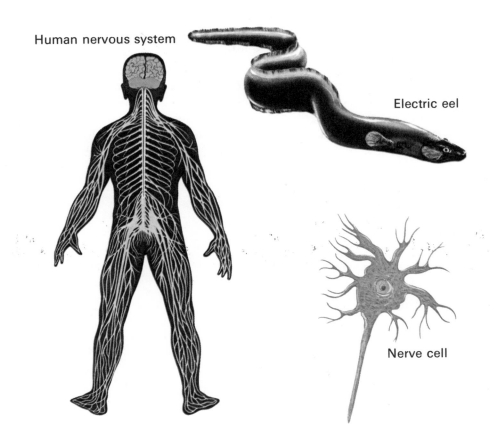

Human nervous system

Electric eel

Nerve cell

Greyhounds at a race track

How fast can a dog run?

Some breeds of dog can run much faster than others, and the fastest dog of all is the greyhound. A fully grown greyhound can run at the astonishing speed of about 56 k.p.h., that is, at nearly a kilometre a minute.

Because greyhounds run so fast, greyhound racing is a popular sport. At a greyhound racing track, the dogs are put in a series of boxes called traps. Then an electrically-driven imitation hare starts to move round a rail running beside the track. As the hare runs past the traps, the doors are released and in their excitement the dogs rush out in pursuit. As in horse racing, people place bets on which dog will be first past the winning post.

Where is the Pampa?

The Pampa is a region of grassland in Argentina. It runs inland from the towns and cities, such as Buenos Aires on the Atlantic coast, and stretches for hundreds of miles up to the foothills of the Andes. The Pampa is very like the great plains, or prairies, of North America which stretch across the states of Texas, Kansas and Nebraska. Like the prairies, the Pampa is most famous for its cattle ranches, and the cowboys which look after the herds of cattle

A cowboy at work on
the Pampa

as they roam across the plains. One of Argentina's most important exports is beef, which comes from the huge cattle ranches which are situated on the Pampa.

What is a rodeo?

Ever since the early days of the cattle industry in the western United States, cowboys have gathered together and organized exhibitions of the best of their skills. The word rodeo, of Spanish origin, came into use in the 1920s. There are five standard events at a rodeo: calf roping, steer wrestling, bareback riding, saddle bronc riding and bull riding. Today, rodeos are highly organized affairs, and contestants are no longer only cowhands but professionals from all parts of the country.

English flag of St George

Scottish flag of St Andrew

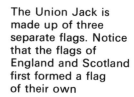

The Union Jack is made up of three separate flags. Notice that the flags of England and Scotland first formed a flag of their own

First Union Flag

Irish flag of St Patrick

Why is the British flag called the 'Union Jack'?

The Union Jack, the official flag of Britain since 1801, is really three separate flags in one, for it combines the English cross of St George, the Scottish cross of St Andrew and the Irish cross of St Patrick. England, Scotland and Ireland were originally independent countries, and the Union Jack symbolizes the fact that they now form the United Kingdom, another name for Britain. Although generally known as the Union Jack, this is incorrect because it is the term for a flag flown only from the jack staff in the bows of a ship to indicate it is a man-of-war. Through popular use, however, the Union Jack has become the accepted name for the flag.

What do charts tell us?

Charts are maps of the sea. As maps show distances, roads and railways, hills and woods and many other features of the land, so charts show distances over stretches of sea, the depth of the water round coasts, dangers to shipping such as rocks and sand banks, tidal currents, the positions of lighthouses, marker buoys and other information vital to a sailor.

Charts are essential to the navigation of a ship. The navigator is the man who must plot the course of the ship, know exactly where the ship is and which direction she is travelling in, at every stage of the voyage. One of the most important items connected with charts is the compass rose, which shows all the principal points of the compass. A navigator needs this in order to relate his chart to the North Pole and so check the direction of the ship's course. Another important item is a set of compasses, or dividers. With these the navigator can measure off distances from the chart, so that he can then calculate how fast his ship is moving and how long a voyage will last.

Special charts for yachtsmen include extra, useful information. Such charts will indicate which courses to follow if the yacht is under sail, and which stretches of water along the coast are safe and suitable anchorages.

The corner of a chart,
showing a compass rose
and a pair of dividers

457

How do hovercraft work?

Hovercraft are often thought of as a type of ship, but they are much more than this. Up to the present, most of them have been built to travel over water, but they can travel over land as well. When it is not running, a hovercraft rests on the water or the land. Underneath it, however, are special motors, and when these are switched on they create what is known as a 'cushion of air'. This 'cushion' is so strong that it lifts the hovercraft right off the water or ground. Other engines then propel it forward.

There are two different types of hovercraft: one which rises only a few inches and travels over prepared, smooth surfaces, and the other type which rises several feet, and operates over every kind of ground, water, or snow, such as this one

Hovercraft are most often used on water because they are much faster than ordinary boats. They do not have to move through the water, they simply move over it. Hovercraft services are now in operation on several short sea routes. One hovercraft service carries both cars and passengers across the English Channel, like an ordinary ship, but the journey is covered in about half the time. Other hovercraft have been built for naval purposes. One type is equipped with missiles. Because they move over the water instead of through the waves, these hovercraft provide a much steadier firing platform. They can also change course far more quickly than conventional naval craft like torpedo boats.

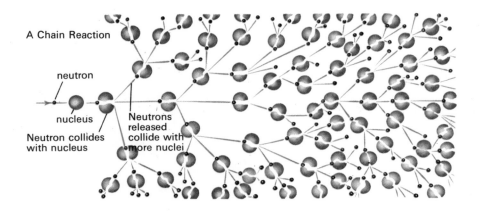

A Chain Reaction

neutron

nucleus

Neutron collides with nucleus

Neutrons released collide with more nuclei

What happens in a chain reaction?

An atom is the smallest unit of true matter, but even it is made up of different parts. The most important part of an atom is the nucleus, which consists of units of energy called protons and neutrons. Earlier this century, scientists discovered that it is possible to hit the nuclei of certain atoms with neutrons taken from other nuclei. A nucleus bombarded in this way splits up and in turn releases more neutrons. Once the process of hitting a nucleus and splitting it up (called nuclear fission) has started, it will continue at an increasing rate. More neutrons from more split nuclei will hit still more nuclei and release yet more neutrons, and so on. This is a chain reaction.

The energy released by the countless millions of split atomic nuclei in a chain reaction is enormous, and takes the form of heat. In an atomic bomb the reaction is immediate and uncontrolled. A flash of light as bright as the sun is followed by a huge fire cloud. In a nuclear power station, the reaction is carefully regulated so that a steady flow of heat can make steam to drive the electric generators.

A single neutron hits the nucleus of another atom and splits it up, releasing more neutrons

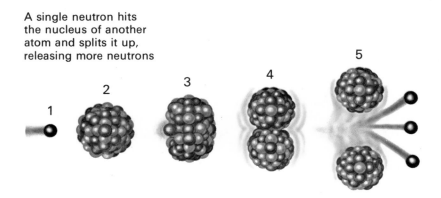

1   2   3   4   5

A rack railway line
in the Alps

What is a rack railway?

Ordinary railway lines usually look as though they are laid on
level ground. In reality most stretches of railway track have a
slight gradient, so that during a journey of any reasonable length,
a train will be running up and down a number of very gradual
slopes. However, there is a definite limit to the degree of steepness
a train can manage going up hill before its wheels start to skid on
the tracks. In mountainous areas especially, it is not always possible
to avoid gradients which a normal train simply could not climb,
even by carrying the track through deep cuttings and tunnels.
To overcome this difficulty rack railways have been built. Locomotives intended to run over such sections of track have a toothed,
or cog, wheel fitted between the normal running wheels. This
connects with a third rail, also toothed, fitted to the track itself.
This is the rack rail. When the locomotive runs along the track,
its cog wheel engages the rack rail and so holds the train to the track
with no risk of skidding.

Some rack railway lines pass through mountainous regions such
as the Alps. Others have been built to carry passengers to the actual
summits of mountains, such as Snowdon in North Wales, and Mount
Washington and Pike's Peak in the United States.

A Rotodyne machine

What is a VTOL?

The letters VTOL stand for the words 'Vertical Take-Off and Landing'. They describe a type of aeroplane which can move straight up or down like a helicopter and also fly forwards like an ordinary aircraft. Their great attraction is that they do away with the need for long runways.

Aircraft engineers are still experimenting with VTOLs, and several types have been built. Perhaps the most successful of these is the Harrier jump-jet. This versatile combat aircraft has rotating nozzles to its jet engines. These can be positioned so that the same engines lift the aircraft vertically or push it forwards in normal flight. The Harrier proved to be very effective during the Falklands Conflict and is in use by the armies of several countries. Other experimental VTOL aircraft include the Rotodyne machine and a number of designs with tilting wings.

Two other types of experimental VTOLs

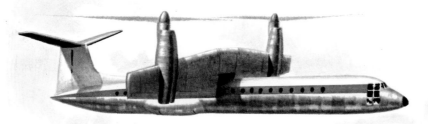

Where is the Camargue?

The Camargue is an area of flat grassland, lakes and swamps in southern France, formed by the various streams of the River Rhône as they flow into the Mediterranean Sea. It is one of Europe's most important nature reserves and is the home of such animals as wild horses, wild boar and flamingoes. Cattle are also reared there by the local cowboys, called *gardians*, and rice is grown in the marshy fields between the numerous lakes and streams.

Historically the Camargue is also a place of great interest. The walled town of Aigues Mortes was the starting point of one of the great Crusades. At that time the town was by the sea, but the streams of the Rhône have deposited so much mud and silt in the area that it now stands high and dry several kilometres inland. Another celebrated town of the region is Arles. The great painter Vincent van Gogh lived and worked there for some time.

In the summer the Camargue is extremely hot, but during the winter months it can be cold and bleak. One of the disagreeable features of this area is the relentless Mistral, a strong wind which blows down the Rhône valley from the snowy peaks of the Alps.

A cowboy in the Camargue rounding up a young bull

The cross-section of
a tree trunk

How can we tell the age of a tree?

As a tree grows it does not just grow taller, its trunk thickens as well. This is due to the fact that with each year of growth new wood is created in the middle of the trunk, pushing the existing layers of wood outwards. There is no sure way of telling the age of a tree just by its height, the thickness of the trunk or toughness of the bark. But if it is cut down, a number of roughly concentric circles will be seen in a cross-section of the trunk, growing from the middle outwards. The space between any two of these circles represents each annual layer of wood, and by counting the circles themselves the age of the tree can be discovered. If the circles inside the trunk of some giant fir trees were counted it would show them to be many hundreds of years old.

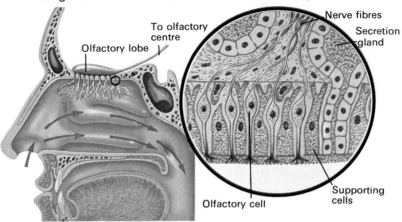

Endings of smell are situated in the nasal cavity

To olfactory centre

Olfactory lobe

Nerve fibres

Secretion gland

Olfactory cell

Supporting cells

How do we taste and smell things?

We can taste things with our taste buds, goblet-shaped clusters of cells on the tongue. These taste buds appear on the surface of the tongue, and different groups of them react to the four basic types of taste – sweet, sour, salt and bitter. They are clusters of cells all connected to a special kind of nerve. This nerve transmits messages to the brain as soon as the cells in the taste buds are stimulated, and the brain interprets them as particular tastes.

Our sense of smell is maintained by what are called the olfactory nerves, and these are located right at the top of the nose. The senses of taste and smell are very closely related. When we have a cold, the nose gets clogged with mucous, which prevents the proper functioning of the olfactory nerves. This, in turn, lessens the effectiveness of the taste buds on the tongue.

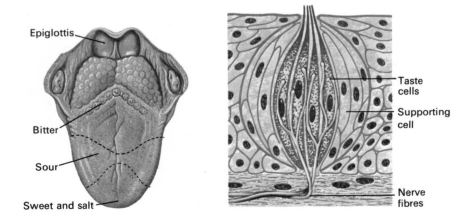

Epiglottis

Bitter

Sour

Sweet and salt

Taste cells

Supporting cell

Nerve fibres

How do our ears work?

Sounds travel through the air as vibrations, or sound waves. High-pitched sounds cause rapid vibrations, while deeper sounds cause much slower vibrations. The vibrations of a sound enter the ear and strike the ear drum, a delicate membrane which itself starts to vibrate when vibrations from the air reach it. The ear drum's own vibrations are then transmitted by a series of three equally delicate bones – the hammer, the anvil and the stirrup – to a coiled tube called the cochlea. The cochlea changes the vibrations into electrical impulses which travel along nerves to the brain, where they are interpreted as different kinds of sound. The outer ear,

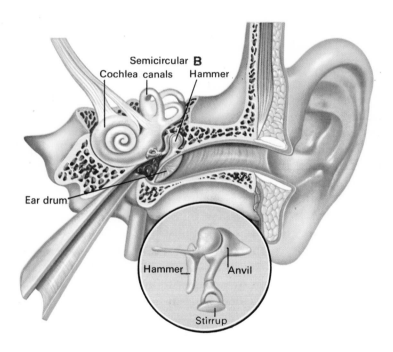

that is, the part of the ear that we can see, is shaped so that the ear drum picks up the clearest impression of the sounds that reach it.

Some sounds are either so low or so high that the human ear drum is not sensitive enough to pick them up. They are said to be beyond the threshold of hearing. The ears of some other animals, though, can pick up such sounds, especially very high-pitched ones. Bats make such high-pitched squeaks that most of the time we cannot hear them at all. But the bats can hear themselves and each other perfectly well.

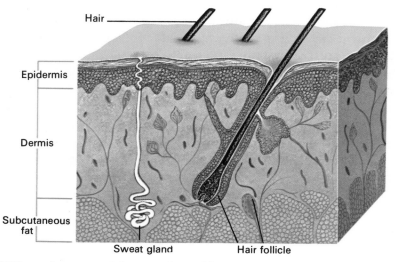

Hair

Epidermis

Dermis

Subcutaneous fat

Sweat gland   Hair follicle

What is our skin made of?

The surface of every part of the body, inside and out, is covered with a protective layer, or layers, of tightly packed cells called epithelia. The largest, thickest and most complex of these epithelial tissues is the skin which covers the whole of the outside of the body. The skin itself is made of two principal layers. The outer layer – the part of the skin we actually see – is called the epidermis. The softer, more delicate inner layer is the dermis.

It is in the dermis that the roots of the hair are contained. In other mammals the hair is far more important than in man. It helps to regulate the heat of the body. In cold conditions the skin tightens. This raises the hair from the surface of the skin and creates an insulating layer of air which helps the body to retain its heat. In cold weather our own skin still behaves in the same instinctive way and we experience what is known as 'goose flesh', or 'goose pimples'.

When the body needs to lose heat rather than retain it the sweat glands start to function. Sweat is largely water, and as it comes to the surface of the skin through the sweat glands it carries with it excess body heat which then evaporates into the surrounding air, thus acting as a method of cooling.

What are vitamins?

In addition to giving us the necessary balance of carbohydrates, proteins and fats, the food we eat must also contain an adequate amount of vitamins if we are to remain healthy. The action of vitamins in the body is very complicated, but what they do is help the body to make full and proper use of the food it has digested in the building of new cells and resistance to disease. Lack of vitamins belonging to any one of the four main groups, A, B, C and D leads to ill health of one kind or another. For example, a lack of vitamin B₁ weakens the nervous system. An insufficient amount of vitamin D in children can prevent bones and teeth from forming properly, causing a disease called rickets.

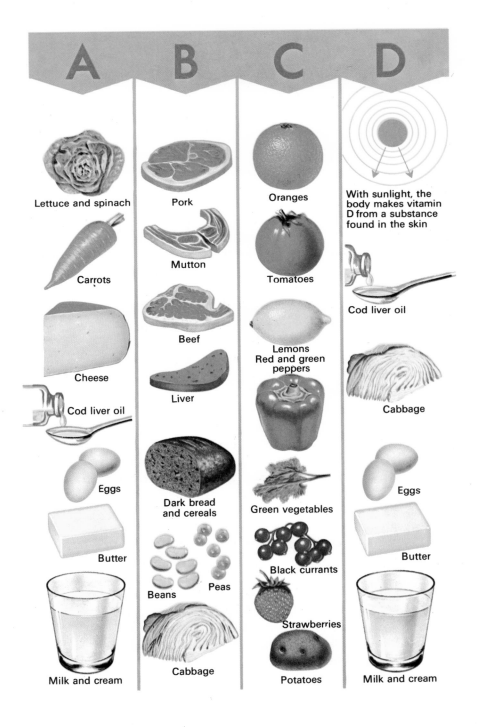

A

Lettuce and spinach

Carrots

Cheese

Cod liver oil

Eggs

Butter

Milk and cream

B

Pork

Mutton

Beef

Liver

Dark bread and cereals

Beans   Peas

Cabbage

C

Oranges

Tomatoes

Lemons
Red and green peppers

Green vegetables

Black currants

Strawberries

Potatoes

D

With sunlight, the body makes vitamin D from a substance found in the skin

Cod liver oil

Cabbage

Eggs

Butter

Milk and cream

A Bertin aerotrain, steered by a central fin, is a six-seater vehicle which travels on an air cushion

Can trains run without rails?

For many years railway engineers have been thinking about new kinds of track for trains to run along. The parallel metal rail tracks with which we are familiar are not very efficient by modern standards. Because wheels are needed to move the trains along, a good deal of power is lost through friction in the moving parts. Ordinary railway tracks also set a limit to the speed that trains can go, especially round curves. They take up a lot of room, and they are expensive to build and keep in good repair.

Some trains, such as those operated on the Paris Métro, run very efficiently on rubber tyres. Other even more interesting advances in this field have been the experiments with monorail systems. Monorail means 'one rail', and several types of train have been designed which are suspended from an elevated monorail track. Spectacular results, in terms of speed and comfort, have been achieved.

Yet other trains have been built which sit astride a single metal or concrete track and slide along it. Called aerotrains, they have been designed to move like hovercraft. Their weight keeps them safely close to the rail or track, but they can glide along a 'cushion of air'. An even more advanced idea is to suspend a train from a monorail by magnetizing the rail. In all these cases there is hardly any friction to overcome, and much greater safety.

New forms of motive power are also being considered, including jet propulsion. The day may come when trains will be able to move almost as fast as aircraft.

Left: Astronaut's hand-operated rocket device
Below: Astronaut 'walking' in space

How do astronauts 'walk' in space?

If an astronaut leaves his spacecraft during a journey, he cannot walk about in the ordinary way. There is nothing but empty space. There is not even any gravity to pull him in one particular direction. He can only guide himself by the same means as the spacecraft itself – by rocket propulsion. So when astronauts do leave their spacecraft during a flight – perhaps to help in docking operations with another spacecraft – they carry specially designed hand rockets with them. If they point the rocket exhaust in one direction, and give the engine a burst of power, they will move in the opposite direction. In this way they can steer themselves.

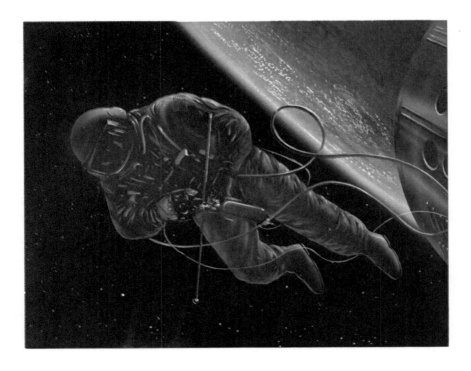

Who started the Olympic Games?

The Olympic Games started thousands of years ago in ancient Greece. They were held every four years as a religious festival in honour of the supreme Greek god Zeus, and included racing, wrestling and jumping contests.

The modern Olympic Games, intended as an international festival of athletics, started in 1896, in Athens. Once again, they are held

What is a swing-tail aircraft?

Aircraft have now been designed to transport almost every kind of freight. There is hardly anything today so large and bulky that it cannot be handled by air transport.

Some freighter aircraft still have doors in the side of the fuselage, as do passenger aircraft. Foodstuffs, medical supplies, even cattle and horses, can easily be loaded and unloaded from air freighters of this type. Other freighter aircraft have been built with great doors that swing open in the nose of the fuselage. This type is designed to transport cars, tanks and lorries, which can be driven up a ramp, through the nose doors and straight down into the fuselage.

Yet another special type of freighter aircraft has been built in which the back section of the fuselage, including the tail plane, swings to one side. This makes freight handling at airports extremely easy and quick, because both the front and rear portions of the

every four years, but each time in a different city. Almost every athletic sport is now included. Only during the First and Second World Wars was the holding of the Olympic Games interrupted.

The Olympic flag is a very distinctive one. A white background is used so that each of the other colours may be clearly seen. The colours of each of the five circles have been selected because they are the ones most commonly used in national flags throughout the world. The chain they form is a symbol of unity.

fuselage can be loaded and unloaded at the same time. Aircraft like this are called 'swing-tail' aircraft. One type of 'swing-tail' aircraft can carry nearly thirty tons of freight. An aircraft of this type was designed as long ago as the 1920s, but at that time nobody could imagine a situation arising in which it could possibly be used.

A 'swing tail' aircraft
ready for loading

Where are the headquarters of the United Nations?

The headquarters of the United Nations Organization are in New York City. Representatives of every member nation have a place in the great conference chamber where debates on matters of world importance are held. There is also special accommodation for language interpreters, so that whatever languages are being spoken by delegates, every other delegate can receive an immediate translation through his earphones.

Another part of the headquarters is the tall Secretariat Building, shown in the picture. The Secretary-General of the U.N. has his offices in this building.

The United Nations Organization was founded in 1945, just after the Second World War. The flag adopted for it, also shown in the picture, represents the world surrounded by two olive branches, traditional symbols of peace.

Who founded the Red Cross?

The Red Cross was founded by a Swiss, Jean Henri Dunant, after he had witnessed the terrible plight of the wounded at the Battle of Solferino in 1859. Five years later, in 1864, the first Geneva Convention was called to establish a code of conduct for nations at war, and Dunant obtained the convention's agreement that both wounded soldiers and medical services should be treated as neutrals.

The flag chosen to represent the international medical service that grew out of Dunant's work was a red cross on a white background, this being the reverse colours of the Swiss flag. It also gave the organization its name. In Moslem countries, however, the flag is a red crescent on a white background, to distinguish it clearly from the Christian symbol of a crucifix.

A Red Cross unit in war-time action

The Pont du Gard is
a favourite spot for
sightseers
Inset: Some methods
of Roman stone and
brick construction

Where is the Pont du Gard?

The Pont du Gard is in the south of France. It is a Roman aqueduct
– a bridge for carrying water – almost perfectly preserved, and so
is one of the most significant of all Roman remains. It was built
about A.D. 150 as part of a much more complex system of canals,
tunnels and bridges designed to convey water from the hills down
to the town of Nîmes.

What are truffles?

Truffles are an edible fungus, similar to a mushroom. However,
truffles cannot be found growing in woods and fields like other fungi.
They grow some way under the ground. They also only grow in

Aided by a dog,
a man searches
for truffles (*see
inset*) in a
Beech wood

certain places where the chemical composition of the soil is just right, so they are comparatively rare. Many people maintain that they have the most delicious flavour of all the edible fungi. For these reasons they are very expensive. Generally they are used to flavour pâté, and appear in the pâté as small, black lumps or flakes.

Traditionally, people went truffle hunting with pigs. The idea was that the pig would smell where a truffle was growing and dig it out of the ground with its snout. Dogs can also be trained to sniff out truffles in the ground.

Who built the Eiffel Tower?

Gustave Eiffel was a famous nineteenth century French engineer. He built a number of impressive railway bridges and other ironwork constructions. For the Paris international trade exhibition of 1889 he was asked to design a special tower made of a combination of iron and steel. The result was the Eiffel Tower. It is about 352 m in height and was for many years the highest structure in the world.

The Eiffel Tower remains one of the most celebrated of all landmarks, and symbolizes Paris just as Big Ben is often felt to symbolize London. There are several floors to the Eiffel Tower. On the first floor is a restaurant, while the view from the top floor is breathtaking. The Tower is also used for radio and television transmissions.

The Earth and Man

How do you put a mountain on a piece of paper?

Compared to the size of the Earth, man is minute. Compared to a mole hill in a meadow, man is much bigger. We can look down on it, and see it clearly. If you were the size of an ant, however, and you had not climbed that particular mole hill before, it might not be quite so easy. In man's case, we would find a mountain that we had never seen before as difficult to explore as an ant would a mole hill. We need something to help us find our way over the mountain without taking the risk of getting lost or falling over a dangerous precipice.

Some animals are able to find their way by smell. When a badger goes exploring, for example, it leaves a scent trail behind it. If the badger wants to re-use the path it simply follows its nose. Some birds are even more clever at finding their way from one place to another. Swallows for example, travel hundreds of kilometres from Africa to Britain and Europe each spring to lay their eggs and rear their young, and then fly back again each autumn. We do not know exactly how birds migrate huge distances without getting lost, but it is likely that they navigate using the Sun and the stars to guide them. It has even been suggested that they are able to detect the Earth's magnetic field to help them find their way.

Man is not so clever. If you did not know your way from one place to another, you would look at a *map* to help you. A map is simply a way of showing the three-dimensional countryside on a small scale in two dimensions.

What is a typical map? In Britain, for example, a typical map is an Ordnance Survey map. If you look closely at one you will notice that the map is drawn to a scale. It could be

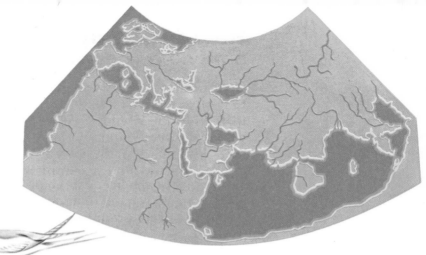

1:50,000, for example. This means that something which measures one kilometre from end to end in the area shown on the map would measure two centimetres on the map sheet.

What is shown on a map? Of course, this depends on the purpose of the map. But look at your Ordnance Survey map again. You will see roads represented by red, orange, or yellow lines depending on how big they are. You will see railway lines marked by black lines, either dashed or un-interrupted. Rivers, lakes and the sea are shown in blue. Woods are shown by areas of green. Then, of course, there are a number of symbols to indicate such things as churches or hotels, quarries or telephone boxes and much more besides. Perhaps one of the most interesting things you will notice on the map are the faint orange lines that seem to form irregular loops. They are called *contour lines*. Each contour line marks the particular height of the land above sea-level. They are usually marked at intervals of 50 feet. It is these contour lines that mark the position, extent, and height of a mountain on the piece of paper.

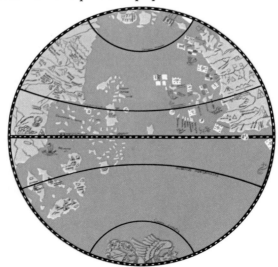

How do geologists help us?

All the sciences, mathematics, physics, chemistry, and biology, are playing an increasingly important role in our way of life, as the years pass and we become more dependent upon the products of science and technology. Geology, too, has a vital part to play in living today, apart from its value in furthering our understanding of the way in which our Earth began, developed, and is in constant motion to this day. For example, few of us could imagine living now without the vast network of roads and railways that span the land surface. But these roads and railways require bridges and tunnels which cannot be built in some areas or they may collapse.

By careful surveying, the geologist is able to tell what kinds of rocks there are in an area, and can suggest to the engineer the best site for their construction. Before geologists were consulted, huge constructions were often erected on sites quite unsuitable for the purpose with disastrous results. A famous instance is the San Francisquito Dam disaster in America. A quick survey was carried out on the proposed site during the dry summer months and it was decided that the narrowest part of the river channel was ideal. Unfortunately, the rocks on one side of the canyon were clays, with schists on the other. When the water filled up behind the dam the clays became soft and flowed away so that the schists broke away and the whole dam collapsed.

Geologists can also help to avoid the terrible loss of life which occurs as a result of earthquakes. So far they have not been able to perfect methods of actually preventing earthquakes, but at least with the methods now available (remember 'What makes the ground tremble?') people can be warned of a coming disturbance in time to escape.

Perhaps today the geologists' skill in finding raw materials is even more important. Industrialized society depends on the raw materials that the Earth provides – nowhere else can provide our needs. Our society with its demands for more energy, more water, more iron, more aluminium, more chemicals from oil, and so on, now asks the geologist to find more sources for all these materials and many others. Obviously it is becoming more difficult and more costly. In time, of course, unless our demands are reduced, not even the cleverest geologist will be able to find new supplies. They will have all been used up.

How do we look for the raw materials we need?

You have already seen that the geologist has an importan part to play in the modern world; one of his most vit functions is to find deposits of raw materials for our industrie The deposits should preferably be in a place which is eas to get at so that materials can be transported cheaply. The should also be in concentrations that are rich enough allow the mining or oil company to remove them at a prof In fact, deposits of this kind are very few and far betwee because they have all been used up. The geologist mu work harder and harder using better and better technique But what are the methods of the modern exploratio geologist?

The geologist's method depends on what he is looking fo and the type of countryside he is exploring. It cannot b stressed too strongly, however, that with all the advance that have been made, there is still no real substitute for th geologist's experience and ability to prepare a real accurate geological map. (You have already seen how a ma can be prepared.) If the geologist is looking for minerals ores such as iron, copper, or tin, a chemical analysis of th soils and streams in an area can provide very valuabl

information. For example, if he takes samples of the water from selected points up a stream, he may find that there are traces of copper in the water in the lower reaches and that much further up-stream there are not. He knows, then that the source of the copper must be between those two places. It is possible to track the origin down quite closely in this way.

You have already seen that when an earthquake occurs, the waves produced travel through different rocks at different speeds. This property can be used on a much smaller scale. If a shock is produced in the ground with a hammer or explosives, measuring instruments can record the waves at selected points and a good idea can be gained of the geology below the surface. It is also worth noting that the pull of the Earth's field of gravity is not constant over the whole of the Earth. It varies with the distance from the centre of the Earth and with the geology of the area which is measured. Denser rocks exert a stronger pull than lighter ones, and sensitive instruments can be used to measure these tiny differences.

A direct look at the rocks below the surface can be made by drilling, and even when oil wells have proved to be dry they are not completely wasted because they can reveal a great deal about the geology. An instrument like a giant corkscrew called an *auger* can be used by the worker in the field for very shallow investigations.

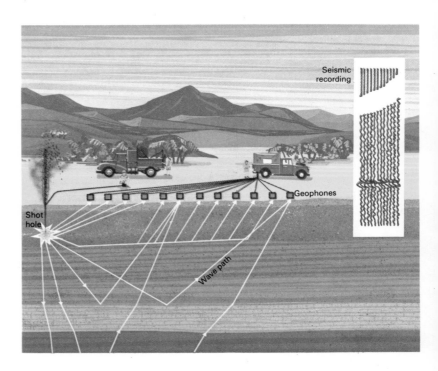

What are ores, and where might you expect to find them?

You must realize that the Earth provides us with all the raw materials swallowed up by our industries. Many of these materials are minerals. The meaning of the word 'mineral' has already been explained, but sometimes it is used to denote any substance obtained by mining. It is clear that the words mine and mineral have similar origins. You might expect that minerals would be spread throughout the Earth, and indeed, this does happen. Occasionally, however, (and fortunately for our present needs) minerals may accumulate in sufficient quantities for man to be able to remove them comparatively easily. When this situation arises, the deposits are usually known as *ores* or ore bodies. The minerals associated with the ores that have no real economic value are usually referred to as *gangue* minerals. Today, because of the greater demand for minerals, the consequent scarcity of them, and improved methods of mining and refining, material that was once thrown on the spoil heaps can now provide valuable sources.

Above:
This typical poor quality iron ore can be found in western Australia.

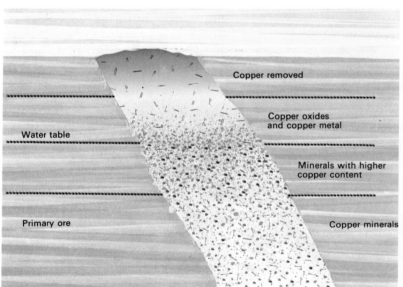

Right:
The concentration of a metal such as copper can be changed by the movements of water and by weathering.

Ores can occur in a variety of ways. With ores of iron, for example, the same ore can arise as a result of different methods of concentration. Many ores other than iron are formed in association with magmatic processes (you have seen the word magma before – look at the questions on igneous rocks if you cannot remember it). If you remember the way in which a magma cools and forms crystals, it will come as no surprise to you to learn that metals such as chromium and nickel result from the settling into bands of the relevant crystals as the magma cools. There are often watery solutions charged with minerals coming from magmas and these also provide supplies of metals such as

Right:
A banded copper ore vein.

Right:
Deposits of ore may be associated with large igneous intrusions.

mercury or copper. Both these minerals are in short supply, and in fact, deposits of mercury are almost completely confined to areas in Spain. Not all ores have been formed by igneous activity, however. Important deposits of iron in England have resulted from concentration by sedimentary process. Deposits known as *placers* are typical sedimentary ores. Of course, oil and coal must be considered as economic minerals and these have obviously resulted from sedimentation.

The sea may one day provide much of the world's minerals. It has been known for some time that there is great richness of gold in the sea but as yet it has not been worthwhile nor even possible to exploit this mineral wealth. Even uncommon metals like vanadium, which is used for the nosecones of spacecraft, is concentrated in the blood of an unexciting sea animal – the sea cucumber.

What is ecology?

You have seen the way in which the first primitive forms of life first arrived on our planet, how they multiplied and became more complex. You have learned something about the main animal and plant groups, and in particular, about those fossils that are of special importance to the geologist. You have even looked at the origins and the evolution of man himself. Each animal or plant has been considered separately, however, and only in terms of its biology and evolutionary history. You know, of course, that no living organism lives a totally independent and isolated existence. Even man depends on other animals and plants for food, and clothing; even the fossil fuels come from living things long dead.

Right:
People and governments are becoming more aware of the importance of protecting our natural environment, as these recent international conferences indicate.

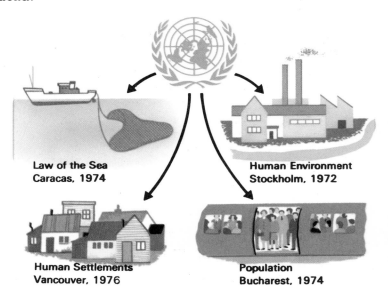

Law of the Sea
Caracas, 1974

Human Environment
Stockholm, 1972

Human Settlements
Vancouver, 1976

Population
Bucharest, 1974

The study of plants and animals in relation to their environment (and this includes other animals and plants) is known as ecology. The word comes from the Greek *oikos* meaning the home and *logos* meaning discourse or speech. You probably do or have done nature study. Ecology really just applies scientific methods to this basic study. Instead of considering just animal life as does the zoologist, or plant life as does the botanist, or where animals and plants live on the Earth as does the biogeographer, the ecologist must have a working knowledge of all these and many more sciences in order to come to an understanding of the nature of all living things. The ecologist must look at the way all animals and plants depend upon each other for their very existence in a complex natural web.

The ecologist does not confine himself or herself to other life forms. Man is an animal and must be looked on as such. Perhaps it is worth remembering that while all animals try to change their environment to suit their own needs, man is able to exert a much greater influence in his attempts to improve his lot. Man has been able to achieve this because of his intelligence and his ability to make and use tools – once just simple stone hammers and axes but now computers and guided missiles. A song thrush may use a particular stone time after time to break the shell of a snail to remove the soft body inside. Thus, it is making use of a tool. A badger may build its sett in a bank and line it with dry leaves to keep itself and its young warm. Thus it is making a home. Man does all these things but on a larger scale, more quickly, and more permanently.

You can see then that the ecologist's knowledge of living creatures could become more and more vital to man as he needs to grow more food and find room for more and more people.

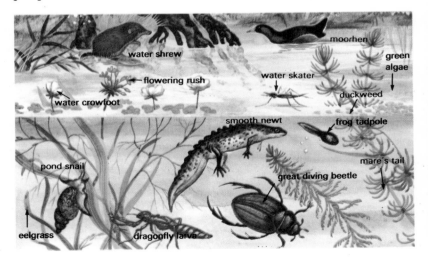

How do animals and plants depend upon each other?

The sun is the driving force in all of the Earth's processes. It is the sun's rays that keep our planet warm enough for us to be able to survive, it is the weather's motor, and provides energy for the most important process of all so far as plants and animals are concerned. The sun provides plants with the energy for *photosynthesis*. It is by photosynthesis that plants use the sun's energy to convert carbon dioxide taken in from the air, and water from the soil into the sugars and starches that make up their stems, leaves, and roots. It is a little more complicated than this, and plants need other substances as well, but this is the important process. Photosynthesis only occurs in plants that contain the complex green pigment *chlorophyll*, in other words in green plants.

Other types of plants depend on other means of manufacturing these materials. It is interesting to note that green plants can store energy so that photosynthesis can even occur at night. You have seen, too, how the first plants evolved in the sea. This is because water is needed to provide the hydrogen to form the sugars and starches.

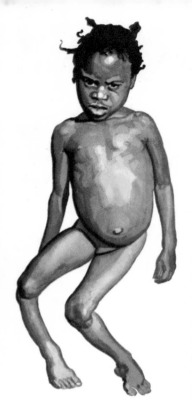

Above:
We all depend on our natural environment. This child is suffering from a disease called rickets, a softening of the bones due to lack of a certain vitamin and sunlight.

Right:
Carnivores, animals that eat other creatures, depend upon animals that eat plants, herbivores. Herbivores in turn, depend on creatures in the soil that release food for them. There must be fewer carnivores than herbivores, and so on.

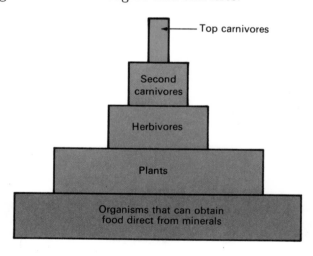

Top carnivores

Second carnivores

Herbivores

Plants

Organisms that can obtain food direct from minerals

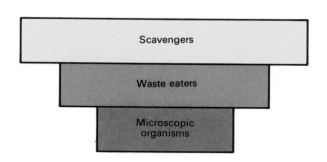

Scavengers

Waste eaters

Microscopic organisms

We now have the basic food supply for the rest of the planet's life forms. You know that cows, for example, eat grass. Without grass or other plant material available, cows could not survive. We then make use of the cow's ability to digest grass and convert it into meat and milk which we eat and drink. Thus, the cow is a herbivore, that is, an animal that feeds on plants. When we eat meat, we are behaving as carnivores or meat eaters. This demonstrates a simple chain of events, in fact, it is known as a *food chain*. The grass grows and is eaten by the cow which is eaten by man.

There are many other such chains. A fox may feed on rabbits, which may be eating clover. The clover may be dependent not only on the sun, water, and the air, but also on bees for pollination. These chains can be disturbed quite easily sometimes with far reaching effects. For example, should bees become reduced in number for any reason, such as a farmer using insecticides, in time the amount of clover would fall back and the rabbits might be forced to feed on the farmer's lettuces. Obviously, the farmer will not be happy about this and may set about reducing the rabbit population. If he was too enthusiastic and all the rabbits in an area were to be wiped out, the fox would have to look elsewhere for its meals – it might even be the same farmer's chickens.

Try to imagine multiplying these simple chains thousands of times to take the multitudes of different animals and plants into account. Now you begin to have some idea of the complicated nature of life on our planet, how animals and plants depend upon their surroundings and each other, and how easily the balance can be upset.

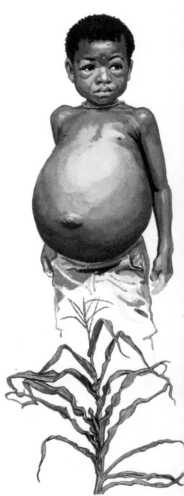

Above:
This child is suffering from a lack of protein. Even plants require the correct nourishment or they will become diseased.

How can you help to look after our Earth?

The first thing to remember is that human beings are animals. Admittedly, humans are very intelligent and adaptable animals, but animals just the same. Our species has evolved on the Earth as part of the Earth's web of living things. We were not born somewhere else in the Universe and then landed on Earth later. This means that we are adapted to living in the conditions which the Earth provides for us. After all, any animal that is not fully adapted to its surroundings or which cannot compete with its rivals in the struggle for food and shelter eventually ceases to exist. We depend upon the energy provided by the sun to keep us warm, we need water, and we need food in the form of vegetable materials or other animals. If the time came when we were the only living species on the planet our days would be numbered.

You can see, then, that in order to protect ourselves we need to look after the Earth and all its creatures. To do this the first step is to try to understand a little more about the way in which living things behave, and to try to appreciate the beauties of the world. This requires us to go out into the countryside and watch and listen. Unfortunately, by going into the areas that we are seeking to protect it is all too easy to cause considerable disturbance. When you go into the country, remember that it is living and growing, and follow the Country Code:

Below:
If areas of countryside are burned repeatedly, the soil can be eroded away leaving desert conditions.

Above right:
Carelessness in the countryside can lead to forest fires killing thousands of plants and other living things.

1. Guard against all risks of fire – do not, for example, throw down lighted matches or drop any glass which may act as a burning lens, and try to see that other people are just as careful.

Left and below:
Nature reserves like the three shown here can help to protect areas of outstanding beauty or plants and animals that are in danger of extinction.

2. Fasten all gates – animals straying into the wrong field may eat grass that is too lush and become ill and even die.

3. Keep dogs under proper control – a dog may easily frighten domestic or wild animals, and this is even more serious if it is during the breeding season.

4. Keep to the paths across farm land.

Below:
Marshy lands at river estuaries are particularly rich in wild life. These areas are decreasing because the land is suitable for reclamation by man.

5. Do not damage walls, gates, hedges, or fences.

6. Take all your litter home. Animals can be cut by broken bottles or cans, or choke on plastic bags.

7. We need water – look after all possible sources.

8. Protect all wild life, plants, and trees – there are laws to protect many species of birds, plants and animals that are in danger of dying out.

9. Go carefully on country roads – if you are in a car, particularly at night, it is all too simple to run over a hedgehog or a fox.

10. Respect the life of the countryside.

These are just a few of the points to remember, but before you do anything, just stop to think of the consequences *before* you do it.

Which parts of the Earth are in most need of protection?

There are certain areas around the globe that are particularly vulnerable to disturbance whether it be by man or such factors as climate. Some areas, such as deserts or the ice caps of the Arctic and Antarctic have definite characteristics of their own, but what of the areas between? Take, for instance, the boundary between the oceans and the dry land. This is where you would expect to find the estuaries of rivers and coastal wetlands generally. In the past, these areas have been considered to be of little value. It was thought that by reclaiming them from the sea, the land could be put to better use whether as farming land or land on which to build a new airport.

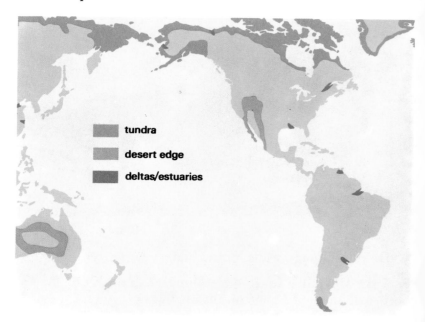

tundra

desert edge

deltas/estuaries

In reality, however, these regions are not the waste lands that they at first seem to be. We depend upon the fishing industry to supply us with food and fish products for fertilizers and so on. Many sea fishes spend much of their development period in the estuaries, and if estuaries were to be destroyed, it would not be long before the stocks of fish became exhausted. Even animals like prawns depend upon the very rich supplies of food in estuaries to survive.

The mudflats surrounding river mouths provide feeding grounds for an important section of the bird community, the waders. Waders include birds such as the redshank and the dunlin, the oystercatcher and the godwit. You have seen

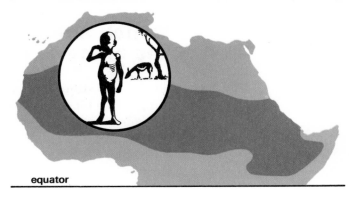

right:
The southward spread of the Sahara desert means the loss of food supply to people that live close to this area with obvious consequences.

equator

in the previous question what can happen to a food chain if it is interrupted in some way. It is important to remember that the destruction of any species of animal or plant by any but purely natural causes does not only remove something beautiful from the Earth but may even affect our own food supplies.

On a somewhat more local scale, it is important that our farmland should be used sensibly, and protected to supply our needs for generations to come. It is easy to see the effects of carelessness. With the coming of the tractor and then even larger and more complex farm machinery such as the giant combine harvesters, it seemed that the bigger the fields, the easier and cheaper it would be to manoeuvre the machinery. As a consequence, many kilometres of hedges were uprooted, to remove obstacles to the progress of the combines. This meant that a great deal of important habitat was lost to wild life. In addition, there was a more direct result. It had not been realized that these hedges acted as windbreaks, and their removal led to widespread soil erosion. The lesson to be learned once again is to think of the consequences before acting.

right:
Notice that those areas that are particularly vulnerable to changes in the environment are generally relatively small. They include deltas and river estuaries.

Which animals and plants are in the most danger?

red helleborine

Cheddar pink

monkey orchid

In this question, the word 'danger' does not refer to the danger to which individuals of any species may be subjected. Danger in this case means the danger to which a whole species is liable. In other words, species may be in danger of becoming extinct, and disappearing for ever from the face of the planet. Of course, we can tell from the fossil record that hundreds of species of animals and plants have come and gone throughout the span of life on Earth. In the past, however, those species that have died out have done so as a result of natural causes. The animals and plants that disappeared were those that were unable to adapt fast enough to changing conditions or were unable to compete with their rivals for the available food supplies. There are instances, however, such as that of the dinosaurs, in which it is not at all clear why they became extinct. Many ideas have been suggested, but none of them is wholly satisfactory.

For today's wild life, there is another, more terrible threat to their existence – man. Man is endangering the lives of many species of animals and plants which are unable to adapt to the pressures of man's increasing numbers and his changes to the natural environment. On the other hand, there are those species that have certainly benefited from man's activities. In Britain, for example, birds such as the black headed gull have increased in numbers quite dramatically in the last fifty years, adapting well to a semi-urban environment and feeding on man's waste. Even the fox has been able to survive by adapting to become an urban scavenger in many large cities. Unfortunately, the lack of suitable foods has led to the foxes becoming deformed so that individuals probably spend a great deal of their lives in considerable pain.

But man is threatening wild life in many ways. Firstly by his spread further and further into the rural areas, man is reducing the areas in which wild life can live. This also includes the effects of widespread farming where forests and heaths come under the plough and many kilometres of

tufted saxifrage

alpine catchfly

alpine gentian

lion

leopard

ocelot

puma

leopard-skin coat

hedges are removed. Secondly, man has hunted many animals to extinction. A good example of this is the destruction of the great auk during the last century or perhaps even more famous the death of the dodo. More recently the fate of many species of the giant sea mammals, whales, has been in the news, as their numbers fall to the more efficient whaler's harpoon gun with its explosive harpoon. Pollution is also affecting the lives of many animals. Millions of sea birds die very unpleasant deaths as a result of their feathers becoming covered in sticky, black oil waste.

It is sometimes argued that if an animal or plant cannot survive man's ravages, then this is just the course of evolution. Unfortunately, many beautiful and valuable species, on which man himself depends, may never be seen again.

Above:
Many wild animals have been hunted almost to extinction and even put to horrible deaths to satisfy the demands of fashion.

Left:
This bird, the great auk, was the northern hemisphere's counterpart of the penguin. Egg collecting and hunting drove it to extinction in 1844.

Who helps to look after the Earth?

You have seen how much we depend upon our planet and its other inhabitants in so many different ways, and although this seems obvious enough, most of us take our environment very much for granted. How many of us stop to wonder what the products of industrial living have cost in terms of loss of countryside or polluted oceans or dead animals. The need to be concerned about the delicate balance of nature cannot be stressed too strongly, although some people feel that because man is as much part of the natural world as any other creature then his widespread interference with the systems of life is acceptable. There are others who lack concern completely.

Right:
Seabirds like the guillemot are in most danger of oiling because of the way in which they feed. They dive under the sea and then surface some metres away, perhaps into an oil slick leaked from a tanker or an oil rig. Volunteers save the lives of many birds by cleaning them with detergent.

It may not yet be time to despair, however. All over the world there are men and women, scientists and non-scientists who have taken it upon themselves to act in such a way as to protect some part of our environment, often at considerable personal cost. In Britain, for example, there are many organizations that are concerned with various aspects of the living world. On a national scale there are bodies such as the British Trust for Conservation Volunteers to which people are able to offer their services for many kinds of conservation work. No experience is required, and volunteers learn a variety of skills from pond clearance to tree planting. The gatherings are usually arranged for week-ends, and during the holiday periods residential trips are arranged at low cost. On a more local scale in Britain, there are the county naturalists' trusts such as the Berkshire, Buckinghamshire, and Oxfordshire Naturalist Trust or BBONT for short. The main aim of these groups is to obtain, whether by gift or by buying with their own funds, areas of particular natural interest which can then be protected as reserves. It is hoped that in this way many of the animal and plant species that might not otherwise survive will be given a better than even chance. This means that these groups must try to have as many of the different types of habitat as possible and must have funds enough to employ people to manage them. There are of course the better known groups that are concerned with particular types of species. The Royal Society for the Protection of Birds is one of these.

Right:
Animals such as the elephant that were once mercilessly hunted just for their ivory are now afforded some protection in national parks and game reserves but these areas have to be looked after very carefully.

The Friends of the Earth are concerned with all things environmental. They are a limited company rather than a charity which means that any actions that they take can be completely independent. Recently they have campaigned against such things as the use of no deposit bottles for beer and fizzy drinks and have been quite successful in their efforts to save the whale from extinction.

These are just a few of the people and organizations that are concerned with looking after our planet, but there are still many ways in which we all can help.

What dangers does the Earth hold for its peoples?

We are intelligent animals that have evolved on the Earth. We have adapted to suit its requirements and we have tried to change our own environment to make our lives more comfortable with varying success. The Earth is our provider. At times, however, it is also our enemy.

The dangers which the Earth holds for its peoples depend to a large extent upon which parts of the globe we are talking about – the areas where there are extremes of any kind are the most dangerous! In talking about some of the processes of the Earth, we have also mentioned the terrible forces locked up and the havoc which they can wreak. We have, for example, already mentioned earthquakes. Scientists watching the earthquakes in Chile in South America described the earth beneath their feet as 'slow and rolling like that of the sea during a heavy swell'. Can you imagine how terrifying that might be? In very thickly populated areas such as Tokyo in Japan, the people there live their whole lives under the threat of an earthquake which could send the whole city toppling with awful loss of life.

Although earthquakes are very dramatic, they are not the only natural disasters which threaten life on Earth – the weather can also play its part. In tropical areas close to the oceans, whirling winds can tear down buildings, rip up trees,

Right:
People living in this area might suffer with drought for most of the year, and when it finally does rain, flooding might take place (*see* facing page).

and pick up motor cars as though they are toys. They are caused when the air has been heated more than normal, sending up twisting streams of air. Around America, they are usually known as hurricanes and around Australia and Japan they are referred to as typhoons. They usually affect quite small areas, usually no more than 400 kilometres across, so that the air pressure gradient is very steep and in the eye or middle it is quite calm, but around this, winds may reach speeds of 350 kilometres per hour. There is also the tornado which usually occurs on land and may begin as an off-shoot of a hurricane. This is a very narrow column of spinning air, perhaps no more than a kilometre across, but causing dreadful damage to all in its path.

In the temperate regions of the Earth such as Britain and Europe, there is generally a good steady supply of rain and temperatures that are neither very low nor very high. In some hot dry areas, such as India and Pakistan or Ethiopia, they are very dependent on the rains for their water for drinking and irrigation of their land to grow food. Sometimes the rains do not come, the people cannot grow food, and thousands die of starvation, the very old and the very young suffering the most. When the rains do come, they may be so intense that flooding occurs, making the situation even more horrifying.

These are just a few of the ways in which the Earth can endanger us, but there are many more.

Above:
Here are three more ways in which the Earth can endanger us:
(1) The tremendous winds and flying objects that are associated with tornadoes can cause severe loss of life.
(2) Waterspouts are not so dangerous because they can be seen and avoiding action taken.
(3) The strong winds that sometimes accompany dust storms can cause the dust to do a great deal of damage, especially to delicate machinery, by penetration and abrasion.

Who are the vanishing peoples of the world?

It is not only animals and plants that are in danger of disappearing from our planet in the face of the industrial 'advanced' nations. There are many races of people that have survived in a very simple, stable way of life for many centuries only to be threatened with destruction in the space of a few decades.

A good example of a vanishing people known to most of us is the case of the Indian of North America. Until Christopher Columbus landed his ship upon the shores of the Caribbean Islands in 1492, the New World and its peoples were virtually unknown, and now less than 500 years later most of the Red Indian tribes are no more, and those that are left have retained little of their culture. Even the surviving tribes have such small populations that many of them may soon disappear. And America is the most powerful industrial nation on Earth.

There are many reasons for the loss of these tribes. The white men came from Europe with the hope of building a new life for themselves in the New World and escaping the poverty of the Old. In most cases, they were welcomed by the Indians. Unfortunately, the white men brought diseases with them. The Indians were not immune and thousands of them died. The coming of the railway opened up the West and supplies of food were required for the rail-

Right:
Many tribes of North American Indians once depended upon the huge herds of roaming bison for their livelihoods. The coming of the railway meant that workers had to be fed and specialist hunters killed millions of these animals. This and loss of their traditional hunting grounds led to the break up of these tribes.

way workers and the new settlers. As a result millions of bison which had provided the Indian with many of his materials, were slaughtered. Slowly, the Indians were driven off their natural hunting grounds on to poorer and poorer lands, and when they tried to fight back, the white man with his army and superior weapons won again.

Above and right:
The sudden coming of industrialization may lead to the destruction of small, self-sufficient communities as people are attracted to factory centres where they may then find themselves living in the terrible squalor of a shanty town.

This is a sad tale, and although it does not happen quite like this today, there are other tribes that are dying out because they cannot adapt quickly enough to the changing conditions which are being forced upon them by industrial man in his search for new lands for building, farming, and natural resources. The Bushmen of South Africa, the Pygmies of central Africa, the Aborigines of Australia, and the Eskimos are just a few of the more well-known races that are dying out or interbreeding with the white men with the loss of their own ways of life. It is thought that there are still tribes of Indians left in the Amazon jungles of South America that have not yet set eyes upon a white face, but these areas are in danger of being opened up.

As is the case with wild life, the loss of these peoples could be thought of as the natural course of evolution, because they are unable to adapt to changing conditions. Generally, however, it is better to have variety of blood, ways of life, and cultures so that there is more chance of man surviving any disaster.

Where does our energy come from?

There are two other questions here which need to be answered at the same time. First of all, what do we mean by energy? And secondly, what kind of energy are we referring to in this question? There is a very exact scientific meaning of the word energy, but for our purposes it is enough to say that energy is the power of doing work. Work can be of all kinds. When you breathe you are doing work and your body is using energy. When you are cleaning the family car, you are working quite hard and using quite a lot of energy. Even when you are sleeping, you are using energy to breathe, digest your food and so on. We get the energy we need for the workings of our body by 'burning' fuel. In other words, we eat food which contains energy locked within it, and as it is digested, the energy is released.

Right:
The long hours of sunshine in tropical zones provides enough energy for a rich growth of plants in which many species of animals can survive.

scarlet macaw

sulphur-breasted toucan

boa constrictor

ruby-throated hummingbird

iguana

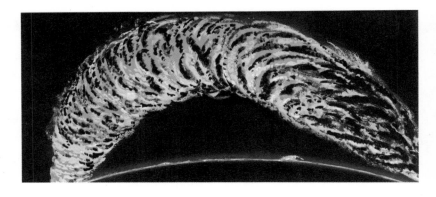

Right:
Originally it is the sun that supplies the energy we use at such an alarming rate. This picture illustrates solar prominences (*see* page 14).

But from where does the energy contained within the food come from? We have already answered this question. The energy is provided by the sun. Plants use the sun's rays to convert carbon dioxide and other materials from the air and soil into proteins. These proteins are then eaten by other animals which we eat together with certain plants. You can see, then, that the energy we use every day comes from the sun through various stages. It is worth bearing in mind that all living things use energy.

Man is rather different to other life forms, however. Have you ever stopped to think how much energy we use in all sorts of ways. Let us list just a few: railways, roads, and ships; electric lighting; all the different forms of heating in industry, in the home, and for hot water; many electrical gadgets. Where does the energy come from? To a great extent we rely upon what are usually referred to as fossil fuels, such as coal and oil. When we burn a piece of coal, in effect, we are releasing energy from the Sun that has remained trapped for millions of years. You have seen how long it takes to lay down the huge reserves of coal, but we are using them up much faster than they can be replaced. The same is true of oil, upon which we rely not only for petrol, but also for many other chemicals. There are also other problems which arise from the widespread use of these fossil fuels. There is the destruction of the countryside in mining for coal and there are all the different forms of pollution that have already been mentioned. Perhaps the next time you switch on an electric light, you could consider the costs to the Earth of our use of electricity on such a vast scale, sometimes for little good purpose.

There are other ways in which we can make use of the energy from the sun. It is possible that in the future we may be able to make greater use of tidal power, wind power, or even solar collectors to convert sunlight directly into electricity. But whatever the source, it is likely that there will be some environmental cost.

Above:
Harnessing water power can provide us with electricity but large areas of land often have to be submerged behind a dam to do it.

503

How clean is the ocean?

Perhaps it is worth remembering the historic voyages of Thor Heyerdahl in his reed boat, known as the *Ra* expeditions. Thor Heyerdahl had more of a chance to take a closer look at the Atlantic Ocean while he was sailing his fragile craft than anyone in a larger boat would normally have. He was shocked to discover that even in the middle of the Atlantic there was considerable pollution with oil!

The sea has always been thought of as a bottomless pit for all of the waste that man cared to throw into it. In the past, the processes of the sea have been able to cope, carrying waste out and allowing it to decay with the aid of bacteria in the normal way. Now, however, the situation is different. From every country, millions of litres of sewage pour into the sea (some of it via the rivers), some of it treated and some of it not, but this is not the only way in which the sea is made dirty. If you were to go to many of the beaches along the south coast of Britain hoping to lie on golden sands and swim in crystal clear waters, the chances are that you would soon find your clothes caked with sticky black tar-like material and you would be swimming in dirty brown water.

Right:
We have often been tempted to treat the oceans as a giant dustbin. A walk along any beach will convince you how clean the oceans really are.

More recently another problem has arisen. The North Sea Oil discoveries would seem to have been made at a very opportune moment with fuel shortages and rising prices, but they do not come without their price. More and more fishing boats have been finding their nets entangled in debris from the drilling rigs, and the catches of fish are being affected.

Right:
Dispersing an oil slick with
detergent can often cause
more damage than the oil
itself would have done.

Atomic energy seems at first sight to be a much cleaner
way of producing the much needed electricity to light our
streets, warm our homes, and power our industries, but
once again there is a cost to the environment. Unfortunately,
nuclear power stations produce materials which cannot be
used further for power but which are still radioactive, and
which can remain so for hundreds of years. What is to be
done with these waste products? One solution has been the
bottomless sea again. The wastes are sealed in stainless steel
containers and dumped in the ocean. It has been suggested,
however, that the containers will have corroded away long
before the products are safely non-radioactive.

All the wastes from many factories are transported by the
rivers into the sea. Detergents are used to disperse oil slicks,
but may even cause more damage than the oil itself. Apart
from the thousands of seabirds that die each year as a result
of oiling, there may be other effects that we do not know of.
It seems that the days of 'sailing the ocean blue' are over.

Right:
Oiled birds die terrible deaths
but they are only indicators
of other harm that is being
caused.

Is fresh air really fresh?

How many times have you heard someone say, 'I think I'll go out for a breath of fresh air'? Have you ever stopped to think what this means in our industrialized world? Of course, if you happen to be living high up among the mountains where there is little or no industry and few people, your chances of finding fresh air are quite good. But what of the built-up areas of Britain and Europe or America? Even if you have not experienced it yourself, we expect you have heard of *smog*. This word is a mixture of the words 'smoke' and 'fog', which is very apt because smog really is smoky fog. London was once famed for its 'pea-soupers', that is, fog containing so much sulphurous waste that it resembled the yellowish green colour of pea soup and was almost as difficult to breathe and see through. These smogs usually occurred during the early months of winter when the fogs that would normally be present at that time of year became contaminated with all the smoke from cars and factory chimneys.

It is interesting to note how much influence pollution of the air, at first by smells of household waste and later by pollution, has influenced the distribution of people in cities like London. As you probably know, London has an 'East end' and a 'West end'. Until quite recently the East end has been by far the poorer half of the city. This is because winds usually blow from west to east carrying the dirty air with them. People who could afford to choose where they wanted to live went to the western side leaving the smelly east for those with smaller incomes. In Los Angeles, in America, which is also famed for its smogs, the prevailing winds are from east to west so that the London situation is reversed.

Above:
Clean Air Acts in many areas have led to fewer scenes like this and smogs are less frequent than they were. However, if we use large quantities of fossil fuels it will be at some cost to our environment elsewhere.

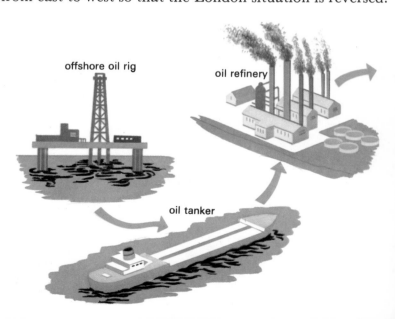

offshore oil rig

oil refinery

oil tanker

Left:
When no wind blows, smoke may rise higher, but in calm, cold weather the smoke may not disperse and smogs could arise.

Today, many industrial countries have introduced 'Clean Air Acts' preventing the burning of ordinary coal in homes in certain areas and controlling the amount of smoke that factories can release. This means that some areas, such as London, certainly, have air containing much less dust and dirt, and smogs are almost a thing of the past. In general, however, the air in our countries is far from fresh. The millions of cars on the road pour vast quantities of poisonous carbon monoxide gas into the atmosphere. It has even been suggested that if supersonic flight became popular, with the 'planes flying at such high altitudes, the upper atmosphere could be affected in such a way as to permit deadly cosmic rays to reach the Earth.

The next time that you see some plants or trees next to a busy road, take a closer look at the leaves. You will probably find that they are covered with a film of black, oily dust. Remember that this is the same air that we are all breathing.

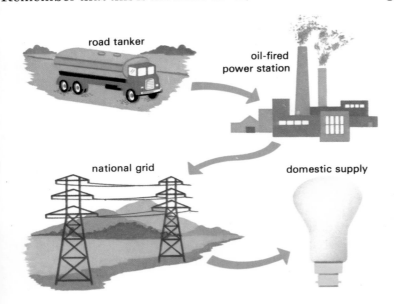

road tanker

oil-fired power station

national grid

domestic supply

Left:
The next time that you switch on a light try to think of all the processes that have been involved to produce the energy.

Why do we use the land?

Throughout this book, we have looked at many aspects of the Earth, its place in the Universe, its life, its oceans, the upheavals which mould the planet's surface, and so on. Like every other form of life, man has a place in the natural web. Also like most other animals, man tries to change his environment to suit his own needs better, but man has been much more effective in changing the shape of the Earth than any other creature.

We use the land for all kinds of purposes. First of all, we need the land for food. In the past, man has lived a hunter/gatherer type of existence filling his belly by hunting animals and catching fish, and gathering nuts and berries from the woods in which he lived. He did not always find it easy to ward off the pangs of hunger, particularly in times of drought or following unusually hard winters.

The next step was probably towards some primitive kind of agriculture. Primitive man would clear areas in the forest by slashing and burning so that he could then plant his corn, and when the land was exhausted of its goodness he would move on to another area to begin again. This was the technique used by men of the Bronze Age, and led to a more settled existence. Instead of men finding shelter wherever they happened to be and leading a nomadic life, towns and

Above and right:
Thousands of hectares of land are being consumed every day as our villages grow into towns and cities and large areas of good soil are stripped off for certain kinds of mining.

villages grew up, and as we are only too aware, these small settlements have expanded into the vast industrial cities that most of us live in today. This is a second use to which we put the land. As the population of the world grows and there is a demand for ever-improved living conditions our cities eat up more and more of the countryside. Land that once was thought of as waste now provides us with valuable building plots, and we are even claiming back land from the sea.

Food and shelter are, of course, our main requirements, but these are not the only claims we make upon the Earth's thin skin. Modern living with its electricity, motor car, and industries means that we need to drag many raw materials from the land. We need the fossil fuels for energy so that the land is dotted with oil rigs and slag heaps and pitted with mines and open cast holes. With the coming of the petrol shortages, it has even become an economical proposition to mine the oil shales to extract this valuable commodity. This requires the stripping of hundreds of square kilometres of its vegetation and topsoil, perhaps never to recapture its former beauty.

In addition to all these things we need the land to look at. We have evolved as part of the Earth, and despite urban living we still need to be able to take pleasure in the beauties of the countryside. We use the land for many other forms of recreation such as football and cricket, athletics and even motor racing.

Right:
We need rural areas not only to grow the food we require but also to provide us with areas where we can get away from the stress of urban life for a short time.

What foods do we eat?

In answering this question, it is worth taking into account first of all, that generally speaking man is an omnivore, that is, he does not confine himself to eating just animal flesh like a carnivore, nor does he just eat plant material as does a herbivore. We eat all kinds of foods. The type of food we eat depends upon a number of conditions, such as where we happen to be living, what kind of work we are doing, and even taboos placed upon certain foods by religion or culture. For example if you were living in China a good proportion of your diet might be rice; if you belonged to the Jewish faith you would not be able to eat any part of the pig – in other words no pork sausages or rashers of bacon; if you were a Hindu living in India you would not be able to eat beef because the cow is sacred; some religions prohibit the eating of meat altogether in the belief that it tends to make people more aggressive.

Right:
Small scale farming like this had very little impact on the natural environment.

Right:
Modern methods of farming put millions of hectares of wild land to the plough with the burning of forest and the uprooting of hedges. However, it is now being realized how important hedges are to prevent soil erosion.

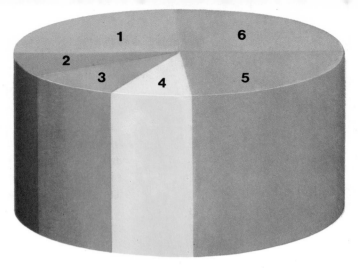

Despite all of these conditions, the world's population depends on a small number of foodstuffs. Most atlases will give you a good indication of what foods we eat and in what amounts. In Britain and Europe people are fortunate to enjoy quite varied diets, but half the people of the world depend on one plant crop for their staple diet – rice.

Rice is a grass which can only be grown in warm climates so that people living in places like India and China rely on it. We need only to include a few other crops such as wheat, maize, sorghum, and barley and we have catered for more than two-thirds of the world's people. With the rapidly increasing world population, crops such as soya beans are being increasingly grown to supplement the proteins provided by meat.

There is also quite a small number of animals that most of the meat eating peoples of the world consume. We expect that you can think of many of them: on your list you might include cows (for milk and butter and cheese as well as for meat), sheep, pigs, and perhaps goats and even deer. (The meat from deer is known as venison.) It has been suggested that as the population rises, with an ever-increasing demand for food, it would be better not to farm animals such as cattle which are not very good at converting grass into protein for us, and it might be preferable to farm animals like rabbits which give more protein per hectare in a shorter time.

Try for a moment to think of your daily intake of food. You might have a cereal for breakfast (probably from wheat) followed by bacon and eggs and toast. For lunch you might have some kind of meat and two vegetables such as peas and potatoes. For tea, a boiled egg and bread and jam might be typical. In addition, there might be some kind of fruit during the day and various drinks such as milk, tea and coffee. All this comes from quite a few plants and animals.

Where do we get the water we drink?

No life on Earth can exist without water. Some animals and plants live in it, others need to drink it either through their roots in the case of plants, or in our case from a glass. But it is not only for drinking that mankind uses water. Try to list all the different ways in which you make use of it. When you get up in the morning, you will wash in water, use water to flush the lavatory, the milk that you pour on to your breakfast cereal is mostly water, there will be water in your breakfast drink, you may boil an egg in water and finally use water to wash up. During the day, you might have many different drinks, use water for cooking, washing your hands, perhaps bathing. You may clean the family car with a considerable amount of water and in summer you may use a hose to keep the garden looking fresh and green. If your family uses a washing-up machine, remember that some types need seventy litres of water to complete the cycle, and of course, there is always the washing machine.

But it is not only in the home that we use water. Industry requires water for all kinds of purposes from cooling to cleaning. Water is also a source of hydrogen.

Where, then, does all this water come from? Of course, in a country such as Britain, this does not seem to be a very sensible question to ask. Britain is an island surrounded by sea and with quite a lot of rain that falls in moderate amounts throughout the year. On the other hand desert areas receive less than 30 centimetres of rain every year, so that if we were living in, say, the Sahara, almost all the available water would be used for drinking purposes.

In Britain and Europe most of the water we use is obtained from the rivers. Of course, as we are all becoming increasingly aware, our rivers today are not very clean, so that the water that comes out of our water taps has been treated very carefully to make sure that it is pure enough to drink. The water then passes through our bodies into the drains and often back into the same rivers from which it was drawn, but a little further downstream. It has been estimated that in a city such as London, drawing water from the River Thames, every cup of water a Londoner drinks has already been drunk seven times before. This does not mean that the water in London is any less clean than further upstream because sewerage works are so good and purifying so effective, but all but the most modern need energy.

Some water can come from other sources, however. As we have already explained, some of the rain falling over the land soaks into the ground to build up a natural reservoir

or aquifer. Again referring to London which lies in a natural basin structure, rain falling on the Chiltern hills and the North Downs percolates into the chalk which forms the bedrock. The level of the water-table at the Chilterns and Downs used to be higher than in London, so that if a well was drilled in London, the water would be under pressure and forced up in an *artesian well*. Now, however the water-table has fallen.

What do we get from the sea?

The first thing to remember, of course, is that the oceans and seas of the world existed long before man was walking the Earth; in fact, long before any other form of life had evolved at all. All life on Earth is believed to have originated from what is commonly called the 'primordial soup'. The first thing that we get from the sea, then, is ourselves in as much as we have evolved from primitive sea-dwelling creatures.

Right:
Salt is very important to us. The word salary comes from the Latin *salarium*, that is, the money that Roman soldiers were given to buy salt. Here salt is being removed from an ancient deposit and from a modern salt pan.

The seas have always been important to man, perhaps of most importance as a source of food of seemingly endless amounts and varieties. When we think of the sea as a larder, the first thing we think of is fish. And every year the sea does yield enormous quantities of different species, but there are many other animals which we eat in large numbers too, such as crabs and lobsters, shrimps and prawns, cockles and mussels, and even octopuses and squid. It has been estimated that in 1968 the world catch of fish and these other marine animals reached a total of almost 60 million tonnes. With improved fishing methods, particularly among the main fishing nations such as Britain and Japan, the catches are still increasing although British fishermen have been having difficulties in maintaining this rich harvest in recent years.

Even the largest of all the animals that live in the sea, the great whales, have long been hunted for meat and oil

Unfortunately, the increased efficiency of the modern whaling ship has meant that in the last seventy years more whales have been killed than in the previous 400 years, so that two species have already been hunted to extinction and a further five species are seriously threatened. In fact, there was so much call for concern that in 1972 the United Nations called for a ban on all whaling for ten years to give the remaining species a breathing space. Russian and Japanese whaling ships continue to sail, however.

Food is not the only thing we get from the sea. Man needs salt to survive, and of course, the sea is a vast storehouse of it, although in many parts of the world it is easier to mine underground salt deposits. This is particularly true in areas which are not hot enough to cause the sea to evaporate naturally in man-made shallows. The world is now faced with an ever-increasing demand for fresh water. In Israel, for example, and the oil-producing countries of the Middle East, it has become worthwhile to build huge plants to distil fresh water from the sea. It may be that the salts remaining could then be used to provide various elements which are found in the sea.

Sand and gravel are often obtained from the sea floor by dredging ships, and these materials are essential to the building industries. Metals such as copper and manganese may be extracted from nodules that can be found on the ocean floors in some areas. Other metals such as vanadium are concentrated in the blood of animals like the sea cucumber. There is even gold in the sea in far greater quantities than on land although it is very widely dispersed.

Finally, the seas provide us with a place to dump our wastes and highways on which to travel.

Left:
Manganese nodules like these found on the ocean floor contain deposits of important metals including copper and nickel. As copper and nickel are becoming more expensive, it may soon be economic to exploit these riches on the ocean floor.

What makes a desert a desert?

If you were asked to name a typical desert, which one would you choose? Probably the most likely choice would be the great Sahara desert of north-west Africa or the Kalahari desert to the south, or perhaps you might even think of the interior of the Australian continent. What do all these areas have in common? You might be tempted first of all to say that they are very hot. Of course, in the deserts that have been mentioned this is true with temperatures soaring to more than 42°C. In fact, we have it on good authority that in the bush of Western Australia, in the mining communities, it becomes so hot that it is possible to fry an egg on a bare rock and door handles become too hot to hold. Even the main motor route running hundreds of kilometres from north to south, the Great Stuart Highway, is a dirt road because a normal tarmac road would melt. In the houses there, with air conditioning full on, the temperature rarely falls below 22°C, or the average summer temperature in Britain.

Right:
The map shows the desert and semi-desert areas of the world.

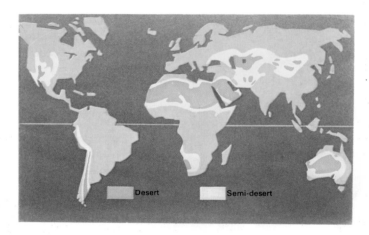

Desert   Semi-desert

Right:
An oasis in a desert.

The next point you might make about these deserts is that they are extremely dry, and it is on rainfall that deserts are defined and not on temperature. A desert is usually defined as an area that receives less than 250 millimetres of rain per year. This is only an average figure. It may be that it may not rain for some years, and then a few years worth of rain may fall all at once. When this happens, temporary rivers form. They may be quite fast-flowing torrents sweeping away the previously dry rocks and eroding quite deep valleys. The waters soon dry up again, however, leaving the valleys dry, the typical *wadis* of desert scenery. Not all deserts are hot. Some are extremely cold, and it is usual to think of the Arctic and Antarctic regions as cold deserts because all of the available water is locked up in the icecaps.

Even in the hottest, driest deserts, not everywhere is dry, dusty, lifeless and strewn with great sand dunes. Rain may fall on the highlands which surround some deserts and percolate into the rocks to form ground water. The sandstones easily absorb the water and an aquifer may develop a few hundred metres beneath the floor of the desert. Where there is an anticline bringing the aquifer close to the surface, or a hollow in the desert taking the desert floor down to meet the aquifer, an *oasis* may develop. This is an area where artesian water reaches the surface. In these areas, the vegetation thrives around the water hole, desert animals use oases to supply them with water to drink, and human settlements may form around them. Sometimes when the rains come in a desert after a number of completely dry years, the water causes seeds that have been lying dormant in the sand to suddenly spring to life and a barren wasteland may appear quite fertile almost over night only to die as soon as the water dries up again.

Where might you expect to find jungles and swamps?

We expect you have read stories of explorers with their native bearers hacking their way through hot, steamy jungles and being plagued by poisonous snakes and spiders, beset by disease and being attacked by savage jungle animals or even head-hunting natives. Perhaps you have read the stories of Tarzan of the Apes by Edgar Rice-Burroughs where a white baby was brought up by a tribe of apes. Most of these stories were set in the jungles of west-central Africa.

Ocelot

Above and right:
A forest like this can support many animals and plants. But there are also tiny communities of animals and plants such as in the human skin (*left inset*) or in a drop of water (*right inset*).

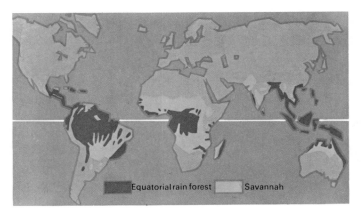

Equatorial rain forest | Savannah

Jungles are to be found in the hot, moist climates of the equatorial belt of the Earth; that is, the region adjacent to the equator. There is probably as much sunshine in these equatorial regions as there is in the hot deserts, but because they are so much damper, the temperatures seldom rise above 35°C. Although, as we have seen, deserts become extremely hot during the day, they can become very cold at night (you will remember the effects that this has upon the rocks). On the other hand, the added moisture in the jungle climates helps to retain the heat built up during the day, and jungles never become very cool. Most Europeans would be able to adapt to the heat of the desert because it is a dry heat, but would soon give way to the steamy heat of the jungles. But it is just this hot moist climate that enables the vegetation to become so dense and provides so many species of birds, reptiles, mammals and insects with such a richness in food.

In some of the great river basins of these equatorial climates, a different type of vegetation may be present. These are the mangrove swamps such as you might find in the delta regions of the Amazon river of South America. The delta itself is formed at the point where the river meets the sea, at the mouth of the river. A delta can only occur where the amount of sediment that is being brought down to the mouth by the river is greater than the amount that can be carried away to sea by the tides and the currents. This means that sediment will be deposited at the mouth of the river.

There are three different types of deltas and two of these are clearly illustrated by the deltas of the Mississippi and the Nile. These muddy swamps may be covered by salt water at high tide and it is under these conditions, along tropical coasts that the mangrove trees thrive.

You can see, then, that in these tropical rainforests the habitat is a very rich one indeed. Tall trees shade the smaller plants, and the area provides homes for animals like the orang-utan and the hippopotamus.

What does the future have in store for our planet?

This question has many parts to it. We know, for example, that eventually our star, the Sun, will die and in doing so will destroy the Earth. The very distant future, then, means the end of the Earth, but this will not occur for many millions of years and need not concern us here. It has also been suggested that our climate is changing and that we are at the beginning of another Ice Age, but opinion is divided. It is enough to say that large scale changes to the planet as a whole take place so slowly when compared to our short life span that they may go unnoticed, disguised by the much more rapid changes which man is causing to his own life and that of all other living creatures on Earth.

The usual way of attempting to 'see' into the future is to look at the way changes have occurred in the past up to the present day and then try to project into the future, but this is not easy because it is not always possible to anticipate the effects of a particular set of circumstances. Try a simple experiment. Draw two lines on a piece of paper at right angles to one another to form the axes of a graph. The graph could represent, say, the rate at which a hot water bottle cooled after it was placed in your bed. Suppose one axis represented temperature and the other time. Suppose also that you had measured the temperature on two occasions so that you could plot two points on your graph. These could be joined by a straight line, and if you wanted to know the temperature of the bottle sometime later, you would simply project that straight line to the required point in time. But if, in the meantime, someone removed the blankets from the bed, the bottle would cool much more quickly and your prediction would be wrong.

Right:
Our wildlife communities are very important to us and to guarantee our own future we need to look after them very carefully.

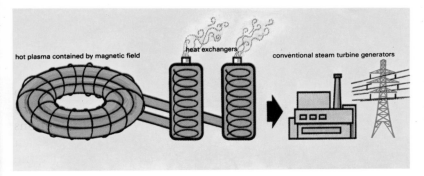

hot plasma contained by magnetic field heat exchangers conventional steam turbine generators

Left:
It has been suggested that the energy released when atoms join together (nuclear fusion) could be used to fuel our power stations. Nuclear power stations today rely on the energy released when atoms are split (nuclear fission).

The subject of many science fiction stories deals with ideas of what conditions might be like in years to come. Some suggestions seem to be wildly far fetched, but a hundred years ago who would have believed in the possibility of supersonic flight or submarines that can stay under the Arctic ice for two years without surfacing, or even in satellites circling Venus? On the other hand in the heyday of the motor car a few years ago, most of us would have laughed at the idea of fuel shortages. How do we know what the world's population might be in a hundred or even twenty years time? Can we predict whether science and technology will be able to find solutions to the problems of overcrowding, food shortages, and pollution choking our rivers and seas, or the ever-decreasing numbers of wild animals and plants with the accompanying dangers to our own species. Will we be able to take a rocket to a distant planet as easily as we can now take a bus to the next town, or will we return to more rural living, each community growing its own food and making clothes by hand? Then there are the dangers of nuclear war. If man is to survive in peace and plenty, the watchword seems to be to try to foresee the consequences of any action rather than wait and see, by which time it may be too late.

Above:
It is possible to cause rain to fall in areas of drought, provided that there are clouds in the sky, by seeding them with dry ice sprayed from an aircraft flying above the cloud cover.

Index

Index

Exploration and Discovery

Index

The Past

The World Around Us

Index

The Earth And Man